ORTHO'S GUIDE TO CREATIVE HOME LANDSCAPING

Created and Produced by
the Editorial Staff of Ortho Books

Writers

Eric Clough

Dr. Michael A. Dirr

Manuela Anne King, A.S.L.A.

Robert J. Mowat, A.S.L.A.

William J. Newton, A.S.L.A.

Illustrators

Larry Blake

Donald Blayney, A.S.L.A.

Craig Bergquist

Tony Davis

Ron Hildebrand

Mitzi McCarthy

Deborah Russell

ORTHO BOOKS

Publisher
Robert B. Loperena

Editorial Director
Christine Jordan

Manufacturing Manager
Ernie S. Tasaki

Managing Editor
Sally W. Smith

Editors
Robert J. Beckstrom
Michael D. Smith

Prepress Supervisor
Linda M. Bouchard

Publisher's Assistant
Joni Christiansen

Graphics Coordinator
Sally J. French

Sales & Marketing Manager
David C. Jose

Address all inquiries to:
Ortho Books
Box 5006
San Ramon, CA 94583-0906

© 1987, 1996 Monsanto Company
All rights reserved

2	3	4	5	6	softcover
97	98	99	2000		

2	3	4	5	6	hardcover
97	98	99	2000		

ISBN 0-89721-279-7 softcover
ISBN 0-89721-289-4 hardcover

Library of Congress Catalog Card Number 95-68606

THE SOLARIS GROUP
2527 Camino Ramon
San Ramon, CA 94583-0906

Consultant
Eric Clough

Editorial Coordinator
Cass Dempsey

Copyeditor
Elizabeth von Radics

Proofreader
David Sweet

Indexer
Frances Bowles

Special Thanks to
California Redwood
  Association
Deborah Cowder
David Van Ness

Designer
Barbara Ziller

Cover Design by
Hespenheide Design

Separations by
Color Tech Corp.

Lithographed in the USA by
Banta Book Group

Photographers

Photographers' names are followed by the page numbers on which their work appears.
William Aplin: 13, 25B, 185, 219BR, 227TR, 228BR, 231BL, 251TR, 235BR, 237TR, 237BR, 240BL, 242BL, 248TL, 249TR, 251TR, 254TR, 260BR, 262BR, 268TL, 268BR, 274TL, 275TL, 281TR, 281BR, 298TL, 300TL, 305BL, 305TR, 306TL, 307TR, 308TL, 309BR, 310BL, 310BR, 311TR, 313TR, 315TL, 316TR, 317TR
Jean Baxter, Photo/Nats: 249BL
Heidi Bishop: 66R
Laurie Black: 18, 29, 31, 65, 77, 79T, 125T, 126, 127, 151, 197, 254BL, 265BR
John Blaustein: 66L, 69, 277BR
Karen Bussolini: 14T, 14B, 64, 83
California Redwood Assoc.: 157
Clyde Childress: 229BR, 240TR, 254BR, 256BR
Richard Christman: 195
Mary Clay, Photo/Nats: 318BL
Barrie Coate: 238TR
Josephine Coatsworth: 223BL, 236TL, 259BL, 275TR, 286TR, 288TL, 293BR, back cover L
Alan Copeland: 137
Gordon Courtright: 252BR
Chuck Crandall: 216BL, 318TL
Crandall & Crandall: 239BR
Michael Dirr: 214TL, 214TR, 216TR, 216BR, 217TR, 225TR, 228BL, 232TL, 233BR, 235BL, 242TL, 243BL, 247TL, 247TR, 248BL, 269TR, 277BL, 282TR, 287BR, 289TL, 290TR, 297BL, 299TR

Christine Douglas: 41, 50
Derek Fell: 215TR, 221TL, 222TL, 237TL, 239TR, 247BR, 259TR, 267TL, 274BL, 285TR, 296BR, 310TL, 311BL, 312TL
Jennifer Graylock, Photo/Nats: 319TR
Saxon Holt: Front cover, 20B, 30T, 36, 39L, 39R, 46, 57B, 58, 62, 166, 208T, 208B, 217TL, 217BL, 217BR, 218BR, 220TL, 223TR, 223BR, 224BL, 251TL, 232BL, 233TR, 236BL, 238TL, 238BL, 238BR, 239TL, 241BR, 245BL, 251BL, 255TL, 255BL, 255TR, 255BL, 258TL, 261BL, 266TR, 267TR, 272TL, 273BL, 275BL, 275BR, 279TR, 284BR, 288BR, 295TL, 295BL, 297TL, 297BR, 303BR, 304TL, 304BL, 313BR
Susan Lammers: 294BR, 302BR
Michael Landis: 3CB, 6, 16, 17, 26, 33, 34, 54, 59, 70, 74, 75, 96-97, 104, 165, 175, 189, 198, 207, 218TR, 226BR, 257BL, 257TR, 260BL, 263TR, 270TR, 281TL, 291BR, 292TR, 297TR, 300BL, 301TL, 303TL, 307BR, 310TR, 314TL, 314TR, 314BR, 315BL, 315BR, 316TL, 316BR, 316BR, 317BL, back cover C
John A. Lynch, Photo/Nats: 243TL
Michael MacCaskey: 234TL, 241TL, 258TR
Peter Margosian, Photo/Nats: 264BL
Colleen McBride: 250BL, 242BR
Michael McKinley: 3CT, 3B, 10C, 27, 28, 37, 44, 45, 48, 52-53, 57T, 60T, 63, 68, 79B, 85, 98, 122, 124, 125B, 159, 199, 210-211, 224TL, 230TL, 233TL, 234TR, 234BR, 239BL, 241TR, 244BL, 246BL, 246TR, 248BR, 249BR, 250BL, 251TL, 252BL, 253BL, 259BR, 260TL, 265TL, 265BL, 267BL, 268TR, 269TL, 269BR, 273BR, 276BL, 278BL, 279TL, 280TL, 280BL, 280TR, 283TL, 286BR, 288BL, 290BL, 291BL, 292TL, 293TL, 295BL, 296BL, 303BL, 303TR, 304BR, 311TL, 312TR, 313BL
James McNair: 42, 223TL, 291TL
Robert Mowat: 10B, 20T, 60B, 132L, 132R, 155, 174, 183, 191, 192, 205
Jack Napton: 233BL
Bernard Nist: 269BL, 272BL, 283BL, 283BR, 284BL, 284TR, 294BL, 298BL
Ortho Photo Library: 22, 38, 73, 154, 221BR, 224TR, 226BL, 229TR, 235TR, 236BR, 237BL, 243BR, 246TL, 249TL, 250BR, 256TL, 256TR, 257BR, 260TR, 279BL, 290BR, 291TR, 292BR, 299BR, 300BR, 302TL, 306TR, 308BR, 311BR

Pam Peirce: 214BL, 215TL, 215BR, 218TL, 218BL, 219TL, 219BL, 219TR, 220TR, 220BR, 221BL, 221TR, 222BL, 222BR, 224BR, 225TL, 227BR, 228TR, 229TL, 229BL, 230TR, 230BR, 231BR, 232BR, 235TL, 236TR, 240BR, 244BR, 245TL, 248TR, 250TL, 252TR, 253TL, 253TR, 254BL, 256BL, 258BR, 262TR, 263TL, 263BL, 263BR, 264TL, 264BR, 266TL, 266BL, 266BR, 267BR, 270TL, 270BL, 271TL, 271BR, 274BR, 276TR, 276BR, 278TL, 278BR, 280BR, 281BL, 282TL, 282BL, 282BR, 284TL, 286BL, 290TL, 292BL, 293TL, 293BL, 294TL, 294TR, 295TR, 296TL, 296TR, 298TR, 299TL, 299BL, 301BL, 301TR, 301BR, 304TR, 305TL, 305BR, 306TL, 306BR, 307TL, 307BL, 308BL, 308TR, 309BL, 309TR, 312BL, 312BR, 313TL, 314BL, 315TR, 317TL
Jerry Pavia: 10T
Bill Reasons: 247BL
Susan Roth: 215BL, 220BL, 225BL, 226TL, 226TR, 227BL, 232TR, 236TL, 242TR, 243TR, 244TL, 244TR, 245TL, 245BR, 246BR, 250TR, 252TL, 254TL, 257TL, 258BL, 259TL, 261BL, 261TR, 262TL, 262BL, 264TR, 265TR, 268BL, 270BR, 271BL, 271TR, 272TR, 272BR, 273TL, 274TR, 276TL, 277TL, 277TR, 278TR, 279BR, 283TR, 285TL, 285BL, 286TL, 287TL, 287TR, 288TR, 289BL, 289TR, 289BR, 298BR, 302BL, 302TR, 309TL, 319TL
Anita Sabarese: 214BR, 500TR
Richard Schiell: 222TR, 253BR, 285TR, 318TR, 318BR, 319BL
Martha Schwartz: 51
Michael Smith: 273TR
Stark Studios: 3T, 4–5, 108
Tim Tabke: 261BR
Tom Tracy: 9, 25T, 80, 216TL, 225BR, back cover R
Wolf von dem Bussche: 227TL, 228TL, 241BL
Jeff Williams: 47
Min Yee: 251BR

Front Cover

Landscaping provides many benefits including a creative challenge, an opportunity to increase your living space, and an important financial return on investment of the overall value of your home.

Back Cover

Ortho's Guide to Creative Home Landscaping does more than inspire, it guides you every step of the way to a beautiful landscape.

CONTENTS

CREATING YOUR DESIGN

Your home is your special environment for enjoyment and relaxation. When landscaping, consider how you want to use your property and who will use it.

Your home landscape should be the place where you are most comfortable. It should provide you with areas to rest and to play. It should make your home attractive to visitors and reflect your sensitivity to nature. The goal of landscaping is to provide a functionally effective, aesthetically pleasing place in which you and your guests can relax and enjoy life.

Landscaping is not a simple endeavor, but it can be an enjoyable one. Designing and installing a landscape will take time, effort, and money. It will also be a creative challenge. Landscape design can be an outlet for your artistic talent—a way of expressing yourself that also serves a practical purpose. If you look at it that way, the hard work ahead will not seem so daunting.

Before you can create your landscape, you must know what you want from it. Landscape design is the process of turning what you have into what you want it to be. The site and the desires you have for it are unique. Each design process is an individual one, and your results will be unlike any other. Consider this book your guide, providing you with many ideas and the technical information necessary to produce them.

HOW TO USE THIS BOOK

Landscaping requires an understanding of basic design and construction principles, as well as a knowledge of plants. These disciplines interact at every step in the process. Although the subject matter is complex and does not follow a straight line to completion, but rather circles back on itself at many points along the way, this book aims to make the process as simple as possible.

The basic sequence of events in creating, designing, and installing a landscape follows the chapters of this book. First, you must get ideas for the design; this involves determining what elements you want and deciding on the landscape style that is best for you.

Next you design the landscape, measuring and specifying all of the features you want and drawing them all on paper to see how they will fit into the yard. To do this you must understand the principles of both design and construction.

Finally, you have to install the landscape or have it installed. Once again you will need to consider landscape style and the principles of design as you choose the materials. Plants will be a major feature. The Landscape Plant Guide, beginning on page 211, describes hundreds of plants that can be used in home landscapes.

In making all of these decisions, you will need to go back and forth among many disciplines. You will also find yourself going back and forth between the various areas of this book, finding design ideas, checking construction techniques, and obtaining horticultural expertise.

Although this process may seem fairly complicated, the steps involved are logical and orderly. Each

Careful planning and thoughtful placement of landscape elements have turned this yard into a peaceful retreat.

chapter ends with a checklist for the stage it describes. These lists include everything you need to have done to that point in the process of creating, designing, or installing your landscape. You may not need to perform all of the steps in each chapter. Make copies of these checklists, and check off each step as you complete it.

As you read each section, you will notice references to other pages on which additional information about the subject matter can be found. These references are provided to help you through the myriad decisions you will be making as you design and install your new landscape. When you need to know all the information provided on a given subject, check the index, which begins on page 321. More help can be found in the Reading List (see page 320), which lists other books on design, construction, and horticulture. We encourage you to consult these books when you need more in-depth information about a given area.

You'll notice that plants mentioned throughout this book are listed by their common name, often followed by their scientific, or botanical, name in parentheses. This has been done because the common names of plants vary in different parts of the country. If you know only the common name, refer to the index. If you are unfamiliar with a plant that is described by its scientific name, check the Landscape Plant Guide, which begins on page 211.

The first step in creating a landscape is to dream of your perfect environment, the most comfortable place you can imagine. As you develop the landscape, keep this simple idea in mind: This is your design, for your home, in your world. It should be a place where you can be at peace.

THE IMPORTANCE OF DESIGN

THE BENEFITS OF HOME LANDSCAPING

A new landscape can beautify your home, increase your property value, and add to your usable living space. Planning and executing your own landscape design can be an artistically fulfilling endeavor. By designing the landscape that surrounds your home, you create an aesthetic environment that is well worth the time and effort you have invested.

Landscape design is an art. A pleasing landscape uplifts the spirit and adds to our day-to-day well-being and health. It encourages thought and contemplation. Gardens, natural landscapes, and greenery all have a soothing, relaxing effect. They put us at ease. Beautiful spaces, art, and landscapes enrich our lives.

Although there is a scientific and technical side to landscape design, the resulting product is meant for enjoyment. Landscape design plays more than a merely functional role in society and our lives; it serves humanistic needs and values as well. Your home landscape should refresh, relax, comfort, and uplift. Of course, the knowledge that you have designed and installed the landscape yourself will greatly enhance your pleasure in using it.

Make a Personal Statement

Your landscape is a creative statement. The form you give to your home's exterior reflects who you are. It speaks of your thoughts and wishes and provides an insight into your personality. Like people, no two landscapes are the same. Your landscape is also an opportunity for you to enrich the global community. Every small effort aimed at adding living beauty to the world helps the global ecosystem maintain its fragile balance.

Increase Your Living Space

Creative landscape design is an opportunity to conquer the physical constraints of your site, providing you with more meaningful living space. Golden Gate Park in San Francisco was once a series of sand dunes. Both Central Park in New York City and Disney World in Orlando, Florida, were once swampy bogs. These are extreme examples, but most pieces of property can be improved upon in some way. You can often turn a drawback into an exciting opportunity. Enclose a noisy front entryway and it becomes a Moorish courtyard; redirect the drainage in a swampy area and you have a beautiful stream; anchor a deck on a steep slope, and your entertaining area doubles in size. You will find that there are creative landscape design solutions to most site problems.

Enjoy a Return on Financial Investment

Landscape installations are well worth the financial investment they require. The most evident return on a new landscape is the increased property value of your home when you decide to sell it. In addition, a well-planned landscape will render a positive first impression that may result in a faster sale. According to a study by the American Association of Nurserymen, an attractive yard can increase the value of a property by up to 30 percent, with the average increase being about 12 percent. Landscape conveniences, such as automatic irrigation, lighting, and gates, can add immensely to the resale value. In addition, your new landscape installation may inspire your neighbors and hence raise the property values and overall image of the neighborhood.

SOURCES OF DESIGN INSPIRATION

Landscape design, like any complex endeavor, will be most successful if the planning process is complete and well researched. The first step in creating a landscape design is determining exactly what your needs and wants are. Ask yourself what you want the garden to do for you and what you want to do in the garden. You may be tempted to rush through the planning stage so you can get started with the work. Resist this urge, however, and give your plan the time and thought it deserves. Think about who you are planning the garden for. Are you a young family with small children who need safe play equipment for a few years? Are you an older couple who want and need an easily maintained landscape and a quiet, shady patio? Are you a family in their active years with athletic children (and lots of their friends) who would spend their weekends at home if they had a pool and recreation room? Is a close friend or member of your family in a wheelchair? Remember, too, that gardens mature and change with time, just like people and other living things. Today's children's play area may be the ideal place for a hammock when the trees and the children are grown large.

Contemplate your psychological needs as well as the obvious physical and functional ones. Allow yourself to daydream and explore your inner wishes and desires—the ones you usually do not listen to. From this deep part of yourself, you

may find true inspiration, yielding a garden design that is uniquely your own and which will give you years of satisfaction. Ask other members of your family to do the same thing, and add their creative comments to the design process.

Consider the climate, microclimate (the "climate" of different places in your yard), topography of the site (do you live on a steep hill or a flat lot?), and—very important—the size of the proposed garden area. Contemplate your budget, both short and long term. How does your landscape rate in priority compared with that new car you were looking at the other day?

Do you enjoy spending your weekends working in the garden, or would your rather have friends over for a barbecue on Sunday afternoons? Do you spend Saturdays coaching a Little League team?

Begin designing your landscape by looking for inspiration—an idea

One way of vastly improving the appearance of your property, is to cover an existing concrete path with patterned brick.

or theme to act as a catalyst to get you started. It should be something you feel excited about and that provides a realistic goal toward which you can work. If an idea of what you want is already stirring in your head, you may simply need to find examples of landscapes similar to the one you have in mind, so you can get an idea of the direction you should take.

Keep a record of ideas in a scrapbook that you can refer to as you formulate your landscape design. Various environments—from the public Butchart Gardens on Vancouver Island, British Columbia, to a rural meadow, or even a Santa Maria, California, mall—suggest forms and colors. Inspiration can also come from popular culture, such as an abstract print or a poem.

The following pages feature some common sources of design inspiration. Your inspiration may come from an area that another person would not have considered. Everything that surrounds you is a possible source of ideas. Like your landscape setting, the source of your inspiration will be individual and unique.

Make a Scrapbook of Inspirations

As you look around you, make a scrapbook of ideas for what you want to achieve with your landscape design. Cut out pictures and articles from magazines. Research family albums for favorite photographs. Search your memory for a favorite place. Take snapshots, make quick sketches, and jot down notes, saving everything in a file or loose-leaf notebook. Some of the items you choose may seem totally unrelated to one another, yet as you look through your inspiration scrapbook, you will probably find a common thread in these various sources. It may be a certain color, a yen for something wild and different than any garden you've ever seen, or the peaceful sense you get when gazing at symmetrical and ordered scenes. This "look" or "feel" is the landscape style to which you are most attracted.

Choosing a Landscape Style, which begins on page 20, is a collection of landscape design ideas for a variety of homes, lifestyles, and site problems. As you look through it and your own scrapbook, you'll find that you like some ideas more than others. You will also discover that some styles are more appropriate to your home than others, and these must be noted as well.

Save your scrapbook after your landscape is designed, to use in developing design details and to take with you when choosing materials. Keep it even after the design is installed and perhaps keep adding to it. You may have reason to remodel or add to the landscape you are currently designing, or someday you may want to design another landscape in another situation. You may be able to include an idea in a future design that you couldn't incorporate into this landscape. If nothing else, you might enjoy seeing how your taste and needs may have changed over several years.

Later in the design process, you will make an itemized account, or wish list, of all of the elements you want in your landscape (see page 55). Your scrapbook of design inspiration will help you choose these favorites. These ideas, developed according to the opportunities and constraints of the site, will become your landscape design.

Art The art world has long been a trendsetter for architecture and landscape design, providing new combinations of color, form, and composition that can be abstracted or applied to landscapes. Look to paintings, sculpture, and photographic art for design inspiration. Monet's paintings of water lilies, for example, may provide you with a pleasing color composition for part of your garden. Your task would then be to find plants in those colors.

Literature Fiction alters your state of mind, transporting you to another time and place. You may find inspiration for a landscape through your reading. Writers are able to evoke visions of places and endow them with strong feeling. You may have come across a description that was so striking that it implored you to be there or to recreate it. This can be a starting concept for your design. Works by

the great authors, such as Shakespeare, may induce you to install a garden using plants drawn from a particular play or piece, or you may want to base your landscape design on an author's depiction. Thoreau's descriptions of settings in his stories include many plants that can be used in the American landscape. Imagery of nature has long been used as metaphor in poetry. The boundaries are limitless; literature provides you with an abundant source of inspiration.

Popular Culture Many books and magazines deal with the home, its interior and exterior, and the landscape that surrounds it. These are, of course, the most logical sources to look to for inspiration, but do not ignore books and magazines on other subjects. Advertisements for a variety of products often feature photographs of beautiful homes and private and public gardens. The art directors of music videos, television shows, and films spend a great deal of time combining looks and colors and choosing locations. All of these are sources of outstanding design ideas.

Public and Private Gardens The design of the landscapes you encounter, whether in your community or around the world, offer many suggestions for your own landscape. Just as you look through a number of different media for design ideas, observe the places around you, paying particular attention to how the different elements are situated.

Become keenly aware of how certain landscapes make you feel. Look at their overall schemes, but also closely inspect the fine details. When you find a landscape you like, carefully document the design of the constructed elements, the plant selection, plant composition, and the landscape layout. If possible, sketch or take a snapshot of the landscape so you can analyze it at your leisure.

Your community is filled with landscape examples. Most public parks, urban plazas, office buildings, commercial and industrial parks, and shopping malls employ professional landscape architects. Each project will offer you a distinct viewpoint on landscape design and installation.

Look around your neighborhood as well. Homes near your own will have many of the same physical restrictions as yours and will certainly have the same climate. Look to everything around you, and you will undoubtedly find something of use and value.

A Memory A recollection of a special place may provide you with a design catalyst. A favorite childhood haunt, your grandmother's garden, or a Spanish courtyard you visited during your last vacation can all become part of the new landscape design. Take some time to analyze the exact reasons why you remember the place so fondly. What was it about that spot that endeared itself to you? What materials, colors, and forms made it exceptional? How were the elements laid out and placed to make it fun, intimate, or meaningful? By analyzing these attributes, you will come to understand them and be able to apply them to your design.

Friends and Family The people you know can be excellent sources of inspiration. Although the merits of design by committee are debatable, a finished design almost always benefits from a critical review and analysis. You will certainly want input from those who will use and enjoy the finished landscape. Children, especially, should be consulted as to their desires in play

areas and planting beds. The inspiration phase is the perfect time to welcome ideas from everyone, well before construction is started or money spent.

Landscape Professionals Many people practice residential landscape design professionally. Some have substantial formal education and design training, and some approach landscape design from backgrounds in construction or a specialized knowledge of plants. Many others design residential landscapes after years of experience working as gardeners or maintenance personnel.

Landscape architects usually have a degree in their specialty and are able to provide comprehensive design assistance. Increasingly, however, most are focusing their practices in commercial, industrial, or public landscape projects and have less time available for residential designs. Their services may be especially relevant if you are planning to build a home and develop the surrounding land. These professionals are competent to answer technical questions about grading, utility lines, and the placement of buildings. You can contact the local office of the American Society of Landscape Architects or check the telephone directory for landscape architects in your area.

Landscape contractors are licensed individuals who can provide expertise in the installation of your landscape. Their emphasis may be in the purchase and installation of plants, they may do some construction work, and many perform maintenance tasks as well. Their practical experience may also be helpful during the design of your landscape. You can contact the local office of the Associated Landscape Contractors of America or check the telephone directory for contractors in your area. See page 107 for additional information on hiring installation help.

The staff of a garden center can offer advice that may turn your project into something quite original. Garden centers often employ professional designers, and many individuals who work in garden centers are trained horticulturists.

Specialists with knowledge based on training and experience will be inspirationally invaluable to you. They can spot needed improvements, modify your plan with technical expertise, and help you foresee problems. Their involvement can be continuous from the inception or it can be minimal, limited to review and advice. Always remember that when it comes to knowing your lifestyle and personal needs, *you* are the expert.

YOUR HOME AND YOUR LAND

Although this phase of the design process emphasizes your wishes and dreams for the ideal landscape, you must consider certain constraints, even at this stage. It is best to think of these factors as opportunities or as starting points for inspiration. Your land, home, and location present a discrete situation that the landscape style must address.

You will have no control over most of the site factors discussed in this section. The climate, the region in which you live, your neighborhood and immediate neighbors, the size and shape of your lot, and the style of your house are, for the most part, unchangeable. However, if you design your yard with these factors in mind, you can modify them somewhat. Ignoring these factors can lead to both functional problems and aesthetic incompatibility.

Your landscape design will also be affected by whether you are beginning a design on a new lot or remodeling an existing one. There is very little difference between the design process for a new installation and that for a remodeled one. Both will benefit from an inspired landscape design.

The different site factors you must consider as you develop a landscape plan are discussed in the sections that follow. As you seek design inspiration, keep in mind the characteristics of your home and your land.

Climate and Seasonal Change

Climate and weather affect outdoor living spaces dramatically. They will make your landscaped spaces either

Working with your neighbors can give your street a grander and more unified look with one long stretch of front yard rather than a choppy series of plots. Some areas have guidelines concerning what you can install in your yard, so it is a good idea to check community regulations as you develop your landscape design.

Opposite: A landscape must be planned for year-round interest. The stairway and May flower beds in this Connecticut yard are transformed into patterns in the January snow. Deciduous trees further accent the seasons.

comfortable or unbearable. Most people are extremely aware of temperature and the comfort level associated with it. And it is important that you and your visitors feel at ease in the landscape. How you adapt your garden areas to climate and weather will determine the amount of use those spaces will receive.

The climatic factors that will affect your design are patterns of sun and shade, temperature, annual rainfall, snowfall, humidity, wind, fog, and smog. Later in the design process you will perform a detailed site analysis (see page 89) of all the elements, including climatic ones, that may affect your design. At this point you need only be aware that the climate will make a difference in your final design choices.

If you are new to your area, you can look up general climate statistics in an atlas. Neighbors are also a good source of this type of information. You can begin researching your own landscape by installing an outdoor thermometer and recording temperatures at the times of day you will most often spend in the yard. Keep a record also of rainfall and snow levels, the first freeze and thaw for the year, the direction of prevailing winds at different times of year, and dates when fog and smog appear, if any. This research will come in handy during the site analysis.

Choosing plants that will grow well in the given climate is crucial to the success of any landscape design. The U.S. Department of Agriculture has devised a map that divides the country into different growing zones according to the normal low temperatures for each region. The plants you buy should be adapted to your zone. This system is explained and utilized in the Landscape Plant Guide beginning on page 211.

Regional Character

The area of the country you live in, its history, and its general character should serve as part of the inspiration for your landscape design. The lifestyle of the region—be it the East, the West, the Midwest, the Southeast, or the Southwest—will have a great impact on your landscape style. Your design should reflect the regional character. A landscape with a tropical character looks and feels inappropriate in an oak woodland setting, for instance. If your home is sited in a clearly identifiable landscape, you might want to mimic it completely or at least use it as a starting point for your landscape design. For the design to be successful, you must understand the topography, elevation, soil type, and native plant communities of the region.

Each region is characterized by certain forms, colors, and topography. It is especially important that you understand these characteristics if you wish to re-create a native landscape style, which requires that you imitate or replicate the forms of the region. In order to deduce the true natural environment of your region, you may need to visit local parks or more rural areas of the community, especially if you live in an urban area.

Neighborhood Character

Every neighborhood has an identity and flavor unique to its location. The home styles, topography, plants, and layout of streets all affect the image of the community. The houses are likely to be similar in size and possibly similar in style. Although the landscape design may be different for each home in your neighborhood, certain elements or styles may be prevalent.

Survey your neighborhood, preferably on foot, and take note of the

Neighbors with lots in the same shape have chosen to use the areas similarly, but both the front lawns and back patios reflect the homeowners' specific tastes and needs. The potential for your lot is limited only by your ingenuity.

affect where you place plants as well as social, storage, and recreation areas. Beyond merely wanting to look and feel a part of the neighborhood, you also want to get along with your immediate neighbors.

Your next-door neighbors' landscapes may be attractive and appealing enough to act as a catalyst for your design. If so, you can coordinate your landscape design with theirs, especially in the front of the house. You may want to select similar plants and construction materials. This will add to the overall impact your landscape has on your home and neighborhood. If the disparity between styles is too great, the only answer may be to screen out your neighbors' landscapes. In any event, seek out your immediate neighbors and explain your intent.

You'll want to take note of features in your neighbors' landscapes that will affect your design. Note the shade cast by neighboring buildings. In hot regions you can use the shade cast by the buildings next door to great advantage in your landscape layout. Notice the location of areas in your neighbors' yards that are designated for socializing, recreation, quiet, storage, and children's play. You will want to consider these functional areas when designing your own. The success of an outdoor dining area planned for elegant entertaining could be destroyed, for example, if it is located just across the fence from a neighbor's garbage cans. Similarly, neighborly goodwill will not be served if you place your basketball court right outside their master bedroom. Your neighbors' landscapes have an effect on your life, and the installation of your landscape will have an impact on them. Further discussion of the good-neighbor policy begins on page 102.

common threads among the homes. Although you want your landscape to be original, you probably do not want it to be too unusual for the neighborhood. Some communities, in fact, have specific rules about various aspects of outdoor decoration. So before installing your landscape, be sure to check into community codes and regulations (see page 99). As you look around your neighborhood, note the use of plants (including street trees), planting styles, lighting, paving materials, fence heights and materials, gate styles, and other structures. Make sure to jot down the names of any plants that are growing exceptionally well. You will want your landscape design to complement the context in which it is located.

Your Immediate Neighbors

The homes adjacent to yours will have an impact on your landscape design and installation. They will

Your Lot Size and Shape

Landscape design is appropriate for all sizes of yards, even ones with no land at all—just a rooftop, patio, or balcony. Regardless of whether your land consists of several acres or only a few dozen square feet, the style and scale of the landscape should suit the size of the lot. The shape of the site will also influence the layout of the landscape style you have chosen. Fitting your style to the edges or boundaries of your property requires an artful touch. You must tailor the style to the space rather than the space to the style.

Later in the design process you will physically measure the size and shape of your site (see page 87). At this point you should simply have a sense of how large or small your space is. You must always consider whether a particular style is appropriate for the amount of land with which you are working.

Your House

The outside of your house presents a particular identity, and the landscape should work to reflect that character. A truly successful landscape design provides a perfect blend of architecture and environment. The landscape styles appropriate for particular styles of houses are discussed in Landscapes for Your Home (see page 40). Determine whether the layout, materials used, or architectural details give your home a distinct style. Books from the local library may help you to correctly identify styles and details.

If the style of your house is contemporary, you will be able to choose from many landscape styles. Remember, however, that house style is not the sole determining factor in the selection of a style for the landscape. Your lifestyle and

desire to make your yard more functional may take precedence.

The relative size of your home is also important to bear in mind as you begin creating a landscape design. A large house usually benefits from some vertical elements to provide balance and make it more aesthetically pleasing on a human scale. Conversely, if the house is small, very tall elements should be

An unusually shaped lot gives you the opportunity to delineate areas for different uses. This property has been enhanced with a patio in colors that echo the existing tree colors.

The softening effect of vines makes this large house less imposing on its rather small lot. The white picket fence reinforces the architectural style of the house and gives an open, friendly feeling while diffusing street-side activity.

avoided, unless your intent is to lose the house within the landscape. Be careful not to build landscape structures that dwarf the house.

In addition, you should evaluate the overall scale of your house in the context of the neighborhood. A small home that is dwarfed by others will not need a plethora of plants to accentuate its isolation. A few well-placed arbors and trees may be all that is needed for privacy and shade. Similarly, a large home sitting among a group of smaller structures will need to relate well to the neighboring buildings—avoid a landscape design that makes the house seem more imposing.

Take a good look at your house and its features as you imagine the new landscape. Would a large expanse of wall unadorned by windows or architectural features

benefit from a vine? Could a few shrubs or planters be used to camouflage an unattractive foundation?

Consider the layout of indoor rooms when designing the landscape. The influence of access, views, and climate control on activity areas will be discussed in more detail later. At this point spend some time simply looking out the windows of your home. Imagine what you would like to see in the landscape. Also take note of the interior design. The coordination of interior design and landscape design in the use of color, texture, and plants can have a stunning effect.

Consider the age of the house as you look at landscape styles, construction materials, and plants. The use of weathered building materials and large plants will give you an established look even if the house

is brand-new, but the decision to use new or weathered materials will ultimately depend on the design you adopt. Another way to create an established landscape instantly is to retain some of the existing features and plants. The extent to which you use such features will depend on whether you are creating a design for a new lot or remodeling an existing yard.

Designing a Landscape on a New Lot

Creating a landscape design for a new lot gives you the advantage of dictating style and overall layout within the confines of the influences previously discussed.

If you are at the blueprint stage or have just started to build your house, you have the freedom to alter or modify the plan to suit your ultimate landscape installation. You can, for example, adjust entries, exits, walks, and driveways to better integrate them with your landscape choices. Look around your lot for existing features, such as large trees, rocks, and streams, that you can incorporate into the landscape design. Make sure that the house construction accommodates these elements so you do not risk destroying them. Although you may feel that the design and construction of the house is taking up all of your creativity, try to decide on at least the major features of the landscape design while the house is being planned.

You can have some of the landscape construction done in conjunction with the building of the home, while you have the equipment on-site. Grading and other earth moving, for example, is considerably easier for a professional to do with a backhoe brought in for foundation work than for you to do later using a shovel and wheelbarrow.

Remodeling an Existing Landscape

Your project may involve remodeling or renovating your existing yard. If so, you have some established elements that you will want to integrate into the new design. Existing trees, paving, or structures may provide a starting point from which to work. Even if you think that nothing in the yard is salvageable, take the time to look at every feature before you begin demolition. Consider remodeling the house at the same time so indoor and outdoor spaces can interact with each other in a harmonious way. Perhaps you need a sliding door to access your new patio, or a new window in the dining room so you can see the new gazebo you are adding to the garden.

If your landscape has a personal or public history, you may decide to accentuate or preserve this identity. Whether it is the overall design that has historical value or just a single tree, let these earlier features inspire your creativity. Relocating a historical structure or plant is well worth the effort. A landscape with a history is a valuable personal and public treasure.

If you are lucky enough to have major landscape elements, such as existing irrigation valves or mature trees and shrubs, that you can use in the new design, you will be able to save a great deal of money. Buying full-grown plants is very expensive. Look to see whether pruning isn't a better idea for an overgrown shrub, or if you can replant a large tree in a different location. During the remodel, you will need to make an extra effort to preserve the plants and structures you want to keep; these expensive items are easily damaged or destroyed in the process of new landscape construction.

Remodeling an existing yard also allows you the opportunity to reflect on the success or failure of the previous design. It will be painfully obvious which plants grew well and which did not. Check access and circulation routes by walking around the yard. Look to see that parking isn't a nuisance. Your analysis of certain landscape influences will not need to be detailed or laborious, because prior experience will have already provided you with many answers.

This Northern California landscape was remodeled with a contemporary emphasis that complements the house, projects a refined presence, and solves site problems. The concrete walk was covered with brick, implying permanence and adding color, and attractive entry lights were installed to guide guests and further enhance the path's appearance. The design satisfies the needs of the homeowners in a handsome way.

CHOOSING A LANDSCAPE STYLE

Attractive residential landscapes don't just happen—they are the result of a great deal of planning. After you have analyzed your planning and design goals, it's time to choose a landscape style. (Of course, it is not necessary to copy a style, but a free rein can result in an incohesive and haphazard outcome for all but the most experienced designers.) Allow the style you like to influence the character of your design. A Japanese lantern and a bamboo do not make an oriental garden, but that feeling may please your senses. This will allow you to combine the various elements—structures, paving, plants, furniture—into an attractive whole. The character and style you choose for your landscape will provide a basic framework, or skeleton, giving it the unity that is essential for a successful design. You can think of landscape style as the broad description or "identity" of a landscape.

Style is an elusive concept that has very real attributes. The most successful style for your landscape design will be one that reflects the style and character of your home, the physical attributes of the site, and the lives of the people who will use the yard. Maximize the potential of your site by choosing a landscape style appropriate to the land, the climate, and the amount of available space. Try to design with what you have rather than working against nature. And, most important, choose a landscape style that you like and will enjoy for years to come.

Once you have chosen a landscape style, all your decisions will be easier. Once you know, for example, that your landscape will be in a contemporary style using native plants, you will be able to narrow down the elements that are appropriate for your yard. Although the range of options will still be quite extensive, having selected the style will give you a design focus.

If your outdoor space is large enough, you have the option of combining different styles in one setting. This will require more thought and finesse on your part in order to create a landscape that is neither out of context with its surroundings nor disharmonious within itself. Native plants and an informal style may be in one area, while another location may be formal and contemporary in style. A small nook might become an oriental rock and sand garden for quiet thought, whereas the remainder of the yard could be composed of active sports areas. Or you may wish to install a rock grotto in some out-of-the-way area in your desert landscape. Tread carefully here—it is much more difficult to successfully combine styles than it is to use a single, unified one.

HOW TO USE THIS GALLERY

Planning your landscape is the best part; you can consider all the possibilities as you decide upon the look, the feel, and the atmosphere you want to create. It is also the least expensive part of the process—dreaming costs nothing.

This gallery has been divided into three sections. Landscapes for Problem Solving features solutions to common landscape liabilities, although the ideas in the section can be incorporated into many situations. Landscapes for Your Lifestyle, as the name implies, consists of design ideas for areas that will serve a purpose—whether practical or recreational. Landscapes for Your Home presents traditional and modern landscape styles that you can consider for the look and feel of your site.

These three sections present a treasure trove of design possibilities. Borrow freely from these ideas, altering them to fit your situation. Designers are constantly taking a good design element and then trying to improve on it or make it work for them.

In browsing through these pages, look for elements that you like and that feel right to you—a favorite plant, for example, or a style that reminds you of a special place. Then ask yourself if this particular style will suit your lifestyle and the way you plan to use your yard. Determine whether the installation and maintenance of a particular landscape style will fit into your budget and time schedule. Another factor to consider is the surrounding context of your landscape. Not all landscape styles will be successful in all climate zones or on all sizes and shapes of lots. Designing with nature rather than against it will make the whole process much more enjoyable.

As you pore over the photos and text, you'll begin to see the unifying themes that tie each landscape together. Look at the details. Notice how plants are used differently for different effects, and see how they can be used to fulfill a purpose or function. Note, for instance, the different ways in which lawns are laid out. A lawn designed in a geometric pattern has a much different feel from a lawn with loose, wavy curves. Trees in straight rows suggest a formal style; groves give a more natural look. If you break the landscape into parts, it will become much more comprehensible to you. Once you understand the parts that

This small-space garden in San Francisco is shared by two homes. A discussion of the needs of both families and of the characteristics of the site determined that the busy families had little time for gardening, making a low-maintenance landscape very important. A few big plants keep gardening chores to a minimum and also avoid making the space seem even smaller.

you like and need, it's just a short step to arranging them in a successful landscape. Keep in mind your choice of landscape style later, as you make design and material decisions.

LANDSCAPES FOR PROBLEM SOLVING

Almost every landscape situation has some constraint or problem. You can turn some of these drawbacks into assets by choosing an appropriate landscape style. You may have functional difficulties, such as noise or poor drainage, or aesthetic concerns, such as dilapidated plants or a bad view. Your landscape problem may be a small plot or even a complete lack of land. The ideas in this section include design solutions for small spaces, balconies and rooftops, large spaces, edges, zero-lot-line homes, hills and slopes, lack of privacy, parking, noise, drainage problems, and obtaining views. The solutions shown here have merit for all locations once you adapt them to the size of your site, the materials, and the climate.

Looking through the photographs in this section, you may find it difficult to tell that these yards were ever problematic. Find the section that describes your landscape problem, and examine the various options for a solution that may be applicable to your design.

Small Spaces

Although urban sites most frequently present a small-space challenge, in some cases a portion of a larger landscape, such as a side yard or enclosed patio, needs to be designed separately as a small space. If you choose to combine a separate small-space design within a larger context, the transition from one space to the other must be smooth and natural. Provide a feeling of continuity among the various parts by using similar materials or plantings.

Small-space landscapes are best used for intimate socializing or as viewing gardens only. These small gardens are good places to show off a favorite sculpture or highlight details such as a specialty plant or fountain.

The greatest challenge in small-space design is the aesthetic problem of scale. If possible, don't have walls or screens that overpower the space. Use several small planting pots instead of one oversized container. Install lightweight, white metal tables and chairs rather than bulky redwood furniture. Small, fine-textured plants, rather than broadleaf ones, are better for a small space. If your goal is to give the illusion of more space, try

affixing mirrors to screens, fences, or house walls. Be careful that the mirror does not face the sun and that it does not become too obvious that it is a deception.

Plantings should tolerate the cramped conditions. If the landscape is in an urban area, you have the added constraints of smog, harsh winds, and limited sunlight. Consult your local garden center for plants that tolerate these conditions. In general, it is better for the unity of the landscape to keep plantings to the same species.

By the very nature of its size, the installation of a small-space landscape usually goes very quickly and, depending on the materials and objects you choose, requires little investment. The amount of maintenance will depend on the type of plants you install. Watering may be your most time-consuming task.

Although many people think of small-space landscapes as a limitation, you should be aware of their advantages. Condensed space means that less of every material is needed, which is nice on the budget. In addition, the time needed for chores is lessened, meaning that you can have an attractive yard with plenty of time left over to enjoy it.

Balconies and Rooftops

Don't let a complete lack of land prevent you from creating a landscape design. Balconies and roofs present especially difficult situations, but they also offer great opportunities for specialty plants and added color while providing a place to get away from it all in the midst of the city. Along with the problems usually associated with small-space landscapes, balconies and rooftops have the added problems of water, drainage, lighting, weight loads, and access. The design of these

LANDSCAPE PLANTS FOR CONTAINERS

In a garden center, you will find countless plants growing in pots and planters. All plants can be grown in containers, at least when they are young. But when you select plants for container culture, choose dwarf or slow-growing types, which will accept container conditions for years. Annuals, bulbs, and perennials are excellent container plants, but many woody species will also adapt to containers. Listed below are some of the best.

Trees

Abies concolor (dwarf forms)	White fir
Albizia julibrissin	Silk tree, mimosa
Araucaria heterophylla	Norfolk Island pine
Chamaecyparis obtusa	Hinoki false-cypress
Citrus limon	Lemon
Cornus florida	Flowering dogwood
Diospyros kaki	Japanese persimmon
Fagus sylvatica (dwarf forms)	European beech
Ficus elastica	
Malus sargentii	Sargent flowering crab apple
Pinus bungeana	Lacebark pine
Pinus sylvestris	Scotch pine, Scots pine
Podocarpus macrophyllus	Yew-pine

Shrubs

Aucuba japonica	Japanese aucuba, spotted laurel
Berberis thunbergii	Japanese barberry
Camellia sasanqua	Sasanqua camellia
Fuchsia hybrids	Fuchsia hybrids
Gardenia augusta (*G. jasminoides*)	Gardenia
Hibiscus syriacus	Shrub althea, rose-of-Sharon
Hydrangea macrophylla	Bigleaf hydrangea
Lagerstroemia indica	Crape myrtle
Mahonia aquifolium	Oregon grape
Nandina domestica	Nandina, heavenly-bamboo
Osmanthus fragrans	Sweet olive
Picea glauca 'Conica'	White spruce
Pinus mugo	Mugo pine
Pittosporum tobira	Japanese pittosporum, mock orange
Potentilla fruticosa	Shrubby cinquefoil
Rhaphiolepis indica	Indian-hawthorn
Rosmarinus officinalis	Rosemary
Tsuga canadensis 'Pendula'	Sargent's weeping hemlock

Vines

Bougainvillea hybrids	Paper flowers
Clematis species	Clematis species
Ficus pumila	Creeping fig, climbing fig
Hydrangea anomala ssp. *petiolaris*	Climbing hydrangea
Jasminum polyanthum	Pink jasmine
Parthenocissus species	Star jasmine

areas is virtually preordained, although you may be able to add flower boxes to extend the planting space. Planters, large pots, and similar heavy objects must be kept over load-bearing walls or near the building edges.

Installation of both constructed elements and plants may be difficult due to the problem of access. Plan all your actions in advance to avoid unnecessary trips through your home or apartment carrying building materials and plants. Storage of unused materials can also be a problem; plan your installation schedule to reflect the need to use everything as soon as it is purchased.

Choose plants that can tolerate crowded root conditions as well as wind, partial shade, and little water. Some plants are more tolerant of these conditions than others. Soil for pots and planters should be lightweight and continually supplied with fertilizer. Vines and ivies are good choices because they are tough, tolerant plants that can climb, screen, and provide blossoms or fragrant blooms without taking up a great deal of room.

Large Spaces

Large-space landscapes present unique problems—mainly the need for intimate spaces and climate control and the huge investments in both installation costs and maintenance time. However, a large property offers the ability to combine many landscape elements or to choose any landscape style. You may also decide to develop only a portion of your land, leaving the rest in a fairly natural condition.

Designing the large-space landscape involves a great deal of thought regarding continuity between areas. The transitions must be smooth and logical. Edges of

areas will need to be addressed, especially the border between a developed area and one left undeveloped, even if it will be developed later.

You will probably want to install this type of landscape in stages, both for financial reasons and for the opportunity it provides you to reflect upon the portion already installed and reconsider what remains to be done. The level of maintenance your grounds require will depend on the landscape style and the proportion of paved to planted areas.

More than any other design situation, large-space landscapes need good initial planning and a well-thought-out installation plan. To keep installation and maintenance costs down, try to work with the present form, size, and type of existing plants. Working with native and low-maintenance exotics can decrease the costs of maintenance as well. Finally, try seed rather than sod to develop the lawn.

Edges and Zero Property Lines

Every piece of property has an edge, of course, as do the various use areas within a landscape. Every edge must be dealt with in some fashion, and some edges present more difficulty than others. Houses that are too close to the house next door, that are adjacent to a commercial or retail establishment, or that are next to a busy street present some of the more common edging problems. Zero-property-line issues occur when a building is constructed exactly on the lot line. This is a problem for the home-owner next door, who is presented with a tall, blank wall.

The solution to these edging problems mainly involves blocking out the landscape beyond your property line. This must be done in a manner consistent with the overall landscape style.

Your solution will vary, depending on your specific edging problem. Low retaining or freestanding walls in a variety of materials can serve as physical breaks between properties or use areas without entirely blocking views or light. Higher brick, masonry, or stucco walls, or wall systems of wood or dry-stacked stone, will block sight lines and noise and act as a passive security system.

In areas where there is no clear indication of a property line, edges are an equally important, though slightly different, problem. If no clear property line exists, and if fences are not allowed, it will be important for you to match the character of the surrounding landscape. When planting these areas, determine if there are any elements or views that you would like to highlight or frame. Plant selectively to provide privacy to the rooms you use the most, and leave the remaining landscape in context with the neighborhood. If there is an existing landscape next door, design the edge so that your property flows into the next in an orderly fashion. Matching one landscape to another might require some cooperation on the part of your neighbors.

Zero-property-line situations may also require cooperation between neighbors. If possible, grow a vine on the offending wall to soften the view. Trees or tall shrubs, if there is enough ground space, will also lessen the impact of a building.

The edge of your property may be large enough to be considered a side yard, providing an extra, albeit limited, area for socializing or outdoor use. Narrow side yards are excellent for storage or as a pet area. If the sun exposure is favorable, you may opt to locate the vegetable

garden here, out of sight from the rest of the landscape. A side yard just off a bedroom may make a cozy private patio. The solutions for small-space landscapes also apply to side yards.

It is important that edges look good, yet the landscape design should not be overly complicated or elaborate. Access to small areas can be difficult, so you must consider installation requirements during the design process. For example, you may want to prefabricate a portion of a structure, if possible,

Top: The designer of this landscape made the lot look larger by providing views and camouflaging the property boundaries with plantings. Bottom: The pond directs attention away from the property edge and offers an excellent view.

Terraced retaining walls aid in preventing erosion on hills and slopes as well as providing an attractive transition between slope and parking area. Timbers are easy to build with, and they blend well into any garden setting. You can use irregular and rugged timbers for a rustic look or milled timbers for a more formal setting. They can be stained to match the color of the house or other garden features, and their appearance improves with age as they weather and take on a more permanent look.

before installing it permanently. Maintaining edge landscapes can be a difficult proposition. Poor access makes getting to plants for maintenance awkward. Avoid using lawn or any other ground cover that requires constant care.

Hills and Slopes

Steep terrain poses particular opportunities and constraints for landscape design and construction. Slopes may present a hazard or limit the usable outdoor space. To extend the usable area, you can install decks, terraces, steps, or walls. However, design and installation of these elements will require thought as to costs, erosion problems, engineering, reinforcement and drainage of retaining walls, and means of getting from one level to another.

Decks lend an informal feel to a landscape; paved levels or terraces achieve a more formal look. Decks and terraces should be designed to complement the character of the home. A stately masonry home will require terraced levels of brick or stone. Decks are best for homes with wood siding, especially those on steep, wooded sites. Painted wood decking allows you to fit

wood into situations that require more formality.

Plan decks and terraces to the topography of the slope. Terraces designed to the existing slope level require less cutting and filling. Multilevel decks that are close to the existing topography require less engineering and will lower material costs.

Installing decks requires only basic carpentry skills. Maintenance of decks involves resealing and painting the wood periodically and examining the footings and beams for dry rot. Terraces require a minimum of cleanup and periodic maintenance.

Pay attention to existing plants when designing decks and terraces. It may be worth building around an established tree, especially one on land that may not support many trees. Terraces can support annual or perennial beds, vegetable gardens, or any low-level shrub. Deck plants should be in pots or boxes, much the same as for rooftops and balconies.

Ground covers as well as shrubs and trees can control erosion. Trees that provide slope stabilization and protection include strawberry tree (*Arbutus unedo*), eucalyptus species, and pines; shrubs include rock rose (*Cistus purpureus*), ceanothus species, cotoneaster species, and junipers; ground covers include bearberry (*Arctostaphylos uva-ursi*), dwarf coyotebrush (*Baccharis pilularis*), ceanothus species, and cotoneaster species.

When planting on slopes, avoid erosion or slumping problems by spreading jute mesh netting over the disturbed soil.

Need for Privacy

Creating privacy in a landscape is simple. In general, areas of high use need privacy the most. You will want to screen your outdoor patio

or entertaining areas from the views of others. You might want a feeling of intimacy and protection at your front door, and you may also wish to enclose your favorite spot in the landscape. In addition to blocking eye-level views, you may need to screen views from buildings above your grade, or from upstairs windows that look down onto your patio or deck.

Privacy does not always mean unneighborly fences and walls. Screens or open baffles with intricate patterns of espaliers or vines can also block views. Fences can be constructed with visual interest on both sides, whether plantings or architectural detail.

Designing for privacy is as simple as laying out the areas you wish to cordon off. The position of landscape plantings, fences, walls, and garden structures will divide private and public spaces. Views from above can be blocked with an overhead arbor or grove of canopy trees. Remember that canopy trees leave the trunk area open for circulation.

Constructed elements will yield instant privacy, whereas hedges and other planted screens will take months or possibly years to grow to the point where they provide adequate screening.

Plant screens can be the least expensive to install if you can afford to wait until they reach maturity. Don't use deciduous plant materials as visual buffers. Consider the overhead and eye-level views when you choose plantings. Coniferous trees normally grow slowly, but they screen from the ground level to several stories up. In time, however, many conifers lose their lower branches, making additional understory planting necessary.

Wood can also be an inexpensive way to create a privacy screen or baffle. With the wide range of possible designs and colors of paint and stain, wood fences and screens will fit into almost any style of landscape. Masonry walls and structures are generally more difficult and expensive to install, but they provide immediate screening and may solve other functional problems—especially regarding drainage. They also open up terracing opportunities in the landscape.

As with other functional elements, it is vitally important that structures remain in context with the landscape style you have chosen, in order to keep that all-important unity of design. If you need to partition only a small portion of the site, select screening materials that complement the other plantings and constructed elements. A small gazebo or bench hidden under a tree can be an intimate, private space for yourself.

Constructed elements will require only periodic painting or minor maintenance, whereas plantings may require somewhat more care to maintain the visual barrier.

Parking

Although automobiles are crucial to our livelihood, they make poor garden sculpture. We require space in

Flowering shrubs screen the sidewalk from the house, providing some privacy while treating those passing by to as nice a view as the one seen from inside.

Wild, grassy plains inspired the design of this driveway. A screen (rear) delineates the parking area for the resident so that circulation of visiting cars is unobstructed.

our landscapes to park our cars, work on them, and secure them. You may require additional storage and access space for a recreational vehicle, a boat, motorcycles, and guest parking. The amount of square footage given up in garage space, driveway paving, and walks to and from these areas is considerable, so some thought must be given to these circulation problems during your landscape design.

In most cases the driveway will be an established element of your lot. Removing an existing driveway is hard work, and you should probably attempt this only if relocation of the garage is also in order. If you are planning a new home, give some thought to the position of the driveway and garage as the home is being designed. Consider a side entry to lessen the impact of the driveway on the landscape at the front of your home.

By experimenting with the surface of the driveway, you can create new patterns in the landscape. Try using colored concrete or other surfacing materials to tie the drive into the design of the home. Soften the effect of paved areas by turning the driveway into a lawn with the

installation of concrete turf block, inside of which you plant grass. This looks like lawn yet provides a hard surface to drive on. Guest or additional parking can be added in this manner without making the yard look like a parking lot.

For continuity in your overall landscape design, carry the patio paving material over into the surface of the driveway; or line the driveway or paths to and from it with concrete bands, pavers, bricks, or interlocking stones that match materials from the house siding or a landscape element such as a garden wall.

The shapes of both the driveway and connecting paths should be in context with the overall landscape style. If the rest of the landscape is loose and informal, for instance, use curved edges for the driveway and paths. If the landscape design is formal and symmetrical, a straight-lined driveway would be more in order.

Locate parking for ease of access, yet enough removed so as not to overpower the home and yard. Although it is natural to want to screen automobiles from sight, you may want to leave a portion of the view open for security reasons. Provide open views between the driveway and the door you will be entering at night. Make sure drives and paths are well lighted for night entry. Be careful of trees and overhead wires—and the birds they attract—just above the parking areas.

Locate extra parking and access areas away from the major plantings. In fact, try to plan these areas so that they act as buffers between you and undesirable neighboring uses and noises. Arbors make excellent screens for extra vehicles if a garage is not available, but choose vines that will not drop fruit or sap onto the cars. Be careful not to locate sprinkler heads and fragile landscape accents too near driveways, and especially too close to the turning area from street to driveway. If possible, provide drivers with at least a few extra feet of room for maneuvering.

Installing driveways is difficult, time-consuming, and expensive. You want to be very careful of grading and drainage needs, especially in areas that freeze in winter.

Noise

Many American homes are afflicted with undesirable noise from a variety of sources. Highways, street frontages, commercial or industrial neighbors, playgrounds, and neighboring homes all present potential sources of noise.

Completely walling in your property is one means of noise control. This is a rather drastic and expensive proposition, however, and one properly used only on large lots. Walls would overpower a medium to small yard. Your solution should reflect the style and character of your landscape. Noise reduction can be achieved in any size and style of home.

Water is the easiest way to mask unwanted noise. A small, strategically located fountain in your yard can divert attention away from unwanted clatter. Installing bird feeders and plants that attract birds can also provide a diversionary source of sound. Locate your social areas closer to the source of the noise, and your intimate areas in places of relative quiet. Use storage areas, driveways, and other areas that do not require a lot of human use as buffers between you and the noise source.

A variety of methods for reducing noise is available. Of these, a masonry wall is the most difficult to install and construct, but it offers the greatest potential in noise

abatement. Simple closed-picket fencing also helps keep out sound and is relatively inexpensive.

It may be that noise control is needed in only a portion of your yard. If this is the case, create a buffer, baffle, or screen so that its beginning and end have logical conclusions in the landscape. Because this is a very functional element, it is easy to overlook the visual aspect of a noise-reducing structure. It should look like a part of the whole, not like something tacked on at the last moment.

Vines on or along bare walls serve to deaden ambient sound, reducing echo effects and noise reverberations. Traditional plantings of trees, shrubs, and ground covers offer little in terms of noise reduction; however, such plantings do offer a great psychological buffer between you and the source of the noise. Use trees, shrubs, and vines to soften the hard surface of a noise-reducing stone or concrete wall.

Drainage Problems

Almost all lots have some form of drainage problem. These range from patios that have settled to major grading problems throughout the site. Low spots or areas that

A tall, solid wall blocks street noise and increases security. Plants soften the barrier and enhance the qualities of the wall.

Dry creek beds aid drainage as well as enhance appearance.

do not drain are found in most lots. You may need to regrade, repave, and add drain line and drain rock.

Regrading the yard for positive drainage is an easy operation that can often be done with a number of hand tools and a line level (see Grading and Drainage, page 109). Once the grading and drainage have been done for a piece of property, there is rarely a need to regrade. You may have to clean and flush area drains and their respective lines periodically.

When diverting water remember to respect its destination once it leaves your property. You may cause a disastrous situation—and possibly commit an illegal act—by directing the flow to another person's property.

Areas that do not drain can be turned into decks, patios, or berms to be planted. By adding soil and a new paving surface, you may be able to raise the existing grade enough so that water will flow away from the home.

Designing around drainage problems can be tricky. If you cannot

find a suitable cost-efficient solution, you may want to work with the wet spot or problem runoff area. If you find that it is too costly to install area drains and tile, try redesigning the area for water-tolerant plantings or a rock and sand garden. If you have a large area that does not drain, it may be possible to construct a pond or small lake. Creating small, dry creek beds or natural-looking drainage swales will divert water and solve problems with wet areas.

If your yard has clay soil or an impenetrable hardpan, you may want to incorporate more constructed elements than plants into your design, as these areas will require plants that can tolerate waterlogged conditions. A wildflower seed mix is an inexpensive solution to large areas with tough soil conditions.

Obtaining Views

Views in the landscape are created by the addition or enhancement of some particular element worthy of interest. A central focus in the landscape provides a topic for conversation and a point for contemplation. Obtaining views involves both finding the point of interest and a method of framing it.

Hilltop sites make obtaining a view an easy task. Design strategically placed constructed elements, such as archways, fence cutouts, and trellises, to frame an existing or planned vista. Keep surrounding plants trimmed and pruned so that they do not obscure the view. Broad-headed canopy trees offer trunks that can split a view into many-faceted frames. Lawn and ground-cover patterns can lead the eye to the view beyond or to a particular landscape element. Fine-textured (small-leaved) plants give the illusion of depth and can focus a view to a particular vantage point.

When topography or neighboring homes prevent a panoramic view, you need to create your own focal point within the landscape. This can be done in any size garden or yard. In small-space landscapes, a fancy flowerpot filled with blooming annuals can become a worthy focus. In most locations a fountain, sculpture, or specific planting can do the trick. A multitrunk specimen tree with night uplighting can be a spectacular focal point. Or turn your view onto your house—especially if it has an interesting architectural feature such as gables or window details.

Topiaries make an interesting focal point, but the plants must mature before they can function as true landscape accents. You may want to use a constructed element as a temporary focal point or framing device while waiting for a specialty plant to grow.

Installing a view can be as expensive or inexpensive as you like. Framing a view with a smattering of trees and shrubs is, for instance, considerably less expensive than constructing a gazebo at the end of a long axis. A viewing opportunity may be just a simple element of your landscape—a single bench or small fountain—that one finds by surprise on turning a corner along a garden path.

LANDSCAPES FOR YOUR LIFESTYLE

Your particular lifestyle should dictate the elements to be included in your landscape design so your yard becomes usable and functional, rather than just an aesthetic statement or a backdrop for your house. Entertaining, growing food, and just plain relaxing are activities common to landscape spaces. Children use some landscapes, handicapped

Some thinning of trees was needed to reveal a view from this deck.

people others; and some people like to play volleyball. A single family may desire a number of different activity areas within one yard. All activity areas and lifestyle needs require consideration in order to be integrated within the design.

During the design process, you should evaluate yourself and the outdoor activities you enjoy. Your landscape style must incorporate these activities. Here we discuss landscape design ideas for playing, relaxing and entertaining, growing flowers, low-maintenance gardening, growing food, and providing access for those with mobility problems. You will be bound by certain constraints, such as lot size, climate, and budget. The best way to provide space in your yard for all the activities you desire is to have them in mind from the beginning of the design process. Look through this gallery to find solutions that can work for you.

A Place for Playing
The type of play activity you include in your landscape will depend on your needs and the

Opposite: The best landscape design reflects the needs and tastes of the owners. If a shady outdoor eating area, combined with a place for the children to play, is what is most important to you, make sure you plan carefully to achieve those spaces.

amount of space you have to work with. A tennis court, for instance, takes much more space than a tot lot for small children. Almost all homes can have some type of play area. Even small homes can usually have a basketball hoop, a tennis backboard wall, a volleyball net, or a play fountain. Integrate play areas into the site so they neither overwhelm nor alter the landscape style. Even traditional Colonial-style homes can integrate a tennis court, provided fencing materials, plantings, and location are carefully thought out.

When designing play areas, always keep in mind the need for unity of style. Areas for lawn sports can be laid out in both formal and informal gardens. Children's play areas can be worked into your style so long as you keep materials, colors, and forms in context with the rest of the garden space. Tennis or sports courts can be effectively screened from the other parts of the landscape, if necessary. Colors can be applied to the surface of a court so it will recede into the landscape.

Locate activity areas close to the rooms in the house to which they relate. Think of the impact of the play activity on the house and the house activity on the play area. For instance, you may want to avoid attaching a basketball hoop near the master bedroom if you know that teenagers will be playing early on Saturday mornings. Most lawn sports can be situated in any area that offers sufficient space and that can be integrated into your chosen landscape style. For safety's sake, locate children's areas where they can be watched from either the family room or the kitchen. In addition, choose the materials to be used in children's play areas with care and always bear in mind that play equipment for small children serves them for only a short time.

All play areas are best located in the path of the sun (unless you live in the southwestern United States). Lawns, courts, and tot lots will dry faster, stay warmer, and be used more often if sunny.

Play areas for lawn sports may be the easiest and quickest to install.

PLANNING FOR DOGS . . .

Dogs that live outdoors require a snug doghouse and a well-fenced enclosure. The doghouse should have a windbreak at the door or should face away from the wind. The inside should be only slightly larger than the dog when it is curled up to sleep, in order to maintain body warmth. The walls should not be insulated except in very cold climates; otherwise, humidity and condensation will cause problems.

Build a flat roof with a slight slope. Despite the antics of Snoopy on his peaked-roofed doghouse, a flat roof provides a better platform for a dog to lie on. A slight slope allows for drainage. Make the doghouse portable, and move it periodically to aid in parasite control and allow the surrounding lawn to regenerate.

Controlling your dog is essential for its safety and the safety of other animals and people. Perimeter fences and dog runs are two common methods of control. The

size of the dog run will depend on the size of both the yard and the dog. In general, however, allow an area 6 feet wide and at least 12 feet long for a medium-sized dog run. Enclose the area with a fence that is at least 6 feet high and made of chain link or sturdy welded-wire mesh. Concrete floors are the easiest to clean and to keep free of parasites, although gravel is easier on the dog's paws. Some combination of the two is preferable. If the

dog run does not include a doghouse, provide a shaded area, such as canvas stretched across the fencing, under which your dog can relax during hot weather.

When placing a doghouse or dog run in your yard, keep in mind that you will need to get to it for watering and feeding throughout the year. You may want to include an all-weather path to it. If you're installing a sprinkler system, consider adding a hose bibb near the dog run for watering and ease in cleanup.

Choose irrigation heads that don't protrude and that feature a protective rubber cover. Position sprinklers on the outer perimeter of the play area.

Preplanning the orientation, location, and means of access to a play area will save you money and possibly time when you are ready to implement your full scheme. If you are adding a play area to an existing yard, either design it to work with your layout, or screen it to hide paving and apparatuses.

Maintenance of play areas will depend on the design you have chosen. Tennis and sports courts will need to be swept and hosed down regularly and resurfaced and repainted periodically. Tot lots should be constantly examined for sharp objects, and play equipment inspected for signs of wear or potential failure. Lawn areas that are used for play or sports will require more maintenance than a typical lawn. Installation of a tough rye or fescue grass may help keep the lawn area from looking too battered after weekend sports.

. . . AND OTHER PETS

Due to their independent nature, cats are easier to provide for in your landscape than dogs. If your cat spends time outside, plan a sheltered place that it can get to in case of rain or snow and a shaded area in which it can relax during hot weather. A small patch of catnip will provide a welcome tonic for your cat.

Rabbits should be kept in small wire-and-wood hutches protected from wind and direct sun. Hutches are best located several feet above the ground for ease of access, to allow droppings to fall below, and to provide protection from predators. Rabbit droppings can be used for soil conditioning. As with dog runs, remember your need to have year-round access to the rabbit hutch.

Chickens are more demanding than most outdoor pets, but this extra effort is offset by the eggs they provide. Chicken coops should be kept within a temperature range of 50° to 70° F the year around; they should be cool and airy in the summer and warm and dry in winter. Add an outside pen of woven 12- to 14-gauge wire fencing that is 6 feet high.

Ducks and geese, because of their built-in insulation, are more hardy than chickens. A simple wood box located out of the wind is adequate for bedding. A small pond is desirable but must be cleaned periodically. Some species of ducks—especially mallards—are preferred by gardeners because of their great appetite for snails and slugs. Geese eat foliage and will strip plants they like. Be careful in purchasing ducks or geese, however, if any kind of creek or drainage canal passes through your property. Loyalty is not a trait of waterfowl.

Consult the local park department about wild predators; in some areas the abundance of animals such as raccoons makes raising rabbits and poultry a stressful task. Some communities have rules prohibiting farm animals in residential areas. Check with local officials before purchasing these as pets.

This outdoor design brings together all the elements of the yard, from house to patio to garden and trees, into a balanced statement. The patio size approximates that of an indoor room, which tends to make people feel most comfortable.

The cost of installing a play area will depend on the size and style, as well as the region you live in and the materials you use. Any lighting, drinking fountains, drainage systems, and storage facilities will affect your budget and schedule.

The plantings around play areas should not be thorny, poisonous, attractive to bees, or allergenic. Also avoid high-maintenance deciduous trees that drop litter. Strong-limbed trees such as Italian alder (*Alnus cordata*) and scarlet oak (*Quercus coccinea*) are suitable. Shrubs such as Japanese aucuba (*Aucuba japonica*) for semishade locations, and vernal witch hazel (*Hamamelis vernalis*), northern bayberry (*Myrica pensylvanica*), and English laurel (*Prunus laurocerasus*) are safe bets for borders and backgrounds. Sturdy ground covers include English ivy (*Hedera* species), lamb's ears (*Stachys byzantina*), and zoysia-grass (*Zoysia* species).

Areas for Relaxing and Entertaining

You will want to provide areas in your landscape to which you can bring family, guests, or just yourself when you wish to relax. Activities involving sitting, introspection, or conversation can also be associated with pool and spa use in the landscape.

Any style of home and most lot sizes can be designed with some sort of patio, pool, or spa complex. Your lifestyle, lot size, and budget will determine whether your place for relaxing is a small planted area with a simple bench or a large spa complex that accommodates swimming and sunning. Pools and spas are a considerable landscape expense and may be phased in to lessen the initial cost.

An area for reading or introspection may require little more than additional plantings for a screening effect. Built-in or movable seating is all that is needed to complete this simple area, which can double as a social space for entertaining. Pool and spa areas require fencing, storage areas, utilities, and pump and filter enclosures.

The design of areas for relaxing and entertaining should be in keeping with the character of your home. Maintain the unity of the landscape by working with the same materials, degree of formality (or informality), and scale as the home. Design pools and patios with the same flow of lines as the rest of the landscape. Continuity of spaces and visual connection is important to these areas. Look at the edges and see if what you have designed fits with the adjacent space or use.

When laying out a patio area, keep the space small enough to give an intimate, cloistered feeling. The patio should not look empty and barren. Remember that people feel most comfortable when rooms, including outdoor "rooms," are designed to a human scale. Think of the indoor space you use for the same kind of entertaining, and design the outdoor space accordingly. Lighting, climate control, and easy access to the kitchen are essential to the success of outdoor entertainment areas.

Place outdoor entertainment spaces adjacent to indoor entertainment rooms. The patio space beyond the doors and windows of the home will give the illusion of a larger indoor room, and the access will provide easy spillover during parties.

Pools, which are great for relaxing, can also double as sculptural elements in the landscape. The pool may become a focal point of your chosen landscape style. As a reflecting pool or formal-looking centerpiece, it can serve not only a recreational purpose but an aesthetic one as well.

Locate the pool where you can view this important feature from the home. Situate it close enough to the changing, bath, or family rooms for easy access. Place the pump and filters away from rooms that would be disturbed by the noise. A pool should be oriented so that it receives full sun most of the day. The absorption of heat keeps energy costs down and helps prevent algae growth.

Locate the patio between the pool and the house for easy access, and place it so you can face the pool and the path of the sun at the same time.

If you're installing your landscape in phases, with the pool as a later stage, leave at least a 10-foot easement around the future pool area for excavation and truck access.

Although patio areas can be installed successfully by anyone with some basic construction experience, pools and spas are probably best left to professionals. In addition to the expense, a great number of safety factors are involved in their design and installation, and there is often a wealth of engineering data to be handled as well. Both pools and spas require constant litter removal, controlling algae, and the maintenance of chlorine levels. Pumps, filters, and heaters require routine adjustment and sometimes repair as well. See page 81 for more information on planning swimming pools.

The maintenance of patio areas simply involves weekly sweeping or washing. Plant shade trees that will shield some of a patio area from the sun in hot weather. Line a patio or pool area with shrubs and hedges to add privacy, control wind, and screen objectionable views. Vines will soften fences, arbors, house siding, and other constructed elements, providing a cozier atmosphere. If the pool decking drains into the planted areas, check for plant species that tolerate chlorine. Colorful annuals and perennials in pots or planters can add a festive look to patio areas as well as aid in controlling the size of the space.

Because these areas are best landscaped with low-maintenance, thornless plants that don't shed leaves or attract bees and other pests, appropriate trees are evergreen pear (*Pyrus kawakamii*), leyland cypress (× *Cupressocyparis leylandii*), or white spruce (*Picea glauca*); shrubs include common boxwood (*Buxus sempervirens*),

This dazzling floral display flourishes because of the well-drained hillside soil. The types of flowering plantings you use in your landscape will depend on your house, your gardening expertise, and the amount of time you have for care.

English laurel, and yew species. Suitable ground covers include coprosma, English ivy, Japanese spurge (*Pachysandra terminalis*), and periwinkle (*Vinca minor*).

Growing Flowers

Almost any home benefits from the addition of flowers. If you wish to grow flowers, you must give extra thought and care to their selection and integration into your landscape design. You may wish to select plants that fit into a specific color scheme or composition, that have a seasonal blooming period, or that provide a year-round display of color and texture.

Every region has its own variety of flowering plant species that do well. Your choice of plants will depend primarily on the amount of time you want to spend on maintenance and the types you wish to grow. In general, every type of flowering plant can be adapted to every landscape look.

Water and rich soil are general requirements for seasonal displays of color. For maximum bloom, annuals and perennials require full sun in a southern exposure.

Flowering shrubs and trees can provide color in spaces where annuals and perennials find it hard to blossom. For continued visual interest, choose plants that have an interesting form and foliage when not in bloom.

It is possible to grow flowering plants in any size landscape. In small areas, use planters and pots for year-round color. Flowers may be limited to only a portion of the yard to keep down initial costs, avoid hours of maintenance, and increase the impact of the color display.

Low-Maintenance Gardening

Designing a low-maintenance landscape requires thought as to access, paving materials, landscape elements or structures, and plantings that can not only survive but continue to look good with minimum upkeep. Low maintenance need not be associated with any one particular landscape style. Even formal gardens can be designed so that the only maintenance is occasional mowing and clipping. More than the look, your choice of elements, materials, and plants will determine your long-term maintenance responsibilities. Pools, spas, and fountains may need to be drained during the winter months in regions with freezing weather. Wood structures need periodic repainting, and vines that cover walls may have to be removed if painting or repair is necessary. Wood is perhaps the least durable of all the patio or deck surfaces, whereas a concrete patio will need little care.

Watering systems need periodic repair, especially in landscapes that endure a lot of use and activity. Keep maintenance time down with the installation of automatic watering systems.

Purchase plants that require only simple watering, occasional fertilizing, and periodic spraying. This does not mean that all of your plantings should be cacti and succulents. Low-maintenance trees for these areas can be Norfolk Island pine (*Araucaria heterophylla*), strawberry tree, incense cedar (*Calocedrus decurrens*), chamaecyparis species, and ilex species. Drought- and disease-tolerant shrubs include rock rose, euonymus species, savin juniper (*Juniperus sabina*), and dwarf rosemary (*Rosmarinus officinalis* 'Prostratus'). A wildflower hydroseed mix may substitute for annuals and perennials if you desire strong shows of color.

A low-maintenance landscape is no more difficult to install than any other style you may choose. Initial costs for elements such as paved areas, structures, irrigation, and plantings will be the same. The follow-up costs may in fact be substantially lower.

Low maintenance can mean different things to different people. What might seem a low level of maintenance to a person who enjoys gardening can seem quite time-consuming to a nongardener.

A series of brick stepping-stones creates interest without upkeep at one end of this low-maintenance garden in Charleston, South Carolina. The bricks are set below the level of the mower blades, eliminating the need for trimming.

This backyard has been carefully planned to accommodate a variety of vegetables, and with successive plantings will keep fresh ingredients on the table all season long.

Growing Food

Depending on the size of the yard, edible plants will generally be only a part of your design. Their seasonality may make these sections of the landscape unsightly during certain times of year, so you must carefully consider their placement in your overall design. In choosing a location, pay particular attention to the amount of sun exposure—many food plants require full sun.

Integrate edible plants into the broader context of the landscape. Vegetable beds, herb gardens, and fruit trees can be placed throughout the site. Angles and curves used in other areas of your design should be reflected in the planting beds as well. Plant low shrubs or build garden walls on the border of the vegetable beds to hide the area

when it is dormant in winter. Herbs as accent edging plants provide interesting color and fragrance when in flower, and pattern and texture throughout the year.

When planting fruit trees, consider their size, form, and flowering period so they can be an integral part of your landscape concept. Be careful of the placement of fruit trees near patio, pool, or parking areas. Falling fruit and the birds that fruit trees attract can be hazardous to guests and automobiles. Storage facilities for tools, fertilizers, and other gardening implements should be located near planting beds.

The timing of food plant installation is probably more important than for other landscape plants. When purchasing edible plants, be sure to check for exact planting times.

Gaining Access

People with less than full mobility can find moving about in gardens to be cumbersome and potentially dangerous. Sudden grade changes, rough pathways, poisonous or thorny plants, and planting arrangements that are all at ground level make enjoying and maintaining a home landscape difficult for the disabled or elderly. If your landscape goal includes the enjoyment of your yard by people who use wheelchairs or walkers or have other limitations in mobility, your design should include the principles of whole-access landscape design. Whole-access gardens, like any other landscape, should be designed with the opportunities and constraints of the individual situation in mind.

The layout of a whole-access landscape should allow for easy accessibility and enjoyment by everyone entering the site. Your landscape should have a clear organization of space and circulation. In small lots this is not a problem. In areas where space is abundant, paths, patios, activity areas, and seating areas must have connections that are clear and understandable to those whose vision or mobility is impaired.

Every size of landscape can include aspects of whole-access design. If the space is especially limited, install table-height planters on a balcony or terrace. Build beds for flowering or food plants at waist height for easy maintenance and accessibility. Tailor wide, bench-style edges on the planting beds so someone can sit on the edge while

Left: This entryway was designed for a wheelchair with no compromise in appearance. The path uses flat-edged stones that are placed level enough to provide a smooth surface; the border offers colors that change throughout the year.
Right: Matched concrete integrates a wheelchair access ramp with the existing entryway steps, and provides a level rolling surface.

caring for the plantings. Freestanding furniture must be solid and should be carefully placed to avoid collision. Paths should be wider than normal to allow for wheelchair access. Use concrete paving materials, as they are most easily leveled, and keep all paths clear of debris.

Your needs may include the use of ramps instead of stairways and steps. All inclines should be gradual and include frequent landings. Provide handrails on all stairways and on paths as needed. Pools and spa equipment must be safe for use and allow easy entrance and exit.

Take care in the selection and construction of the details of a whole-access landscape. The plantings chosen should reflect thought as to their characteristics. Avoid thorny, poisonous, allergenic, or difficult-to-maintain plantings. Also important are trees that do not drop litter or have roots that heave paving.

Review the site periodically for needed improvements, restricting conditions, or hazards that may have recently appeared.

You may encounter additional expenses in the installation of this type of landscape because of ramps, handrails, and other such construction, but costs for the remainder of the landscape installation will be the same as for any other style.

LANDSCAPES FOR YOUR HOME

Your home has a style and character all its own. That style—with its architectural forms, layout, details, and colors—will suggest the general direction you should take in choosing a landscape style. Your home may be constructed in a clearly identifiable design type or historical style. Many such home styles lend themselves to a particular type of landscape. If your home is part of a neighborhood constructed by one builder or in a planned development, it may be identical to many others. Yet its form and style, considered on an individual basis, will help you decide which landscape style is right for you.

Let your tastes and travels influence your decision as to landscape style. The design ideas in this section are based on Italian, French, English, oriental, Early American, Moorish, native and natural, contemporary, and avant-garde landscape styles. Many, if not all, will be familiar to you, and it should be readily apparent whether a style shown here is right for your house and yard.

Italian

During the Renaissance, the renewed interest in art, business, literature, and philosophy spread into the outdoors. Looking to the past, the Italians were influenced by the Greeks and the Romans. The design principles they uncovered in their study of the ancients led directly to the Italian landscape style. Their use of classic forms, symmetry, columns, and sculpture reflects this inspiration.

The classic Italian garden utilizes a single or double axis to divide the entire site. An axis in the landscape can be thought of as a dividing line creating equal parts on both sides of the landscape space. A balance results when the area of one side equals the area of the other. Symmetry and balance are paramount in the Italian style. Slope, sculptures, plantings, and walks are balanced on either side. If six trees are located on the right side, six should be on the left.

Hills and mountainous terrain surround the major centers of culture and commerce in Italy. It was in these hilly environs that Italian landscape design developed to complement the villas, and thus slopes and tumbling water play a major part in this style.

Because wood was a rare resource in Italy, most constructed landscape elements were made of local rock. Although marble and travertine may not be readily available in the United States, suitable substitutes such as concrete and masonry are fairly easy to come by.

Landscapes in the true Italian style fit wonderfully into sloped or hilly yards. Multilevel terraces joined by steps are typical of the Italian villa and garden. Some of the early Italian gardens used ramps instead of stairs to connect one level to another. Gardens in this style make for excellent strolling and easy viewing of landscape patterns or flowers. Playful, moving water is also a major feature of these gardens.

The Italian garden is easy to lay out because it is centered around a main axis, with all the landscape elements balanced on either side. Installation is easy because you work with straight lines and right angles. Curves in a parterre are easily laid out in simple geometric forms. Landscape parterres are the formal geometric gardens laid out with clipped boxwood hedges. These are commonly planted with brightly colored flowers within their borders.

Although this type of landscape style is best suited for a sloped site, it can be implemented in most yards, large or small, flat or sloped,

Although the extravagance of large public gardens, such as this one at Villa Mansi, Italy, cannot be duplicated in the residential landscape, the details can. Take note of the way the white statuary and flowering bushes on the path lead you to the fountain, which provides a focal point in the center of a sight plane to deemphasize a narrow lot.

A carefully worked out design, this formal French-style garden is intended to be enjoyed from an upstairs window.

so long as the principles of balance and symmetry are maintained. This style is most compatible with a house of masonry or stucco with a clay-tiled roof, but can also work with many other American home styles.

A wide variety of plant materials is adaptable to this style of garden. Typical trees include Italian cypress (*Cupressus sempervirens*), olive (*Olea europaea*), and citrus trees. Shrubs include common boxwood, Japanese privet (*Ligustrum japonicum*), holly, (*Ilex* species), and English yew (*Taxus baccata*). Lan-

tana species and dwarf rosemary are common ground covers.

The cost of installing this type of garden is moderate; the majority of your investment will be spent on the terraces, walkways, steps, and pools or fountains, if any are included. Maintaining a traditional Italian garden consists mostly of trimming boxwood and hedges along with the routine garden upkeep (fertilizing, weeding, and spraying).

French

France was greatly influenced by the Italian Renaissance, and travel and trade between the two countries led to a sharing of ideas and styles. French landscape design thus has much in common with the Italian style. Because the great gardens of France were built in areas devoid of hills and mountains, however, the simple geometry and balance of the Italian villas did not work well in every situation. Without natural level changes to create interest, the French established a more complex and elaborate system of landscape geometry.

Both palaces outside Paris—Versailles and Vaux-le-Vicomte—are prototypes of the French formal garden. Although the designers adhered to the principles of symmetry and balance on which the Italian landscape is based, they enlarged upon them to develop multi-axis and complex woven patterns. Parterres of intricate design, flowers of many colors, long vistas, and tree-shaded alleys became the symbols of traditional French landscapes. As in Italy, water had an important role, not so much for its playfulness but for its use as a design form on the land. Long reflecting pools, moats, and diverted rivers took water to a grand scale and became a major element of the French style.

Flat sites with grand views are well suited to the French landscape style. Flat planes of water and intricate designs of boxwood with perennials typify this style. This type of garden is suitable for strolling and for displaying perennial or annual collections. The French style is also appropriate if you wish to use plants as an architectural statement. The intricacy of this style and its emphasis on symmetry, balance, and order make it the perfect setting for long rows of trees, perennial beds, clipped hedges, and large expanses of lawn.

The French style is a bit difficult to draw on paper due to the intricately interwoven designs, but you can easily copy a design that is already laid out. Look for one that you can adapt to fit your garden. Once it is laid out, the garden is simple to install: Trees, shrubs, and lawn are planted in straight rows; irrigation heads are installed in simple patterns.

This type of garden may be more difficult to maintain due to the large expanses of lawn and the amount of water required. Trees, hedges, and boxwood must be trimmed approximately every three months. Planted beds must be maintained frequently and replaced at roughly the same interval.

This style is not suited to the arid southwestern United States, where dry winds and hot sun can deplete lawn areas and pools of water at a rapid rate. It is well suited for a flat site with a view. Large, traditional homes sit grandly in this type of landscape.

The most costly features in the French landscape style are the pools or fountains and the sculpture, if any are planned. The remainder of the landscape is relatively inexpensive to install,

LANDSCAPE PLANTS FOR FORMAL USE

Plants for formal gardens usually have neat, symmetrical forms or lend themselves well to intensive shearing and training. They also tend to grow relatively slowly. Other than that, plants are often chosen for formal gardens on the basis of tradition.

Trees

Acer species	Maple species
Araucaria heterophylla	Norfolk Island pine
Cedrus species	Cedar species
Chamaecyparis pisifera	Sawara false-cypress
Cupressus sempervirens	Italian cypress
Juniperus virginiana	Eastern red cedar
Magnolia species	Magnolia species
Picea species	Spruce species
Quercus species	Oak species
Tilia cordata	Littleleaf linden

Shrubs

Berberis thunbergii	Japanese barberry
Buxus sempervirens	Common boxwood
Daphne odora	Winter daphne
Gardenia augusta (*G. jasminoides*)	Gardenia
Ilex crenata	Japanese holly
Ilex vomitoria	Yaupon
Ligustrum species	Privet species
Myrtus communis	Myrtle
Paeonia suffruticosa	Tree peony
Photinia × fraseri	Fraser photinia
Pittosporum tobira	Japanese pittosporum, mock orange
Potentilla fruticosa	Shrubby cinquefoil
Prunus laurocerasus	English laurel, cherry-laurel
Rosa hybrids	Rose hybrids
Taxus baccata	English yew
Taxus cuspidata	Japanese yew
Viburnum tinus	Laurustinus

Vines

Ficus pumila	Creeping fig, climbing fig
Hedera helix	English ivy
Parthenocissus quinquefolia	Virginia creeper
Parthenocissus tricuspidata	Boston ivy
Rosa hybrids (climbing hybrids)	Rose hybrids
Wisteria species	Wisteria species

Ground Covers (Perennials)

Achillea tomentosa	Woolly yarrow
Ajuga reptans	Carpet bugle
Calluna vulgaris	Scotch heather
Hosta species	Plantain lily species
Santolina chamaecyparissus	Lavender cotton
Thymus pseudolanuginosus	Woolly thyme
Thymus serpyllum	Creeping thyme, mother-of-thyme, wild thyme

Without a strong overall design, the effect of a landscape will probably be nothing more than a confused jumble. This cottage garden is composed of a variety of carefully arranged plants that bloom at different times for an ever-changing show.

although bedding plants will need replacement periodically.

Trees found in the French landscape typically include red horse-chestnut (*Aesculus* × *carnea*), London plane tree (*Platanus* × *acerifolia*), and Lombardy poplar (*Populus nigra* 'Italica'); shrubs are often common boxwood, holly (*Ilex* species), and yew. Coniferous trees such as pines, false-cypress (*Chamaecyparis* species), and cypress (*Cupressus* species) can be used if installed within the parameters of this formal style. Perennials and annuals contribute seasonal color.

English

Balance and symmetry took on new meaning in the English landscape. Tired of the contrived geometry brought from the European continent, English landscape designers began to experiment with the idea of re-creating nature as closely as possible. Although early attempts at English landscape design included formal parterres, evergreen hedge mazes, topiary, and knot gardens, the style most closely associated with the English is decidedly informal and natural looking.

Horticultural knowledge and a developing interest in the aesthetic arrangement of plants led to a distinct English style. Plants chosen for their form, color, texture, and size were grouped to imitate the English ideal of nature. Dead trees, picturesque ponds, and romanticized gazebos and colonnades were included in this ideal. Curving lakeshores and pathways planted with a menagerie of trees and shrubs created the large English landscape.

This landscape style works well with a gently rolling site. A flat site can also be used to picturesque effect if you create mounds or walls through excavation and special grading. Steep slopes do not work well since this style requires an even flow of spaces and forms—one space must flow effortlessly into another. Although the early English landscape centered around lakes and ponds, a large, irregularly shaped lawn will substitute quite well. Not a particularly functional garden, it does offer stupendous viewing points and a wonderful atmosphere for strolling. It also allows you the opportunity to create compositions of varying colors, forms, and textures.

A traditional English landscape requires careful thought as to the placement and juxtaposition of plants. Layering of the plants requires moderate to large open spaces to achieve the effect of foreground, middle ground, and background. Installation takes time and patience, since the true effect is seen only after a few years of growth. Pruning, fertilizing, and spraying take more time than in other garden styles.

This type of landscape is well suited to the northern regions of the United States. The topography and climate constraints of the southern states make this style hard to achieve and maintain in that part of the country. The lush growth typical of these landscapes looks out of step with the regional character of the Southwest.

With the exception of the small lot, most home lots can work well with this type of garden style. The English style requires space for all of the various plant masses and lawn or pond areas. Tudor, château, and large masonry-style homes work especially well with this landscape concept.

Installation expenses for this style are moderate—about the same as for a contemporary garden of comparable size. Although this style may be a part of a larger landscape scheme, it requires a large component of space to be successful. Normally, the entire front or rear of the property will be required for the full effect.

All types of native or exotic plants will work with this style, so long as the principles of loose space and large lawn areas are considered. The deciduous weeping willow (*Salix babylonica*) combines wonderfully with evergreen hedges such as euonymous and holly. Coniferous trees that are particularly well suited to the English landscape include firs (*Abies*

species), cedars (*Cedrus* species), false-cypress (*Chamaecyparis* species), and yew (*Taxus* species). Native flowering shrubs such as redosier dogwood (*Cornus stolonifera*), witch hazel, native azaleas, and Carolina rose (*Rosa carolina*), can also be integrated into the landscape.

Oriental

A traditional oriental landscape can take many forms: a garden for strolling, a tea garden, or a Zen meditation (rock and sand) landscape. It is a landscape composed for the picturesque, with meaning behind every element. Plants take on special importance as specimens in the landscape, and these gardens almost always contain water or the illusion of water, such as a dry rock stream. An oriental garden can be a place to sit, think, stroll, or converse with a friend or guest.

The size of your yard is not important; this style is easily adaptable to many spatial situations. What is important is the careful placement of landscape elements. Each element must be given care

Graceful simplicity may be difficult to attain and keep, but here the efforts yield a meditative expanse of smooth lawn, on which the sun plays patterns. In Japan the appreciation of subtlety in nature has reached its peak.

The shrubs, trees, and pathway at the front of your house all aid in clearly directing guests to your entrance. The symmetry and evenness of this front lawn typify the Early American landscape.

as to its use and aesthetic implications. The installation requires craftsmanship and careful attention to detail. The placement of plants and rocks and the art of wood joinery should all be done with an eye toward quality and originality. Pruning takes on a creative style and execution.

Various oriental styles are adaptable to all climates and locations. A rock and sand garden is perfectly suited to the desert conditions of the Southwest, whereas a strolling garden can be used for a steep wooded site. A small courtyard or a secluded corner of the yard may be the perfect place to add an oriental touch to the landscape. This style is compatible with contemporary and modern homes. Installation costs may be somewhat high due to the time and materials necessary to produce a high-quality project.

Trees traditionally used in the oriental garden are Japanese maple (*Acer palmatum*), pines, maidenhair tree (*Ginkgo biloba*), and Japanese flowering cherry (*Prunus serrulata*). A variety of shrubs can be incorporated, although a few of the most popular are glossy abelia (*Abelia × grandiflora*), camellia, Japanese andromeda (*Pieris japonica*), and mugo pine (*Pinus mugo*). Excellent ground covers include blue fescue (*Festuca glauca*), Hahn's ivy (*Hedera helix* 'Hahn's Self-branching'), evergreen candytuft (*Iberis sempervirens*), lilyturf (*Liriope muscari*), and mondograss (*Ophiopogon japonicus*).

Early American

This style reflects the quintessential American home landscape. It is the traditional backdrop and framework for Colonial-style homes.

Usually designed for a lot that slopes gently toward the street, the home features a front entry that faces and looks down upon the street level. The Early American style is not socially functional; it provides a setting for the facade of the home.

An Early American landscape is suitable for any site on which a traditional American home is built. Because it is so familiar, you may find that this is the easiest style for you to design. Use simple geometric shapes and curves to lay out this landscape style. Foundation plantings, a few large trees in groupings, and a straightforward walkway to the front entry are the main design elements.

Any number of other features can be added to this basic style. If you are interested in growing flowers, for instance, you may want to incorporate flower beds or boxwood parterres. Depending, of course, on your design choices, installation and material costs are minimal. Because of its simplicity, this style may be the best one for getting an established look quickly. Maintenance consists of weekly mowing, and regular clipping and fertilizing.

The large shade tree, a staple of this style, may be red maple (*Acer rubrum*), silver maple (*Acer saccharinum*), white alder (*Alnus rhombifolia*), or European beech (*Fagus sylvatica*). Foundation shrubs include garland flower (*Daphne cneorum*), winter daphne (*Daphne odora*), euonymus, holly, and azaleas. Most ground covers are compatible; the lawn is always located at the entry as a welcome mat and foreground setting for the home.

Moorish

Walls and water in a courtyard setting are the main features of the Moorish style. Originating in the Middle East, this style has also

come to be associated with Spain, Mexico, and the American West. Colored tile, stucco walls, grillwork, and fountains are integral to the Moorish garden.

Designed to provide a shelter from harsh winds, sun, and noise, this style is perfect for the southwestern and southeastern United States. It is also useful in some urban settings. The Moorish style provides a setting for small groups and intimate conversations. It can consist of a series of landscaped spaces or one focal point within the landscape.

A fountain or pool serves as a central focal point in the Moorish style, with stucco walls and lush plantings as a backdrop. Once the main elements are in place, the surrounding landscape areas will be easy for you to design and plant. Use drought-tolerant plantings and paved areas to keep maintenance to a minimum.

This landscape style may work with a sloped site, provided you create a series of level terraces. Walls can retain soil as well as serve an aesthetic purpose.

Paving, arbors, walls, and fountains raise the cost of installation.

The elements that Spain adopted from the Moorish landscape style were later introduced to California and the American Southwest by Spanish missionaries. Water, a bit of bright color, and adobe walls are still found in all of these arid climates and can be modified according to your inclinations—in this case geraniums were included.

The native plantings at the Arizona-Sonora Desert Museum look natural, even though the plants have been selected to include a wider variety than would normally appear together. The cacti obstruct intruders so that the fence need not be very high.

Walls and fountains may require special construction. In a small space, however, the cost may be well worth the final result. Small entries, courtyards, and atriums are perfect settings for a Moorish landscape. Contemporary, Spanish, and stucco-style homes are all compatible with this style.

Trees common in the Moorish-style garden are trident maple (*Acer buergeranum*), silk tree (*Albizia julibrissin*), common hackberry (*Celtis occidentalis*), river she-oak (*Casuarina cunninghamiana*), citrus species, mayten tree (*Maytenus boaria*), and black locust (*Robinia pseudoacacia*). Moorish-type shrubs that tolerate drought and hot conditions include rock rose, Spanish broom (*Genista hispanica*), oleander (*Nerium oleander*), and pomegranate (*Punica granatum*). Bougainvillea and scented vines cover and add texture to the walls.

Native and Natural

Native landscape design is not the same as natural landscape design. A true native landscape is one that uses only indigenous plants and building materials. A native landscape will thus take on the quality of your particular region. A natural landscape is one that uses plants and building materials that are free-form and natural looking but not necessarily indigenous to the region.

Although these styles are slightly different, the aesthetic effect is the same. Both native and natural landscape settings are, for the most part, informal, loose, and unstructured, and appear as though the home were built around the landscape, rather than vice versa.

A natural-looking cactus garden in a nondesert region is one example of a natural landscape. Another is an evergreen forest in the plains of the Midwest, where there are

no natural forests. When designing a natural landscape that is not indigenous to your area, be especially careful of plant needs. Your maintenance costs may be overwhelming.

You may choose to plant a mix of natives and nonnatives; if you do this, be sure to keep the cultural requirements of the plant groupings (sun, water, soil, fertilizer, and so forth) in mind. Another option is to install native plants without placing them in a natural landscape setting. Instead, you can plant them in a different, perhaps more formal, style.

The style of your home will dictate whether this loose style of landscape is appropriate for you. Rural and rustic settings are especially suited to the native and natural style. Urban lots and tight suburban areas may not look "natural" enough for this style. A native or natural landscape will work with any size yard. When planting in small spaces, pay particular attention to the size and final form of the plants.

If your yard is large enough, you may wish to install a natural landscape on only a portion of the property. To integrate two styles properly, be careful to hide the edges or views of that part of the landscape that is not natural.

The native and natural styles are easy to design. There are no hard-and-fast design rules for patios, walks, and structures. In most cases, you will want to design to your yard, rather than making your land fit a preconceived idea. Landscape accents should reflect the local environment.

You must consider the soil, climate, topography, and sun exposure prior to the design process. Planning the arrangement of the various plants may require more thought than for other styles. The plants should appear as natural groupings; they should look as though they have evolved into communities like those you see in the wild. If you plan a natural landscape using nonnatives, plantings may be more difficult to install and establish because they require special growing conditions and a longer establishment period.

Installing native plants and materials is generally not difficult, but if you are concerned with growing plants that are truly native, you may have to do some research. Many of the listings in the Landscape Plant Guide that begins on page 211 state the region to which the plant is indigenous. You may even be able to incorporate into your design many of the plants growing naturally in your yard, although you will want to verify that they are true natives. Native plants, once established, require little, if any, maintenance.

Contemporary

Contemporary landscapes are usually designed with entertaining and activity in mind. This style originated at the same time as the design rule that "form follows function." That rule is based on the premise that a pleasing design can be the result of a well-thought-out combination of functional use areas.

A contemporary landscape is adaptable to any climate, region, and budget. It is found in all parts of the United States. If your home or neighborhood has a distinct historical character, however, it may not be the right style for you. Sloped yards, drainage problems, noise, and lack of privacy are all easily solved in a contemporary landscape style.

The contemporary landscape is based on simple geometric forms, making it one of the easiest styles to design. Base your design on the existing geometry of your house,

This Wisconsin landscape adapts traditional elements to a contemporary style. Although it is modern in feel, notice the cherubs and the fountain, elements of a French landscape.

and then incorporate into the landscape the building materials used in the home.

The size of a contemporary landscape is limited only by the specific location. You can lay out the modern geometric lines and forms in just about any size yard. All elements should be logical and straightforward.

The contemporary style is very versatile. The majority of plants sold at a local garden center can be integrated into this design. Intermix native plants with exotics to obtain the effects and maintenance level you desire. You can easily incorporate a distinct color scheme or plant collection into this type of landscape. Maintenance is routine,

depending on the amount of landscaping and the elements you decide to install.

Always remember that you, as a designer, do not need to be a slave to any particular "style." You can allow any style to influence your design approach and to interject itself into your garden. Too much diversity in design influence can create disharmony, but a simple contemporary landscape can easily incorporate a stone garden with a Japanese influence or the basic character of a fountain from that favorite Spanish courtyard you visited years ago. With a few bold-leaved plants you can create a feeling you enjoy; it doesn't have to be an authentic tropical jungle.

CHECKLIST:
CREATING YOUR DESIGN
- ❏ Remember that there are landscape ideas everywhere.
- ❏ Start a scrapbook of design inspirations.
- ❏ Record climate changes.
- ❏ Verify correct local USDA plant-hardiness zone.
- ❏ Find out community guidelines.
- ❏ Identify the style of the house.
- ❏ Note the size and shape of the lot.
- ❏ See existing features to save.
- ❏ Check for existing site problems.
- ❏ Ask for ideas from everyone who will use the landscape.
- ❏ Consider professional opinions, if needed.
- ❏ Think. How do I want to use the yard?
- ❏ Listen. Too noisy? Can I fix that?
- ❏ Look. What would I rather see?
- ❏ Inhale. Is this what I want to smell?
- ❏ Choose a preferred and appropriate landscape style.

Avant-garde

The avant-garde style is whimsical and fun. It can be functional, or you can design it so that it does not invite human use or presence.

An avant-garde landscape incorporates both traditional and nontraditional landscape materials. Color, texture, and light play important roles in this artistic style. You can even design a landscape without plants. In this case, the "garden" becomes whatever the designer chooses.

This is the most difficult style to design. It requires strong personal convictions and the ability to live with adverse reactions and criticism. This style challenges you to be different, unique, and, above all, creative. Proceed boldly when designing in this style and, once you feel you have arrived at your "answer," stick to your beliefs.

Remember, many landscape styles we now consider traditional were avant-garde when they were originally developed.

As in all landscape design, you will be limited by climate, location, and budget. The amount of space available will dictate the scale of the landscape but not the design or forms. A traditional or historical style of home may not be appropriate for such a radical design. More than other landscape styles, the avant-garde style is a statement. Be aware of reaction from neighbors.

Installation will be easy or difficult, depending on your concept and the process involved in carrying out your ideas. The level of maintenance required will also depend on your design. It may require constant care and attention or none at all.

The expense involved in this style depends on how you plan to execute your ideas. You may be able to institute an avant-garde landscape in only one portion of the yard, perhaps where only you can view it. It can be as little or as large a statement as you like.

Avant-garde landscaping encourages experimentation. The Stella garden was designed by landscape architect Martha Schwartz for her mother. The multicolored acrylic plastic sheets, which enclose the area, are sunk in clay for easy removal. The brightly colored material inside the edging is aquarium gravel, purchased in bulk.

DESIGNING YOUR LANDSCAPE

Landscaping requires an understanding of basic design principles and careful consideration of all of the elements you wish to include in your yard.

Residential landscaping is similar to many of the other activities you undertake in your day-to-day life. Although designing a landscape is not the impossibly mysterious or inscrutable task that many people think it is, it does require some time and some mental and physical effort. You need to understand certain principles of design and be able to apply those principles to the elements of your landscape.

This chapter guides you through the design process. It will help you understand the principles involved in creating an aesthetically pleasing design, give you a feel for how all of the landscape elements can be put together appropriately, and teach you how to draw your ideas on paper. These are the necessary steps you must consider before finalizing your plan and certainly before purchasing materials or breaking ground. The design process rarely proceeds in a straight line. You will find yourself making many adjustments and choices along the way.

AN APPROPRIATE FIT

A landscape design has an appropriate fit when the functional needs, the wants of the users, and the physical conditions of the property combine into an aesthetically pleasing site.

You will find it easy to keep the goal of an appropriate fit in mind as you proceed with the design process if you realize that it is a goal you strive for in many other things you do. Consider, for example, the decision process you use to select a new pair of shoes. This process probably includes questions such as: Do they fit my feet comfortably? Does the color complement the clothing I want to wear with them? Does the style project the image I would like? Can I afford them? If your answer to all of these questions is positive, the shoes are

likely to satisfy your definition of an appropriate fit. If there are no comparable alternatives, you will probably decide to buy the shoes.

Notice that in this example, appropriate fit means more than merely whether the shoes fit comfortably on your feet. It also includes the need to satisfy the number of additional requirements you have set.

The general sense of appropriate fit is determined by the landscape style you have chosen. You choose the style appropriate to your home, lifestyle, and physical site, just as you choose a shoe for a particular need—you don't buy running shoes when you need something to wear to a formal dinner. There are also certain basic design principles, or rules, that make up the more subtle requirements of appropriate fit. You probably know how to use these

As this landscape shows, many different activities can be accommodated in one area. These homeowners wanted to supervise their children while relaxing in the spa.

principles when buying shoes, but understanding how they apply to landscape design may take some time. The rules of form, scale, rhythm, axis, color, and texture are the fundamental, aesthetic areas of design that you must incorporate into every decision, both now, in the planning stages, and later, when you install the landscape. You will want to come back to these basic design principles when you choose materials in order to guarantee a truly creative landscape.

Creating Your Wish List

One of the most useful aids in determining all that your design must accomplish is a list of absolutely everything you want from your landscape. In making this list, consider both the opportunities open to you and the constraints of the site. You may have already started thinking about some of the elements you want to include—that's probably why you are reading this book—but it's a good idea to make a formal, written list of these ideas before beginning your design.

Develop your wish list as you read through the principles of design and the discussion of the various landscape elements. Look at all of the opportunities landscape design presents. People who study the human creative process have adopted the following four rules to guide brainstorming. Use these rules as you create your wish list.

▐ There are no bad ideas at this point; list everything you have ever wanted.

▐ The wilder the idea, the better; it's easier to tame down an idea than to dream one up.

▐ Go for a quantity of ideas; the more ideas you have, the greater the likelihood of useful ones.

▐ Combination and improvement will be necessary. At this point involve everyone and everything that

---

LANDSCAPING WISH LIST

Write a wish list of all the things you can think of that you would like to include in your landscape design. Keep adding to this list as you read through the Elements of a Landscape (see page 63). Later, delete from this list as you determine what will actually be appropriate for your yard. Use the list and your scrapbook of design inspiration to fit all of the elements you desire into the design of your new landscape. This sample list shows all of the wished-for items the owners wanted to incorporate into their design. Keep in mind that not everything on a wish list ends up in the final design. Without making a complete list, however, some good ideas might be forgotten.

For My Home
Contemporary style
Low-maintenance
 front yard
Natural area
Entrance from street
 to front door
Preservation of
 full-grown trees

For My Lifestyle
Small putting green
Swimming pool
Storage space
Vegetable garden
Patio for entertaining
Built-in barbecue area
Hot tub
Flowers

For Problem Solving
Block view of
 construction site
Screen road noise
 (northeast)
Control erosion
 (southwest)
Add privacy off
 master bedroom

Keep view from
 living-room window

---

will be part of the final product. In addition to contributing ideas of their own, participants should suggest how the ideas of others can be improved upon, or how two or more ideas can be merged into yet another one.

Remember that this is *your* list, made specifically for *your* site. There is no magic formula to follow. Note the sample wish list above. Do not hesitate to put something on your list and try to fit it into your plan. Take as much time as you need to create a list that is specific to your situation. The time will be well spent and will later provide you with a way to check your accomplishments.

PRINCIPLES OF DESIGN

FORM

The principle of form relates to the shape and structure of the various elements in a design, rather than to the materials used for those elements. A well-designed landscape contains forms that balance and complement one another. Too much of one type of form—such as too many tall elements, too many curves, or too many rectangles—will make a design uncomfortable. The forms in a landscape should be in keeping with the overall landscape style.

Certain types of forms have deep-seated symbolic connotations that we all intuitively comprehend. For example, vertical forms induce a sense of awe. You may be able to capitalize on this feeling by planting a column of tall trees, placing a slender statue in a spot that emphasizes its form, or painting the high wall of your garage to exaggerate its height.

Diminutive and intricate forms evoke curiosity and interest. Put this to use in a small-space landscape or in the creation of detailed patterns in a pavement design.

The static nature of the horizontal plane promotes feelings of peacefulness or passivity and gives the appearance of permanence. Water rests at a horizontal level.

Eighteenth-century garden designers believed that geometric forms made of straight lines were the ultimate expression of reason and represented the straightforward character of nature. A square lawn, a rectangular pattern of boxwood hedges, angled planting beds, or a patio with geometric interest can give a landscape an ordered and formal air.

Circular forms give a feeling of closure; they are complete in themselves. Some think this is quite comforting. A circular entryway implies that it is a place to wait. When the door opens, the circle is broken, along with the sense of closure.

Curves are visual symbols of harmony. A garden can have many curved shapes in it, such as leaves and pebbles, a billowing mass of foliage, or a terrace with rounded edges. When you design a paved walkway or the edges of a narrow planting bed, consider using gentle, sweeping curves that flow from one to another.

Projecting and jagged forms suggest dynamism and may imply speed, strength, and power. If they are not used carefully, however, they may merely look sloppy. A cantilevered deck, for instance, the footings of which are not visible, will seem to defy gravity. This may produce an exciting element in your design but an undesirable feeling of anxiety in your guests.

Low, shelflike, covered forms, such as caves and canopied walks, imply protection. In contrast, the freedom of the open desert under starry skies can be oppressive in its abundance, causing us to yearn for mountains or buildings that have the capacity to hold us in. In a very open and level site, the juxtaposition of open spaces against covered ones makes both more interesting.

Forms need to relate well in size to one another. A circular flower bed that is 10 feet in diameter might work well next to a bed that is 5 feet across, because there is a significant difference in size between the two. If you place two circles together that are 10 and 8 feet across, however, it may look like you made a mistake, because there is not enough difference in size to create an interesting contrast.

In the same vein, try to use angles repetitively, but be careful not to mix too many different-sized angles in a limited amount of space; it will weaken your design considerably. Stay with angle families, such as 30, 60, and 90 degrees or 45, 90, 180, and 360 degrees. When you plan odd angles, try to tie them into right angles at some point.

Reinforce two-dimensional forms, such as a circular lawn or a rectangular patio, with three-dimensional masses of shrubs and other solid forms. For example, if you lay out a circular lawn, plant the trees and shrubs in curved patterns that accentuate the main circular design.

Plant Forms

The form of a plant is its shape or silhouette. The arrangement of branches and leaves also contributes to the form of a plant. Plants have a wide variety of forms, including vertical, columnar, round, vase shaped, weeping, pyramidal, and horizontal. Plants that are tall and thin are said to have vertical form and add a strong accent to a design. Plants that are wider than they are tall have horizontal form. Massing of plants can accentuate their form. The use of contrasting forms can create focal points in a garden. For example, a group of tall trees has a strong vertical form and will draw the viewer's eye in a landscape in which most of the plants have a horizontal form.

SCALE

Scale is an expression of relative size. The principle of scale refers to the relationship between something being looked at or experienced and something else that acts as a reference. The most comfortable reference point in a residential landscape is the human body. Properly scaled spaces, ones that relate

well to the people using them, are necessary for a successful landscape design.

Scale affects our emotional response to a place. For example, if you were to walk through a high-rise district, you would probably feel dwarfed and overwhelmed. This is because few buildings in such districts are designed to be in scale with pedestrians. On the other hand, a single-family residence is designed so that its mass, height, and distance from adjacent houses are at a more human scale. Accordingly, we are likely to feel more

Top: A successful landscape contains forms that balance and complement each other. Consider form when planning and purchasing plants.
Bottom: A scale established by plants of various sizes makes this house seem accessible rather than intimidating.

This contemporary house and landscape give an impression of unity and order through the rhythmic repetition of plants—birches and flowering ground covers appear on both sides of the entryway—and the consistent use of building materials; brick is used in the house and steps.

comfortable within this environment than in a high-rise canyon.

Getting the scale of spaces and materials right is a concern that all designers share. However, as with so much else in design, there is no one right scale for each type of space. Decisions or feelings regarding whether a space is in scale with its occupants often vary. For example, an adult will have a different feeling of comfort in a given space than a child will. Therefore, it is important that you take note of the outdoor spaces that make you feel most comfortable. Probably the easiest way to set the scale of your landscape is to base it on the scale of your house.

Planting to Scale

The scale of plants refers both to the size of the plant and to the size of its leaves and branches. In a

small garden, plants that are too large will seem out of scale and will make the garden appear smaller. Likewise, in a larger garden, smaller plants may be lost within the space. When massing plants, using a gradual transition in scale from the larger trees down to the shrubs and ground covers will seem most natural. Remember to allow space in your design for plants according to their full-grown size.

RHYTHM

Like the ordered flow of rhythm in music, the principle of rhythm in a landscape involves the ordered regularity of the elements in the design. The use of similar forms in the same scale will create a constant beat, so to speak, uniting the landscape. The rhythm will tie together the various parts of the landscape—

and the home. Devise clear connections between spaces, and repeat construction materials and plants to create a unified design. With a large piece of property, it is especially important to consider the rhythm among the various activity areas.

You can design a change in rhythm where one space ends and another begins. A change in material occurring at a logical place—for example, a brick path leading to a concrete patio can keep your design from becoming monotonous.

Planting With Rhythm

Each part of your planting design should be related to the other parts through a recognizable pattern of color, texture, form, or location. This perceptible pattern will help establish the rhythm of your design. Too many varieties of plants can lead to visual confusion. Plant massing of a single species will enhance unity. Another way to achieve unity is to orchestrate the planting design so that one or two species of plants recur throughout the landscape.

AXIS

The principle of axis is a visual orientation that relates to the way in which objects in a setting attract the eye, causing you to focus on them. The axis of a landscape is determined by your line of sight as you view these focal points. In formal landscapes, axes and cross-axes form pleasing patterns, partly because of their strong geometric simplicity and partly because they emphasize the naturally straight line of sight.

In an informal garden, axis lines are created by suggested lines of sight. Although they are not apparent, they are still significant. Suggested axes can be formed by pavement patterns, night lighting, the shape of a clearing through the woods, lawn areas, foliage patterns, and many other contrived and natural occurrences. Even though they are only suggested, the interconnections of axes can be quite powerful, particularly if they are emphasized and remain uninterrupted. For example, a specimen shrub can be pruned to open up a distant view, or a few strategically placed container plants can help to move the eye along an entryway. Look for the natural axes on your site and find ways of strengthening them.

You can achieve some mystery in your landscape through the manipulation of axes. An axis may end at the point where a lawn disappears around a mass of shrubs, leading the viewer to wonder where the lawn actually ends. It may appear that the lawn extends for some

Square pavers, set diagonally, clearly point the way to a destination around the bend.

distance, when in reality it ends a few feet behind the shrubs. A lawn that disappears is interesting to look at precisely because we cannot see all of it. Paths that curve away from sight and private sections of decks and patios can take advantage of similar design tricks, disappearing from sight and urging visitors to search out the hidden parts of the landscape.

The axis lines of your design should reflect the lines of the yard and the landscape style you have chosen. In general, design axis lines that can be easily understood. Figure out what you want people to see and where you want them to go, and then guide their eyes accordingly. A complex set of lines in a landscape may be too busy for a clear and unified composition. Keep your lines simple, and add complexity in the plantings and activity areas.

COLOR

The use of color in a landscape makes a distinct statement and affects the mood of the home. A yard done in shades of green will be more soothing than one in a bright color. Cooler colors, such as greens and blues, tend to recede into the distance, whereas warm colors, such as reds, oranges, and yellows, advance, making distances seem shorter. Following this principle, a small garden can be made to seem larger if cooler colors are used in the design. Color can refer to subtle variations in leaf color as well as to the bright colors of flower beds. Simple color combinations, with one color dominant, are generally the most successful. Contrasting colors can be used in certain situations to accentuate landscape elements. For example, a gray slate patio next to a red brick wall will intensify the colors of each.

Opposite top: The brick walk forms an axis that helps focus attention on the fountain at the far end of the landscape.
Opposite bottom: Use color to give continuity to different areas and materials. Here the retaining walls were painted white, extending the horizontal line of the house and making it seem much larger. Note that the wall in the foreground, which borders the street, was left dark to blend with the gray street and sidewalk.

LANDSCAPE PLANTS FOR FALL COLOR

The leaves of many deciduous plants turn breathtaking shades of red, orange, or yellow in the fall. Other species contribute brightly colored fruit or branches to the autumn kaleidoscope. The plants in the list below, selected from the Landscape Plant Guide (see page 211), are some of the most spectacular species.

Trees

Acer buergerianum	Trident maple
Acer campestre	Hedge maple
Acer platanoides	Norway maple
Acer rubrum	Red maple, swamp maple
Acer saccharinum	Silver maple, soft maple
Cercis canadensis	Eastern redbud
Cornus florida	Flowering dogwood
Crataegus species	Hawthorn species
Diospyros kaki	Japanese persimmon
Franklinia alatamaha	Franklinia
Ginkgo biloba	Maidenhair tree
Larix kaempferi	Japanese larch
Liquidambar styraciflua	American sweet gum
Liriodendron tulipifera	Tulip tree, yellow poplar, tulip poplar
Pistacia chinensis	Chinese pistachio
Pyrus calleryana	Callery pear
Quercus palustris	Pin oak
Quercus rubra	Northern red oak
Zelkova serrata	Sawleaf zelkova, Japanese zelkova

Shrubs

Abelia × grandiflora	Glossy abelia
Berberis thunbergii	Japanese barberry
Cotinus coggygria	Smoke tree
Cotoneaster horizontalis	Rockspray cotoneaster
Euonymus alatus	Burning bush, winged euonymus
Fothergilla major	Large fothergilla
Hamamelis species	Witch hazel
Lagerstroemia indica	Crape myrtle
Nandina domestica	Nandina, heavenly-bamboo
Rhododendron calendulaceum	Flame azalea
Rhus aromatica	Fragrant sumac
Rhus typhina	Staghorn sumac
Spiraea japonica 'Bumalda'	Japanese spirea
Tamarix hispida	Kashgar tree
Vaccinium corymbosum	Highbush blueberry

Vines

Celastrus orbiculatus	Oriental bittersweet
Lonicera sempervirens	Trumpet honeysuckle
Parthenocissus quinquefolia	Virginia creeper

Ground Covers (Perennials)

Ceratostigma plumbaginoides	Dwarf plumbago, blue leadwort
Cotoneaster conspicuus 'Decorus'	Necklace cotoneaster
Cotoneaster horizontalis	Rock cotoneaster
Euonymus fortunei	Wintercreeper
Gaultheria procumbens	Wintergreen, teaberry, checkerberry
Nandina domestica 'Harbour Dwarf'	Nandina, heavenly-bamboo

The color of your house has a significant impact on the appearance of your landscape. Here, the color that links the concrete path and steps and the flower boxes to the blue facade of the home completes a well-composed entryway.

Although contrasting color in the landscape can provide a stimulating show, an overabundance of color can become contrived and tedious. The eye seeks a restful composition, and while vivid colors provide a spectacular display, the effect may be overbearing. It is best to use restraint when mixing a number of colors together. Choose hues that are close together for a unified effect. The result will still be an explosion of color, but the overall composition will be more successful.

To find color combinations to use in your landscape, seek out examples of compositions that you want to re-create. Look to your inspiration scrapbook (see page 10) for these. If you have the time or are installing your project over a long period, you will want to observe how the colors work together over the length of an entire season or a full year, if possible.

TEXTURE

The principle of texture refers to the visual and tactile surface of all the materials installed in a landscape. Use texture to create interest in your design. Juxtapose rough-textured paved surfaces with constructed elements made of smooth, more refined materials. Heavy timbers and unfinished woods have a rougher texture that should be placed in proximity to durable, heavy-use paving such as rough-finished concrete or cobblestones.

Although the surface texture of paving and structures requires thought and preplanning, textures among plants are the predominant tactile feature in a landscape. Plants may have a texture that is coarse, fine, rough, or smooth. Adjacent plants with sharply contrasting textures may seem jarring to the viewer. On the other hand, installing plants with leaves that are similar in size and number will result in a flat-looking surface. In general, it is wise to use a range of textures, gradually shifting from the coarse textures of larger-leaved plants to the fine textures of lacy foliage.

In some instances, however, a sharp contrast in texture can be used to accentuate a specific element, if done carefully. Plants with smaller, more numerous leaves can be placed next to large-leaved plants to provide contrast.

Texture can also be used to increase apparent distances in the garden. Placing fine-textured plants, such as Japanese maple (*Acer palmatum*) and smaller varieties of rhododendron species, near the end of an axis induces the appearance of distance, tricking observers into thinking that the end of the property is farther away than it actually is. This can be used to great advantage in a small space. Larger spaces are more conducive to coarser-textured plants, such as Norway maple (*Acer platanoides*), which are more in keeping with the overall scale.

Large-leaved plants used against a smooth wall or fence also create a textural composition. Consider the shadow patterns that the sun will create as it filters through the leaves when you plant next to paved areas or walls that provide a surface for shadows.

ELEMENTS OF A LANDSCAPE

ACTIVITY AREAS

Thoughtful design of your outdoor living areas will provide you with years of pleasant recreation. Activity areas are similar to the rooms inside your home; they are the places in which you will spend time outdoors. Major activity areas include patios, decks, and sports areas, but the specific types you include in your design will depend on your needs and interests. If you know that you want to grow food, a vegetable garden will be an activity area in your landscape design. If you have young children, include some kind of children's play yard. Generally, activity areas fall into the categories of social areas, such as patios and decks; planting areas,

This backyard patio area has the appeal of a wild landscape even though it is located in Washington, D.C. Contrasting textures and forms with subtle color variations change constantly with the seasons—an outdoor bouquet in summer is a big dried arrangement in winter.

As you plan your landscape design, consider how the inside of the house relates to what is on the other side of the wall or window, and envision the view you would like to see from within the house.

including food gardens and flower beds; play areas, such as tot lots and sports courts; and access areas, such as driveways and storage lots. Your choice of activity areas centers on how you plan to use your landscape, the site conditions, the coordination of the various areas, and how the areas will relate to the rooms inside your house.

The placement of outdoor areas is critical to their success. You must consider the topography, light, and temperature plus the condition of the soil when placing various activity areas. In the design process,

you'll be asked to spend some time walking around your garden to see how it is affected by sun and shade patterns and prevailing winds. You can use overhead structures to modify some of the effects of the microclimate, but a proper location to begin with will give the most satisfactory results. You probably want a sunny play area, for example, and in most cases you want your vegetable garden both to have the benefit of good soil and to be away from the main entrance to your home. And although you may desire one large entertainment area,

your sloped site may be more appropriate for several smaller, terraced areas. In addition to learning about the microclimate, you must observe the views, both of the rest of the landscape from the activity area and of the outdoor activity area from the house and street.

In planning activity areas, you need to consider your lifestyle. For example, you may know that you want a patio, but should it be a large space for large-scale entertaining or one on an intimate scale for family dining? You may have to choose among various activity areas if there is not enough space for everything you want to include. However, you may be able to combine different activities within the same area—a lawn may fit both a Saturday afternoon touch football game and, with the addition of lawn furniture, a Sunday brunch.

You must also consider how your desired outdoor activity areas relate to the interior of the house. Many older houses were designed with only a narrow door connecting the house to the backyard. If your landscape design includes a patio just off the back of the house, you may wish to modify the door—replacing it with a sliding glass one, for instance—to open the house up to the outdoor activity area.

In addition, consider the location of individual rooms of your house that will be used in conjunction with an outdoor activity area. Locate a kitchen garden near the kitchen, an outdoor dining area near a passageway for food and serving equipment, and a patio or deck near an indoor entertainment room that can be opened up for large gatherings. You will want to keep some activity areas separate from your house, if possible. For example, try not to place a play area just outside your home office;

a dog run near the master bedroom; or your garbage storage just outside your formal dining room.

The juxtaposition of different activity areas within your landscape and with the activity areas in your and your neighbors' yards is also noteworthy. For example, try not to place your flower garden, which is going to attract bees, right next to your swimming pool or other leisure area. And unless you enjoy the sound of teenagers playing ball while you are trying to nap in your hammock, avoid placing quiet areas next to play areas.

Preserve your relationship with your neighbors by obliging their land uses. Here, a well-maintained storage area has little effect on the quiet-use activity area on the other side of the fence.

Left: Location and ground surface are especially important in the design of children's areas. Sight lines from the deck and the kitchen window permit unobtrusive adult supervision. Sand beneath the swing and playhouse softens possible falls and adds another activity—filling pails and building castles. Right: Safety factors and the age of the children using the treehouse must be considered before construction. Children can enjoy years of imaginative games in this "home" of their own.

The shape of each activity area should relate to your house, be in keeping with your overall landscape style, and be in scale with surrounding areas. Simple shapes are usually best. Align the edges of the outdoor space with existing features in the house or landscape. For example, the corner of the house may be the logical extension line for the edge of a deck or patio. Planting beds and benches can help subdivide a larger deck or patio into smaller areas. This allows you to separate activities such as barbecuing from the main seating area.

You will place the various activity areas into your landscape design during the process of developing your ideas (see page 90). During this process you will be asked to refer to your scrapbook of landscape inspirations (see page 10) and your landscaping wish list (see page 55). These will help you determine the type, placement, and size of each activity area.

Children's Activity Areas

Everyone needs a place of his or her own, and children are no exception. Creating a special area in the yard for your children can satisfy their needs for adventure and fantasy while helping to keep the toy trucks out of your prized perennial bed. A child's age and interests are key factors in determining an appropriate play area; since both change rapidly, build multiple uses and flexibility into your design.

The style of your children's play area should complement your overall landscape style. Match the fencing, surrounding plantings, and the size and color of a piece of play equipment according to the principles of design you follow for other activity areas.

Complexity is not necessary for a successful children's activity area. For example, sandboxes are very simple, and children truly enjoy them. Three general categories of children's areas are play structures, playhouses, and free space.

Play structures have evolved rapidly in a few years, from low-cost metal swing-and-slide sets to elaborate structures constructed of heavy timber or colorful steel and plastic. The basic elements, however, are still swings, slides, and climbing structures. Your choice of materials will depend on

your budget, how long the structure will be used, and whether it is to be located in a visible area.

Site selection is an important consideration for children's activity areas, and especially for areas of active play. For safety, most active play equipment should have at least 6 to 8 feet of clear area beyond the maximum swing arc or landing area. Soft surfaces, such as deep layers of bark chips or sand, are recommended for cushioning inevitable falls.

Playhouses are wonderful vehicles to fulfill a child's need for fantasy and personal space. They can range from a carefully detailed miniature house to an overturned cardboard shipping crate. In constructing a playhouse, think of providing a stage set that your child's imagination will fill; the space itself is more important than the detail.

Tree houses provide an additional element of adventure and privacy for older children and save ground space in your yard for other uses. Think of tree houses for uses beyond children's play areas. A well-built tree house can provide an interesting space for adults to retreat to for a few hours of quiet reading.

Free space is just that—an area set aside for your children to dig holes, build forts, or lay on the grass and look at the sky. Since the emphasis is on satisfying personal interests, no set size or shape is required for this type of area. A play area should contain sufficient objects to create a miniature world. The natural environment is complex; something new can be found under every rock. The goal of a play area should be to come as close as possible to reproducing the richness of nature.

When deciding where to place the child's play area in your landscape,

consider supervision as well as your children's desire for a certain degree of privacy. Also consider the surrounding plantings—avoid delicate plants that damage easily and thorny plants that could cause injury. Finally, strongly encourage your child's participation in the design and construction of the play area; it will be more rewarding for all of you and will instill a proud feeling of ownership in the child.

FLOORS

Once you have determined the various activity areas of your site, you must determine the appropriate surface for each area and for the connections between them. A wide range of options is available for landscape floors. The first choice you need to make is whether a given area will be surfaced with plants or with constructed material. Your final decision will depend on the site conditions (Will a ground-cover plant grow in this part of the yard?); on how you plan to use the area (If this is to be the play area, do I really want concrete under the swings?); on your budget (A brick patio is beautiful, but how much does it cost?); on the ease of installation and maintenance (How much time do I have to care for that huge lawn?); and, of course, on the landscape style you have chosen (Will a constructed floor fit in with my natural landscape?).

It is important to consider the whole yard when selecting flooring material. The final result should be an integrated design, with all ground surfaces in harmony.

Plants as Floors

The most common living landscape floor is a green lawn. Lawn grasses visually unify areas and provide a soft surface for playing and relaxing. Lawns are adaptable to many

This patio provides privacy without blocking the view.

landscape styles. They can be close-sheared for a formal look or left to grow as natural meadows with a scattering of wildflowers. A

PLANNING PATIOS AND TERRACES

A well-designed patio serves as a ground-level extension of the house, adding space for outdoor living and relaxation. A patio can serve as a transition area between the house and the garden, or it may connect directly to a major lawn or pool area. Planting beds, container plants, garden furniture, and paving patterns can add texture, color, and visual interest to patio areas. Low garden walls, fences, and hedges can be used to provide enclosure and privacy. Low walls topped with benches can be used for seating. If you're adding on to an existing patio area, match the materials of the existing patio as closely as possible. However, do not limit yourself just to save a small, old patio. It may be far more satisfying in the long run to tear it out—or use it as a foundation for a new patio—and develop a design specifically suited to your needs.

A terrace is a patio that is raised above the level of the main garden area. A terrace is most appropriate on a gradually sloping lot where a level surface is needed for outdoor living and entertaining. Low steps and walls are used to connect the terrace to the main garden area.

An elevated terrace has visual prominence in the landscape. It provides better views of the garden and creates a focal point. Steep sites may require a series of terraces that step down the slope. Classic examples of these are found in the gardens of Italian villas. Each terrace in such a series may have a distinct function and style. Terraces are most successful when they have a simple shape. Detail can be added through the use of materials and accents such as planters and benches.

lawn area can provide a visual foreground for the house, dramatizing it in its setting. A lawn is most effective when it is a simple shape, is relatively large, and is on fairly level ground. Too small a lawn area can be aesthetically unappealing and is seldom worth the effort required to maintain it. In any case, a lawn is the most expensive way to cover an area if maintenance over a period of time is figured into the cost equation.

Ground covers make a good flooring material in areas that will not be actively used. Ground covers add interesting textures to the garden and can provide additional treats such as flowers and fragrance. They are well suited to areas where mowing is difficult, and they usually require less maintenance than a lawn except during the first year or two when weeding between the small plants can be onerous. Ground covers are also an excellent form of erosion control on sloped sites. For the most part, ground covers are quick to become established. You may want to take advantage of this by planting an inexpensive ground cover temporarily in an area of your landscape that you plan to develop in the future. As a general rule, avoid mixing several types of ground covers in a small area of the landscape. Mass plantings of a single species are more visually effective.

Constructed Floors

In areas that receive frequent foot traffic, hard-surfaced paving is the most practical flooring material. A wide variety of paving materials are available. Paving should be durable, easy to walk on, and aesthetically appealing. A large area of paving, such as a patio, may be a focal point and as such should be congruous with the rest of the design but should not overwhelm it.

PLANNING DECKS

Decks are especially useful on steeply sloping sites where the construction of a patio or terrace would be difficult, if not impossible. In these situations, the deck may be the only place in the yard that is suitable for outdoor living.

Decks can range from small, simple structures to wide, open areas. The design of the deck should harmonize with the house and garden in both scale and materials. When you are planning a deck, consider the topography of the land. The deck may be shaped to fit the natural curves of a surrounding hillside or designed to work around existing rock formations. Consider how the deck will look from above as well as below.

As with patios and terraces, the intended use of the deck is a primary design consideration. If it will serve as an outdoor eating area, the deck should be easily accessible from the kitchen. Similarly, a deck around a pool or hot tub may require a screened area for sunbathing.

A deck can be a freestanding platform that provides a sitting area in a separate part of the garden. This type of deck can be located to capitalize on a dramatic view or an especially sunny garden area. You can use a series of smaller decks that step down a hillside as a means of drawing attention to specific garden features or of separating family functions, creating private spots for play or relaxation.

Decks can be constructed around existing trees, whereas a patio or terrace might require that you cut and fill earth, which would injure the tree. Leave a hole in the deck large enough to allow for future tree growth and wind movement. You can also incorporate planting containers into the design of a deck, providing visual interest, enclosure, and room to grow plants on steeply sloped sites. Low planters, railings, or walls will give a deck an added sense of security and comfort.

Whenever possible, choose materials used in the exterior construction of the house as the flooring material for outdoor areas. If this cannot be done, select complementary materials to help achieve overall unity. You can further strengthen the visual connection between the interior of the house and the landscape by carrying the flooring material of the house over to an adjacent outdoor terrace, patio, or deck. Rooms with slate floors are lovely with adjacent outdoor terraces paved in slate. Wood indoor floors that lead to wood decks visually extend the indoors to the outside. The flooring material should complement the exterior of the house and the landscape as well as the indoor flooring.

It is also important to consider the shape of the paved area when selecting paving materials. Flowing curves may be difficult to construct from brick but are relatively simple to achieve in poured concrete or with gravel.

Design paved areas to drain quickly in order to avoid puddling and slippery spots. Paving next to trees should allow sufficient air to get to tree roots. Paving units should be in scale with the rest of the garden. Smaller unit pavers, such as bricks or granite sets, will seem more in scale with smaller sites.

Decks such as this one provide the perfect setting for a relaxing evening meal.

You must decide early what you'll use for "carpeting" for the floors of your outdoor "rooms." The color, texture, and pattern of the materials in each area should compliment other areas in the landscape. The various floorings used here were chosen for high contrast. Select materials that will serve the needs of the area and suit the level of maintenance you are able to provide.

There are many ways to combine different paving materials to add interest to a landscape floor. The hard characteristics of stone can be visually softened with low ground-cover plantings between the stones, concrete walks can be edged with brick or wood to add texture and color, and brick patterns can be punctuated with colorful tiles for an ornamental effect. As a general rule, it is best to keep the design simple, using one main paving with a second paving as an accent.

Paving materials vary greatly in their cost and ease of installation. The latter is an especially relevant consideration if you plan to install the pavement yourself. The construction aspects of specific materials are discussed beginning on page 156.

WALLS

Once the surfaces and connections of your activity areas have been determined, it is time to specify the walls in your design. A wall is any vertical surface that serves to block views, either completely or partially. Landscape walls include fences, garden walls (meaning walls that are not of wood and that do not retain earth), screens, and hedges in a variety of plant materials. They have in common their ability to give structure and definition to the yard, provide privacy and security, and—if designed correctly—help provide a more pleasant microclimate for outdoor activities.

There are numerous ways to place walls in an outdoor activity area. Your design choices will include the style of wall (fence, garden wall, or hedge) and the type of material to be used (wood, masonry, or plants). The purpose the wall is to serve, such as blocking wind or providing security, will determine its height.

The most common use of a wall is to provide privacy and enclosure for the whole yard or a particular activity area. Walls designed for enclosure do not need to be solid. A latticework fence can still offer privacy and will let in light and breezes as well. Perimeter fences mark the boundaries of your property and define the spaces they enclose. Fences and garden walls screen the garden from strong winds, undesirable views, and noise. They can also provide security, helping to keep children and pets in and intruders out. South-facing brick walls can store the heat of the sun and reflect it back during the night, an ideal situation for heat-loving plants. Walls suggest paths of movement in the landscape, both visually and literally. In addition, partial walls, archways,

PLANNING CONNECTORS

The connections between activity areas lead people through the landscape, both visually and literally. The form of the connector relates directly to the landscape style—geometric shapes appear more formal, and curves are more natural. The paving material can also, to a large degree, influence the character of the design; log rounds set on a bed of sand create a rustic feel, whereas a smooth, mortared slate walk is more elegant.

You can introduce color and texture into a path with different paving materials. Select materials that complement the overall landscape style. The configuration of the connector will reinforce the organization of the design. For example, straight paths parallel to a wall, fence, or landscape axis will give strength to a design based on geometric patterns. Curving paths will be more comfortable in an area of rolling topography or when they follow the lines of a meadow or forest edge.

In general, a landscape should have as few connectors as possible to eliminate confusion. The layout of paths and steps should be as close to the natural lines of movement as possible. Connect major destinations, such as entries, driveways, patios, and service areas. Smaller secondary walks can lead to other activity areas.

The shortest line between the two destinations may not necessarily be the best location for the connector. For example, a curved path that accentuates an especially attractive view will make the route more interesting. If there is an obvious shortcut between two points, the design of the connector should take it into consideration by either following the natural lines of movement or by screening the shortcut to make it less desirable.

One of the most important things to remember when designing connectors is that the space itself is the most important element. Do not design the landscape around connectors, leaving other areas as leftover space. Instead, use connectors to enhance and accentuate landscape features.

Planning Paths

Use accents to entice people down a path. At its end, provide new focal points that draw them down different paths. This allows the yard to be revealed gradually, leading the viewer through a sequence of spaces and providing places to pause, rest, or admire a particular view. A path that terminates in a specific place, such as a bench on an overlook, or at a landscape accent, such as a specialty plant, will give the terminus greater importance in the design. For safety and to add drama to your nighttime landscape,

consider lighting the paths. Paths should be comfortable, well drained, and easy to walk on.

The width of the path will depend on its use in the landscape. Major paths should be wide enough for two people to walk side by side—at least 48 inches and preferably 60 inches. Secondary paths can be as narrow as 36 inches; and paths in seldom-traveled areas can be even narrower. Paths are comfortable on slopes of up to 8 percent. Steeper slopes should incorporate steps.

Planning Ramps

Ramps are ideal in designs that require wheelchair access. They are also quite useful in sloped areas through which you might need to wheel equipment—mowers, wheelbarrows, items being taken to a storage area, or sports accoutrements. Ramps are dangerous when they are too steep; an 8-percent slope is the maximum desirable. For safety reasons, paving materials used for both ramps and steps should be nonskid. Ramps designed for equipment moving can also be installed in conjunction with steps for ease of movement.

Planning Steps

Steps add drama to your design, are an architectural element in your landscape, and accentuate changes in level on the site. Steps must be designed to fit in with the overall landscape style. In general, regular, symmetrical steps of concrete or brick are found in formal styles. More irregular, rough-hewn stone or wood steps are appropriate in informal designs.

Whenever possible, avoid using a single step. Two or more steps are easier to see and are less likely to be tripped over. Outdoor steps should be a bit broader than their indoor equivalents to invite informal sitting and to make them more visually appealing and comfortable to walk on. If there are more than eight steps, a landing should be incorporated to break up the climb. The rise of each step is usually 4 to 6 inches, and the tread should be at least 12 inches wide. In general, the lower the riser is, the wider the tread should be. Riser height times tread should equal close to 72 (for example, $6 \times 12 = 72$).

The scale of the steps should relate to the scale of the surrounding garden. Wide, substantial steps are far more pleasing than constricted ones. Steps that flare out as they near ground level add interest and indicate that a major path or terrace has been reached. Many variations of step layouts are possible. Above all, the form and materials of the steps should harmonize with all other parts of the design. Simplicity, rather than complexity, is usually most successful.

PLANTING HEDGES

The most common living wall is a hedge. There are two basic ways to plant a hedge—you can dig a trench the length of the hedge, or you can dig individual holes. Although the methods are interchangeable, the trench method generally works best for bare-root plantings, and the hole method works best for plants from containers. Generally speaking, the width of the trench should be two times the width of the rootball. For detailed information on installing the plants in the ground, see page 201.

A double, staggered row of shrubs results in the rapid growth of a thicker, denser, and wider hedge, but involves twice the initial expense and effort. If you plant a double row of shrubs, stagger the plants so that no two are directly opposite each other.

The spacing between individual plants will depend partly on how wide the branches spread in that shrub variety and partly on how fast you want the hedge to fill in. Spacing can be from 18 to 30 inches apart. Most gardeners recommend a spacing of 18 to 20 inches within a row to avoid root crowding. Some dwarf varieties are planted on 12-inch centers. Ask at your garden center for advice on your particular plant variety.

When considering a hedge, remember that a formally pruned hedge requires constant maintenance. Select plant material that grows naturally close to the shape you are looking for.

and screens can add to the mystery of the garden, framing distant views and suggesting garden areas that wait to be explored.

When you are deciding on a type of wall, it is essential to consider your functional goals. Walls of solid construction will physically prevent movement between two spaces as well as give a strong architectural flavor to the landscape. Less structured walls of plants may provide spatial definition while still allowing some views and movement between adjoining spaces. If the garden wall is designed as a backdrop for a particular landscape accent, it should be as simple as possible so as not to compete with the object it is meant to highlight.

You must also consider the relationship between the wall and the rest of the site. As with other landscape elements, walls should be compatible with the architectural style of the house and your overall landscape style. A white clapboard fence might be elegant in one yard but completely out of place in another. Coordinate your choice of wall materials with the materials of your house.

It is particularly important for walls along property lines to be integrated with their surroundings. Look around your neighborhood to see what other people have done. Choosing materials and styles that are similar to those you like in neighboring landscapes will enhance the neighborhood character. You may wish to talk to your neighbors when designing a fence that will affect their views. If you agree on a design, they may offer to help with costs or construction. If you are constructing your own wall, the method of installation is an important factor. Materials vary greatly in both ease of installation and cost. Construction principles for some of the more common types of walls are discussed beginning on page 176.

Plants as Walls

Evergreen shrubs are the most common plant walls, acting as year-round visual barriers. They may be clipped into hedges in formal gardens or massed in borders and left untrimmed. Deciduous shrubs, such as forsythia and common lilac (*Syringa vulgaris*), provide privacy during the spring and summer months, when they have their leaves, and allow sunlight to enter the garden after their leaves drop in winter. If you wish to discourage animals or people from entering your yard, dense plantings of shrubs with thorns will deter intruders. Living walls have the advantage of providing texture, color, and fragrance as well as acting as barriers. Flowering shrubs, such as eastern redbud (*Cercis canadensis*) or flowering dogwood (*Cornus florida*), will enrich the landscape with their beautiful blooms during the spring months. Espaliered plants, ones that have been trained to grow in a flat, horizontal direction, create more formal garden walls, but time and effort are required to train them. Dramatic effects can be achieved with a deciduous plant, such as an apple tree, that has been espaliered against a wall. The silhouette of the bare branches in winter can be striking.

Pleached trees are trees that have been pruned to create architectural forms. Pleaching is commonly used to provide vertical definition in formal gardens. Rows of trees are pruned so that their lower trunks are bare and their top branches form a dense, boxlike hedge. The trunks of the trees resemble the columns of a building, creating strong spatial definition for garden areas. Pleached trees require continuous maintenance and should be used only when you have the time to continue this practice.

Vines can soften the hard architectural lines of many houses and garden walls. Vines require less maintenance than clipped hedges and are fast growers, providing leafy coverage and flowers within a few years of planting. There are many types of vines, and they vary in their means of supporting themselves. Some, such as wisteria, climb by twisting and require a trellis or arbor for support. Others, such as creeping fig (*Ficus pumila*), cling directly to a wall with tiny discs.

Constructed Walls

Walls can be constructed of a wide variety of materials, ranging from wood, brick, and stone to metal pickets and chain link fencing. When deciding between a garden wall or a fence, consider the purpose you want the wall to serve. If you desire absolute privacy, a solid wall would be your first

choice. If the wall is to serve more as a deterrent than a means of gaining privacy, an open wood fence or low brick wall that allows your neighbors to spot intruders may be more suitable.

Your landscape style will be a determining factor in your choice of a fence or a garden wall. Another factor to consider is installation cost and overall maintenance. In most cases brick is more expensive than wood pickets, and unless you have some masonry experience the installation of a brick wall will be more difficult. However, the brick wall will require little or no maintenance for years, whereas the pickets will need periodic repainting.

The height of the wall will have a strong impact on the landscape. Low walls suggest enclosure without constricting small gardens. Higher walls may increase security but can seem overly confining. Other factors will also affect the design of walls in the landscape. Codes and zoning ordinances set limits for fence and garden wall height, usually 6 feet for side yards and 42 inches at the sidewalk line. You will probably need a building

Given time, plants make wonderful, sometimes aromatic walls that create discrete areas within a yard. Low parterres define specific planting areas and contribute colorful patterns to the ground level of this French landscape. Higher hedges hide the less colorful vegetable garden.

PLANNING GATES

Gates are a necessary part of walls. They affect the direction in which people move through the landscape and can serve as focal points in a design. Many types of gates are possible in varying styles and materials. A gate constructed of materials similar to those used in the fence will be less obvious than one made of a contrasting material. The height of the gate can accentuate its position within the fence. A gate that is slightly taller than the fence, with an arched lattice above it, will draw attention and frame the entry walk. Additional trim, color, or latticework on the gate can also make it more of a focal point.

A gate can either swing open or slide open. Entry gates that swing open should always swing inward toward the private space so guests do not have to back up in order to enter. If the gate is across a driveway, it can be as wide as 20 feet. Openings wider than 4 feet can have double gates. A garden gate should be wide enough to allow for easy entry. Garden entries are not always gates; they can also be arched openings. These can be constructed of wood, brick, or stone, they can be openings cut through a dense hedge, or even two columnar plants on either side of a path. Whatever style of opening you choose, it should, of course, match the overall landscape style.

An attractive fencing choice for screening a small garden is wood lattice. Note how the gate, when constructed of the same material, blends into the fencing.

permit if you build above a certain height, typically 3 feet. Ordinances frequently require that a masonry retaining wall taller than 3 feet be designed by an engineer.

If the fence or wall is to act as a windbreak, careful positioning is required. A solid fence will not screen the wind from a patio located 20 feet away. The wind will simply swirl over the top and sweep down again to the patio area. An open fence or hedge will provide better protection, slowing the wind down but still allowing it to pass through, forming an actual cushion of air to deflect the currents curling over the top of the barrier.

If a wall is low enough, it can provide a place to sit as well as an enclosure. Sitting walls are effective in areas where minimal enclosure is desired, such as around a children's play area. The ideal height for sitting walls is about 16 inches, with a flat top that is at least 12 inches wide.

Screens

Another consideration when determining the walls of activity areas is whether you need them to be permanent. Garden screens are temporary or even portable partitions constructed of lightweight materials. They can be placed in a landscape to serve the same function as permanent walls—they can block views, provide wind resistance, and act as a deterrent to passage—without the design commitment of a fence or garden wall. Screens can be constructed of a variety of materials. Use screens to enclose a dining area or to hide stored items. Position portable screens in places where you are considering a more permanent wall, to determine the scale, size, and form of the enclosure. Temporary screens are also ideal for blocking unsightly areas during the process of installing the landscape. A screen that partially blocks a view can provide a sense of mystery about what is beyond and create the illusion of implied larger space.

CEILINGS

As in interior rooms, part of the sense of enclosure in activity areas is determined by the ceiling. The sky is, of course, the most natural ceiling for a garden. There are times, however, when you will want shelter from the sun, rain, or wind. You may also need to block views from above if, for example, your neighbors are on a higher slope than you or they have a taller home with a deck that extends from an upper floor. Developing a place in the landscape with a more permanent ceiling will satisfy these needs. Ceilings can be portable, such as a patio umbrella, permanent, such as a built shade structure, or seasonal, as the beautiful branches of a deciduous tree.

If a garden ceiling is partially open, the sun/shade patterns that it casts become significant design elements. Shadow patterns can be the lacy filigree of a honey locust tree or the striking alternating bands of sun and shade cast by the wood beams of a pergola or gazebo.

Plants as Ceilings

The overhead canopy of a tree is the most basic of garden ceilings. A tree allows sunlight to filter through its leaves, providing patterns of sun and shade for garden interest. In addition, certain types of trees can add color and fragrance to the garden. When selecting a shade tree, consider how its mature size will relate to the garden in form and scale. An overly large tree will dwarf a small garden and may eventually cover the entire area with shade. The overall texture of the tree as well as the amount of shade it provides are other factors in tree selection. Check the water, soil, and sun requirements of each species you are considering, as well as their tolerance for wind if that is a problem of your site.

There are three basic types of landscape trees. Deciduous trees, such as beech and maple, lose their leaves during the winter. These

A beautiful landscape ceiling is a natural canopy of branches and leaves. Trees provide cooling protection from the sun, while enlivening the area with texture and ever-changing patterns of shade.

PLANNING SHADE STRUCTURES

A trellis is a simple structure designed for the specific purpose of supporting plants. Trellises are generally built of lightweight construction materials and are placed overhead on supporting columns to provide filtered shade and visual interest.

Arbors are structures designed with open canopies that may or may not support plants. Arbors define a space, usually a patio area or a path. They can be either freestanding or attached to the house.

A pergola is an arbor constructed of open beams that rest on two parallel rows of wood or stone columns. Pergolas are frequently used to cover a segment of a path or as a ceiling for a passageway that connects an outbuilding to the house. True pergolas have flat roofs; those with arched roofs are sometimes called galleries. Pergolas provide spatial definition while allowing access and visual continuity. They contribute little protection from the rain, but they do help to screen sunlight and some wind.

A pergola can link the house with the yard. You can strengthen this link by building the pergola of the same materials as those used for the house. A simple design is usually the most successful. If the pergola is over a path, a destination should be visible to attract the viewer. A pergola in a small garden can be placed next to a garden wall or boundary to avoid cutting the central area in two. Use a pergola to separate the flower garden from the vegetable garden or to enhance a long, linear walkway.

Gazebos have been part of gardens since the Renaissance. Eighteenth-century French garden pavilions were traditionally designed as places where the nobility could hide away from life at court. They ranged in size from single rooms to fairly large structures. During the nineteenth century, the gazebo acquired its more contemporary meaning as a small, permanent structure, frequently having open sides. A gazebo adds romance to a garden, often with an old-fashioned air reminiscent of the Victorian era.

Your gazebo can serve as an overlook, an outdoor dining area, or a poolside retreat. Because gazebos create strong focal points in a garden, they must be sited carefully. If you include a gazebo in your landscape, it should be an integral part of the design. A gazebo in an open lawn area becomes a centerpiece, drawing attention to itself. Placed in the corner of a walled area, a gazebo can serve as a retreat. You can also use a gazebo to terminate an axis or highlight a vista, uniting distant parts of the landscape.

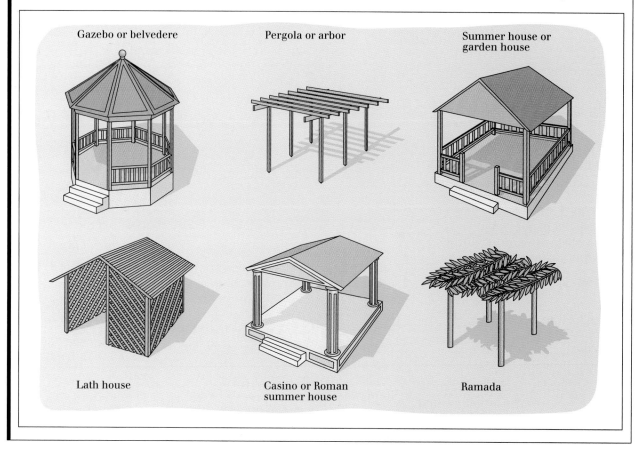

Gazebo or belvedere

Pergola or arbor

Summer house or garden house

Lath house

Casino or Roman summer house

Ramada

trees can be used to advantage in spots where you wish to have shade in the summer and sun in the winter, such as near a patio or living area. A disadvantage of deciduous trees is that you may need to rake up the fallen leaves in autumn, but remember that leaves make great compost and all trees replace their leaves sometime during the year.

Broadleaf evergreen trees, such as holly (*Ilex* species) and southern magnolia (*Magnolia grandiflora*), are clothed with leaves the year around. This type of tree is valuable in warm-winter climates where year-round shade is desirable.

Coniferous evergreen trees have needlelike leaves that they retain all year. These include pines and spruces. Although coniferous evergreens can provide deep shade, their continuing needle drop can be messy for patio areas.

A grove of six or more of the same type of tree planted relatively close together will create an inviting shaded garden area. Many varieties of trees are suitable for grove planting; birch and maple trees are especially attractive. Another option in living ceilings is a single shade tree with limbs that spread wide. A shade tree can be a beautiful addition to a garden but may require many years of growth before it can provide adequate shade. Fast-growing species, such as northern red oak (*Quercus rubra*), will show the quickest results.

Constructed Ceilings

Ceilings can be constructed of wood, fiberglass, plastic, or canvas. These architectural structures are appropriate in areas where year-round protection from the elements is needed. Constructed ceilings provide full-time enclosure of activity areas, shelter from rain or snow, and protection for shade-loving plants (and people) against the hot rays of the summer sun. They may also support climbing vines. You can build a constructed ceiling over all or part of a patio, deck, or play area.

Constructed ceilings can be solidly roofed for complete protection from the weather, or they can provide broken cover that allows sunlight to enter. If you design more than one ceiling in your landscape, be sure they harmonize in style and materials.

Solid-wood ceilings over porches or pavilions will be architecturally dominant features in the landscape and may also affect the structure of the house. Although these ceilings

A constructed ceiling can be implemented more immediately and controlled more easily than a ceiling of plants. This pergola-style shade structure is strategically placed to allow morning sun and afternoon shade on the east-facing patio.

provide the greatest amount of protection from the weather, they are permanent and should be planned with care. To be successful, ceilings over porches and pavilions must harmonize with the architectural design of your home. The form, scale, size, and color of all constructed features must be in keeping with your overall landscape style.

LANDSCAPE ACCENTS

Use landscape accents to direct attention and reinforce your landscape style. An accent can be any of a wide range of elements, including an unusual tree, a brightly colored planting bed, a work of art, a splash of water, or a play of light. You may have a landscape accent already picked out—a piece of statuary or an antique park bench, perhaps. If so, you must consider this piece as you determine your landscape style, and you will want to provide a special place for this accent in your design. If you do not have a particular accent in mind, consider the types of accents that best suit your landscape style and keep your eyes open for such pieces as you choose your materials.

Plants as Accents

Specimen trees, particularly the more exotic or unusual varieties, create natural landscape accents. Locate these visually prominent trees where you wish to draw the viewer's attention, and do not make them compete with surrounding plants. For example, you could plant a brightly colored 'Sunburst' honeylocust (*Gleditsia triacanthos*) against a row of green conifers to show off the accent tree to its fullest. When selecting a species of tree to use as a specimen plant, consider its mature size, which should be in keeping with the scale of the rest of the landscape.

Flower beds of brightly colored annuals or perennials also make effective accents. Annual flowers have a rapid growth rate, are available in a wide range of colors and textures, and can be changed from season to season to provide a continuous display of garden color. Biennials, perennials, and bulbs provide the same effect when in bloom, but they do not provide as constant a show as annuals. Container plants are useful as accents because you can move them into prominent locations when in full bloom and relegate them to more remote parts of the yard when they lose their flowers. A variety of containers can be used for container plants. Select ones that harmonize with your garden style for the most attractive results.

Constructed Accents

Not all landscapes require an accent. If you decide to use one, be sure to locate it where it receives all the attention it deserves. Well-placed benches or statues are enticing elements of design. A bench provides a spot to relax, focuses attention on a particular view or activity area, and acts as a focal point when no one is sitting there. An ideal location for a garden bench is in a sheltered spot overlooking an activity area or a distant view. A tremendous variety of seating styles is available, both fixed in place and movable. Whatever seating arrangement you choose should be in keeping with general design principles. In particular, bear in mind the sense of scale when you build or purchase benches—don't overwhelm a small area with large patio furniture or place a small bench in a large expanse without some kind of enclosure to keep it at a comfortable human scale.

Sculpture or statues used as landscape accents can evoke many moods. Classical figures, works of modern art, and wood carvings are strong design elements and should be used with discretion. As a general rule, one well-placed statue is far better than several scattered randomly throughout the landscape. A large statue or sculpture is probably best used to highlight the end point of an axis. Make sure it is of sufficient size to be noticed from a distance. Use smaller pieces to create an element of surprise along a garden path, perhaps sheltering the sculpture in a shady nook surrounded by plants. Choose the texture of nearby plants and paving to complement the accent.

Temporary landscape accents can also be very effective. Colorful flags, streamers, banners, and wind socks lend a festive air for special occasions. However you use them, constructed landscape accents should be chosen with a careful eye toward appropriateness and authenticity. Of course, your choices in design and materials of accent pieces should be in keeping with the overall landscape style.

Accent Lighting

Although you will figure your lighting needs well after you have chosen activity areas, keep outdoor lighting in mind as you select landscape accents. Patterns of sun and shade can be used during daylight hours to create dramatic effects. Leave an open, sunny area at the end of a shady walk to attract people in that direction, as there is a natural inclination to be drawn toward the sun. Well-placed light fixtures can spotlight activity areas, guide movement through the yard, and provide security at night. Decorative fixtures act in much the same manner as statuary and should be in keeping with the landscape style. Concealed lights can highlight plants or a constructed

Top: Underwater lighting and a grazing uplight create stark drama at this fountain. Bottom: Accent lighting can add sparkle to an outdoor scene. Small, low-voltage lamps highlight plantings and spotlight artwork.

Water as an accent can have many faces; this small, concrete reflecting pool is strategically placed along a path of concrete stepping-stones. Building a reflecting pool is a fairly simple construction project. The pool is also a great attraction to passing birds in need of a bath.

landscape accent. More information on the design and construction principles of outdoor lighting begins on page 120.

Remember that the process of fitting the elements of a landscape into your site is just that—a process. As you now begin actually designing your landscape, you may have to modify the ideal—your wish list and all the beautiful pictures in your scrapbook—to fit the reality of your site.

Water as an Accent

Water can be used in the landscape either as an activity area or a landscape accent, and it is delightful in its many forms and uses. Classical gardens through the ages have incorporated water as a major design focus for both practical and aesthetic purposes. Water can have myriad characters, ranging from the serenity of a reflecting pool to the playfulness of a bubbling fountain. It provides a cool and refreshing landscape element, particularly in hot climates. The sound of water splashing in a basin invites relaxation and contemplation and helps overcome noise problems. If you are lucky enough to have a running brook or natural pond on your property, you should capitalize on this valuable asset. Planting near water features should not be overdone,

PLANNING SWIMMING POOLS

An attractive pool area can increase the value of your property and often its marketability; conversely, a pool that is poorly designed or constructed will be frustrating to use and maintain and could lessen the marketability of your home.

Pool Use and Size

Three general uses of recreational pools are shallow-water play, diving, and lap swimming. Each has different requirements that affect pool dimensions.

Depths of 3 to 5 feet are recommended for shallow-water play. Because this type of activity does not involve much formal swimming, the length and width of the pool can vary.

If you dive, you must carefully coordinate the length, width, and depth of the pool with the height and location of the diving board or platform; a poorly designed diving area can result in serious injury. To meet your particular needs, obtain the booklet entitled *Suggested Minimum Standards for Residential Swimming Pools,* published by the National Spa and Pool Institute, 2000 K Street N.W., Washington, D.C. 20006. Also, check with your insurance carrier about the liability of diving boards.

The main requirements for a lap pool are a length of at least 25 feet, and a depth of at least 3½ feet to safely accommodate end turns. The end walls of the pool should be perpendicular to the lap direction to facilitate turning. The width of the pool can vary depending on your needs and site conditions. Be aware that very narrow lap pools are single-purpose pools and may not suit the tastes of others should you decide to sell your house.

If you wish to enjoy a multipurpose pool accommodating shallow-water play, diving, and lap swimming, the pool should be at least 16 by 32 feet.

Pool Shape and Style

A simple pool shape is most easily accommodated in the yard. The water itself becomes the focus and complement to the garden, rather than an eclectic pool that dominates the landscape. Often the architectural lines of the house or the layout of the yard will give you clues as to a good shape and style for the pool. Most pool contractors have a book of popular pool shapes to study. Once you have a shape and style in mind, test it out in the yard. Using garden hoses or agricultural lime, lay out the pool and deck area in accurate detail. Adjust the size and shape until it feels right.

Pool Configuration and Materials

The most common construction materials for pools are air-sprayed concrete and vinyl lining, but fiberglass-shell pools are also becoming popular.

Air-sprayed concrete is applied over a steel reinforcing web; with this material it is easy to achieve almost any shape, and it is permanent. The interior pool surface is generally plastered with a smooth finish in either the traditional white or the increasingly popular dark colors.

Vinyl-lined pools consist of a vinyl liner supported on the sides by walls of aluminum, steel, wood, or plastic. Sand or vermiculite is usually packed under the liner bottom. The cost of vinyl-lined pools can be considerably less than air-sprayed concrete pools. Vinyl liners vary in life expectancy. Vinyl-lined pools are more restricted in shape than air-sprayed concrete pools due to fabrication and installation limitations.

Fiberglass-shell pools are increasing in popularity in some areas of the country. These are prefabricated containers that are trucked to the site and dropped into place. They are very durable. Like vinyl-lined pools, their size and shape is limited by fabrication and transportation considerations.

Decking material is an important part of the design, especially for fully in-ground pools. In general, the decking should be nonslip, fairly uniform in surface, resistant to chemicals and algae, and sloped away from the pool for drainage.

Other Considerations

Safety is a critical aspect of the design of every pool area. Self-latching gates and perimeter fencing are usually required to keep unsupervised children and pets away from the water; refer to local codes and regulations for detailed information.

Heating a pool requires a considerable investment but it extends the pool season into the cooler months. It also makes swimming in the evening more enjoyable. Solar pool heating is a simple technology that can be utilized for a substantial amount of the required heating.

Pool covers can also extend the swimming season; they keep a pool 10° to 15° F warmer than an uncovered pool. Covers also reduce evaporation.

Plants Near Pools

When you plant around a pool, select specimens that are relatively litter free or that have litter large enough to be caught in a strainer basket so the filter will not become clogged. Avoid thorny plants around heavily used areas as well as those that attract bees. Keep fruiting plants back from pool areas to avoid slippery and stained decks. Desirable trees or shrubs with litter problems can be planted on the downwind side of a pool so that most litter blows away from the water. Evergreen shrubs provide simple, clean planted areas. Limit color accents to containers placed in key areas.

but should instead highlight the natural beauty of the water. The reflection of the surrounding plants or buildings on the water is a particularly pleasing aspect of pools.

A pool or fountain doesn't have to be large to be effective. The sound of a simple jet of water splashing into a small pool will attract attention and add life to your yard. Maximize the effects of sunlight glinting off the water surface. Pools in the shade of trees may be difficult to keep clean and can appear dark and murky.

PLANTS

Plants can be used in a landscape in a number of ways. An architectural approach to planting design uses plants in much the same way as walls, columns, and roofs of a building. A hedge used in lieu of a constructed fence, shrubs pruned to mimic construction, or trees planted in straight lines to emphasize a formal style are examples of the architectural use of plants.

A horticultural approach to plant design uses plants as botanical specimens. A native landscape style, that is, using only indigenous plants throughout the design, is one example of a horticultural planting approach. The use of a particular plant as the focus of a view is another. Designing a completely edible landscape is yet another.

Use plants in your design to solve functional problems as well. Plants can block wind, provide shade, and aid in erosion control.

As you begin your design, think of plants as sculptural masses rather than individual specimens. This will make it easier for you to achieve overall unity. Imagine pleasing combinations of texture, color, and form that will work to fulfill the functional uses.

Trees These form the backbone of the planting design. Large trees will give the landscape its structure. Smaller trees can be used in masses to create enclosure and scale. Place trees according to their mature size.

You can combine trees in groupings of a single species or in combinations of up to three different species. Any more than three species will cause the grouping to lack unity. To be most effective, the trees within a grouping should have different design characteristics. For example, a grouping of conifers with dark green color and a pyramidal form placed behind a group of flowering dogwoods (*Cornus florida*), with white flowers and a horizontal form would accentuate the best qualities of each plant.

Shrubs As landscape accents, architectural edges, foundation plantings, privacy screens, or natural borders, shrubs should relate in form, texture, and scale to the surrounding trees and structures. A shrub used alone as an accent should have a unique form, scale, texture, or color. Shrubs are frequently massed in borders or foundation plantings. The success of such a grouping will depend on the combination of textures, colors, and forms in it. It is best to avoid using too many different types of shrubs in a grouping. Three to five different species, with three or more plants of each species planted together, is quite attractive. Massings of shrubs of a single species make an effective and simple background for an activity area. This is particularly desirable if the foreground of the massing has a great variety of plants or colors, such as a flower border.

Shrubs used in foundation plantings should not grow rapidly or require continual pruning. If you want an immediate effect, infill with fast-growing plants that will be removed later. In general, lower plantings are better than taller ones, which would eventually make the house appear to be buried behind the shrubs. Hedge plantings form a strong architectural element and should be used to enhance the lines of the garden. Hedges can be formal or informal. Formal hedges require a great deal of maintenance. Informal hedges make excellent privacy screens and backdrops.

Ground Covers The use of ground covers is an excellent way to add interesting colors and textures to a design. They are useful in areas where lawn grasses would be difficult to establish or where foot traffic is undesirable. A single ground cover under shrubs and trees throughout the landscape can help unify the planting design.

Lawns A large expanse of open lawn can visually unify various activity areas, provide a surface for many different activities, and serve as a foreground for an architecturally interesting house. Use lawns in both formal and informal designs. Although large lawns are visually effective, in climates that are dry in summer a large

When choosing landscape floors, consider function and aesthetics. Keep in mind that nonliving surfaces require good drainage and should not be laid too close to the trunks of trees or shrubs. Consider whether the area will receive much foot traffic.

LANDSCAPE PLANTS FOR FRAGRANCE

Most of your landscape design will center on visual effect, but you shouldn't neglect the sense of smell. Although the flowers of some plants are inconspicuous, their fragrance may fill your senses more completely than the showiest blossoms. Other plants may delight you throughout the year with their fragrant foliage. The plants in the list below all have fragrant flowers or leaves. To learn more about them, see the entries in the Landscape Plant Guide beginning on page 211.

Trees

Abies concolor	White fir
Acer tataricum ssp. *ginnala*	Amur maple
Eriobotrya japonica	Loquat
Eucalyptus species	Eucalyptus species
Magnolia species	Magnolia species
Malus hupehensis	Tea flowering crab apple
Malus sargentii	Sargent flowering crab apple
Pittosporum tobira	Japanese pittosporum, mock orange
Prunus caroliniana	Carolina cherry laurel
Pseudotsuga menziesii	Douglas fir
Robinia pseudoacacia	Black locust
Tilia cordata	Littleleaf linden

Shrubs

Buddleja davidii	Butterfly bush
Choisya ternata	Mexican orange
Daphne species	Daphne species
Elaeagnus pungens	Silverberry
Gardenia augusta (*G. jasminoides*)	Gardenia
Hamamelis species	Witch hazel species
Magnolia stellata	Star magnolia
Myrica pensylvanica	Northern bayberry
Osmanthus fragrans	Sweet olive
Pittosporum eugenioides	Tarata pittosporum, lemonwood
Pittosporum tobira	Japanese pittosporum, mock orange
Rhus aromatica	Fragrant sumac
Syringa vulgaris	Common lilac
Viburnum × *burkwoodii*	Burkwood viburnum

Vines

Beaumontia grandiflora	Herald's trumpet
Clematis armandii	Evergreen clematis
Gelsemium sempervirens	Carolina jessamine
Jasminum polyanthum	Pink jasmine
Lonicera sempervirens	Trumpet honeysuckle
Rosa banksiae	Banks rose
Trachelospermum jasminoides	Starjasmine
Wisteria sinensis	Chinese wisteria

Ground Covers (Perennials)

Hosta plantaginea	Fragrant plantain lily
Mentha requienii	Corsican mint
Sarcococca hookeriana var. *humilis*	Small Himalayan sarcococca
Viola odorata	Sweet violet

Opposite: A curving border of flowering annuals provides a dramatic display of color.

lawn may prove environmentally and economically impractical. When planning a lawn, select a type of grass that grows well in your area and that is durable enough for your needs.

Vines Incorporating vines is a useful way to add color and texture to the small garden. Vines can disguise unsightly areas and climb trellises and arbors to provide a light overhead canopy. The texture of vines against a brick or stone wall can be enchanting.

Flowers Although flowers are not thought of as traditional landscape plants, the location of flower beds is essential to the success of a landscape design. Poorly located beds can ruin an otherwise successful design. If you want to grow flowers in your garden, they must be considered as part of the overall landscape design. Too many flowers will overpower a design and appear gaudy. Use flower beds as accents, directing views and movement. Mass the flowers in large drifts rather than spotting them here and there.

Other nontraditional plants can also be used effectively in a landscape. Tree and ground mosses, lichens, and mushrooms and other forms of fungi will add interest when used in an appropriate setting, such as in the midst of a rock garden. A vegetable such as ornamental cabbage is handsome as a border or ground cover. Peas and beans are quick-growing annual vines. Swiss chard provides outstanding color. Berries, as a group, make good barrier plants and can be used as mounding ground covers. Wild berries are thought by some to be a scourge of the garden, but if left alone they can be quite attractive. Besides enjoying their unusual ornament, you can also enjoy the bounty of their harvest.

DRAWING PLANS

Plans are drawings that translate the three-dimensional objects in a landscape into lines and points on paper. Plans will help you visualize the existing patterns on your site more easily, develop new ideas quickly, and guide you while you are installing your design.

Taking the time to draw plans will actually save you many hours of construction time, because you will know exactly where all landscape features belong and precisely how they fit together before you ever break ground. Those hours can be put to better use enjoying your new landscape. Drawing plans before attempting installation will also allow for more accurate materials estimates, so you don't spend more money than necessary on expensive items such as concrete, wood, brick, and plants.

You can draw plans freehand, or you can draft them. Freehand plans are drawn quickly and loosely, without the aid of mechanical drafting tools. If your design is fairly simple, and especially if you will not be changing utility lines, adding an automatic watering system, or building large outdoor structures, freehand drawings may be all that you will need.

Drafted landscape plans are precise and professional and may be necessary for detailed construction drawings where accurate measurements are required.

A compromise between freehand and drafted plans may ideally suit your needs. For these, your house and the constructed landscape elements should be drawn with a straightedge and the trees drawn with a circle template. Everything else on the plan, such as planting beds and nonpaved activity areas, may be drawn freehand. In any case, draw your plans to scale. The only way you will be able to determine if a desired feature will fit in your landscape is to accurately measure the lot and existing features and plot new elements to size on your drawing.

Before you begin drawing your plans, purchase a few basic materials, available at any art-supply store: one pad of 1000H tracing paper with a grid (graph paper), one pad of plain tracing paper (both pads of the same size), an architect's scale (if your plan is at a scale of 1 inch to 10 feet or greater, you will also need an engineer's scale), a roll of drafting tape, an eraser, a drafting pencil (softer leads are better for designing), a circle template (used to draw perfect circles for trees and shrubs), a 6-inch 45-degree triangle (used to draw right angles), and a compass (to make circles larger than those possible with a circle template). If you want to draw parallel lines accurately, purchase an inexpensive tool known as a rolling parallel glide. This tool allows you to draw parallel lines without using a T square and triangle.

There is an alternative to the above methods if you are computer literate and have a moderately sophisticated computer at hand. Several low-cost CAD (computer-aided design) software programs are available for simple drafting, some specifically for landscape drafting. These programs come equipped with all the symbols you'll need for accurate landscape design and construction drawings.

Architects use some basic symbols to represent objects typically found in a landscape. You can purchase a template for drawing these symbols at an art-supply store. A general rule to follow in drawing your plans is to use the thickest line for the building walls; the second thickest to outline trees; a medium line for shrubs, garden walls, fences, and paved paths; and the finest line for paving patterns and ground covers. Using these different lines widths, and keeping them consistent, will make your plans much easier to understand.

Drawing Your Plan

To draw your plan, tape a sheet of grid paper onto your drawing board. Begin the plan by laying out the property lines and walls of the house. Use the scale to get accurate measurements and the triangle to draw right angles. A rolling parallel glide will help you to draw the parallel building walls. Draw one building wall to scale, running a pencil along the straightedge of the parallel glide to get a straight line. Roll the parallel glide to the correct location for the opposite wall and draw it. This line should be parallel to the one you previously drew.

To draw trees, shrubs, ground covers, and lawn areas, find a circle on the circle template that represents the diameter of the crown of each tree or shrub when it is about 10 years old, and use that circle to lay out trees and shrubs with a light pencil line. If the circle template is not large enough to draw the trees, use a compass.

Finishing Touches

After you lay out the various elements, label your plan by neatly printing any pertinent notes directly on the activity areas, or by printing all your notes on the side and drawing arrows to indicate the area to which they pertain. Be sure to include on all your plans a scale and an arrow indicating north.

You'll need to make additional copies of your master plan to use for drawing a grading plan (see page 118), lighting plan (see page 128), irrigation plan (see page 147), and planting plan (see page 182), and to make notes on. Blackline prints will most closely resemble your original drawing. If you wish to add color, get a print of the master plan and color it with marking pens or colored pencils.

THE DESIGN PROCESS

As you design your landscape, you will find that you need to make many decisions along the way. In most cases these decisions will fall into one of three categories: those related to the overall layout of the property, those related to details, and those having to do with materials.

There are no set rules that tell you how to create a design. The best way to develop a landscape design that meets your needs is to follow a logical design process involving five basic steps: understanding existing conditions, analyzing appropriate fit, defining locations for all of the items on your landscaping wish list, drawing a detailed plan, and producing working drawings. You do not need expert drawing skills to use the design process successfully. With a few simple tools, available in any art-supply store, anyone can produce a creative and workable plan.

Every design, whether for a new lot or for a remodel of an existing landscape, can benefit from a thoughtful plan. The process described on the following pages can be completed in a few hours or can take as long as you like.

The process of design involves fitting many different items into a set space. Save hours of frustration by experimenting on paper instead of attempting to install your landscape from just an idea.

PREPARING A BASE PLAN

Although you have studied the existing conditions of your lot by looking around to see what you have, you will need to translate these observations into two-dimensional drawings before you can begin designing. Architectural plans are drawings that show an area from a bird's-eye view—that is, looking directly down on the site. Such a plan will help you see planting areas, lawns, paths, and the house and how they relate to one another in your final, installed landscape.

The first thing you need to begin your plans is an accurate base plan. A complete base plan will show your property line, any easements or underground utilities on your lot, existing contours (lines that connect points of similar elevation,

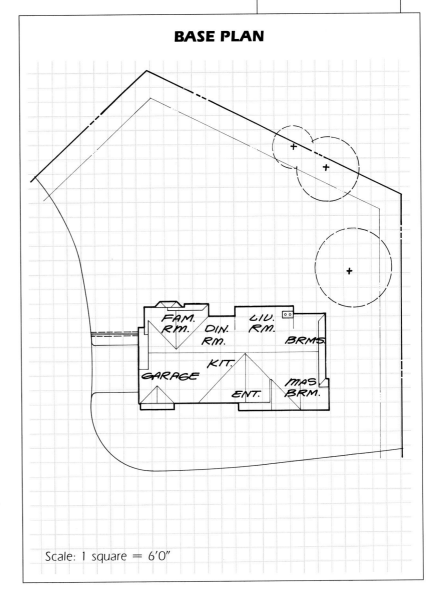

BASE PLAN

FAM. RM.
DIN. RM.
LIV. RM.
BRMS
KIT.
GARAGE
ENT.
MAS BRM.

Scale: 1 square = 6'0"

indicating the formation and slope of the land), existing trees and shrubs that you plan to save, the outline of the house, and any paths or structures on the property.

The local building department or assessor's office may have a copy of your plat plan on file. This plan normally would not show your house or any improvements made to your lot, but would indicate a property line and any underground utilities or easements. If your house was designed by an architect or builder, that office may have a plan of your property. Old plans should be verified to ensure that whatever is indicated is still part of your landscape and that any new structures or plantings are included. If a copy of your plat plan is not available, you may need to have your property professionally surveyed. A topographic survey will show the property boundaries and contour lines of the site. This is particularly important if the lot is on a steep slope. A relatively flat site won't need a plan that shows contours.

Many aspects of drawing a landscape plan can be done freehand, but drafting tools will enable you to draw straight lines, precise angles, and circles. Even a freehand plan must be drawn to scale. Scaling aids accuracy when you are locating areas on a plan, helps you visualize the relative size of landscape elements, and is necessary for determining the amount of materials needed for construction. See page 86 for more information on the tools you'll need for drawing plans.

To draw plans to scale, you will need graph paper, with each square representing a set measurement. A scale of 1 square equaling 6 feet is an especially easy scale to work with when roughly measuring activity areas in your yard, as six feet is approximately two adult strides.

For more-detailed drawings, you can also use an architect's scale, a tool for converting real dimensions into a relative scale. For example, if you are using a scale in which ¼ inch equals 1 foot, the architect's scale would represent a 4-foot length as 1 inch, an 8-foot length as 2 inches, and so on.

When choosing a scale for your drawing, consider the size of your property and the amount of detail you need to show. A large lot will require the use of a smaller scale, such as 1 inch to 20 feet, in order to fit the entire site on one piece of paper. A smaller lot or detailed areas would be better at a larger scale, such as ⅛ or ¼ inch to 1 foot. Construction details should be drawn at a 1-inch-to-1-foot scale.

To begin measuring your site, you will need a baseline, or datum line, on which to base the measurements. A wall of the house or an adjacent building will make an adequate baseline. Draw this line to scale on a sheet of graph paper, being sure to leave enough room around it to include the rest of the lot. Always draw a north arrow on all your plans and indicate the scale you are using. This is a standard practice and will make it easier for builders or city officials to read and understand your plans. It is also a standard convention to use the top of the drawing as the north direction; sun and shade patterns can then be determined at a glance.

Beginning from the baseline, use a 50- or 100-foot tape measure to locate everything on the lot that seems relevant. This includes the property line; all walls of the house, including the locations of doors and windows; the driveway and road; paths and pools; the location and diameter of tree trunks and the spread of overhanging branches; shrubs; fences; overhead and underground utility lines; easements and setbacks; existing irrigation and hose bibbs; and any other structures on your lot. Mark down all of these locations as you measure them. To draw curved walks and driveways, locate a series of points along the curve and then draw a line connecting them. The more points you locate, the more accurate the curve will be.

In addition to horizontal dimensions, you may wish to include some vertical measurements on your base plan. The best way to do this is to set an elevation for the floor of your house and take the measurements from there. For example, assume that the finished floor of the house is at an elevation of 100 feet. If the deck is 6 inches below that, its elevation would be listed as 99 feet 6 inches. If the lawn is 1 foot below the deck, the elevation of the lawn would be 98 feet 6 inches. If the site has many elevation changes, you will need an accurate topographic survey produced to convey this information.

After you have taken all the measurements, trace this information onto a clean piece of paper as neatly as possible.

ANALYZING THE SITE

The existing conditions of your property are some of the strongest influences on your final landscape design. Even if you're very familiar with your lot, it will be to your advantage to record all your observations. Use the principles of design (see page 56) to help you analyze your site; look for things such as natural axes, rhythms, scale, and so on. You may discover aspects of your lot that you had never thought about before. The better you understand what you have, the easier it will be to develop a sensitive and appropriate design solution.

To conduct a site analysis, overlay your base plan with a piece of tracing paper; write down your observations on this. Note on the plan the following information: the location of sunny and shady areas; any areas with poor drainage; views, both good and bad; the direction of prevailing winds and wind-free areas; steep slopes and level areas; access points and circulation routes; and any features you might wish to accent, such as a rock outcropping or a pond. Also record any improvements you find desirable,

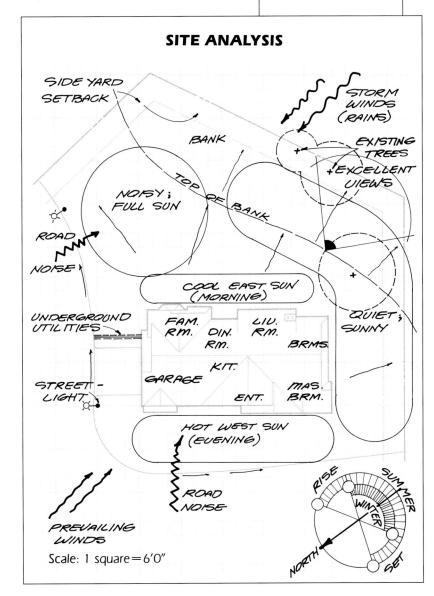

SITE ANALYSIS

SIDE YARD SETBACK

STORM WINDS (RAINS)

BANK

EXISTING TREES

EXCELLENT VIEWS

TOP OF BANK

NOISY; FULL SUN

ROAD NOISE

COOL EAST SUN (MORNING)

QUIET; SUNNY

UNDERGROUND UTILITIES

FAM. RM. DIN. RM. LIV. RM.

BRMS.

KIT.

GARAGE

STREET LIGHT

ENT.

MAS. BRM.

HOT WEST SUN (EVENING)

ROAD NOISE

PREVAILING WINDS

RISE SUMMER WINTER NORTH SET

Scale: 1 square = 6'0"

CHANGING NEEDS

Your landscape needs may shift over time. As you design your site, consider not only how you will use it today, but how you may use it in the future. A well-thought-out initial design will be flexible enough to accommodate changing needs.

A family with young children may require space for active play, with hardy plants and open expanses of lawn. As the children grow older, it may be necessary to enlarge the terrace, providing more space for family functions and entertaining. Family members may develop new hobbies, such as vegetable gardening, that require more garden space. After the children leave home, aging couples may desire less maintenance, more privacy, and quiet areas in the garden for relaxation.

The simplest way to allow for flexibility is to limit the construction of architectural elements such as walls, patios, and planters. These landscape improvements, although desirable in some contexts, are more costly to remove when needs change. Certain construction materials allow for greater flexibility. You can alter the size of patios made of brick or stone laid in sand or stone dust by adding or removing individual pieces; with concrete, however, large areas must be destroyed if your needs change.

Planting beds are easily altered with changing needs. The framework provided by large, mature trees is less amenable to change, however. Careful placement of trees during the design process can reduce future conflicts.

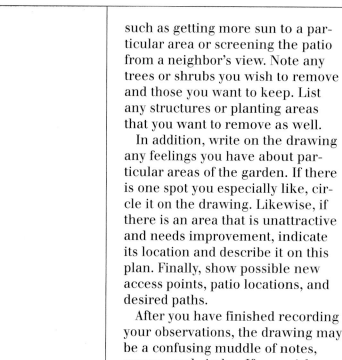

such as getting more sun to a particular area or screening the patio from a neighbor's view. Note any trees or shrubs you wish to remove and those you want to keep. List any structures or planting areas that you want to remove as well.

In addition, write on the drawing any feelings you have about particular areas of the garden. If there is one spot you especially like, circle it on the drawing. Likewise, if there is an area that is unattractive and needs improvement, indicate its location and describe it on this plan. Finally, show possible new access points, patio locations, and desired paths.

After you have finished recording your observations, the drawing may be a confusing muddle of notes, arrows, and circles. If you wish, you can redraw your analysis onto a clean sheet of tracing paper, including the rough outline of the lot,

house, and other fixed points. Don't throw away your original drawing, however; it will be helpful as you develop your ideas into a final plan.

DEVELOPING YOUR IDEAS

The next step will be the most challenging and the most exciting in the design process. Now is the time to fit into a cohesive design all of the elements you want in your landscape. Gather together your scrapbook of design inspirations (see page 10), your landscaping wish list (see page 55), and your site analysis drawing. These three guides will help you develop design alternatives for a successful landscape.

Draw a bubble diagram to locate the activity areas you wish to develop. To construct a bubble diagram, lay a new sheet of tracing paper over your site analysis and base plan. Rough-in the locations of the proposed design elements, but do not concern yourself with the actual shape or size of the areas. Experiment. Try various locations for different use areas. Using loose bubble forms, locate elements such as a patio or deck, swimming pool, storage shed, lawn area, planting beds, play areas, entries, and screening. Draw arrows indicating general path connections between areas.

In order to achieve appropriate fit, locate each area according to its specific needs. Adjacent areas should have compatible uses. For example, if your children are young, you will probably want to locate the play area near the house so you can supervise it from indoors, but away from an area you might wish to use for quiet relaxation. Planting beds can provide screening for privacy as well as separation between areas within the landscape.

After checking the compatibility of adjacent use areas, make sure that the areas are compatible with the information you discovered during your site analysis. You would not want to locate a major outdoor seating area in the windiest part of the lot; similarly, you don't want to put a service area in your favorite part of the garden.

Remember that the shape and existing conditions of the site are some of the strongest influences on design. Relating new areas to the conditions suggested by the existing natural features will make them more appealing and appropriate. Spaces should have continuity and should flow together to create a cohesive environment. Experiment with different shapes and forms to find the ones that appeal to you most. Use the natural edge of an adjacent forest to define the curve of a garden path. A distant view may suggest a location for a bench. Likewise, existing features in the architecture of the house can give you clues for the landscape design. Extending the walls of the house to create low patio or deck walls will visually link the house and garden. Relating landscape accents to views from the windows of the house will enhance both your garden and indoor living experience.

Make notes on your drawings to help you to keep track of your ideas. Record what the areas are and general ideas about how they will look, and use arrows to indicate relationships among areas and major circulation paths.

Do not limit yourself to your first solution. Instead, develop several different bubble diagrams and compare their advantages and disadvantages. Doing this will open you up to new ideas. Draw your chosen alternative on a clean sheet of tracing paper to use as a base for your master plan.

DRAWING YOUR MASTER PLAN

The final product of the conceptual design phase is a plan that accurately shows the location and shape of all the elements of the new landscape. This plan is called a master plan. Lay the bubble diagram over your base plan, and place a clean sheet of tracing paper over that. Using an architect's scale, begin to assign dimensions to the different areas of the garden. The average dimensions of activity areas (see

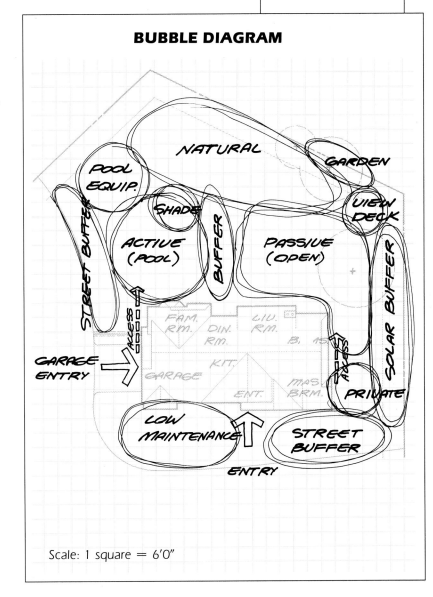

BUBBLE DIAGRAM

Scale: 1 square = 6'0"

sidebar below) is a good reference point from which to start.

Begin placing the elements of the design onto your plan. Draw floors, walls, outdoor rooms, ceilings, accents, and plant massings. Remember to base the size and position of each element on the principles of design and appropriate fit. Some

---

STANDARD DIMENSIONS

The amount of space you devote to each area of your landscape will depend, of course, on your priorities and on the total square footage available to you. There are some standard dimensions you must keep in mind, however, so your design will be functional as well as aesthetically pleasing.

Path Widths

For one person: 24 to 30 inches.

For two people side by side: primary walk, 4 to 6 feet; secondary walk, 3 feet.

Step Rise and Tread

Recommended riser-to-tread ratios: a 6-inch rise to a 12-inch tread, a 5-inch rise to a 15-inch tread, a 4-inch rise to an 18-inch tread, or a 3-inch rise to a 24-inch tread. Never use more than a 6-inch rise. The product of the rise and run should be between 72 and 76 inches whenever possible.

Ramp Rise

Recommended maximum rise is 12 feet over 100 horizontal feet (12 percent), and that is pretty steep; 8-percent maximum for wheelchairs. Create flat landings every 20 feet or so for wheelchairs unless the ramp is 5 percent or less.

Driveway Width

One-car garage in urban area: minimum 9 feet wide, centered on the door.

One-car garage in suburban or rural area: 12 to 14 feet wide, centered on the door.

Two-car garage: 18 feet wide, centered on the doors.

Curved driveway: 14 to 18 feet wide.

Auto parking space: 9 feet wide and 18 feet long, minimum.

Planting Beds

For shrubs: minimum 1 foot wide.

For flowers: 1 to 5 feet wide.

For vegetables: about 10 feet by 10 feet for a small garden; about 20 feet by 20 feet for a large garden.

Fences and Gates

Recommended fence height: 6 feet. Fence should be built to either above or below eye level. You will find that a fence built at eye level is uncomfortable.

Width of a typical single, hinged gate: 4 feet. Any wider will require additional support.

Width of a vehicle gate: 10 feet.

---

types of uses will strongly influence the forms your design will take. A tennis court is a good example—a large and dominant rectangular form. Swimming pools may take many shapes.

At this point you should think about your preferred style for the landscape. For example, if you have decided that you like a French-style landscape, use geometric lines for the site areas, shaping them based on the principles of symmetry and axis. On the other hand, if your home is most suited to an English style, design a large, irregularly shaped lawn, plenty of planting areas, and curved paths for strolling.

Although the characteristics of the construction materials you choose will influence the forms of the landscape, at this point in the design process you should concentrate on the form of the space and the aesthetic relationships rather than on actual materials and construction. Similarly, think of plants more as sculptural elements in the garden, don't weigh their horticultural merits now. You will consider specific materials and plant characteristics later.

It may be easier for you to visualize different shapes if you draw them to scale on separate pieces of paper and then cut them out and lay them on your plan. When you develop a solution that you like, trace it onto your plan. This method is particularly valuable when you are designing a deck, patio, pool, or outbuilding.

Consider how you would logically move through the garden, locating paths as close to these natural lines of movement as possible. Try to visualize what it will feel like to be in the spaces that you design—what you will see, where you will want to sit, and where you would like to walk. Visualizing in this way will

MASTER PLAN

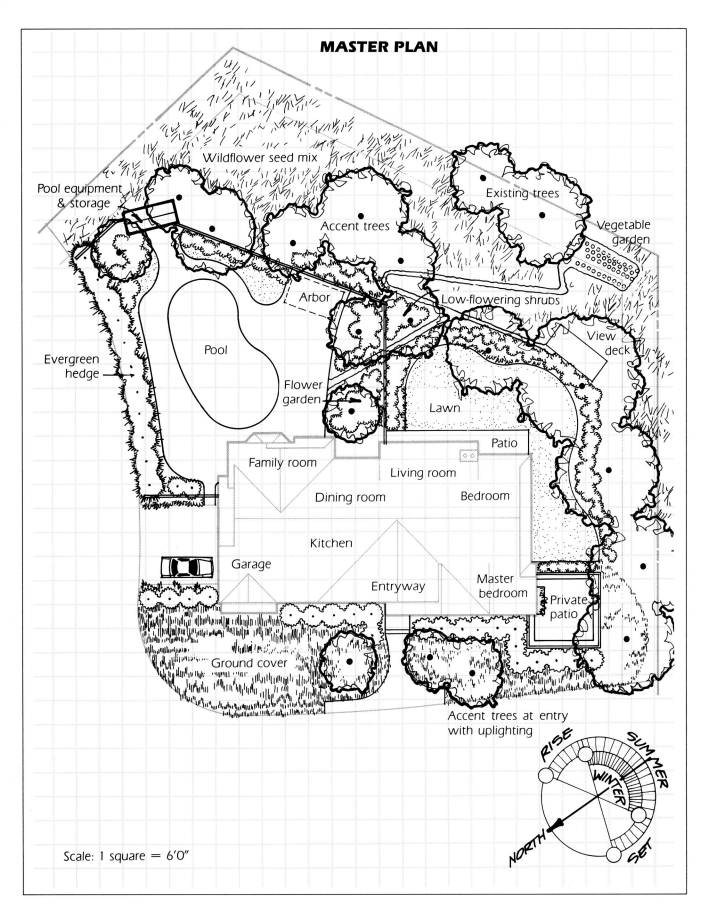

Wildflower seed mix

Pool equipment & storage

Accent trees

Existing trees

Vegetable garden

Arbor

Low-flowering shrubs

View deck

Evergreen hedge

Pool

Flower garden

Lawn

Patio

Family room

Living room

Dining room

Bedroom

Kitchen

Garage

Entryway

Master bedroom

Private patio

Ground cover

Accent trees at entry with uplighting

RISE SUMMER WINTER NORTH SET

Scale: 1 square = 6'0"

help you analyze each solution effectively to see whether it fits your design intentions. There is usually more than one solution to a given design problem. Develop many solutions, saving each sketch for further consideration.

During this design phase, you may find it helpful to use other types of drawings. Don't worry if you don't draw well—you are doing these sketches only for your own use so you can visualize your plan.

Sections are drawings that show a cut profile of an area. They are useful when you have changes in elevation or are interested in seeing how objects relate vertically. To draw a section, imagine that you have cut through your plan vertically with a knife. Show everything that you would see, such as the cut walls, the ground line, decks, trees, and shrubs. It may be helpful for you to draw the outline of a person in your section to give it relative scale.

An elevation is a scaled drawing of the side, front, or rear of a structure or landscaped area. Elevations are similar to sections but include everything you would see when looking at the site from a particular direction. Thumbnail sketches are rough, quick sketches showing different views of a finished design. Thumbnail sketches are helpful when you're trying to imagine how certain aspects of the design will look.

You can also use photographs as a design tool. Take snapshots of your garden as it exists now; then use marking pens to draw the new trees, fences, or patios onto the photographs. This may give you a better idea of how your final design will look than the drawings can.

After you have developed a plan that you feel suits your needs, and you have evaluated it through section and elevation drawings, take your plan outside and walk around the spaces that you have drawn. Try to imagine the landscape exactly as you have drawn it, making sure that it is suitable and will satisfy all your needs. You may even want to lay out string or hoses that mark the paths and patio areas to help you visualize the final design.

Trace your final design onto a clean sheet of paper with your base plan elements—property line, house walls, windows and doors, and contours, if necessary. Label the primary new areas and the existing structures and plants that are to remain. This drawing will serve as your final landscape master plan.

Once you have drawn your master plan, you are ready to select materials for construction. In doing this, consider the design properties of each material and how it will enhance your design. Further descriptions of the nature of specific landscaping materials begin on page 156.

After you have selected your materials and before you draw working plans or begin construction, check your design for community regulations and schedule constraints and draw up a cost estimate to make sure you'll be able to install the landscape as planned. These constraints may have a significant effect on your design and should not be ignored. A discussion of what to do before breaking ground begins on page 99.

Working Drawings

Working drawings are accurate, scaled drawings that detail how the elements of your plan will be constructed. The amount of detail shown on the drawings will depend on how they are to be used. If you are making your own working drawings and constructing the project yourself, you may not need a full package of drawings in order to construct the project.

If you are hiring an outside contractor to construct your project, talk to him or her before starting the working drawings to learn what will be needed. If you are unfamiliar with construction methods or if your project has complicated or unusual elements, you may wish to hire a landscape architect to help resolve the construction details. A landscape architect can produce a full packet of working drawings or just the one or two specific drawings you may require. A complete packet of working drawings will contain a copy of the final master plan, a grading plan, a lighting plan, an irrigation plan, a planting plan, and construction details. Depending on your plan and construction situation, all these drawings may not be necessary. Draw grading, lighting, irrigation, and planting plans to the same scale as the final master plan. Have several copies made of the master plan to serve as a reference for working drawings and to use during the installation of your design.

A grading plan shows both existing and proposed contours as well as spot elevations at significant locations. This plan is critical for showing how the site will drain. Drainage pipes, channels, and drain inlets are all shown on a grading plan. If the site improvements are relatively simple, you can combine the grading plan with the planting plan on a single drawing. Instructions for drawing a grading plan begin on page 118.

A lighting plan shows the location and type of each light fixture and switch in the plan. Simple lighting plans are sometimes combined with planting plans. Instructions for drawing a lighting plan begin on page 128.

Irrigation plans show the location and sizes of sprinkler heads, pipes,

controller, and spigots. Instructions for drawing an irrigation plan begin on page 147.

A planting plan indicates the scientific name of each plant, its exact location and spacing, and the number of plants needed. A plant list on the planting plan should indicate, for each plant, the total amount needed, botanical and common names, size, and special features. Simple construction details are sometimes included on the planting plan. Instructions for drawing a planting plan begin on page 182.

Construction details show how driveways and paths, garden walls and fences, decks and patios, and steps and ramps will be built. The details included on this type of drawing include dimensions, type of materials, method of construction, and other relevant information for getting the plans approved, estimating costs, and purchasing materials. Construction details may not be necessary for work you will do yourself on projects where a permit is not needed.

CHECKLIST:

DESIGNING YOUR LANDSCAPE
- List elements for your lifestyle on your landscaping wish list.
- Consider principles of design for your landscape style.
- List elements for your home on your landscaping wish list.
- List site problems to be solved on your landscaping wish list.
- Think about your design style preferences.
- Purchase drawing materials.
- Measure and locate all existing site elements and conditions.
- Draw your base plan.
- Analyze the site.
- Develop a number of design alternatives using bubble diagrams.
- Roughly figure the costs of alternatives against your budget.
- Check alternatives for regulation, easement, and set-back requirements.
- Consider construction principles of landscape features.
- Choose the most workable bubble diagram.
- Create your master plan.
- Prepare working drawings including details.
- Revise and refine your cost estimates (include contingency).

INSTALLING YOUR LANDSCAPE

Brick-floored activity areas, such as this patio, can be installed in phases as time and finances permit.

Your time thus far has been devoted to planning your design. You have evaluated a number of styles and thought about the functions of the various areas in your landscape. Now you must consider the installation of each landscape element. Installation, like design, must be planned carefully in advance.

This chapter not only helps you plan the installation, but also shows you the principles of building so you can make your design a reality. Constructing a landscape involves properly preparing the land through grading and drainage; designing and installing the watering, lighting, and utility systems; building outdoor structures and features; preparing soil for planting; and purchasing and installing the plants.

You must consider the impact that the installation of each element will have on your design. You may have to reevaluate your master plan once you understand the principles of installing a landscape. A certain element may be much more difficult, expensive, or time-consuming to install than you had first imagined.

The sound of water enhances an outdoor environment. Here a simple splash box, hidden among the boulders at the corner of a patio, simulates a mountain stream. Recirculating pumps can be used to pump water for splash boxes, fountains, waterfalls, and even small streams.

It is easier, and cheaper, to make changes on your drawings than it is to make them in the middle of the installation. Many designs are changed at this stage of the process. Once you understand the construction principles involved in installing your landscape design, you will probably want to improve or fine-tune the design.

Before you actually break ground, make a checklist of all the elements in your design and think through the implications of each. One of your first tasks should be to determine whether your design will comply with local regulations. Develop a schedule by evaluating how long each part of the landscape installation will take and then deciding how long you are willing to wait for the landscape to be completed. As you decide on the appropriate effort, time, and budget you can allocate to the project, take into account the length of time you expect to live in the house. After this analysis, you may need to make adjustments to your plan.

Also consider whether your needs will change. Look at who will use or benefit from the project, and for how long. Children grow up, and tastes change. Think of how play areas, for example, will be used or recycled after their heyday is over. The resale value of specific home improvements may also be a consideration. You may choose to undertake a few of the more pressing improvements now and do the more elaborate or time-consuming projects later; or you may wish to do everything at once rather than put up with continuous construction over an extended period.

Determine how much of the landscape installation you can do by yourself and whether you will need to hire professionals for some aspects. You may consider having a contractor do the heavier or more equipment-intensive work, or hiring some carpentry help if that is not your talent, or doing the carpentry but not the masonry. Even if you go so far as to have someone else perform the entire installation, you need to understand the construction principles involved so you know when tasks are being performed correctly.

BEFORE BEGINNING CONSTRUCTION

UNDERSTANDING REGULATIONS

The regulations that will affect your landscape design include zoning ordinances, easements, building codes, and community design guidelines. All are legal constraints that govern what you can build and how you can build it. They are designed to safeguard the community, promote public safety, and protect the homeowner. You may need to obtain a certain permit or attend a hearing if what you request is in conflict with zoning ordinances. The rules of each community vary to some degree; if you've recently moved to a community, do not assume that the rules of your old neighborhood will apply.

Criteria developed by a neighborhood association, historic district, or planned unit development may also govern building activities in your area. If so, you will need to have this organization approve your plan. The review may include the types of materials and the colors to be used in visible elements such as fences, walls, storage sheds, and shutters. Occasionally, even the choice and location of plant material will need to be reviewed.

Often it is not enough to do your homework, but that is precisely where you should start. Find out what your community has published on this matter. The local building department is a good place to begin. Some cities have prepared informative pamphlets that describe in detail the types of drawings and permit applications required in order to make improvements to your property.

The different types of legal restrictions you need to consider before installing the landscape are described in more detail later in this chapter. Your community may have regulations regarding fences, swimming pools, and structures such as gazebos, breezeways, garages, and decks. Find out about easements and any special variances required, and what the setback requirements are for the front, sides, and rear of your property. The community engineering office may have plat plans and utility and drainage maps available, and they may prescribe certain procedures for working around public utilities. You may need permits for curb cuts (for an element such as a driveway), tree removal, electrical work, plumbing, and other utility connections. In addition, you may be required to submit completed drawings, permit applications, and fees before you can start work.

Building codes can be boring to read, and they often are so technical that they are difficult to comprehend. You need to become familiar with them, however, in order to understand the level of construction quality your city requires.

Legal Restrictions

If properly prepared, a certified land survey of your property will document most legal restrictions on a drawing of the site. Often these restrictions are also described in the deed to your home. As you prepare the site analysis, as discussed on page 89, carefully include these restrictions on the survey. Some key types of restrictions are described below.

Easements These corridors along or within your property are defined for a specific use by public entities or private individuals. They vary in width from 10 feet to as much as

200 feet. If it is a public easement, you are constrained from building over or otherwise obstructing it. You may be given permission to plant trees or shrubs in the easement or use portions of it on a temporary basis. Obtain a legal description of the easement in question so you can see what is permitted. Common easements are street and road rights-of-way and easements for electricity, gas, telephone, television, and sanitary and storm sewers. Utility companies and communities have certain rights regarding easements, often including the right to cross your property to service utilities and easements. The utilities can be either overhead or underground.

Setbacks These restrictions legally define the location of a structure with respect to the front, sides, and back edges of the property. They are used to determine how far back additions, garages, fences, and walls must be from the property line, especially if footings are involved. Front setbacks are usually 25, 30, or 40 feet. Side-yard and rear-lot setbacks are generally somewhat less. This information is readily available, usually on city or local zoning maps. Know the exact location of your property lines, and record them accurately on your survey. Property lines are not always correctly indicated by existing fences or hedgerows.

Underground Utilities Throughout your neighborhood and property, there may be a few or many underground utilities of which you must be aware. As you plan your landscape design, you must determine the exact location and depth of any underground utilities on your property. Utility companies and communities have utility hotline telephone numbers. Check

the telephone directory for the number in your area. You are required to call these hot lines before beginning any construction work that involves digging around these utilities. The hot-line office, in turn, will send a representative to your home to locate the utilities. In most cases this is a free service.

Building Codes

Building codes and zoning ordinances describe the uses permitted in a given zone and impose certain restrictions upon development. In some areas, zoning ordinances limit the percentage of the lot that can be paved or covered with buildings. If this is the case where you live, you should measure the elements on your property to determine whether you have already reached this limit. Zoning ordinances may also restrict building height.

Building Permits Most communities base their code on the Uniform Building Code (UBC). You can often obtain the sections of the code that apply to your project from the community engineering office. Check also for specific plumbing and electrical codes if your design will require this type of work.

Whether you will need a building permit depends on the scope of your plan. If the plans call for relatively minor, nonstructural work—such as installing new plants, building a wall less than 3 feet high, and adding a sprinkler system—you probably will not need a permit. You also do not normally need a building permit to install or construct a tool shed that occupies 120 square feet or less of floor space. But if you are putting in outdoor lighting, decks, patios, driveways—anything that involves structural work or changes in plumbing or electrical wiring—you will probably need a permit. If you are in doubt, call the community building inspector's office. The staff there can give you advice on how to comply with the codes.

A permit consists of written approval from your municipality, giving you permission to build. Permits protect both you and the community by stipulating the required performance, level of quality, and methods of installation.

To obtain a permit, you'll need to submit plans (usually two sets) to the inspector's office. If the work to be done is extensive, you may be required to submit a master plan plus specific construction plans, elevations, sections, and details of the electrical system, plumbing, or other components. If the project is very small, a master plan and a description may suffice. Your plans will be checked and either approved or sent back for changes. You may be asked to modify your plan to conform to local codes, or to demonstrate that you are proficient enough to do the work yourself. The permit may require that you start and end the project within a certain time period—usually three months to start work and nine additional months to complete it. If you have not completed the work within the specified period, you will need to obtain a new permit.

Inspections As part of the permit process, the local governing agency will inspect your project at predetermined stages of construction. Features installed without inspection may cause many different problems for you, including the ability to sell your home. These inspections are based upon sound judgment, and by law and common sense you must abide by them.

You must schedule your installation so that you can stop work for inspection. The inspector will tell you at which points during the installation the work should be inspected. If your plan was prepared by an architect or engineer, lay out the work exactly as drawn and execute it per the approved drawings. Inspectors are especially concerned with foundations, retaining walls, and excavations for utilities. For example, any ditch should be excavated to the specified dimensions shown on the plan, which should meet or exceed local code requirements.

The depth and width of footings and foundations for structures are specified in the UBC. Local codes vary, however, and take precedence over the UBC; therefore, it is very important to confer with a building inspector prior to starting a project.

Electrical Inspection Local building codes rarely require permits for a 12-volt lighting system. If, however, you are installing new 120-volt circuits to operate a large low-voltage system, or a new ground fault circuit interrupter (GFCI) receptacle to plug in a transformer, check with the building inspector to see if you need a permit. Find out at the same time if local code lists any requirements for low-voltage systems, and if an inspector must come to your site before, during, or after installation or adjustment to your electrical system.

Liabilities
Recently, because of the increase in liability suits, cities and towns have become more cautious in granting permits for construction projects that involve more than the usual amount of risk, such as swimming pools on hillsides, any construction in flood plains or environmentally sensitive areas, and any project that uses particularly innovative construction techniques. You need to be aware of this recent attitude and act accordingly.

Make sure that you and your contractor(s) have proper liability insurance to protect you against lawsuits from anyone working on the project. Protect yourself from potential liens by withholding some of each payment for at least 45 days after the work is done; 10 percent is the usual amount to withhold. Insist that the contractor prove he has used the previous payment to pay for material and labor that have been expended on your project. This 45-day holdback period should allow time to see that everything is in working order and that no liens have been filed. In addition to the holdback for liens, it is important to retain the value of any deficiency in the work until it has been satisfactorily completed.

The Good-Neighbor Policy

Another factor critical to the successful installation of your landscape is that it be pleasing to those who will encounter it most often— your neighbors. This is especially true for visible structures, such as fences, walls, gazebos, sheds, and prominent trees. You want to be certain that your landscape does not have an adverse impact on your neighbors, the neighborhood, and the community. Carefully evaluate the potential repercussions of your project to protect your investment. You do not want to be required to tear down a partially completed project because a neighbor or the entire neighborhood considered it a visual intrusion, and that consideration was later upheld.

Starting from the center and working outward to the perimeter is one way to tackle controversial projects of a different style or scale than the rest of the neighborhood. By the time you reach the perceived perimeter, the impact may have softened.

Most important, talk to your neighbors about what you are planning to do. Although the changes will be on your property, they may have an impact on a neighbor's home. The removal of significant trees is a common example. Also, find out what is on the other side of the fence. Do not design a play lot next to a neighbor's area for quiet and privacy, for example. Be completely candid with those whose opinion may affect the disposition of your plans. Invite them over and carefully map out the plans. Do this only after you have done your homework and know what objections to expect and how they may be overcome.

You may even find that a neighbor is interested in splitting some of the cost of improvements that will affect both homes. Especially in a new development, many neighbors will be planning landscape projects at the same time; cooperation in buying materials, renting equipment, and sharing labor will save you some money and perhaps even find you a friend.

DETERMINING COSTS

To determine how much your landscape project will cost, you need to come up with a budget. To do this you must consider the prices of all the tools and materials you plan to purchase, equipment rental costs, and possible labor expenses. In order to keep project costs within this budget, you will have to monitor expenses constantly. Pay attention to all of the incidental costs as you do the work. This will make it easier to stay within budget.

The key to estimating both time and cost requirements is to combine work-related projects. Building a brick walk, for example, involves grading and excavation, laying crushed stone, and pouring a

BEFORE REMODELING

If you have recently moved to a home with an existing landscape and are eager to start remodeling it, the best strategy is to be patient. Rather than digging up the existing beds and running off to the garden center with a shopping list of new plants, spend some time in your new home, waiting and watching for the seasonal rhythm of the garden to reveal itself.

Many plants have dormant or off-seasons, when they can easily be overlooked. If you begin remodeling your yard during the winter, for ex-

ample, and decide to remove that overgrown tangle of bare branches against the back fence, you could be missing a spectacular spring show of lilac (*Syringa vulgaris*).

Even warm-season remodeling has its perils. In removing that small deciduous tree outside the breakfast nook window, you could miss the winter pleasure of sipping coffee while cedar waxwings and jays compete for the scarlet berries on the Washington thorn (*Crataegus phaenopyrum*).

Animals use the plants in your yard for food and shelter; while observing

seasonal sights and smells, also notice which plants are important to wildlife.

When you have noted the special character of your site and determined which areas are to be remodeled, carefully consider the plants that will be affected. Many plants in older yards are removed because they are overgrown, out of scale, or located in the wrong place for your design. Careful pruning and/or transplanting can often solve these problems, however, and save you a lot of money in plant replacement costs. Large evergreen shrubs, for example, can be dense and

uninspiring when overgrown; removing the bottom foliage to expose the branching structure and thinning out the top can give the plant a unique character as well as allow a complementary understory of small shrubs, perennials, and bulbs to be planted below.

A plant of any size, from bulbs to large trees, can be transplanted successfully if the proper steps are taken. Relocating plants in an existing landscape is an excellent and inexpensive way to create a garden of mature plants suited to your needs and tastes.

concrete base, in addition to laying the brick. You must consider all of these elements for cost-estimating purposes, although the only part you see is the brick itself. Similarly, installing a lawn involves preparing the subgrade, installing an irrigation system, spreading 6 inches of loam, and placing the sod. Cost estimation is based upon this premise of combining all of the factors involved, and the composite estimate that results is far more useful than a single cost figure for each unit.

Costs in Relation to the Value of Your Home

Although you may want to make improvements to your property, you will also want to keep the costs in proportion to the value of the house and neighborhood. In new construction, the cost of major site improvements, including grading and drainage, is normally between 12 and 15 percent of the cost of a new

home. If the house costs $100,000 to build, the site improvements would amount to between $12,000 and $15,000. The cost of installing the actual landscape elements—the surface treatment—is only a small proportion of the site-improvement cost, usually 20 percent. If you have to overcome difficult site conditions in order to have a decent landscape, this percentage can be even higher, and you may have your work cut out for you.

As you decide what to add to a new or existing home, you will need to evaluate what the return will be in the event that you sell the property. Real-estate agents generally agree that landscape improvements provide the highest return to the investor, more than all other home improvements. Therefore, any improvements you make above and beyond the minimum, such as patios, decorative walls, tennis courts, or swimming pools, are

considered safe investments, especially if they are consistent with the character of the neighborhood and the size and style of the home.

The amount you spend on landscaping can vary widely. Where you choose to splurge and what you splurge on are personal decisions. The landscape should, of course, reflect your lifestyle and the things you enjoy. You should be careful, however, that you do not invest more money in the property than you can recover when you sell it.

The best way to estimate your costs at this point is to use a composite method based on cost per square foot. This method is most useful for developing preliminary cost estimates, when the exact conditions, materials, and methods are not yet known. You can fine-tune the estimate later. This rough estimate will give you the information you need in order to decide how much improvement is warranted.

Researching Cost Figures

The time to make a rough estimate of the cost per square foot is after you have finished the bubble drawings but before you start your master plan (see page 91). For example, in some regions planted areas cost $3 to $6 per square foot; constructed areas range from $5 to $15 per square foot. Assume that you do the work yourself and that the area to be improved is 25 by 40 feet, or 1,000 square feet. If 75 percent of your design is made up of planted areas and 25 percent is paving, the cost estimate would be $3,000 for the plants (750 square feet at $4 per square foot) plus $2,500 for the paved area (250 square feet at $10 per square foot), so the total would be about $5,500.

If the areas were reversed, the estimate would be $1,000 for plants (250 square feet at $4 per square foot) plus $7,500 for constructed areas (750 square feet at $10 per square foot), so the total would be about $8,500. Calculating a rough estimate can help you decide how much money to devote to each item to stay within a budget. Always allow a 10- to 15-percent contingency figure in your estimates. These figures do not include major items such as swimming pools, covered decks, or overhead structures; these must be estimated on an individual basis.

Saving Money

As you budget the work, imagine a triangle, the three points of which are cost, quantity, and quality. If you change one, you affect the other two. For example, if you have a fixed budget of, say, $5,000 for an item (such as a patio), and you want to increase the quantity of the item (make the patio larger), you must decrease the quality of the item in order to maintain the fixed cost. In the case of a patio, you could use concrete instead of more-expensive brick to keep the price at a fixed level. Conversely, if you increase the quality of the material, you need to decrease the quantity in order to keep the item within budget. If you use specialty brick or decide on cut stone, you will have to build a smaller patio. If you manage to decrease the cost of the material (for example, by finding used brick in a salvage yard), you may either increase the quantity (make the patio bigger) or reduce the cost for that item (take the savings on the cost of the patio).

The most obvious way to save money is to do most of the work yourself and choose economical materials that will do the job. Know what materials cost in your area, and shop for the best price. Buy in bulk as much as you can, and simplify your design.

Another way to save is to buy materials before the peak construction season, when prices tend to be higher; or buy from a supplier who brings the material into your area in bulk, such as a discount supply store or lumberyard. There are even suppliers who salvage or otherwise stockpile used landscape materials from construction sites. Used bricks, cobblestones, and railroad ties are common examples. Contractors often advertise the availability of such materials in newspapers and the Yellow Pages.

Remodeling is often the best way to save money. Give existing elements a face-lift to improve their appearance rather than start anew. Resurfacing a driveway rather than ripping it out, pruning a wooded area rather than removing it and regrading, or applying stucco to an old concrete wall can result in a considerable cost savings. Although it is not common, in some situations you will encumber your design if you try to save all the existing elements, and you would save more money simply by removing them. In general, salvage what you can to keep costs down.

Transportation and Installation Costs

Choose locally available materials, if possible, because the savings in doing so can be significant. If you pick up all the material yourself from the supplier, the quantity you buy will not affect the price per unit. However, any material that must be delivered will cost more per unit in small quantities. This is especially true of asphalt and concrete in amounts under 5 cubic yards. If you plan to rent a vehicle to pick up all your materials, add this cost to your total.

If you want to have materials, especially pavement materials, deliv-

Opposite: Existing plants, such as this aged tree, are assets that must be protected during the process of installing new elements in your landscape.

ered on a certain date, try to request at least the minimum load. That way your order will be delivered normally, rather than be combined with another small order, and you will also avoid paying a minimum charge. Be ready for the delivery so it can be placed quickly; you will be charged for the delivery time, usually in 20-minute increments.

If you choose to install the landscape yourself, you need to consider the difficulty of the work and how long it will take to complete. Some materials are easier and faster to work with than others. Design with your abilities and schedule in mind. If you choose to have some of the work done by others, hire experts where your money will be best spent, and secure bids for the work. Page 12 discusses the various types of landscape professionals, and page 107 has information on how to hire construction help.

Maintenance Costs

A wise adage says that you should never build anything that you cannot maintain. We have all seen beautiful landscapes that need a battery of gardeners to keep them looking attractive. Only you can decide what your landscape maintenance time is worth.

If you have time to do only 90 percent of the maintenance in your yard, the 10 percent that you do not do is what will be noticed. Therefore, design according to the amount of effort you are willing to put into maintenance.

Durable materials will hold up longer, can take maintenance without wearing out, and will actually cost less in the long run, although their initial cost may be a little higher. Consider life-cycle cost as part of your design. This analysis is necessary to protect your investment. Selecting materials based on their durability is certainly one way to keep maintenance costs within reasonable bounds, even if it means that you forgo installation in an area until you can afford more durable materials.

Checking Your Design Against Costs

By now you will have asked a multitude of questions, visited sites similar to your own, asked for assistance from many sources, and researched cost data for the materials you plan to use. At this point compare your design to the cost estimate and make a second, more definitive estimate. Before you break ground, decide whether you can afford to install all the elements of your design. Ask yourself if some of the elements can be eliminated or made of less expensive material. Perhaps you can do some construction now and some can wait until later. Your next step is to consider your installation schedule.

ESTABLISHING YOUR SCHEDULE

As you plan your schedule, keep in mind that projects often take much more time than you originally anticipate. This is especially true if you are following unfamiliar procedures and are using tools you have never used before. The rule of thumb is that any task will probably take twice as long as you think it will.

Assess the extent of your construction skills. Ascertain how much time you are willing and able to devote to the project. Large blocks of time over long weekends and vacations are usually necessary to perform the work adequately. Working for just a few hours in the evening is often not very efficient; it is best to use this time for small tasks that are not critical to your schedule.

HIRING HELP

Although this book is aimed at those who want to do the work themselves, everyone has limits. When it comes to doing the physical labor involved in installing a landscape, you can do it all yourself, hire helpers, or contract out some or all of the work.

Because there are no fixed prices in contract work, you should ask at least three different contractors to visit your property and give you a written bid. The bid should include specific information, such as the size and quality of all materials—sprinkler pipe, lumber, brick—called for in your design. Make certain that all bidders are pricing the same items.

Once you select a contractor, request a written contract that specifies the work to be done, the materials to be used, and a completion date. The contract should specify the quality of each material required, to prevent the contractor from substituting materials of a lesser quality to save money. If your schedule depends on work being completed by a certain time, write into the contract a per-day penalty clause for uncompleted work or, better, a bonus clause for early completion. Contractors are licensed, and if contract disputes arise, the matter can be taken to the state licensing board.

The contract should also specify the payment schedule. You'll normally pay a down payment, with the remainder to be paid in installments at specified stages in completion of the work. However, agree in advance that a substantial sum will not be paid until at least 45 days after all work has been completed. This is done because a contractor purchases material and may hire other workers for the job and then, for various reasons, not pay them. Those unpaid workers or material suppliers can file liens against your property, which you must pay before you can sell the property. Any such problem should surface during the waiting period.

An alternative to hiring a contractor, particularly when you plan to do most of the work yourself, is to hire helpers. Good sources for helpers are the classified ads or the nearest high school, college, or technical school, which may have a job placement program for students. Neighborhood youngsters looking for part-time work also make good helpers for landscaping projects.

Hidden Problems

A one-year plan can end up as a two-year project, and a two-year plan, if it is too ambitious, can be a three-year project. This can happen for several reasons. One of them is sequencing problems.

Sequencing involves performing in their logical order all of the various tasks necessary to install a landscape. For example, a swimming pool may require an approach walk, fences, a mechanical and electrical supply, and drainage capacity before it can be rendered useful. The poolside must be finished, a storage and changing area built, plants installed around the area, and furniture purchased and put in place. This related work may take more time than the construction of the pool itself. Many unforeseen problems can crop up during the construction period. You may not be able to hire help in time for a certain task, or delivery of materials may be held up for one reason or another. Build buffers into your schedule to allow for such delays.

Installing your landscape will involve many different tasks. The most basic way to sequence these tasks is from the ground up: grading first, determining drainage, establishing various utility lines, then adding paving, structures, and so on until you are ready to install the plants.

Phasing

Your phasing strategy establishes the projects you start first and the sequence in which you complete them. You may need to delay some landscape installation due to a limited budget, or you may need to put off some work because of lack of time. The construction season is short in some areas; therefore, the time of year that you start the project has a great impact on what you tackle first.

Plan your project well. Make a list (perhaps even a sketch) of the ma-

A recently land-scaped site allows for future growth: The ground covers, protecting the soil, will fill in later; the trees are spaced to allow room for their roots to grow and will eventually provide the desired amounts of shade and sun. Plant annuals for quick fillers and immedi-ate effect, if desired.

terials you will need, possibly label-ing key pieces that have a critical ultimate location. Think through how and where you will store the materials and how you will protect them. This will all culminate in what is called a project schedule. On the schedule specify starting dates and completion dates for the work, and make sure that the mate-rial you need will be available when you need it. For example, in northern climates asphalt plants traditionally close at Thanksgiving, and concrete foundations are not poured before March 30.

The finished schedule should not be complicated but should show starting dates, delivery dates, vacation dates, and other key

target dates for all the phases of the project.

Checking Your Design Against Your Schedule

Once you have a schedule, group all of the projects into related tasks, and be sure that there is ample overlap between each set in case the schedule has to slide by a week or so every now and then. You may want to install a temporary landscape element in an area of the yard that will not be fully land-scaped this season—a ground cover to protect the soil, or a temporary screen to hide construction. Be sure that the final design does not conflict with the schedule, and make any final adjustments.

BUILDING A SOLID BASE

GRADING AND DRAINAGE

Landscaping involves working with the land and understanding its topography. Land is, of course, the basis for all landscape design. It is the stage set for all other elements. Grading, simply put, is remodeling the form of the land. It is one of the most, if not *the* most, important aspects of landscaping; everything else—constructed elements and plants—is in some way tied to the land. Assess your grading needs as soon as possible, because the construction planning will be based on grading specifications.

Drainage depends on grading and vice versa. Flat surfaces rarely occur in nature. In a human-made landscape, even surfaces that appear flat, such as a patio, must be sloped somewhat to provide drainage. Some of the precipitation falling on the ground is absorbed, but much of it must run off. It is critical that you control runoff water adequately and dispose of it properly.

Be sure to investigate any codes, rules, and regulations that may govern grading and drainage operations in your community. Do not do anything that may be illegal or unsafe.

Why You Should Grade

Grading can involve as little as moving a few shovelfuls or wheelbarrow loads of dirt, or it can be a giant earth-moving operation involving thousands of cubic yards of soil. Your landscape project will undoubtedly fall into the "shovelfuls and wheelbarrow loads" category.

Grade to create a house extension. You may need to make a flat area for a garage or extension to the house, or to create an activity area such as a concrete-slab patio or ground-level deck. Grade to produce special effects or preserve special features. Form a "bowl" for a family gathering area, or build a mound for wind protection or to screen a view. You may need to grade to produce a slightly sloping area for a lawn.

Grade to provide circulation around the site and between various structures and activity areas. Create a road, a meandering footpath, or a set of steps.

Grade to ensure that drainage (both surface and subsurface) works properly. Efficient drainage helps prevent structural damage, settling, and erosion, as well as flooding of lawns and patios caused by rain, melting snow, or your own watering system. Grade to divert water from the house to help avoid basement flooding, and make sure that water is not running off your property onto that of your neighbor.

Design and Construction Guidelines for Grading

Before you start thinking about the specifics, such as what to do about the puddle that forms by the back porch, take time to look at the big picture. Find out all you can about the existing grades and drainage patterns on your property. Walk it during different times of year, if possible, in different weather conditions. Look at the pluses as well as the minuses. Talk to neighbors, the developer, the previous owner, city and county officials, and utility districts. And, if your budget allows, seek the help of a professional.

Shaping the land to the best possible use while preserving its natural attributes is critical to the success of the overall design. Although some of the following considerations may not be applicable to your site, read through the list to see whether you need to take any of these into account.

Natural Features Are there certain areas or dominant features that should be preserved at all costs? Are there features that could be eliminated or modified if necessary? What areas and features are least important? Look at large trees, views, rock outcrops, water features, open areas, and exposures to sun and wind.

Human-Made Elements What elements on the site should be preserved, and which should be removed? What elements of an adjacent property can you see that should be enhanced or screened? Try to visualize what the site would be like if these things were removed or modified. Will grading be required to do so?

Access and Circulation What is the best route from the street to the garage or parking area? Is a parking area required? How should foot traffic circulate from street to house and around the site? Will ramps be required instead of steps for the people living in the house? Will the driveway you visualize allow vehicles to enter and exit without scraping their bumpers? Will the driveway be so steep that you will not be able to drive up it when it is slippery? Analyze and visualize to determine the most efficient, aesthetically pleasing, and functional means of getting around.

Existing Utilities Find out the extent and location of drainage systems and utilities, either overhead or underground, through visual examination and by checking all sources. Grading the site may affect existing utilities by, for example, filling them over or exposing them to view. Is there a water course through the property that drains adjacent property, or something similar that cannot be tampered with? Are there any utility easements that must be maintained?

Soils Is there good topsoil that should be saved? Is the soil permeable, soft, sandy? Are there possible slippage planes? How deep is the

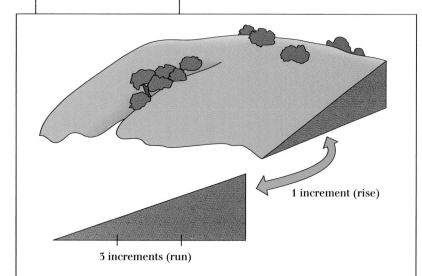

1 increment (rise)

3 increments (run)

The slope shown has a ratio of 3 to 1 and is written 3:1. Another way to express this is to say that for every 3 feet of horizontal distance the ground rises 1 foot.

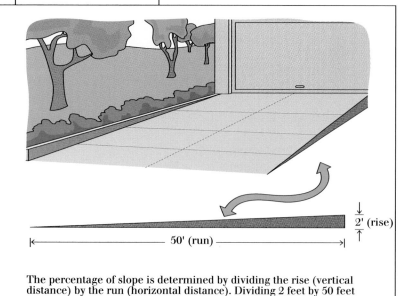

2' (rise)

|← 50' (run) →|

The percentage of slope is determined by dividing the rise (vertical distance) by the run (horizontal distance). Dividing 2 feet by 50 feet gives 0.04, or a 4 percent slope.

topsoil? Does bedrock (or any rock) exist near the surface? The best soil for planting is soft, friable, and free of rocks and weed seeds. It also drains well. A handful of good soil is dark and resembles cake crumbs. Its softness and darkness are due to high humus content. A moist clod should crumble easily and not be sticky. It should not contain rocks, and there should be no trash such as sticks or building material.

Vegetation What is the existing vegetation in the yard—grasses, weeds, shrubs, trees, or a combination thereof? Could there be problems if any of these were eliminated or modified? Do not plan to clear the site of all vegetation until you are ready to install some kind of landscape floor. You may lose precious topsoil if it is not protected by vegetation during even one period of rainfall.

Drainage What is the natural drainage pattern around and across the yard; which way does it slope? Are low areas, bogs, or muddy areas evident? Is some of the site paved, or will it be paved? Pavement and roof areas create large amounts of runoff. Are there any known or suspected springs or underground water sources? If possible, wait to make any landscape design decisions until you have recorded naturally occurring drainage patterns throughout the course of a year or have prepared a very precise topographic survey so that drainage patterns can be accurately plotted.

Test the garden soil for proper drainage. Drainage is how fast or slow water moves through the soil. To see if there are likely to be drainage problems, dig a hole 3 feet deep so you can see the composition, or profile, of the soil. Look at the layers of soil, called horizons, in the profile. Is the subsoil loose

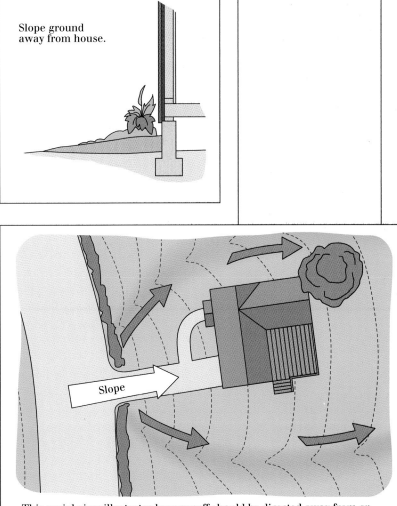

Slope ground away from house.

This aerial view illustrates how runoff should be directed away from or around structures.

and porous, or is it tight and clayey? Drainage problems are caused by hard or impervious layers and by strongly contrasting layers. For instance, if the topsoil is a fine-textured clay and it sits on a sand or gravel subsoil, water will drain very slowly into the subsoil.

Fill the hole with water and let it sit for a day. Then fill it again. How quickly does the water recede? If the water level drops more slowly than ¼ inch per hour, you have drainage problems. If it drops faster than 1 inch per hour, the soil has excellent drainage. If there is standing water, the problem is more serious and you may want to install drainage tiles.

If you strike a layer of very hard soil or rock, try to dig through it with a crowbar. If the layer is a few inches thick and looser soil is under it, you have claypan, a layer of extremely dense clay, or hardpan, which is like rock and is almost impervious to water.

If you hit hardpan, the simplest way to provide drainage is to break up the hardpan with a pick or crowbar under each plant. You do not have to remove or replace hardpan—just provide a way for the water to pass through it.

Be sure to check for cracks in existing paving, walls, or foundations. Look for walls or bulkheads that are tipped, heaved, or settled. Check to see if any topsoil seems to have eroded away. Any of these may indicate that you will have a drainage problem during heavy rains.

Toxic Conditions Ask authorities or neighbors who have lived in the area for some time if any part of your site may have been used as a dump for garbage or chemicals that may be highly toxic. Some problems will be evident from your own examination, but get expert advice if you suspect contamination or if no reliable information is available. Any filled land is suspect. For example, an innocuous-seeming swampy area may have been filled, in the process burying large quantities of organic material. Methane gas, a by-product of rotting organics, is explosive and can accumulate under paved areas. A simple gravel base with some drain tiles to let the gas escape can handle this problem.

Streets The streets of any residential community not only facilitate traffic, they are also the principal drainage arteries. Your drainage should be designed to find its way to the streets and deposit into the community storm sewers. Curbs and gutters are constructed for this purpose, so utilize them whenever possible. Remember that this ready-made drainage system runs right by your house.

Principles of Grading and Drainage Design

Much of the success of a landscape design depends on well-executed grading and drainage. Therefore, it is strongly recommended that grading and drainage be analyzed and solutions for your site be fairly well worked out before you become too involved with the rest of your landscape design. Not all of the following considerations will apply to your situation, but keep them in mind while you walk around the yard, before you start your grading and drainage plan.

Plan the grading operation before you do anything with your landscape—even before you clear the site. You may be able to use some on-site soil instead of purchasing fill to build up certain areas. Your grading requirements may have a big effect on your budget and schedule and must therefore be determined early in the design process. Plans for watering systems, lighting systems, and additional utilities should follow. Find out where underground utilities are located before you start to grade.

Do not grade any more than is necessary to achieve your goals. If the design can be carried out satisfactorily with little or no grading, all the better.

Remember that water flows downhill; drainage works by gravity. This may seem obvious, but it is surprising how often this principle is overlooked or forgotten. It is sometimes difficult to tell the direction in which drainage occurs,

GRADING AND DRAINAGE TERMS

Cleanout: Occurring at turns and at the end of the line in an underground drainage system, cleanouts permit access to the pipe for maintenance.

Concentrated drainage: This drainage is runoff that is collected over an area and directed to a channel; it moves along like a stream. Concentrated drainage should be avoided to prevent erosion.

Drip line: In reference to a tree, it indicates the outermost edge of the foliage. A line projected straight down from this skirt would form a roughly circular pattern on the ground. This is the zone in which most of the tree's roots occur and the area within which grading should be avoided.

Elevation: Numerical values assigned to points on a grading plan to indicate elevation points above or below a baseline and in relation to each other.

Finish floor elevation: The elevation of the floor level of a structure, typically a house. Finish floor elevation should be at least 6 inches (check local codes) above the ground level outside. Plan grading to slope away from finish floor elevation.

Frost line: The frost line is an average depth, depending on region and severity of climate, to which the ground freezes. Foundations and footings are placed below it to prevent heaving; pipes are buried below it to prevent freezing. Compacted areas such as driveways and walks will freeze to a greater depth. Snow cover acts as an insulation blanket.

Gradient or slope: These terms are used interchangeably. They refer to the rate of incline or decline over a surface and may be expressed in such general terms as "flat" gradient or "steep" gradient. Moreover, they are usually expressed as a percentage: 2-percent grade or 5-percent grade.

Grading, rough: Rough grading means moving earth and remodeling land to a general "rough" elevation and surface. It is similar to a sculptor roughing out a statue, chipping away the big chunks to reach the basic form before refining the volume and outline.

Grading, finish: Finish grading, which comes after rough grading, is the finishing or refining of earth surfaces—floating them to much tighter tolerances, smoothing them, and removing irregularities. It involves forming the final surface before planting, paving, or installing structures.

Leach field: A system of pipes extending out from a collection point, perhaps a drain inlet, the leach field disposes of water over an extended area.

Percolation: Refers to the movement of water down through the soil surface.

Sheet drainage: The opposite of concentrated drainage, sheet drainage directs water over a surface in a "sheet." Planted surfaces should be sheet-drained wherever possible to prevent erosion.

Subgrade: A grade or level of ground underneath paving, subgrade is similar to rough grade.

Sump: Sometimes called a "dry well," a sump is a large hole dug in the ground. Sumps hold water and allow it to percolate into surrounding soil.

Surface drainage: Rather than directing and collecting runoff in underground systems, surface drainage directs runoff over surfaces, preferably as sheet drainage.

Swale: A swale is an elongated depression similar to a channel but much shallower, with gently sloping sides. Swales are typically designed into lawns to direct runoff to some disposal point.

Weep hole: This is an opening, hole, or slot that runs through a retaining wall, from back to front, near the base. Weep holes prevent damage by draining off accumulated water.

either because slopes are relatively flat or because they change direction. Virtually every surface must be sloped to some extent to make it drain properly. Always attempt to drain away from structures. Do not take on the extra burden of grading neighboring property. By the same token, do not let your runoff drain onto someone else's property. All grading and drainage must be done within your property lines.

The need to drain is most often thought of in terms of disposing of rainfall, but irrigation water is also a frequent source of problems. Be aware of how changes in grading and drainage will affect existing plants. Do not grade within the drip line of existing trees if they are to be preserved. Many of a tree's roots occur within the drip line; to grade within this zone could expose or bury roots deeper than they are accustomed, and the alteration of the natural drainage patterns could injure or kill the tree. Avoid draining water, especially concentrated runoff, into plant beds.

Don't use paths and walks as conduits for water, and do not concentrate drainage across them. Use curbs where possible to contain and direct runoff into the street. To avoid ice in freezing weather, grade so that water is quickly drained from walks and paved surfaces. To prevent erosion, try to have water drain in sheets instead of in a concentrated stream, and do not drain large areas over unstable embankments.

The critical areas (in terms of washout and erosion) are those in which paved surfaces drain onto earth and vice versa. Plain earth and surfaces planted with grass and other ground covers are the easiest and least costly to grade. Paved areas (depending on the material) are generally the most costly to grade. Paving should be as near flat as possible, both for practical reasons and for appearance, so paved surfaces need to be sloped just enough to carry the water away; they should not vary as radically in slope as earth surfaces. Therefore, it is a good idea to work out the forms and slopes of paved areas first and make earth surfaces conform to and blend with the paving. Because soil is a much less precise surface to work with, steeper slopes must be planned to ensure positive drainage. Soil will soak up some water (until it reaches its saturation point), whereas paved surfaces have 100-percent runoff.

Local codes will vary, but try to keep the soil surface outside buildings at least 6 inches below the floor inside. A great deal of water pours off the roofs of structures. Collect rainwater into downspouts and then run it to the street in a storm drain line. If this is not possible, provide splash blocks at the end of the downspouts to help prevent erosion. Locate the downspouts where they will not be unsightly or interfere with traffic.

Try to use surface drainage as much as possible; underground systems are costly to install and maintain. If you must have an underground system, plan to bury drain lines below the frost line where possible to prevent the line from freezing. Do not connect roof or storm drain lines to the sanitary sewer system; this is generally an unacceptable practice and is illegal in most municipalities.

General Grading Procedures

Two types of grading are performed on a landscape site: rough grading and finish grading. Rough grading consists of moving around quantities of earth to shape the site into a general, rough elevation and surface. It is similar to the work a sculptor does in roughing-out a statue, chipping away at the big chunks to arrive at the basic form. Finish grading is done after rough grading. It consists of refining the surface to tighter tolerances; removing all the irregularities, bumps, and dips; and smoothing the final earth surface where needed for such items as lawns or planting beds.

Before you start moving soil, decide first where you will dump soil you have dug out and where you will store any soil you have to buy. If at all possible, try to balance the amount of soil you dig with the amount you fill. If you need to fill in a low spot, try to use soil from a high spot. Hauling soil to or from your site can add considerably to your expenses.

Check the soil for drainage. You may have several types of soil on your site; if so, you may consider moving the better soil to areas where you plan to plant and the poorer soil to areas where soil quality and drainage are not so consequential. If you have to buy soil, select material that most closely approximates the existing soil on your site so the purchased soil will blend with the existing material as you overlay or mix them. Placing a sandy soil that drains fast over a heavy clay soil, for example, can cause drainage problems.

Check out local soil dealers, and take a sample of your soil with you to compare with the dealer's material. Find out what the minimum delivery is (some dealers have a minimum delivery of 5 or 10 cubic yards), and check the price. Consider whether it would be cheaper to pick up the soil yourself if you have the means. Be sure to have any soil you purchase dumped as close as possible to the area where you are going to use it. Moving soil to make room for other grading operations can be a backbreaker.

In many cases you will be able to make a grade change by eye, so a formal grading and drainage plan will not be necessary. Judge where slopes will occur and about how steep they need to be. Keeping in mind the design principles discussed earlier, estimate where soil must be moved and about how much will be involved, and try to figure out a logical sequence of operations. Once you have walked around and made a few on-site judgments and developed some ideas, you can determine whether the job is large enough to warrant a grading and drainage plan (discussed on page 118).

If you decide to make a critical or extensive grade change, there are

A DITCHING LEVEL: A HOMEMADE TOOL FOR MEASURING DRAIN LINE SLOPE

When bubble in line level is centered, board is at a slope of 1" per 8', or approximately 1' per 100'.

two devices that can help you. For short distances, buy a line level—a small spirit level suspended from a horizontal line by a pair of hooks. Attach a piece of mason's twine to the tops of two stakes or along the side of a 2-by-4, and hang the level at one end of the line.

For more complex jobs or longer distances, rent a carpenter's level. This instrument looks like a surveyor's transit but is much simpler to use. Set the level on its tripod in the center of the yard; ideally, you should be able to see from this location all the points you wish to measure. Next, level the tripod and look through the telescope. You will see a horizontal line on the lens; this line indicates points that are level with the instrument.

Levels are used with a surveyor's rod or a tape measure. Have an assistant stand the rod on a reference point (the corner of a patio or sidewalk works well). Look through the lens at the rod, and record the number intersected by the horizontal sight line. This will serve as your reference number.

Now take sightings of any points in the landscape you wish to measure. The distance above or below

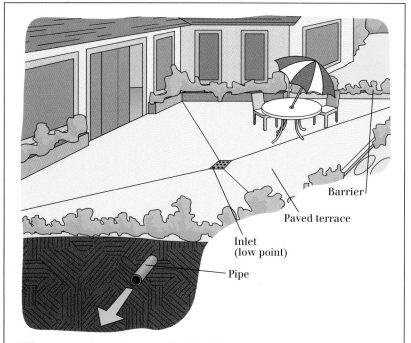

When a paved area is surrounded by a barrier—a wall, a curb—it is best to direct water into a drain inlet at a low point and then pipe it away.

the reference number indicates the height above or below the reference point. Remember, a lower number means that the ground is *higher*. Mark the measured points with surveyor's stakes (available at lumberyards). Write the elevation on the stakes.

Drive stakes in places where you plan to add soil. Their tops should be level with the height of the new grade. These stakes will serve as guides for the leveling process.

Before you remove any large amounts of soil, strip off the topsoil (usually the top 6 to 12 inches) and pile it to one side to redistribute later. This soil is valuable for plant growth—do not bury it.

Grading Costs

The best way to save money in grading operations is to work with the contours of the site. Walls, steps, and ramps are very expensive. If you can use grading to make the necessary transitions

instead of building these structures, you can usually save money.

Make sure you do all of the major grading at once if heavy equipment is involved. This will minimize the daily rental costs. Even on flat sites, balancing the amount of earth you take off with the amount you fill will avoid the extra transportation expense of bringing soil in or taking it away. Because earth material compacts as it settles, plan on purchasing 20 percent more than you need to fill any given area. Usually, it costs about four times as much to import material as it does to have it taken away. The greater the haul distances are from the site, the more this will cost. Importing soil is expensive and should be avoided. If you cannot avoid importing soil, inspect the fill material before you ask to have it delivered. Junk soils with clay and rocks are no bargain and can cause many problems.

Drainage Installation

Most of the drainage work you will do employs pipe (usually flexible pipe) and drain inlets. Drain inlets, sometimes called catch basins, consist of a box (usually of concrete, but sometimes of pressure-treated wood) with an open grate on top. Check with a local building supplier; a great variety of catch basins, grates, and other drainage aids are made with high-density polymeric plastics and fiberglass. These products are lightweight and easy to install, and all the parts fit together. The inlet is placed at a low spot, where water will normally puddle, with the grate flush with the soil level. A pipe (or pipes) installed below the ground surface, with one end protruding into the box, carries the water to another drain inlet or to some disposal point, such as a ditch or street curb.

Drain lines of perforated pipe are most useful for lowering the water table and taking subsurface water away from foundations, terraces, and driveways. Water that gets under these structures can cause them to settle, resulting in structural damage or cracks. If you're installing a drain line behind a retaining wall or at the footing of a basement, install a geotextile fabric on the wall to wick the free water directly to the drain. This will reduce direct water pressure that causes leaks and structural problems.

Drain lines can also be used to prevent puddling in low areas, but this can sometimes be better accomplished with the use of a drain inlet. Drain inlets are most effective where there is heavy surface runoff. Install them where water collects, especially in paved areas where it cannot be drained from the surface and must be collected. Unperforated pipe is usually used for directing collected water away from a drain inlet.

To plan a drain line, first determine where the water will go once it leaves the line. It will usually go into a storm sewer, gutter, or drainage ditch. The point at which the water leaves the drain line is called the outfall. The elevation of the outfall determines the construction of the rest of the system. Because water moves through the line by gravity, there must be a slope from the top end to the bottom end of the line. In addition, there must be enough downward slope to move the water fast enough to keep silt in suspension. This means there must be at least a 1-foot drop for every 100 feet of line, or eventually the drain line will fill up with silt and stop functioning.

To find out how deep you can place the line, start with the elevation of the outfall and measure backward. The deeper the line, the

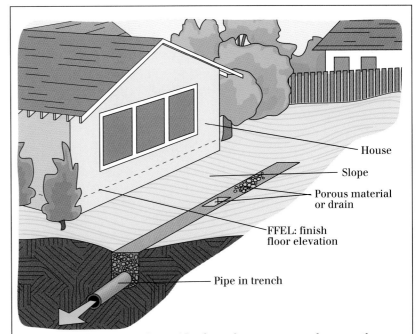

If your yard slopes toward one side of your house, use a swale—a gentle, V-shaped, sloping depression—to intercept runoff. Create another short slope that slants away from the house. This swale adaptation with a trench is even better at capturing surface runoff and directing it safely away from the house.

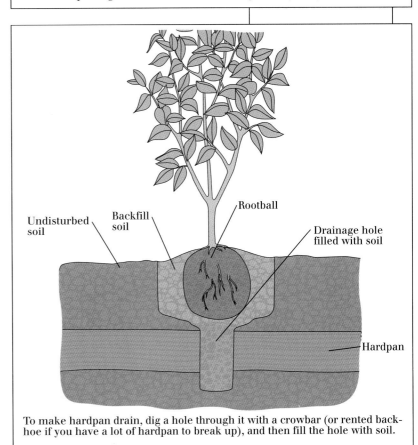

To make hardpan drain, dig a hole through it with a crowbar (or rented backhoe if you have a lot of hardpan to break up), and then fill the hole with soil.

more water will be kept away from the ground surface.

Place the drain lines in a herringbone pattern, keeping them between 10 and 20 feet apart. If you have only one low area in the yard, you will probably need only a single line under it.

Start digging the trench at the outfall, and work back into the yard. Try to maintain a steady slope (a minimum 1-foot rise per 100 feet of ditch, or $\frac{1}{8}$ inch per foot) without dips, no matter what the shape of the soil. Use a level. As you dig the trench, drag the level behind you to measure an even 1 percent.

If the bottom of the trench is rocky or broken, cover it with a 1-inch layer of sand to make an even bed for the drain line.

New drain lines are usually made of a flexible, corrugated plastic hose. This hose will make all but the sharpest bends without needing to be joined, and it is lightweight and simple to install. You can buy it in 3- and 4-inch diameters. The 4-inch hose is less likely to clog if a piece of debris or a small animal gets stuck in it.

Always lay drain line with the holes facing down. This prevents soil from dropping into the line. It also lowers the water table to the bottom of the line rather than to the level of the top, because water rises into the line.

An effective drainage system must be surrounded by an envelope of gravel. This will protect the line, keep soil from entering it, and increase its capacity by conducting water itself. After smoothing out the trench bottom with soil or sand, lay about a 4-inch-deep layer of gravel over the bottom. You can use either clean drain rock or crushed rock; the former drains faster, but the latter stabilizes the pipe better and keeps it from

moving around. Don't, however, use rock containing particles smaller than the holes in the pipe; they will clog the holes or enter the pipe and reduce its capacity to carry water. After you lay the pipe in its bed of rock, backfill the trench with more drain rock to a depth of 4 inches over the line. Then install a cleanout, or access hole, at the highest point of the system.

Next cover the gravel with a manufactured filter cloth; then replace the soil that you removed from the trench, backfilling the trench to ground level. Before the trench is completely full, moisten the soil thoroughly and tamp to settle it. This will help keep it from settling later on, after you have planted a lawn over it. You can also use this method to ensure that any trenches dug for watering systems, utilities, and foundations will not settle. Then fill the trench the rest of the way.

A variation on the drain line involves filling the trench with drain rock up to the surface. This allows surface water to enter the line quickly, and catches the water that runs off a slope before it gets to the garden. To keep soil out of the rock on the surface, place a couple of 2×6 headers on either side of the trench so they extend about an inch above ground level. This will create a gravel path that drains very quickly.

Drawing Grading and Drainage Plans
Grading and drainage can be tricky. Except for minor adjustments, it is best to get professional help, either for consultation or to draw up the grading and drainage plan. This is especially true for steep areas or sites on which many steps, terraces, ramps, or levels are contemplated. Always check local codes.

Many jurisdictions now require retention ponds to temporarily hold runoff water during storms so it can be released slowly into the storm sewers. This prevents overloading, backing up, and dangerous and damaging flooding.

If your yard is relatively flat (remember, although it may look flat, it probably has some slope), try to determine the lowest points. These, obviously, are where runoff will go, and they may require drain inlets. If you are unable to tell the direction of runoff by eye, take some "shots" around the site using a hand level and surveyor's rod, both of which can be rented.

Your grading and drainage plan must be drawn in conjunction with the master plan. The procedures for drawing a master plan begin on page 91. To draw a complete grading and drainage plan, you will need to determine the topography of the site. Pick a permanent point for reference—one just outside the door of the house, on top of a street curb, or some other nearby permanent base—and use it to take elevation measurements around the site. Note where the measurements are taken and their relative height with respect to the reference point. Transfer these elevation values to the drainage plan. These, together with the elements previously drawn on the base plan or master plan, will provide a complete topographic picture of the site.

Using the principles and considerations discussed earlier, try to determine where water will drain naturally and where it must be diverted or controlled. Use surface drainage for as much of the area as possible, and direct drainage to the street where practical.

Make several copies of the master plan so you can sketch on it and work out an overall grading plan.

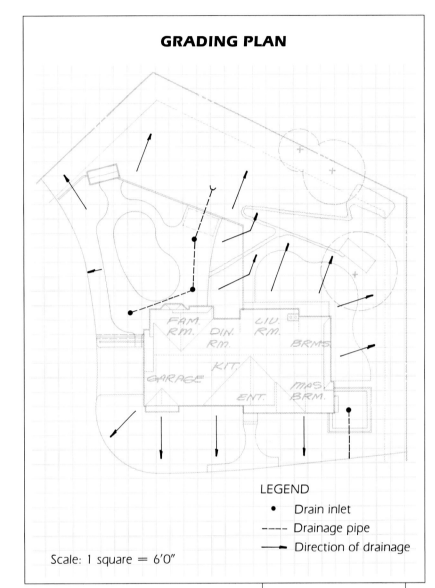

GRADING PLAN

FAM. RM.   DIN. RM.   LIV. RM.   BRMS

GARAGE   KIT.   ENT.   MAS. BRM.

LEGEND
- •   Drain inlet
- ----   Drainage pipe
- ——   Direction of drainage

Scale: 1 square = 6'0"

Walk around the yard, checking grades and looking from the house to the street, from the street toward the rear property line, and from the house toward each side of the yard. Make notes and adjust the concept as necessary, depending on what you measure and see. Draw arrows on the working plan to indicate the direction in which the water should drain or in which it drains naturally. Then proceed with selecting areas for collection, and think about the various methods for conducting and disposing of runoff.

Some landscaping won't affect the established grading and drainage in the yard. This is especially true if you are remodeling established areas. If you're not planning landscape improvements that will affect the grade, you will not have to draw a grading plan. Remember, however, that even minor changes such as pouring a concrete-slab patio will affect drainage.

OUTDOOR LIGHTING

A landscape is one thing by day and something quite different by night. The sun is the great illuminator; at night, illumination comes from the moon and stars or from artificial outdoor lighting. Night lighting brings a garden to life with an aura of soft glows, textures, shadows, romance, and mystery—all quite different from daytime illumination. Lighting can reveal or conceal as much or as little as you want.

Understanding the techniques and principles of outdoor lighting design and installation will help you decide if you want to incorporate night lighting into your overall plan. This section should assist you in deciding how much lighting to use and the type of lighting appropriate to your yard and budget.

Plan your lighting needs before you break ground in the yard. You should have all the elements of the outdoor lighting system that must be placed underground purchased and ready to install along with other underground utility elements so you do not have to dig trenches twice.

Why You Should Install Outdoor Lighting

Light is an important, powerful element and tool. It can create moods of happiness or gloom, serenity or anxiety; it can also have a physical impact, a feeling of warmth or cold, excitement or relaxation. It can make a place safe at night, extend a welcome, guide the way, or widen the use of an area that might otherwise have limited appeal.

Much of what is perceived—physically, emotionally, and intellectually—comes to each individual via sight. Sight is possible only because of light, whether natural or artificial. Natural light, either sunlight or moonlight, can be controlled to some extent through the use of constructed shade structures, vines, and portable accents such as umbrellas and awnings. But the greatest control can be exercised over artificial light.

It is not likely that you will be doing a lot of work in the garden at night; thus, lighting for work is not given much consideration here. Outdoor lighting is usually provided for activities such as strolling, sitting, entertaining, and recreation; for visual effects such as highlighting and concealment, lighting views, and setting moods; and for the practical aspects of security and safety.

Lighting Fixtures and Materials

The world of outdoor lighting systems includes an extremely wide array of fixtures, lamps, enclosures, equipment, and materials. Moreover, the components are constantly changing, with new equipment introduced every day.

The best sources of fixtures and materials are catalogs and lighting consultants. Many home centers and hardware and lighting specialty stores have catalogs and fixtures on display, and the staff in such places can be of great help.

As you plan your outdoor lighting needs, keep in mind two things: the overall electrical needs of your home and the switching and

LIGHTING TERMS

In planning and installing an outdoor lighting system, you will need to understand a few terms. Some of these are used to measure and describe light, and others denote the parts of a lighting system.

Absorption: A measure of the amount of light that is absorbed, rather than reflected, by an object. Surfaces that are black or dark colored and heavily textured absorb the most light.

Ballast: An electrical device used with fluorescent, mercury-vapor, high-pressure sodium, and metal halide lamps to provide the power to start the lamp and control the flow of electricity while it is operating. The ballast is usually built into the light fixture.

Brightness: Also called illumination, this is the amount of light striking a surface or object, measured in units called footcandles.

Energy efficiency: In lighting, energy efficiency is calculated based on the amount of light (measured in lumens) produced by 1 watt of electricity.

Fluorescent lamp: A lamp with a coating on the inside that glows when activated by electric current. Fluorescent lamps require special sockets and ballasts and give an even, glare-free light.

Footcandle: The unit used to measure the brightness of light striking a surface. Specifically, the amount of light that is cast on a surface 1 foot square from a standard candle 1 foot away.

Glare: Distractingly bright light that interferes with our seeing what we need or want to see in an environment.

High-intensity discharge lamp: Also called an HID lamp, this type of lamp produces light when electricity excites gases within a pressurized bulb. Mercury-vapor, metal halide, and high-pressure sodium lamps fall into this category. All high-intensity discharge lamps require special fixtures and ballasts.

Incandescent lamp: A lamp that produces light when electricity heats a metal filament. This is the type of lamp that most people think of as a light bulb.

Lamp: The technical name for what we commonly call a light bulb. It is a tube, usually of glass, in which a filament, gas, or coating is excited by electricity to produce light.

Light fixture: The housing for a lamp, usually containing a reflector and electrical wiring connected to a power source. It may also contain a lens to control light spread and protect the lamp, and a ballast if it is intended for use with high-intensity discharge lamps.

Lighting system: The complete system of lamps, fixtures, wiring, switches, and a power source that supplies light to an environment. A system may also include auxiliary equipment such as transformers, time clocks, and sensors.

Light output: The amount of light emitted by a lamp, measured in lumens.

Light source: The combination of a lamp and fixture that illuminates an environment.

Low-voltage lighting system: A type of lighting that operates on 12-volt current rather than the standard 120 volts. (A few systems use 24-volt power.) Power is supplied by a transformer, which is connected to a 120-volt power source.

Lumen: A unit measuring the amount of light emitted by a light source. Figure a lumen is the amount of light emitted by a standard candle.

Reflectance: A measure of the amount of light that is reflected from a surface. Reflectance is highest from objects or surfaces that are smooth and pale in color, most dominantly white.

Standard-voltage lighting system: Light fixtures and lamps that operate on standard 120-volt house current.

---

control features of the outdoor lighting system. Consider using light switches, including timers and photocells, to turn lights off and on, and dimmers (called rheostats) to control light levels.

Design Guidelines for Outdoor Lighting

The climate and the landscape style you have chosen are important considerations when making decisions about outdoor lighting. In warm regions of the country, where you can use your outdoor spaces nearly the year around, changes in the view aspect are relatively minor (it is, for the most part, green all year), and thus only one lighting plan is needed. In colder areas, where garden use and appearance change significantly with the seasons, consider using different lighting techniques at different times of year. You may not use the garden at all during the winter, but it can have dramatic visual effects—snow, frost, tracery of naked trees—if properly illuminated.

Lighting is not effective unless there is something significant to illuminate. Constructed features, such as fences, decks, walls, and terraces, can be well lighted as soon as they are constructed. Plantings, however, need maturity; if the garden consists of nothing but a flat lawn with small, newly planted trees and shrubs, a lighted landscape will not have much visual interest. Even with careful planning, the ultimate lighting effect cannot be achieved until the plants mature. Plan ahead as much as possible, but remember that your lighting needs may change over time.

Planning an outdoor lighting system requires the same thorough analysis as any of the other landscape elements. Do not be hasty. Live with the yard for a while. Make note of shadows and highlights during different seasons, the effect of moonlight, and the effects of the light that spills over from your house, your neighbor's house, and from the street.

Professional help is available from lighting consultants, contractors, electricians, and lighting specialty stores. If your lighting design is complicated and your budget allows, have a consultant review or perhaps draw up the lighting plan. Check local codes; if you retain a consultant, he or she will help explain codes and requirements and will incorporate them into the plan.

If your budget is limited, draw up a lighting plan to be installed in phases. Light high-priority areas first: entries, heavy-use areas, stairways, and locations where security is critical.

A great deal depends on whether you are adding lighting to an existing yard or designing a new site. In an existing garden, give careful consideration to the routes of underground electrical circuits, since installing them will require that you disrupt, remove, or replace some plantings or structures. Try to plan for as little disturbance as possible, running wires around large trees rather than trenching right through the roots. Avoid running circuits under paving, walls, or structures. To install a lighting circuit under paving, you must cut the paving, dig a trench for the circuit, and then replace the paving after the circuit is installed. It is much easier to route electric circuits around existing features whenever possible.

In some ways planning and installing lighting in a new site is easier than adding lighting to an existing one; in other ways it is more complicated. Work out the lighting installation schedule along with the schedules for grading, drainage, irrigation, and construction so all underground work can be done at the same time, if at all possible. The complicated

Area lighting planned in conjunction with patios increases the usefulness of an activity area. Dining outdoors is a treat on a warm summer night.

part is planning the various systems so they do not interfere with one another.

Outdoor Lighting Costs

Low-voltage (12-volt) lighting systems are the least expensive for the home landscape. The composite cost of a 12-volt system includes the electrical service, the distribution system, bases for the fixtures (usually concrete), the light fixtures and standards, the control switches, the transformers, and the lamps. Because of strict requirements for grounding and wiring standard 120-volt electrical service outdoors, a low-voltage system is much less expensive.

Low-voltage systems have the advantage of being quite safe, but because the electric current drops off somewhat, no line can be longer than about 100 feet, and you cannot have more than three or four 100-watt fixtures per line.

A standard 120-volt system is less limiting. If your property is large and you intend to use the grounds at night for such activities as swimming, badminton, or tennis, or if you plan to light patios and lawn areas with multiple fixtures in order to minimize glare, you may wish to consider a 120-volt system. Because of the high voltage, this type of system is much more expensive to install, and because of the amount of electricity consumed, it is more expensive to run.

In either system you can set all the fixtures and dig all the trenches. Codes may require that you have an electrician do all the wiring and connections for a 120-volt system. Electrical cable should be snaked through a PVC (polyvinyl chloride) pipe for protection, but that cost is nominal. Fixture costs vary, and the choice is dependent on your budget and overall landscape style.

How to Figure Light Levels

Ask five people what they perceive as "dim" light and you will get five different answers. Although it is difficult to define standards for perceptions that are basically personal, you can use the following guidelines. Brightness is measured in footcandles. Footcandles are a function of the brightness of the source and the distance from the source to the surface being lighted.

Dim Generally about 0.4 footcandles or less, this is the equivalent of full moonlight or the light on a street between streetlights. Silhouetting or moonlighting techniques produce about this level of light.

Medium Bright Anywhere from 0.5 to as much as 8 footcandles, this is less bright than interior house lighting. Low-voltage garden lighting is usually from 3 to 5 footcandles. Most standard garden fixtures fall in this range. This level of brightness is used for uplighting, downlighting, and area lighting.

Bright About 8 footcandles or brighter, this is the illumination level of most interior rooms. Lighting in office spaces ranges from 60 to 150 footcandles. Bright lights are used for safety lighting, security lighting, and spotlighting. Except for special areas and security lighting, it is rarely desirable to light any part of the garden brighter than 20 footcandles, and 5 footcandles is a good average maximum. Be aware of glare caused by bright lighting.

Lighting Techniques and Special Effects

Lighting techniques vary as to the position of the light source and whether it is pointed up, down, or across. Each technique brings a different focus to an area. Choose from among the following lighting techniques to accent different elements of the landscape.

Downlighting Simulating natural illumination from the sun or moon, this refers to the illumination of plantings, surfaces, and objects from above. The light source may be a floodlight for safety or security, several lights set high in a tree or on a pole, or light diffused through an overhead lattice, canvas, or arbor.

Uplighting This is the illumination of a tree, wall, or object from below. Light is cast upward in either a broad spread or a more concentrated beam. This can have a dramatic effect and, since uplighting rarely occurs in nature, its appearance may be somewhat unnatural. Hence, areas of uplighting should be carefully planned and selected to illuminate special features.

Backlighting creates an exciting evening view of the trees off this deck.

Backlighting This technique is similar to silhouetting, shadowing, and fill lighting. Essentially, it involves casting light (in any direction) behind plantings or objects. It reveals textures, creates long shadows, and gives a feeling of depth to the landscape.

Each of these basic lighting techniques can be employed for a variety of purposes. You will probably need to use a combination of techniques to light various elements appropriately and create the desired ambience. Safety, security, and nighttime activities will dictate the majority of lighting needs, but lighting can be used for a number of special effects as well.

Safety Lighting Usually a medium-bright or bright illumination of areas, this type of lighting is designed to help people see obstacles

and to allow them to move about the garden easily and confidently. Combining techniques of accent lighting, downlighting, area lighting, and spotlighting, its principal use is to eliminate confusing shadows on steps and paths.

Security Lighting As bright as safety lighting or brighter, security lighting is employed to make one feel comfortable with the dark or what may be hiding in it. Often security lighting is harsh and glaring, so bright that it detracts from the overall garden lighting effect, but it need not be this way. Lights don't have to be placed high on poles or house eaves; carefully placed fixtures at waist or knee level can effectively silhouette possible intruders. Moreover, security lighting can come into play late at night, when other garden lights are switched off and you have retired for the night. If you do this, an efficient switching system is a must, whether you use manual switches, timed switches, or photocells to turn lights on and off at various times and in different areas.

Area Lighting This is soft, uniform, ambient lighting, usually from overhead flood- or spotlights. It is suitable for terraces, lawn areas, entertaining, or games. Illumination is in the medium-bright range. Place fixtures to avoid glare. You may want to combine this type of lighting with other, more decorative lighting techniques.

Accent Lighting This style usually consists of small spotlights that cast a concentrated beam to highlight a plant, object, or work of art. Thought of as small "shots" of light here and there that lend sparkle and life to the night garden, accent lights can include low-voltage fixtures and strings of small, twinkling Christmas-type lamps.

Notice the repeated right angles—the concrete pavers, the 2 by 4 edging, the square light fixture, the lattice fence set straight—in the details of this landscape lit attractively for safety.

When well lit, a distinctively shaped plant can be an interesting landscape accent at any time of day. Plants are especially striking seen in silhouette, as against this stucco house wall.

Spotlighting This technique is more direct, generally more intense, and illuminates a larger range than area lighting. Employing the techniques of down- and uplighting, it provides a focal glow on key garden elements, such as artwork, a wall, or a fountain. Use this technique judiciously; too much spotlighting can ruin the overall effect.

Silhouetting Similar to the technique of backlighting, silhouetting involves placing a soft light behind an object so it glows on a background surface (such as a wall or fence). This allows you to view the object in silhouette, as a black image or outline against a light backdrop. The light source should be concealed. This technique is very effective when you want to emphasize plants that have unusual shapes or textures.

Moonlighting This is a form of downlighting using fixtures placed high above the ground. The effect resembles moonlight: Illumination is dim, and there is a soft background luminescence with focal points and shadows. This can be the most effective type of lighting, and sometimes entire landscapes are illuminated using only this technique. It is important to conceal the light source; the higher above the ground it is placed, the better.

Cross-lighting The illumination of an object from two or more points with beams of light that either cross or converge, cross-lighting uses diffuse sources of light, such as floodlights. This technique is often combined in downlighting and moonlighting.

Grazing Light This mode of lighting involves placing a light source

to cast a soft beam that grazes or slants across a wall, fence, shrub, or other object, revealing surface texture and color. It can also be effective for silhouetting.

Shadowing Essentially the opposite of silhouetting, shadowing involves placing a fixture (usually a flood- or spotlight) in front of an object, such as a plant, and projecting its outline or shadow against a wall. The light source is usually placed low to the ground and aimed up at an angle.

Fill Lighting This is a result of reflectance and spillover from other lighting sources. It is an overall dim, ambient illumination that is most evident on the garden floor. Hidden low-voltage fixtures can be used to enhance this effect.

Vista Lighting Elevated sites, especially ones in hilly areas, often look out on a beautiful view of a lake, bay, meadow, or city. It may be a sweeping view, or it may be limited, framed by buildings or trees. In order to preserve the view at night, nearby lighting should be dim or in the low medium-bright range to prevent glare from obscuring the view. Fixtures should be carefully placed low to the ground, and any lighting within the view should be very dim. Trees may be softly uplighted to emphasize the view.

Perspective Lighting Down-, up-, or backlighting can be used to emphasize an axis—the edges of a lawn area, a path leading to a gazebo, a line of trees on either side of a planted area, or walls that bound an area. In this technique, the lighting is linear, usually consisting of evenly spaced fixtures that lead the eye in a narrowing frame of view—a perspective view—to an object in the distance. The object can be accent-lighted as well. In some

Plan outdoor lighting for the best views from inside your home, being careful not to cause glare on the windows. The lights hidden in the plantings above the swimming pool are tilted to reflect against the brick wall and not into the eyes of viewers.

ways this technique is similar to vista lighting in that it emphasizes or protects a certain view. It can also make the area seem larger because it directs the eye into the distance, giving an illusion of greater depth than what is actually there.

Water Lighting Ponds, swimming pools, and spas can be lit at night and can be very effective elements in your overall scheme. The light source must be concealed. Water is usually lighted with white or slightly yellow lamps; colors such as blue, red, or yellow can look strange, and may even be upsetting. The light produced is much like fill lighting, sending a soft glow upward into overhanging structures or trees. For best effect, the water must be clear.

Mirror Lighting The reflection of lighted trees and objects can be mirrored across water surfaces for a very dramatic effect. The area or object behind (or immediately beyond) the water surface is lighted, perhaps with uplighting, and the reflection is cast across a still water surface. The water must be dark to reflect light.

Designing Your Lighting System

As you design your lighting system, remember the main purposes for outdoor lighting—function, visual impact, and practicality.

Check local codes, rules, and requirements before embarking on a design. Have an electrical inspector, consultant, or contractor check both your plan and your work for conformance with these regulations. They are intended for safety. Do not jeopardize life and property by attempting shortcuts.

Lighting levels vary according to purpose. Generally, lower levels are for viewing; higher levels

are for activity areas. Be careful about beaming light into a neighbor's yard. Light is sometimes difficult to control in a small garden, and it is surprising how much even a dim light can spill over the property line.

Study the natural light in your garden. Notice how the sun and moon cast shadows and reveal textures and tracery, or how the light looks on bright, cloudless days as opposed to cloudy ones. For night lighting to look right, it should simulate natural light as much as possible. The quality of light in the garden depends directly on the surfaces and materials in the spaces to be lighted.

Textured and varied surfaces are good candidates for uplighting. These redwoods also benefit by mirrorlike water in an adjacent pool.

Do not overlight the landscape. When in doubt, err on the side of too little light. Lower levels create effects that look more natural. Carefully select techniques and fixtures that are in scale with the spaces, and avoid glare at all costs.

Bear in mind that insects are attracted to light. If you live in an area where insects are a problem, try using pink or yellow bulbs sold as "bug" lights. If the quality or color of these is not satisfactory, at least place standard-colored fixtures away from windows or doors so you don't invite insects into the house. Avoid lights near outdoor dining areas as they may attract insect dinner guests.

The smaller the garden, the simpler the lighting system should be. Try to stick with one type of lamp for continuity within the landscape. In larger spaces, you can use a variety of techniques and lamp types. Carefully analyze what areas and elements require illumination, and determine light levels and fixture types accordingly. Use bright lights for safety along paths and in entryways, and arrange softer, more subtle accent lighting for special features. You can also use lighting to mask or black out areas that are unsightly by placing bright lights in front of the space. You may want to black out scruffy plants, an unfinished structure, a fence that needs paint, or a storage area.

Place switches and controls in protected, easily accessible locations. Hide light sources to the extent possible. Conceal fixtures under plants or other objects, and always direct the light beam away from the viewer. Position fixtures to bounce light off surfaces or diffuse it through leaves. This helps avoid glare.

Choose fixture locations carefully so they don't interfere with garden maintenance or walkways. Paint fixtures to blend in with plants or nearby structures. If you are installing the landscape in phases, consider using portable fixtures until permanent locations have been determined.

Make the lighting system as flexible as possible. Your landscape is a growing, changing thing, and a lighting scheme that looks good when first installed may not look right once plants mature or your needs change. You can gain flexibility by using some portable fixtures, running several circuits (rather than one), and providing switches and dimmers.

Drawing a Lighting Plan

Like any other plan, the lighting plan is the result of a logical process. It will be based on information from the master plan. The procedures for drawing a master plan begin on page 91. Make several copies of the master plan that you can use for sketching and studying. Your finished lighting plan will show the location of electrical circuits, fixtures, and other equipment.

Consider lighting landscape accents, such as a particular plant, statue, or constructed element. Light a favorite view by figuring out where you would sit or stand to see it best. Plan lighting for special needs, placing a soft, relaxing light outside the bedroom window, for example, or creating a well-lit area for guest parking.

Next, check elements that you will use light to hide. Look at your least favorite feature. Think about hiding power lines, your neighbor's motor home, and other visual nuisances in the landscape. Use light to hide bothersome views of the street, nearby houses, and storage and garbage facilities. Try to light only features that are attractive and

LANDSCAPE PLANTS FOR OUTDOOR LIGHTING

When choosing plants that will be intensified by outdoor lighting, study their forms, branching structures, and the texture and glossiness of their leaves and bark. Each species can be lit to bring out its unique beauty. Below are some of the plants from the Landscape Plant Guide (beginning on page 211) that are particularly beautiful when illuminated.

Trees

Acer species	Maple
Arbutus unedo	Strawberry tree
Betula species	Birch
Cedrus deodara	Deodar cedar
Celtis species	Hackberry
Fagus sylvatica	European beech
Gleditsia triacanthos var. *inermis*	Thornless honeylocust
Lagerstroemia indica	Crape myrtle
Liquidambar styraciflua	American sweet gum
Olea europaea	Olive
Pistacia chinensis	Chinese pistachio
Prunus caroliniana	Carolina cherry laurel
Quercus species	Oak
Salix babylonica	Weeping willow

Shrubs

Berberis thunbergii	Japanese barberry
Cotinus coggygria	Smoke tree
Euonymus alatus	Burning bush, winged euonymus
Ilex species	Holly
Myrica pensylvanica	Northern bayberry
Pittosporum species	Pittosporum
Phormium tenax	New Zealand flax
Prunus laurocerasus	English laurel
Punica granatum	Pomegranate
Pyracantha species	Firethorn
Rhododendron species	Rhododendron
Syringa species	Lilac
Viburnum species	Viburnum species
Xylosma congestum	Shiny xylosma

Vines

× *Fatshedera lizei*	Fatshedera
Hardenbergia violacea	Coral pea
Lapageria species	Bellflower
Parthenocissus species	Boston ivy
Polygonum aubertii	Silver lace vine
Trachelospermum jasminoides	Starjasmine
Wisteria species	Wisteria

Ground Covers (Perennials)

Agapanthus species	Lily of the Nile
Bergenia cordifolia	Heartleaf bergenia
Festuca glauca (*F. ovina* var. *glauca*)	Blue fescue
Hosta species	
Liriope species	Lilyturf
Ophiopogon japonicus	Mondograss

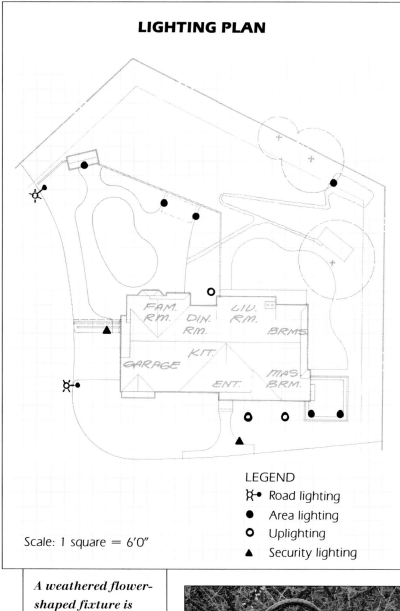

LIGHTING PLAN

Scale: 1 square = 6'0"

LEGEND
☼• Road lighting
● Area lighting
○ Uplighting
▲ Security lighting

A weathered flower-shaped fixture is part of the view in the daytime, a source of light at night.

that will help mask out the undesirable ones.

Look at your planting plan to figure out which plants have textures and colors that light can emphasize. Certain plants look especially good under night light. Keep in mind that many plants have different shapes in different seasons. You may want to light a flower bed for spectacular spring color, but you may not want to see it when it is covered in snow. Just remember to put that light on a different circuit than the porch light, and you will have the effect you want throughout the year.

Think of how you plan to use the new landscape and consider the types of lighting needed for your outdoor life. Determine the light levels for entertaining versus viewing, for example. The light level required for dining on the patio will be different than that needed for a night game of croquet on the lawn.

Do not overlook the safety and security aspects of outdoor lighting. If the entrances to your home are tricky to find, you may need more light along a path than you would need for a fairly straightforward approach. Look for equipment now on the market that is light sensitive, so the light turns on when it gets dark. Or consider attaching timers to some lights and setting them for random or fixed times. These are very effective deterrents for times when you're away from home. Heat-sensitive lights feature a sensor that turns the light on when it detects the warmth of a body. Consider installing heat- or motion-sensitive lights near rear entrances, driveways, and parking areas where lighting is necessary only when someone approaches.

Remember that not all of your lighting needs may be permanent. If you decorate the front of the house with specialty lights to celebrate winter holidays or if you want to add festive lights around the patio for summer parties, remember to include some kind of electrical access for these lights as you plan other lighting needs.

As you plan the lighting system, find out what light already exists. Light may spill onto your site from a neighboring yard, streetlights, or the interior of your house.

Make sketches of lighting needs on copies of the master plan. Jot down all thoughts and possibilities. Try to imagine what the night-lighted garden will be like. This plan should not be rushed.

Take the sketch of your plan outside and walk around with it. To test your ideas, set flashlights, portable lamps, or candles in places you are considering outdoor lights. When all seems workable, draw up the plan in final form on a clean copy of the master plan. Indicate on the lighting plan all of the circuits, switches, fixtures, methods of attachment, and all other items related to outdoor lighting.

Measure the length of the circuits on the plan. Make a list of the different types of fixtures and the quantity of each. Then estimate the cost of materials and installation. Check that the lighting plan fits into your budget. If not, see whether you can put off some of the lighting installation until finances permit.

Also, check local codes again. If you are unsure about some aspects of your lighting plan, consult a licensed electrician or your community inspection department. Make certain that all components are legal and safe. Be sure to schedule the installation in conjunction with construction for other utilities, keeping in mind that work should be done during fair weather.

UTILITY SYSTEMS

As you develop your landscape design, and before you break any ground, you must develop at least a working knowledge of the various utility systems on your site. It is important to know how the utilities are or will be routed to the house, what precautions you should take, and what general components make up any particular system, both during construction and once you want to use the utilities in the landscape.

Every inhabited structure is dependent on utilities that bring water and energy to the site and carry waste products away. Utilities systems comprise any or all of the following: sanitary and storm sewers, electricity, gas, telephone, water, and television cable. They not only make living more comfortable, they protect and serve both you and the community in the areas of health, safety, and public welfare.

Although design implies control, you have little control over utilities. They are almost always laid out and installed by utility companies and will probably be available, if not already in place, when you begin landscape work. Utilities really mean the main feeder lines from the street to the house. Beyond that (within the house and around the yard), utility work is usually called plumbing or wiring or gas-line work. Check the Reading List on page 320 for books that go into much more construction detail than there is room for here. If you want to extend a gas line to the barbecue, run electricity to some outdoor switches, or extend a telephone jack to the terrace, consult a book written specifically for the job you need to do. Any good how-to book will emphasize caution, a thorough knowledge of applicable codes, and possibly

Left: Utilities are a necessity, but they can be camouflaged in your landscape. Painting these irrigation faucets black will make them less noticeable.
Right: Cleverly submerging garbage cans in a deck makes good use of the space below and also allows easy access for both yard and household waste.

inspection by the city building department.

Any major additions to plumbing, gas, or electrical lines will usually require some inspection for approval. Check with local authorities to determine the requirements before proceeding. Both plumbing, which includes gas and water lines, and electrical work involve systems that can be dangerous if you do not know what you are doing. An improperly installed gas line, for example, can be hazardous.

As with the other subjects discussed in this book, if you feel that you do not have the time or skills to do the work, or are not sure what you need, consult a professional—an engineer or contractor with a specialty and license in electrical, plumbing, sewer, or gas work.

Design Guidelines for Utilities

The following guidelines will help you understand what you need to consider when utilities are affected by a landscape installation. You may want to have a landscape architect, designer, or contractor take a look at your design if any of your ideas will have an impact on your home utility systems.

If you want to do your own construction work, especially where wiring, gas, and plumbing are concerned, you should have some experience. Consult a licensed professional, the local utility company, or your community building department for review and approval before beginning work. In any event, for your own safety and the safety of your property, you need to be aware of all utility codes and regulations governing the routing and rerouting of utility systems to and around your house.

Provide valves at convenient points so the system (or any part of it) can be shut down for emergencies or repairs. Make sure that cleanouts are installed at critical points in the sewer and storm drains so pipes can be snaked should they become clogged.

Be aware of any easements along your property or through it. A utility easement is a strip of land along which a utility company has run a line (electric, gas, water, or sewer). A private owner in effect leases the easement (without pay) to the company. The company usually will not permit the construction of any permanent structures, such as buildings or large walls, over the easement but will allow terraces, walks, and plantings. Check with the utility company involved, find out what is permitted, and get approval before making changes on or near an easement.

Carefully calculate the total demand you will make on each utility. If new lines are being installed, you may have some say as to their size and placement; contact the utility company and voice your needs. The important thing is to try to anticipate what your complete needs will be, both now and in the future, so utilities will be adequate and will not have to be augmented or relocated later. In the case of electricity, determine how many switches (both indoors and out) you will need, the amount of lighting and number of appliances you anticipate using, and whether there will be any unusual electrical demands. Do the same for all other utilities—make lists and keep them with your landscape plans.

Coordinate utility installation with other underground work. In some cases certain lines can be installed in a common trench, and it is cheaper and easier to install them together.

Consider what all conduits, pipes, and boxes will look like. You may want to paint them to make them blend in, cover them with a box, mount them on the backside of a wall or fence, or cover them with plantings. For example, if you plan to install a water valve in a given location, think about how you might disguise it while still having easy access to it.

If freezing is a problem in your area, water and sewer lines should be buried below the frost line. The frost line varies from region to region. To find out how deep the frost line is in your area, consult a local contractor, the community building department, or the weather service.

Contact the utility companies before beginning any trenching or grading work. Ask them to verify line locations on your property. The utility company has (or should have) an accurate record of where lines are located and their sizes, and will be able to give you the information over the phone at no charge. If you need more specific information, a representative can probably come to your site to show you where the lines are. Drive stakes into the ground above these lines so you can avoid digging near them. Breaking a utility line can result in more than interrupted service; the company may charge you for repairs and, worse, it may cause personal injury.

While you are dealing with other utilities, you may as well figure out the placement of your garbage facility. Cans or a dumpster should be located for your convenience as well as that of the collector. Check with the service company or community for specific regulations. All garbage enclosures should be located out of view and integrated with the overall landscape design.

Utility System Equipment and Components

You need to be familiar with the components of the various utility systems so you can integrate them into your overall design and discuss them with a landscape architect or contractor, should you decide to hire one.

Sewer Lines Both sanitary and storm sewer systems work on the principle of gravity flow; they are not pressurized and must therefore be laid out so pipes slope down from the collection point to the main sewer. If your site makes gravity flow impossible, you can use force mains to pump the sewage to the main sewer. Unlike standard sewer systems, force mains operate under pressure and require a pump to either pull or push the effluent liquids up the slope. Force mains involving pumps are tricky; a thorough knowledge of hydraulics is necessary. If you foresee the need for such a system, it is strongly recommended that you have an expert advise you or design the system for you.

Sanitary Sewer: Waste that has come into contact with humans is called sanitary sewage. Effluent and solids from both inside the house—kitchen and bathroom sinks, shower, and toilet—and outside the house—pool, spa, outdoor sink, and drinking fountain—are collected via a system of pipes that branch back to a single sanitary line. This line in turn leads to and connects with the main sewer,

TYPICAL UTILITY CONNECTIONS

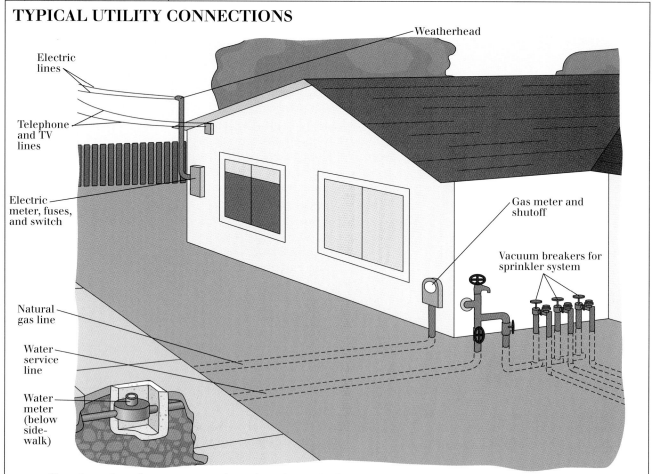

Weatherhead

Electric lines

Telephone and TV lines

Electric meter, fuses, and switch

Gas meter and shutoff

Vacuum breakers for sprinkler system

Natural gas line

Water service line

Water meter (below sidewalk)

Note: A new branch can occur anywhere along the service line to connect an irrigation system. In newer homes, electric, telephone, and TV cable will probably be underground rather than overhead.

which usually lies under the adjacent street.

Typically, the utility company installs the sanitary pipe from its connection with the main sewer to a point just past the property line. From there a plumbing contractor finishes the job, running the pipe to and through the house.

Storm Sewer: Often referred to as a storm line or storm drain, a storm sewer resembles a sanitary sewer in all aspects save one: Its purpose is to conduct runoff from rainfall, irrigation, and seepage away from the site and dispose of it in a common community system. Most communities prohibit the mingling of sanitary and storm sewage; the systems must be separate. In newer or larger developments, storm pipes may connect directly with drain inlets around the property or with downspouts from the roof. The largest storm system is the city streets and the piping under them. Streets collect runoff, direct it to drain inlets along the curb, and pipe it via large conduits to a point of disposal.

Water Lines A communitywide system distributes water through pipes under pressure. Large mains usually lie under the streets. These are connected to smaller pipes that serve individual properties. The utility company makes the connection and extends it to a water meter inside the property line, often just behind or within the sidewalk. A plumbing contractor extends the line throughout the house. The meter is provided by the utility company, and the owner pays a service charge for installation.

The line running from the meter to the house is called the service line and for most residences is from ¾ to 1½ inches in diameter. This is the supply line for all water needs

on the site, both inside and outside the house.

Your water source may be a well rather than a utility company system, in which case a pump and a tank are required to take water from the ground and store it for use.

Electrical Lines Electricity is distributed throughout the municipality via underground cables or overhead lines. The utility company will make the connection to the distribution lines and will run an individual line to the structure to be served, connecting it with a "weatherhead" (a large, vertical pipe structure on the side of the house) and meter. From this point an electrician installs additional lines through the main fuse box and from there to various points within the house and around the site.

Gas Lines Not all homes make use of natural gas; heating may also be accomplished with electricity, fuel oil, wood, or bottled gas (butane or propane). Natural gas is provided by an overall network of pressurized mains and submains throughout the community. Like water, gas is brought to the structure via a service line. From there it is distributed to the furnace, stove, water heater, clothes dryer, and perhaps a fireplace. Gas lines can also be extended from the house to the garden to serve a barbecue, pool, or spa.

Telephone and Television Lines These two utilities serve the property via overhead or underground distribution systems, with individual lines leading to the house. The lines can also be extended to the yard if you desire telephone service or television access outside or in an outbuilding.

Cleanouts Cleanouts are used both on sanitary and storm lines to permit access to the pipe for cleaning should the line become obstructed. For more information, refer to the grading and drainage glossary (see page 113).

WATERING SYSTEMS

The terms *watering, irrigation,* and *sprinkler* are often confused. Actually, a sprinkler system is a special assembly of components that sprinkle water onto planted areas, usually from above. Irrigation is an umbrella word that encompasses all forms of watering systems—agricultural and residential. The distinction is a small one, and these terms will be used interchangeably.

This section discusses the basic design considerations for installing a system to water landscape plants. It is intended to acquaint you with the components of a watering system, how such a system works, and the general principles involved in its design and installation. Both design and installation help is available from experts such as irrigation consultants, component manufacturers' representatives, irrigation supply houses, or landscape contractors.

Why You Should Install a Watering System

Watering can be accomplished by hand, with an irrigation system, or by some combination of the two. Hand-watering is not as expensive as installing a watering system, but is more time-consuming and less efficient. The decision to install a watering system in your landscape will depend on the climate, location, budget, landscape style, and amount of time and energy you want to spend watering your plants. A properly designed and installed system can use less water than hand-watering.

Although watering-system installation is not regulated to the same extent that electrical and garden construction work are, it is a good idea to check local codes. Of particular importance is the connection to the public supply line.

Watering Methods

Your choice of watering method should be based on the functional needs of the site, on your lifestyle requirements, and on your budget. You will have the best chance of success with a self-installed system if the site is not too large or steep and if planted areas are not too complicated.

Conventional Sometimes referred to as overhead irrigation, this is the system that usually comes to mind when someone mentions irrigation. It consists of pipe, valves, and heads that spray water in different patterns over planted areas. It is generally efficient for all types of plants but does have minor drawbacks—it can spray water onto structures, the water can be blown around by the wind, and it generally provides only surface water, which is not particularly helpful to deep-rooted trees and shrubs.

Drip This type of system employs pipe and valves, but instead of sprinkler heads uses small emitters (usually with tubing) placed at the base of trees and shrubs and in planting beds and containers. These emitters dribble water into the soil at the rate of a few gallons per hour. The advantages of a drip system are that it provides thorough, deep watering, loses very little water due to runoff or evaporation, and is less expensive to install and operate. The disadvantage is that this system is inefficient for watering large areas of ground covers and lawn grasses.

If your budget allows, it may be worth considering a combination of conventional irrigation for large areas of lawn and ground cover and drip irrigation for trees, shrubs, and vines.

Manual A manual watering system employs hand-operated valves; that is, you must turn the water on and off. The advantage of this method is in savings; manual valves cost less than automatic valves and there is no need for a controller, but the cost of the remainder of the system—pipe, sprinkler heads, and other components—is the same as for an automatic system. The disadvantage is obvious: You must spend time turning valves on and off.

Automatic Automatic valves are electrically or, in some places, hydraulically operated. They are sometimes called remote-controlled valves (RCVs). The valves are activated by a controller, which can be preset to water any part of the garden for any amount of time at any hour of day on any day of the week. The advantages and disadvantages of this method are just the opposite of those for the manual system, but there is one significant additional advantage: The automatic system can be operated during the early-morning hours, say, from 3 to 7 a.m., when the garden is not in use, when house water usage is lowest, and when the wind is usually lightest. This is also an ideal watering time for plants, because they can dry out during the day, helping prevent mildew and fungus.

Of course, either of the operation methods can be combined with either type of system. You can install a manual conventional system, an automatic conventional system, a manual drip system, or an automatic drip system. Choose the

combination that best serves your landscape design, budget, and lifestyle needs.

Watering-System Equipment

In choosing equipment, look up the specifications of all the components of the watering system in irrigation catalogs, and become familiar with climate and code specifics for your area. You can get catalogs and equipment from irrigation equipment manufacturers or supply houses. Check the local telephone directory for listings. Most home centers and some garden centers offer these products as well.

A tremendous variety of watering-system equipment is available in many styles, sizes, and materials. Quality and price also vary considerably. Irrigation equipment is sold for a variety of residential, commercial, and industrial situations. Choose high-quality equipment that is suited for residential use. Nearly all the components you need, especially heads, can be of plastic (or mostly plastic). Plastic

Pop-up lawn sprinkler heads lie flush with the ground when not in use, then rise a couple of inches when the water comes on, so the spray clears the grass. They are available in full-, half-, and quarter-circle spray patterns, as well as in a few other configurations for odd corners.

components are more than suitable for residential landscape needs.

The most commonly used equipment, materials, and components in a residential watering system are described briefly below.

Pipe Almost all pipe used today is made of polyvinyl chloride, commonly known as PVC, rather than galvanized steel. PVC is easier to handle and is much faster to assemble than steel because it is welded (or glued) together using a solvent. Galvanized-steel pipe requires many hours of cutting and threading and is subject to corrosion and obstruction buildup over time.

PVC is manufactured under two rating systems: schedule rating and class rating. Schedule-rated pipe is rated like steel pipe and has walls of uniform thickness regardless of pipe diameter. The walls of class-rated pipe vary in thickness—the greater the diameter, the thicker the wall—meaning that the pressure rating remains the same whether the diameter is small or large. Class 200, for example, will carry 200 psi (pounds per square inch) of pressure before bursting. Schedule-rated pipe is stronger in the smaller diameters and hence is most often specified for fittings and risers; class-rated pipe is stronger and more dependable in larger diameters and is therefore usually used for main lines.

Residential systems commonly use pipe in classes 315, 200, and 160, and in schedule 40 for fittings and some main lines. Lateral lines use class 200; a less expensive alternative would be 160.

PVC pipe is marked along the side with the size, the class or schedule, the manufacturer, and the NSF stamp showing that it meets the requirements of the National Sanitary Foundation.

PVC pipe is more susceptible to damage than is galvanized steel, so you must exercise some care in handling and storing this material. It will deteriorate and weaken if exposed to sunlight for any period. To prevent this, store all PVC pipe out of sunlight, and always completely cover it with soil anywhere it is used.

Fittings Fittings are the components that join the pipe sections together and connect the sprinkler heads to the lateral line piping. Fittings are sold in a variety of sizes and shapes; there are tees, elbows, sleeves, risers, nipples, and unions. PVC elbows and sleeves are usually "slip-fitted," that is, the pipe slips into the fitting and is glued in place. Other fittings, such as unions, risers, and sometimes nipples, are threaded on one or both ends and screw into the pipe. Some fittings designate whether they are slip-fitted or threaded. For example, a tee might be called SST or SSS. SST indicates that two openings are of the slip type and one opening is threaded; SSS indicates that all three openings are slip-fitted.

Schedule 40 PVC is usually used for fittings; where special strength is required, such as in risers, schedule 80 might be specified.

Valves There are two types of valves: manual and automatic. In either case the operating principle is the same. Like the faucet in a bathtub or sink, a valve connects to a pipe containing water under pressure. No water passes through the valve until it is opened, just as no water comes out of a faucet until you turn the handle.

A manual valve is usually placed in a box just below ground level. You operate it either by turning the handle by hand or by using a valve key (a long rod with a fork on one

VALVES AND SPRINKLER HEADS

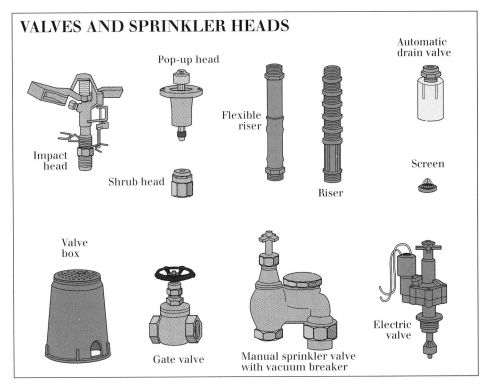

Pop-up head

Automatic drain valve

Impact head

Shrub head

Flexible riser

Riser

Screen

Valve box

Gate valve

Manual sprinkler valve with vacuum breaker

Electric valve

end). An automatic valve operates electrically via a solenoid mounted on top of the valve. The solenoid is connected to the controller by two low-voltage wires buried in the same trench as the pipe. When the controller setting indicates that watering is to begin, an electric current is sent through the wires and the valve opens. When the watering period is over, the current is shut off and the valve closes.

Some automatic valves are hydraulic and operate via small-diameter flexible tubing that runs from controller to valve. Water in the tubing is under pressure. Depending on the manufacture of the valve, the valve opens when pressure is released and closes when pressure is again applied, or vice versa. Hydraulic valves tend to freeze in cold areas and have generally been replaced by electrically operated ones.

Typically, a valve is placed at each juncture between the main line and a lateral line. The main line is under constant pressure; when the valve opens, it allows water to flow through the lateral line and out through the sprinkler heads.

Controllers Sometimes called clocks, controllers have come a long way in the past several years. Originally, a controller was similar to a timer you might use to turn lights on and off for specified periods. Today, state-of-the-art controllers are virtually computers. You can program them for any combination of day, period, and hour. Repeat cycles allow you to water certain areas more than once a day. The latest controllers employ digital readouts, telling you what to do next, what selections are available, and how to set the program. Less sophisticated controllers, which employ dials and knobs, will do the job at a lower cost.

The greatest advantage of a controller is the time it will save you.

The other advantage is that you can program it for night watering, when home usage is down and water pressure is maximized. When you don't have to worry much about heads spraying patios and paths, you can install fewer, larger heads, which will simplify the watering-system plan.

Controllers are available in a variety of sizes and capacities. Capacity is determined by the number of "stations" the controller will handle. Typically, 1 station operates 1 valve; hence, a 12-station controller has the capacity to operate 12 automatic valves. Your watering system's design will determine how many valves are required, which in turn will determine the capacity of controller you will need.

Heads Today, there are hundreds of sprinkler heads available, offering a variety of types, patterns, coverages, materials, internal components, and operational requirements involving pressure and flow rate. Irrigation catalogs are the best source to help you select the proper heads for use in your system.

Type indicates whether the head is to be used for watering lawn, ground cover, or shrubs. Generally, heads for lawns and ground cover are of the pop-up, or impact, type. These heads pop up when water is discharged and otherwise are set flush with the ground surface, making them less visible and facilitating mowing. They are designed to distribute water over a relatively flat area. For large lawn areas, gear-driven heads can be used. These are larger heads contained in a plastic or steel housing; the nozzle is directed back and forth by a system of gears. Shrub heads (also suitable for beds) distribute water in confined areas and are sold in a variety of spray patterns. Bubbler

heads are set close to the ground and "bubble" rather than spray.

Pattern refers to the spray pattern of a head, both horizontal and vertical. Viewed from above, the spray may form a full circle or a half, third, or quarter circle. Viewed from the side, the higher the arc, the farther the water will spray.

Coverage concerns the distance water is thrown from the head. This can be as little as 3 feet or as much as 150 feet. Heads are usually adjustable for a range of coverage, from 10 to 15 feet, for example, to fit within a designated area.

Materials commonly used for heads are plastic (PVC), brass, and steel. Plastic is the least expensive and possibly the most suitable material for home use, because residential sprinklers are not subject to the coverage requirements and wear and tear of systems for large public areas. Moreover, plastic heads are easier to maintain. Brass was once the primary material for sprinkler heads, but its use is diminishing due to cost and maintenance problems. The large heads used in areas such as parks and golf courses to cover thousands of square feet of surface area are made of steel, or a combination of steel and plastic, and are quite expensive. The internal components—gears, springs, nozzles, and couplings—can be of any of these materials.

All of the heads installed to water a lawn area should be of the same type, and they should be attached to a lateral line that serves the lawn only. This line in turn should be activated by a lawn valve. You may need to install several valves and lateral lines to water your lawn area, but do not use one lateral line to water both lawn and shrubs. Similarly, shrub heads should be on

SPRINKLER HEAD PATTERNS

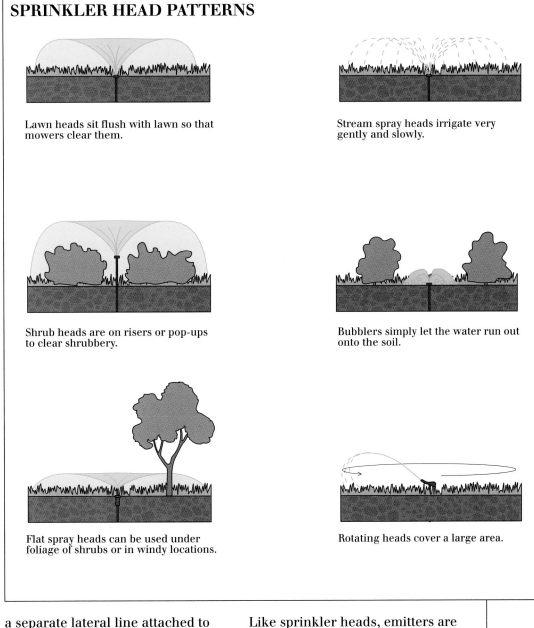

Lawn heads sit flush with lawn so that mowers clear them.

Stream spray heads irrigate very gently and slowly.

Shrub heads are on risers or pop-ups to clear shrubbery.

Bubblers simply let the water run out onto the soil.

Flat spray heads can be used under foliage of shrubs or in windy locations.

Rotating heads cover a large area.

a separate lateral line attached to a shrub valve, and so on. You need to keep lawn and shrub heads on separate lateral lines and valves because lawn grasses and shrubs have different water requirements. Typically, you water lawns more frequently but for shorter periods; shrubs require less frequent but deeper watering.

Emitters Emitters are the "sprinklers" used in drip emitter systems. Like sprinkler heads, emitters are sold in a wide variety of styles. They are usually made of plastic. An emitter is a simple device fitted into a flexible ½-inch or ¾-inch-diameter hose. Some emitters have extensions made of small (⅛-inch) tubing that extends from the emitter. These are used to water various points around a tree or several shrubs. Emitters operate under very low pressure.

WATERING-SYSTEM TERMS

Besides the equipment involved in a watering system, there are some common terms you need to understand to design a system and choose equipment.

Flow rate: The flow rate is expressed in gallons per minute (gpm), a measure of how many gallons pass through a meter, pipe, or head every minute. Every sprinkler head has a minimum number of gallons per minute at which it will operate properly; thus, the system must be designed so the last head (the one farthest from the valve) receives at least the flow it needs to operate. Flow rate is a function of pressure.

Frequency and period: Frequency indicates how often a given area is watered. Period refers to the length of time that a given area is watered. For example, a lawn area might be set up (on a controller) to be watered twice a week (this would be the frequency) for a period of 45 minutes. Many combinations of frequency and period are available if you use a controller.

Lateral lines: Lateral lines receive water from the main line through a valve and are typically smaller than the main line. Each lateral line has its own valve. These lines are not pressurized when the system is not operating. Heads are attached to the lateral lines by means of risers.

Main line: The main line carries the supply of water under pressure from the meter through the back-flow preventer to valves, where it is distributed to lateral lines and then to the heads. The main line is the largest line in the system. There may be only one main line, or there may be several, depending on system design.

Pressure: Pressure measures the force exerted against the walls of a pipe or head and is expressed in pounds per square inch (psi). You must know the pressure and flow rate of your system in order to select sprinkler heads correctly. Typically, a head might be designated as operating with 20 gpm at 40 psi. As pressure is reduced, the amount of flow is usually reduced.

Gate Valves A gate valve is a manually operated valve installed on the main line between the meter and back-flow preventer so that the entire system can be shut down in case of emergency or for repairs. Gate valves are convenient but not required; many systems are installed with no such device. Other systems have several valves at critical points. This device is called a gate valve because of the way it operates: When the handle is turned, a gate within the valve rises to allow water to pass through.

Quick-Coupling Valves Known as a QCV or quick-coupler, this type of valve is much like a hose bibb. It is installed on a main (pressure) line; the top sits flush with the grade, and a flip cap permits insertion of a coupler. The coupler is attached to a hose or sprinkler and, when turned, opens the valve. QCVs are sometimes distributed around the garden so hoses can be plugged in to allow hand-watering where necessary. Some inexpensive systems use QCVs only—instead of permanent sprinkler heads—into which heads are manually inserted and removed.

Check Valves A check valve is a small device installed at the base of a sprinkler head or within a pipe run that allows water to flow in one direction only. Check valves are used on lines that are on a slope to prevent water in the system from continuing to flow out of the heads when the automatic valve is closed.

Drain Valves These valves also come in various sizes and types and are used primarily to drain the system in freezing weather. The valves are set at the low end of the system and can be opened to allow all residual water to drain out.

Hose Bibbs A hose bibb—you probably call it the outside faucet—is perhaps the most common irrigation component around the home. It is a spigot protruding from the house wall or mounted on a standpipe to which a hose can be attached. A hose bibb is a necessity for access to water outdoors, regardless of whether you have a watering system. You may want to add hose bibbs near new activity areas for cleanup and water access.

Meters The water meter is installed on your property between the house and the municipal supply line, ahead of the back-flow preventer and the connection to the house supply. It measures the amount of water being used both in the house and by the outdoor watering system. Meters come in various sizes; the bigger the meter, the more water can flow through it. Chances are, a meter will already be in place when you purchase your house or plan your site. Meters are usually installed by the local utility company; check with them if you cannot locate a meter near your home.

Back-flow Preventers A back-flow preventer is installed in the service line leading from the municipal supply main to the house. It is located on the house side of the meter, downstream from the connection to the house potable water supply. The purpose of this device is to prevent any water that has flowed back into the watering system from reaching the city water supply or mixing with the potable water system for the house. Virtually every community requires that one of these devices be installed if a watering system is planned. This rule is for the common good, to prevent contaminants from reaching general water supplies, and should be adhered to in all cases.

The most common back-flow preventers are also called antisiphon valves, vacuum breakers, and atmospheric breakers. These are simple, inexpensive devices that operate on the principle of atmospheric pressure: Air is allowed to enter the highest point of the system to break any vacuum that could siphon water back into the main supply. The need to mount an atmospheric breaker above the highest point of the system can sometimes be a problem; if it is too high in the air, it may be unsightly. Some municipalities require only an atmospheric breaker for residential use. More sophisticated back-flow preventers, involving check valves and pressure operation, are used on larger commercial systems. Be sure to check local codes for requirements.

Costs for Watering Systems

The cost of installing a watering system depends on the size and sophistication of the system. The least expensive means of getting water to lawns and plants is to hand-water. This involves providing plenty of hose bibbs around the exterior of the house, as well as plenty of hoses, so you can access all of the areas of the site.

Because establishing and nurturing plants and lawns takes a great deal of time, a watering system can save you hundreds of hours of labor over the years. If your free time is limited or you travel frequently, a watering system may be a sound investment, especially if your landscape areas are large.

Quick-coupler systems are the least expensive watering systems. They require a water meter connection, a back-flow preventer and manual shutoff valve, main line, quick-coupling valves, and a supply of plug-in quick-couplers that you move from place to place. Although this is a manual system, it is permanent and takes less time than hand-watering. It can also be upgraded later into an automatic system. Prorate the installation cost over the life of the system and you will find this an especially sound investment.

Automatic systems are more expensive to install than manual ones, and the more automatic the system, the higher the cost. Each sprinkler head, each zone, and each control valve adds to the cost. You can save by minimizing the number of zones.

Because about 50 percent of all domestic water use is devoted to outdoor watering, drip systems can save you money due to lowering water consumption. If you have a heavy financial investment in plants and you live in an area where water conservation is critical, drip systems make sense. The cost of installation is no higher than for other conventional watering systems. The advantage is that water enters the soil slowly and naturally, thereby minimizing runoff, evaporation, and costly erosion.

Design Guidelines for Your Watering System

To be successful, an irrigation system must be carefully integrated with grading, drainage, planting,

DRAINING THE LINE IN FREEZING CLIMATES

In areas where the ground freezes to the depth of the irrigation lines, the lines must be drained each fall to prevent water in them from freezing and rupturing the pipe. This is most easily done with automatic drain valves, which drain the line automatically every time the water is shut off.

To enable the line to drain completely, slope the pipe toward each drain valve. Every low spot in the system of lines must be drained with an automatic drain valve, so the more carefully you plan the slope, the fewer valves you will need.

Wherever a valve is to be installed, dig an area about 1 foot square, to the side of the ditch. It should be about 8 inches deeper than the ditch. Place a tee in the line and install the drain so it slopes down slightly from the pipe. Slip a short length of pipe over it to protect the opening. Add drain rock or gravel, filling the hole and covering the drain. Lay a sheet of plastic film across the gravel. Backfill the hole, covering the plastic with soil. The drain valve will drain the line into the pocket of gravel.

DRAIN VALVE

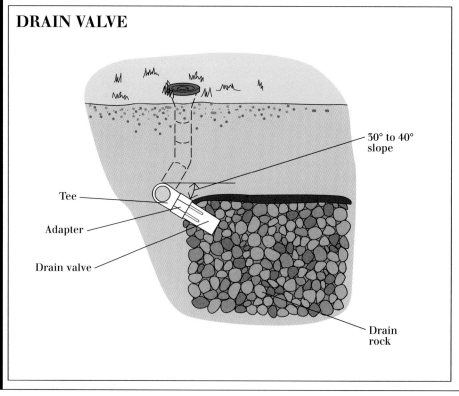

30° to 40° slope

Tee

Adapter

Drain valve

Drain rock

and structures. Since most of a watering system is underground, it is especially important to plan its layout and installation thoroughly so it does not interfere with lighting circuits and drain lines and does not have to be unearthed later for changes or additions.

You must have your planting plan fairly well worked out before you design the irrigation system. The reason for this is obvious—you have to know the type of plants and the extent of planting before you can design a system to water them.

Find out the size of the water meter and of the service line from the street. To do this, locate the meter, open the meter box, and look at the number stamped on the fitting leading out of the meter. It will be ½, ⅝, or ¾, indicating the size in inches. If this does not work, someone at the water company should be able to tell you the meter size and service line size as well as the pressure in the main line. You can use a water-pressure gauge to determine the amount of water pressure you have. It will indicate the pressure in pounds per square inch (psi). Your design will depend almost entirely on the amount and pressure of water available.

If you're contemplating a manual system that will operate during the day, do not fail to take house needs into account. Running sprinklers, a washing machine, a shower, and toilets simultaneously may demand more water than is available through the service line and meter.

Always keep in mind that different types of plants require different heads and separate valves. For example, lawn grass requires more frequent and heavier watering than ground cover, so lawn heads and heads for ground cover should not be controlled by the same valve. Use a separate valve for shrubs as well. Select heads for lawn, ground cover, shrubs, and flowers for their adaptability to watering need. Use lawn heads for watering lawns, and bubblers for shrubs and flower beds. Do not use different types of heads on one lateral line; for example, don't put a bubbler on the same lateral line as a pop-up lawn head.

As discussed in the grading and drainage sections, soil conditions figure prominently in the amount of water you can apply at once. If the site features hard, nearly impenetrable soil, you will probably have to water more frequently and for shorter periods. In such cases it would be better to water twice a day for a short period to allow the water to soak in rather than run off.

Frequency and period are also a function of slope. If the ground is steep, water is likely to run off rather than penetrate if too much is applied at one time. In this case or with hard soils, choose heads that release water at a fairly slow rate, and consider installing more heads to distribute water evenly.

Spacing refers to how far apart heads are placed. The coverage of each head should overlap that of an adjacent head by nearly 100 percent to help prevent dry spots. This means that water thrown from one head should almost touch the next head. Irrigation catalogs specify the diameter of coverage for any given head. When fitting heads into odd-shaped corners, add an extra one when in doubt to ensure complete coverage.

Check for obstructions that might interfere with the spray pattern. Low, overhanging branches, a tree trunk, a large shrub, a retaining wall, or a pole can cause inadequate coverage and dry spots. If this is the case, install extra heads so that all areas around the obstruction are covered properly.

Wind is another factor to consider. If your garden, or any part of it, is subject to frequent strong winds, you must use more heads and make the spacing between them even smaller to account for wind distortion of the spray pattern.

Trimming refers to designing the system and selecting and spacing heads so that water will not be thrown onto paved surfaces or structures. The reason that heads come in full-, half-, and quarter-circle patterns and have different and adjustable coverages is to avoid wasting water or flooding an area where water is not needed. You will want to trim irrigation coverage to the edges of terraces, driveways, walks, and decks. Also be careful to place heads so that water will not backspray onto structure walls, thereby staining or damaging them. Place heads a few feet in from the edge of a driveway or street, so vehicles will not run over the heads and damage them.

Climate obviously has a great deal to do with the extent and type of watering system you'll install. If the site is mostly in the shade, you will not need to water as often and perhaps can get by with a less sophisticated system. Conversely, a sunny garden or one in a hot climate will require more frequent watering and more positive coverage, and hence more heads and larger components. In areas subject to freezing, the system should be designed so it can be drained in the fall—or winterized—to prevent bursting pipes.

Mount the controller in a convenient place where it is out of weather. Inside a garage is a good location. The controller will require 120 volts for operation, which is normal house current. You need to give some thought to the low-voltage control wires that run from the controller to the valves. They must be conducted through the wall or floor slab of the garage or other enclosure to the outside, and they must connect with each of the valves.

If you decide to use a manual system, lay out at least the manual valves so they can be "manifolded," that is, grouped together, so you can turn valves on and off from one location.

Calculate flow rates to determine the system's requirements. Remember that only one valve operates at a time. One sure way to tell whether all of the heads will operate properly is to take the longest line with the most heads on it and determine, using catalog information, how much flow the pipe will carry, how much each head requires, and whether there is sufficient pressure and flow at the last head to operate it. If the last head on the longest lateral will work, all of the other heads on the other laterals will work too.

Drawing Watering System Plans

Your watering system plan will be based on information from your master plan (see page 91). Make several copies of the master plan for sketching and studying.

Begin your sketches by drawing heads for different plant types at the spacing recommended by the manufacturer. Indicate the extent of coverage with circles, with the head at the center. See if the coverage overlaps sufficiently.

After laying out the heads, try connecting them in each area with a lateral line for each type of plant. Calculate the flow rate and pressure each lateral will require to operate the heads connected to it. If there is not enough pressure for all of the heads, try using more laterals until each will operate properly.

The larger the head and the higher the pressure required to operate it, the fewer heads can be installed on one lateral line.

After the laterals are laid out, plan the route of the main line. Strive to cross the shortest possible distance and to avoid obstacles. At every point where a lateral connects to the main line, a valve will be required. Indicate these on your sketches.

Next evaluate the flow through the meter, back-flow preventer, and main line, and see whether the water flowing through the entire system, from meter to most distant head, is sufficient to properly operate that farthest head. If not, try larger pipe sizes, more laterals and valves, and different heads. Try several alternatives. When you are satisfied, transfer the sketch information to a clean copy of the master plan. This is your watering plan.

PREPARING THE SITE

Before you begin installing the new landscape, you must clear the site of all elements you do not intend to retain—debris, weeds, and other unwanted vegetation, as well as constructed items such as old paving, posts, walls, trellises, and buildings. Before you start clearing the site, give some thought to how you are going to remove all the debris and where you will dispose of it. If you plan to use an existing element in the landscape but in a different location, you need to figure out where you can store it while you work out the installation. See the information on page 148 on protecting existing plants.

Whether you choose to clear the site before you finalize your design or wait until you are ready to begin installation will depend on your schedule and the condition of the site. Don't clear away debris until you have decided on a grading plan, as you may be able to use rubble to build up low areas. Avoid clearing away every item on the lot before you decide on the final landscape design—you may change your mind and decide to use an existing structure or planting after all. Obviously, if you do not plan to work on the entire site, you will need to clear only those areas in which you plan to work. However, if you need to work on different parts of the site, either now or in the near future, it is a good idea

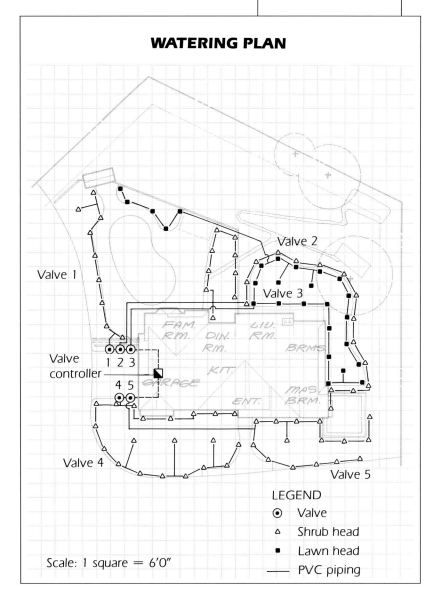

WATERING PLAN

Valve 1

Valve 2

Valve 3

Valve controller

Valve 4

Valve 5

LEGEND
- ◉ Valve
- △ Shrub head
- ▪ Lawn head
- —— PVC piping

Scale: 1 square = 6'0"

PROTECTING TREES

A mature tree is a valuable asset and should be protected during construction as much as possible. Wrapping the bark with tree tape or cloth will help protect it from nicks and cuts. Most of the roots of trees are within the top 2 feet of soil. Care should be taken during construction to disturb this soil as little as possible.

Ideally, no grading or soil movement should be done within the drip line of the tree. To determine the drip line, imagine a perpendicular line dropped from the outermost branches of the tree to the ground. Many trees depend on the roots within this zone to satisfy the majority of their water needs. Keep heavy construction materials out of this area, as the weight may compact the soil and restrict the flow of water to the roots. A temporary barrier can be constructed at the drip line to protect this area.

Never add soil above the existing soil level of a tree, and never cut deeply into the soil around the base of a tree. If it is necessary to have a level ground area around the tree, it is far preferable to construct a low deck or platform around the tree than to attempt to change the soil immediately adjacent to the tree base.

If you need to raise the grade slightly in the vicinity of an existing tree, build a rock retaining wall around the tree to form a well; this will keep soil away from the tree trunk.

Modern equipment makes it possible to move even large trees. If the tree is a healthy, desirable specimen, it may be worth the expense and effort required to move it to a better location. A reliable tree service will be able to evaluate the tree's condition and give you an estimate of the cost to move it.

If there are no other options but to disturb the soil around the tree, leave as much undisturbed soil next to the trunk as possible.

to take care of all the clearing and removal at one time, though constant cleanup during construction is wise as well.

Probably the easiest way to remove a lot of refuse is to rent a debris box from the garbage company. The box is usually delivered to your house, set either on the street or in your yard if access and space are available, and then picked up at an agreed-upon time. These boxes are large, so give some consideration to their placement. If you have access to a truck or if the debris to be cleared away is small, you may be able to bag up everything and haul it away yourself or leave it for regular collection.

First pick up the easiest and most obvious debris and trash. You may want to hire someone to do this, but

supervise the job. Make sure that it is done properly and that your helper doesn't rip out things you want preserved.

Removing structures can take a lot of work. They must usually be disassembled first. For paving, you can try a large breaker bar, pounding it up and down on the surface to break up concrete or asphalt. For large areas or thick paving, you may want to rent a pneumatic jackhammer or hire someone to do the work. If you are removing existing brick or flagstone paving and want to save and reuse the materials, you must remove each piece separately, and carefully chip off mortar and dirt.

Wood structures such as fences, decks, and outbuildings should be knocked apart first and nails carefully removed. If possible, fence posts should be pulled out or at least cut off at the soil line.

Some weeds pose a problem. If you just cut them off or till them in, they will come back. They will return from two sources: from roots and stems of perennial weeds left in the ground, and from seeds in the soil. The best way to eliminate perennial weeds is to spray them with a systemic herbicide—a weed killer that travels through the entire plant, including roots, killing all the parts. This must be done while the plant is actively growing so the herbicide can be carried to the roots.

Seeds are difficult to eliminate as seeds, but easy as seedling plants. Land that has been fallow for more than a few months is probably full of weed seeds. Plan a delay of a few weeks between the final grading and planting. After the final grading is done and the soil is ready for planting, water it well and keep it damp to encourage weed seeds to germinate. After a couple of weeks, but before any of the new weeds have a chance to set seed, kill them with an herbicide. To avoid bringing additional seeds to the surface to germinate, don't stir the soil any more than necessary for planting after this operation.

Shrub and tree removal can be difficult. Small shrubs can usually be dug out, roots and all; at least dig out most of the roots. To get rid of unwanted trees, top them, cut off all large limbs, then cut off the trunk at ground level. You may want to hire a tree service to do the heavy work. Many trees and shrubs will resprout if their roots are left in the ground; to avoid this, apply a brush-killing herbicide to the trunk. If the trunk is not in the way, cut it off just below ground level and leave the stump. Over time, the roots will rot away and leave a depression in the soil. If it is important that the trunk base and most of the roots be removed, you may need to hire help. Trying to remove the stump of a large tree yourself can be an arduous task.

To remove lawn, strip it out with a shovel or, to make a faster job of it, rent a sod stripper. Stripped sod can be stacked upside down and kept moist to make a fine compost. In about a year, add it to garden soil. If you want to save the sod for later use, strip it off, along with about 1 inch of soil, using a sod cutter. Cut it into strips 12 to 18 inches wide, lay them out flat in a shady, out-of-the-way place, and keep them moist.

Establishing the Layout

Once the land is cleared and you have planned your installation, but before you begin buying materials and constructing landscape elements—that is, before you begin spending money—you should do a final analysis of your master plan. This process will take you outside for a final design step known as establishing the layout; it will take only a few hours. This step is done mainly as a reassurance that the master plan has been drawn correctly and that everything will actually fit in the available space. It will also give you a chance to see, albeit roughly, how the new landscape will look. Establish your layout by marking onto the ground the lines of the activity areas shown on the master plan.

First mark on the master plan the definitive points of the landscape— the corners of planting beds and points on the outside curve of a path or the perimeter of a pool, for example. Then go out to the site and, measuring from an established point in the yard such as a corner of the house, place a marker at the points that are represented by the marks on the master plan. Wood stakes or piles of rocks make excellent markers. Once you have established the main points of each activity area, run string between the stakes or lay rope between the piles of rocks to define each element in your design. Rocks, boards, and garden hoses can act as boundary dividers. You can draw lines with agricultural lime dribbled from your hand or a trowel. If none of the existing paving materials are to be retained, establish the layout by drawing lines on the ground with spray paint.

Once all of the lines on the master plan have been repeated on the ground, spend some time walking around the new landscape. Bring out chairs and sit on what will be the patio. Walk down the paths. Verify that everything you have designed feels right before you break ground to install the landscape.

Opposite: Careful planning and installation of electrical lines helped turn this ground-level deck and shade structure into an outdoor dining room.

BUILDING OUTDOOR STRUCTURES

THE IMPORTANCE OF CONSTRUCTION EXPERTISE

If you like working with your hands and have had some experience in home improvements, you can probably install all of your landscaping yourself. In most cases the expertise of general home repair is all that you will need to install outdoor structures. There are exceptions, however. Material choices, some tools, the timing of construction, and construction principles are different for outdoor construction than they are for building most indoor features. A small error in laying out the site of a patio can be disastrous, for instance, as there is no give and take in the construction material: Poured concrete cannot be moved once it is in place. The fact that these elements must withstand all types of weather must be considered in the materials you choose and the locations you select. How deep into the ground footings, edgings, and posts must be trenched and the type of wood, metal, and pipe you choose are dependent on climate.

If you plan to hire someone to build your landscape elements, construction expertise will guide you in the choice of the best workers, how much their work is worth, and how long it should take someone to build various features.

Develop a construction schedule identifying all the necessary steps in the project and identify who will do what and when. You may decide to alter your landscape plans once you have determined the particular needs of outdoor construction.

Safety Tips

"A clean job is a safe job" is never more true than when working on outdoor construction projects. Always begin projects on a clean site, and get into the habit of clearing away all scraps of material, dropped nails, and loose tools at the end of each working day.

Install some kind of barricade or temporary fence around excavations and work-in-progress to prevent accidents. Always wear suitable clothing when doing construction work; shorts and sandals are just not appropriate for this kind of activity. Steel-toed boots and long pants prevent injury. Wear heavy work gloves when handling all construction materials; wear safety goggles when sawing and sanding.

Be sure to use only grounded electrical cords for all power tools. Keep all tools sharp and in good working order. Make sure you have and use the proper tool for each job. Accidents are often caused by the improper use of tools. Remember to check codes and regulations before beginning your project (some even limit the time of day that you can work), and check with your insurance carrier about liability, especially if you are hiring help.

TOOLS FOR BUILDING

To start your project, begin by selecting the right tools, which are very important to any project. The proper selection of tools can help take the mystery out of building an outdoor project. Often just having the right tools will make the difference between a project that is built correctly and one that cannot be built at all. Tasks can be done more quickly, safely, and efficiently with the proper tools.

Years ago there were just a few basic tools, made mostly of materi-

als such as wood and drop-forged steel. Today there are so many specialty tools, made with a variety of new materials such as aluminum and plastics, that it is impossible to keep up with them. The array of tools in a store can be very tempting but, unless you are wise in your selection, tools that may have seemed irresistible in the store can lie unused in your basement for years, or at least until the next garage sale.

Even though the array of available tools is staggering, only a few are absolutely essential. Many others can be rented for a weekend for specialized projects. Start with the basic tools and acquire new ones gradually. When you come across a tool you want, stop and evaluate your needs carefully. When in doubt, ask questions—not just of the store clerk but of carpenters, masons, and others whose livelihood depends on owning the right tools.

When you shop for a hand tool, try it out first to test the feel and see if it is balanced well and feels comfortable in your hand. Any tool that you are going to own for a long time should be sized to your grip and weight. A well-made tool will give you many years of service. After doing research on the right tool selection and brands, look for sales of brand-name tools after the holidays, usually in January and February.

Although your landscape projects may not require all of the tools discussed here, you will need tools for basic measuring, layout, carpentry, general construction, and masonry. Most of these have been around a long time and are the bare essentials of the old-fashioned basement workshop.

You will need utility toolboxes to hold all the odds and ends. They should be large but not so big that they will be too heavy when filled with tools. You will probably end up with two toolboxes—a large one and a small one. The most popular large one is approximately 9 inches by 9 inches by 32 inches. This is sometimes called a carpenter's box because it can hold a standard 28-inch crosscut saw.

A small, general-purpose tackle box with a removable top tray is also useful. You will move items in and out of the box as you move from your indoor work area to the yard.

Tool Maintenance

To keep your tools in good working condition, it is important to clean and lubricate them on a regular basis. This will make them last longer and work better. Learn to sharpen tools and fix any nicks as they occur, being careful not to take off too much metal in the process. Wash tools if they are in contact with the soil. Add some penetrating oil before storage to prevent rust.

Tools for Measuring

Standard household measuring instruments are probably all that are necessary for measuring the site when you determine your base plan and as you lay out your design. As you get ready to install landscape features, however, measurements must be accurate and more detailed. Construction projects such as pouring concrete, lining up a fence, and leveling a garden wall demand precision. High-quality measuring tools are a sound investment.

Steel Tape Get a tape measure that is at least 25 feet long, and preferably 50 feet long. These tapes have been used by surveyors for years.

Carpenter's Collapsible 6-foot Rule These wood jewels are very handy. A carpenter's saying is: "Measure twice, cut once." If you don't, it could easily be "Measure once, buy twice," which can be very expensive and time-consuming. This folding rule is invaluable for confirming those final measurements.

Framing Square Made either of steel or wood (if available), a framing square is essential to laying out the initial work so that it is square and true. Squares are L-shaped for measuring right angles, with inch gradations marked on all sides.

Spirit Levels Ideally, you should own three of these: a torpedo level, a carpenter's level, and a line level. A torpedo level is 8 to 12 inches long with at least three bubble tubes and true edges. It is used for small jobs such as framing fences and setting the tops and vertical sides of walls and steps. A 4-foot carpenter's level is indispensable. Most today are made of aluminum, but a real mason prefers wood because it is permanently true (correct). Levels are essential for concrete and masonry work, but they must be cleaned thoroughly after each job. A little mortar left on a level will distort the reading. A line level is a short piece of metal with a bubble tube that can be hung from a taut line to check for horizontal level.

Mason's Line This is a thin but exceptionally strong nylon cord that supports a line level. To obtain an accurate measurement, the line must not sag. A mason's line has the advantage that it can be pulled taut over a considerable distance without sagging. Do not try to use ordinary string, which will stretch and sag.

Plumb Bob With Sheath This tool is for measuring vertical elements such as fence posts and foundations. The best have a sheath to protect the bob tip and allow the string to wind up for storage.

Carpenter's Marking Crayons Usually red or blue, these crayons are used to mark on wood, pavement, and metal surfaces.

Carpenter's Pencil This flat pencil is used to mark dimensions on lumber. Keep a utility knife nearby for sharpening.

Chalk Line This chalk-coated string marks a long, straight line when snapped between two points.

General Carpentry Tools

The same general carpentry tools used for interior home repairs can be used to build outdoor projects. Designate a specific storage area for your tools. One of your first building projects can be to install a perforated board and hooks along the wall of a garage or storage area, where you can store tools, keeping them in plain view and allowing easy access. It is not a bad idea to imprint your name on tools that may be lent out on occasion.

Hammers You should own three hammers for outdoor construction: the familiar 20-ounce rip-claw framing hammer, a 16-ounce curved-claw finishing hammer, and a heavy-duty sledgehammer. The straight rip-claw hammer is useful for heavy-duty chores; its claw is specially designed to give leverage when pulling wood and nails. The curved-claw hammer is used to do light-duty hammering without leaving indentations on the finished surface. The sledgehammer is used to drive posts and columns, break up pavement, and do other general demolition chores. Store hammers in a moderate temperature. Humidity will cause the wood to swell, weakening the handle. Storage in an overly dry or hot area may cause the wood to shrink and the handle to break away from the head. Inspect hammers regularly; if the head is chipped, replace the tool. Damaged heads result in bad nailing, and they can also chip again, sending out metal fragments that may be dangerous to you and those nearby.

Saws A straight-back crosscut saw is used for sawing lumber, plywood, and general surfaces. For cutting metal and plastics, you will need a hacksaw with replaceable blades, preferably with an alternate set of coated blades. Coated blades are especially good for cutting plastic.

Pliers You will need adjustable pliers, 1½-inch channel lock pliers and vise grips. Also consider picking up tin snips.

Files A basic collection of files should include a 6-inch slim taper, an 8-inch rough file with a 7-inch auger bit, and a file brush.

To cut a brick with a brick chisel, score a line all around the brick where you want it cut, then sever it with a sharp blow. If the brick doesn't break evenly, you can trim it with the chisel peen on your brick hammer.

Chisels You will need a butt chisel and a mason's chisel; these are versatile enough for most uses. Cold chisels can be acquired as needed for cutting and shaping metals.

Screwdrivers A strong, sturdy square-shank screwdriver with a ¼-inch blade is a necessity. You will also need a Phillips screwdriver; buy a high-quality one, because the slots go quickly in cheap ones. Choose only screwdrivers with handles made of rubber or, preferably, wood. You may find that only plastic and rubber handles are available.

Awls An assortment of awls in various sizes will be useful for just about any job that requires punching holes through templates or establishing prepunched screw or nail openings in wood and other materials. You may also want to pick up a center punch and putty knives of various sizes.

Tools for Concrete and Masonry

Masonry tools are used for installing walks, steps, and patios, and for general repairs such as repointing brick or patching pavements. Depending on the kind of construction you plan to do, the tools you need for masonry can vary considerably. In addition to the tools listed below, you will need several buckets and a garden hose to wash away silt and debris.

Wheelbarrow The first and most important tool for concrete work is the wheelbarrow. You will need a sturdy one to carry rocks, boulders, soil, gravel, and other backfill material from the stockpile area to the job site. A 5¾-cubic-foot contractor's wheelbarrow with a 4-ply pneumatic tire is the most versatile size. The larger the tire the better. You will appreciate this the first time you use it. Thick wood handles and stable supports help take the strain off your back. Strong supports give reasonable stability while you mix material in the wheelbarrow. The quality of the metal is also important. Generally, the heavier the gauge of metal the better; 18 gauge is the minimum you should consider. If you will be pouring a lot of concrete, select a wheelbarrow with a deep, round nose for easy pouring. If most of the work will be moving soil, a square nose is easier to shovel soil out of. A general-purpose shape, halfway between these two, is also available.

Shovels The two most preferred shovels are a flat mason's shovel and a spade. The flat shovel is useful for spreading and leveling material, and the spade is used for general digging.

Picks and Mattocks A heavy-duty mattock and a pick are essential for construction. Each has a flat side and a pointed side for maximum versatility. These tools are not only essential for digging in difficult clay and rocky soils, but they are indispensable for lifting and removing pavements if you plan to do demolition work.

Trowels Mortar, steel, and margin trowels are used for spreading and smoothing out mortar and concrete and for applying mastic to the backs of tile. Grooving trowels, also known as groovers and joint fillers, are used to construct the joints between pavers.

Floats Floats can be made of magnesium, molded rubber, cork, wood, and aluminum; each type gives a different finish to concrete without marring the texture.

Edgers These tools give a clean, crisp edge to concrete. They are identified by the type of pavement they edge; the types available include sidewalk, highway, curb, and radius edgers.

Screeds Made of magnesium, screeds are sold in several sizes, including 1 by 4 and 2 by 4 and different lengths, from about 2 feet to 6 feet long. They are used to spread pea gravel, sand, and other base material evenly, and for the first pass at leveling concrete. They can also be built of wood at the job site.

Tampers Flat-grill and roller-grill tampers are used to compact and set in place sand, gravel, and dry paving materials such as brick and stone. Simple tampers, for projects such as installing a fence post, can be made from an old tool handle or length of pipe.

Power Tools

Most power tools can be rented, although you may want to purchase them if you own your home and plan to do more than one project.

Placing a layer of black plastic sheeting with holes for drainage beneath a dry creek bed helps prevent weed intrusion and contain the rocks. Using the proper tools can make your job easier and safer. A flat mason's shovel works well for redistributing rocks. Be careful that you don't pick up too many at once.

All power tools should be handled safely and used only for their intended purpose. Check the power source and make sure that everything is grounded. Buy only high-quality extension cords, especially those that are 50 or 100 feet long. See that the cords are UL approved for outdoor use.

Circular Saw The single best power tool, the versatile circular saw can save hours of lumber and plywood sawing. It can be used like a miter box for making angle cuts, and it can also serve as a radial arm saw when purchased with a bench mate. Buy a 7¼-inch size with at least 2¼ horsepower. Pay a little more for the better model with sealed bearings and other features that will guarantee durability.

Reversing Power Drill The most common power drill is a ⅜-inch size with variable speed. Newer models can vary the torque as the speed is changed, which gives greater versatility. Use one whenever you're working with fasteners, wood screws, and other connections. The ability to reverse direction speeds up installation and correction of errors.

Power Saber Saw This saw is particularly good for sawing in difficult quarters and on vertical surfaces. It is also very light. You will need a medium- or heavy-duty one with ⅓ horsepower and a ⅝-inch stroke. A two-speed reciprocating saw is useful but not as versatile as the saber saw, mainly because there are so many types of blades available for the saber saw.

Renting Versus Buying Tools

The list of basic tools is certainly not a small one. You do not have to go out and buy everything at once. Treat the basic tool needs like a

shopping list that you add to as time goes by. For some projects, you may need even more tools than the ones cited here; or you may just be starting out and choose not to buy many tools because of space or budget constraints. Almost anything can be rented. You should rent rather than buy certain power tools, such as augers and power compactors. They take up a lot of space, are used only rarely, and are very expensive. Most communities have reputable equipment-rental businesses; check the local telephone directory.

Allow yourself plenty of time for constructing your projects when you rent equipment, because most accidents occur when you rush; look for weekend rates to give yourself extra time. If possible, browse around a few places in advance of a contemplated project simply to gain an understanding of what is available and how various tools can help you.

Many tools—especially compressors, generators, sprayers, and sandblasters—are heavy and dangerous to use. Any tool can be dangerous if used incorrectly. Whenever you rent or purchase an unfamiliar tool, be certain that you receive full instruction and have trained store personnel demonstrate the tool before you attempt to use it. Wear appropriate safety clothing and use common sense when working with any tool.

MATERIALS FOR BUILDING

The success of your design will ultimately be based on your installation—on how you execute the design and the materials you choose. The durability of construction materials is vital. Generally, it is better to consider substitutions rather than lessen the quality of materials. There is no excuse for using materials that won't last, because so many durable materials are available. The durability of a material is determined by its life expectancy and how well it weathers.

Permanent outdoor structures must be sealed and protected to keep them from deteriorating in the elements. All materials weather. You must spend a little extra to build permanence into a structure. The more sophisticated the detailing, the connections, and the base or support, the more costly the structure. You can trim costs by keeping the materials and connections simple and minimizing cutting and drilling.

One way to save money while maintaining appearances is to use a lower grade of materials for parts that will not show, such as material that will back up a finished surface or the portions of structures that will be buried, covered over, or otherwise hidden by the finish construction.

Building With Wood

Wood is a favorite material for the home. It exudes warmth, is natural, and is easy to work with. It is also durable, is resilient and therefore comfortable to walk on when used for a deck, and reflects heat, a significant consideration for a seating material. The flexibility of wood allows it to meet a number of budgetary, structural, and appearance criteria.

Wood is manufactured in a variety of ways to frame, underlay, or finish surfaces. All wood can be stained, oiled, bleached, left natural (to weather), or painted. You can paint or stain wood to match existing structures. Wood can be made to look formal or informal, depending on your needs. It is used for fences, screens, decks, trellises,

arbors, and other outdoor structures; railroad ties are often used for steps and walls. Wood, in fact, can be incorporated into almost any outdoor project.

You can install wood at almost any time of year, except during severe winters. You may need help framing decks and the like, but you will soon discover that the primary tasks necessary for success are accurate measurements and sawing and solid connections. Good carpentry takes time. Wood does not have to be expensive to look good, but it is definitely not an inexpensive material. The grade of lumber dictates the cost. High-grade wood can last 50 to 100 years or more in an outdoor setting (think of old barns); cheap wood lasts less than 10 years.

The annual growth rings of a tree determine the grain. If the rings are narrow and close together, as they are in pine, the wood is said to be close grained. If the rings are wide and farther apart, as they are

All fences are made up of the same three components: posts, rails, and infill. The materials you choose, such as the redwood shown here, and the finishing techniques you employ will depend on your landscape style and your construction expertise.

in oak, the wood is said to be coarse grained. Close-grained wood is preferable to coarse-grained wood. This is the difference between softwood and hardwood.

The way a board is cut from a log makes it strong or weak, so it is sometimes the grain in wood that makes or breaks a project. Before a log is sawed into boards, its rounded edges are sawed off to form a square. This square log is then cut into boards.

The grain in each board or joist is visible. If the grain makes an angle of 45 degrees or more with the sides of a board, the lumber is said to be vertical grained in softwoods and quartersawed in hardwoods. If the angle is less than 45 degrees, the board is said to be flat grained in softwoods and plain sawed in hardwoods. When the grain is random and undifferentiated, it is called mixed grain. Boards or 2×4s made of vertical-grained lumber, which has a straight grain at the top, are stronger than those made of flat-grained lumber; quartersawed boards make the best floors.

When the grain runs off to one side, the board may split and look unattractive if given a natural finish. When appearance matters, this "checked" lumber should be avoided. Avoid also, if possible, boards that have knots, are warped, and that show signs of decay. To avoid warp, select cypress, Douglas fir, pine, maple, oak, birch, walnut, or redwood, and use vertical-grained softwoods or quartersawed hardwoods.

Pressure-Treated Lumber Unless it is left to weather naturally, wood will need periodic maintenance. It is flammable and, when in contact with the earth, decays quickly. Termites are a constant problem. However, wood can be treated by a process of injecting preservatives under pressure, causing the preservative to become locked permanently into the wood. Such pressure-treated lumber is far superior to wood that has been merely sprayed or dipped in a chemical preservative. In many cases it will outlast naturally durable species such as redwood, cedar, or cypress. Pressure-treated lumber is recommended when wood will be buried or subject to ground contact; some codes actually demand that it be used.

The most common types of chemicals used for pressure-treating lumber are waterborne salts such as chromated copper arsenate (CCA) and ammoniacal copper arsenate (ACA). These preservatives are recommended where the wood will be close to plants; they can be used safely around the home except on surfaces that will be in direct contact with food or serving utensils. Other preservatives used are pentachlorophenol and creosote, but they are very toxic, prohibited in some jurisdictions, and the lumber cannot be painted or stained as easily as lumber treated with CCA or ACA. Penta applied with liquid petroleum gas is an exception.

Pressure-treated lumber is slightly green or beige in color and does not darken if left to weather. When buying it, specify whether it is for ground contact or aboveground use. Sometimes it is incised or punctured on the surface to facilitate the penetration of chemicals. For projects where a smooth, unblemished appearance is critical, always ask for pressure-treated lumber without incisement. It is also worth the extra cost to buy lumber that is kiln dried after treatment (KDAT) to avoid extensive warping in exposed outdoor applications.

When handling and cutting pressure-treated lumber, wear gloves, goggles, and a dust mask—especially if the wood is damp. Do not leave pressure-treated lumber around the work site where it can be picked up by someone who doesn't know how to handle it properly. Do not burn scraps of pressure-treated lumber; dispose of them in an approved landfill. For best results on outdoor construction projects, coat the ends of cut boards with an approved preservative. For children's play equipment, sun decks, and benches, use redwood or western red cedar (*Thuja plicata*) where the lumber will be in contact with skin on a regular basis.

Building With Brick

Brick is a familiar, warmly attractive building material that ages beautifully and can be used in a variety of ways. The ancient Romans built brickwork 2,000 years ago that still stands today. Brick can be used in numerous construction projects. It can be purchased or cut into many shapes and sizes. The multitude of available colors provide a great variety as well; the color of brick depends on the original clay used. As a paving material, brick outshines all others because it is comfortable to walk on, appears natural, and is easily repaired. If one or two bricks are broken and need to be replaced, the pattern is not disrupted, nor does it look patched as concrete does.

Brick is available in a wide variety of textures; your choice will depend on the intended use. A smoothly finished brick may be perfect for a patio, but because it is slippery when wet and may reflect too much glare in the summer, it is not recommended around a pool. Used brick, on the other hand, is sometimes considered too rough to provide a comfortable playing

surface, but may be perfectly suited for garden walls or edgings.

Bricks for landscape floors can be laid in several basic patterns and can be altered and combined to produce myriad individual effects. Some patterns are more complicated than others and may require more bricks and a knowledge of brick cutting, but the final result may be spectacular. Try different patterns until you find the one that best fits your budget and masonry experience.

When employed as a facing material for a wall, the use of brick can result in multiple patterns and heights. It, like wood, is a relatively easy material with which to work.

Brick is also an interesting edging material for walks, driveways, planting areas, or patios. With brick you will find that placement technique—end-to-end, side-by-side, or face-to-face—greatly affects the final appearance of the element being edged.

In recent years a great deal has been learned about the damage to

When carefully planned and installed, many different construction materials can be successfully combined in one landscape. Brick patches add color and contrast to a concrete slab patio at a lower cost than that required to cover it completely with brick, and the brick accent ties the patio and the path together.

brick walls caused by water. Damage from freeze/thaw cycles, efflorescence, corrosion of metal supports, and differential settling are all a direct result of water damage. In order to avoid these problems when building with brick, it is important to protect wall cavities and use sound design practices.

Paving Brick Your choice of paving brick will depend on absorption rate, compressive strength, and size. Most suppliers will have this information readily available. A low water-absorption rate of 8 percent is desirable. As the

absorption rate goes up, the brick is more susceptible to freeze/thaw cycles and resultant damage.

Compressive strength can vary from 3,000 to 20,000 psi. Good paving bricks will withstand at least 8,000 psi. A woman in high-heeled shoes can exert as much as 1,000 psi. The higher the compressive strength, the better the brick can withstand wear and tear.

All brick sizes are not available from all manufacturers. Familiarize yourself with the sizes available in your area. The most standard size is 2¼ by 3¾ by 8 inches. Others are: Roman, 1½ by 4 by 12 inches; Norman, 2 by 4 by 12 inches; and paving brick, 3½ by 4 by 8 inches. Because the names of bricks vary from place to place, it is better to specify them by size.

Brick to be used in landscaping should conform to the severe weather (SW) designation described as ASTM C 216 or C 652. (These are the standards established by the American Society for Testing and Materials, a national organization of users and producers of materials.) This grade requires a minimum average compressive strength of 8,000 psi and an 8-percent absorption rate. Consider interlocking concrete pavers as an alternative to clay brick.

The use of salvaged brick is acceptable for outdoor construction, if you know where it came from and if you know it has weathered over a long period of time. Otherwise, you have no way of knowing whether it is strong and resistant to weathering unless you test each and every brick. This is a time-consuming task. If you are unsure of the strength of some salvaged brick, consider using it in nonstress features in the landscape such as lawn edgings, to line planting beds, or for some other decorative use.

BRICK PATTERNS FOR PATHS AND PATIOS

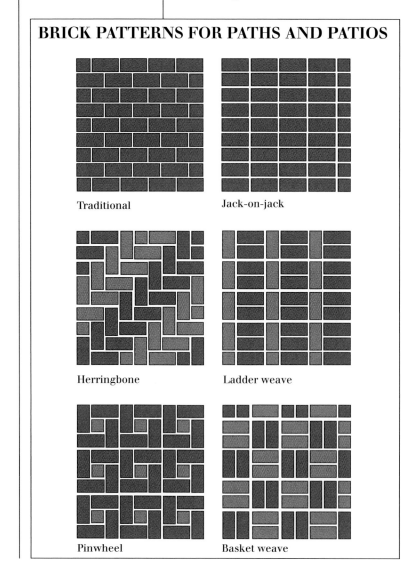

Traditional

Jack-on-jack

Herringbone

Ladder weave

Pinwheel

Basket weave

Facing Brick for Walls Type designations specify the permissible range of color and size variations in brick. Facing brick is classified into three types: FBX, FBS, and FBA. Type FBX brick is used in exposed masonry where a uniform color and size is desired. Type FBS, a general-purpose brick, permits a wider range of colors and sizes than type FBX. Type FBA brick is used in exposed masonry where nonuniformity of color, size, and texture is desired for a particular architectural effect. Hollow brick, used as a wall veneer to reduce weight, is classified into four types: HBX, HBS, HBA, and HBB. The first three types correspond to types FBX, FBS, and FBA. Type HBB hollow brick corresponds to building brick (C 652). Facing brick has been treated to produce a surface that shows a special effect in texture or color. Building brick is "common" brick. Both HBB brick and building brick can be used as backup material or in exposed masonry where color and texture are not a consideration.

Mortar for Brick The primary function of mortar is to cement individual bricks together so they act as one masonry unit. Mortar has a great effect on the performance of masonry. If it does not perform its function properly, undesirable effects may result; for example, moisture may enter a wall, lowering the strength of the masonry and causing it to crack and disintegrate. Masonry that is held together by poor mortar will not last.

High-performance mortars contain four basic materials. These are portland cement (ASTM C 150) Type I, II, or III; hydrated lime (ASTM C 207) Type S; aggregate (sand and/or gravel) with good gradations (ASTM C 144); and water. The five types of mortar—M, S, N, O, and K—are made by varying the proportions of these ingredients. Each type of mortar has specific properties that allow it to perform best under certain conditions. Only types M, S, and N are recommended for exterior use. Type M should be used for below-grade walls, retaining walls, pools, fountains, drainage, walks, patios, and paving. Type S should be used for garden walls that will be subjected to high winds. Type N should be used for garden walls that will be subjected to moderate winds, for masonry elements that will be exposed to weathering on both sides, and for patches, repair, and renovation work when the original type of mortar used is unknown.

Building With Concrete

Concrete is inexpensive, versatile, and very durable. As a material it has often been abused, and it must be placed with considerable thought for lasting results. Concrete is adaptable to a variety of forms and shapes. It is almost plastic in nature, conforming to the shape of its contained form as it sets up.

Concrete is made by mixing specific amounts of cement, sand, gravel, and water. The mix is commonly called 1-2-3 because it is approximately 1 part cement, 2 parts sand, and 3 parts stone. If you are mixing concrete yourself, 1 cubic foot of concrete will require 24 pounds of cement, 39 pounds of sand, and 70 pounds of aggregate stone. With water, the final weight is approximately 150 pounds per cubic foot.

Cement comprises finely ground lime, clay, and gypsum. When mixed with water, a chemical reaction causes it to harden. Type I portland cement is most commonly used in concrete and is best suited for general purposes. Cement has no structure by itself. It needs the

PAVING-MATERIALS COST COMPARISON

A cost comparison of paving materials is given below. The composite estimate for each pavement type assumes a 12-inch base of crushed stone and normal installation. It also assumes that the material is available in your area. Use a factor of $1.25 for each comparative index below. A price index of 1 indicates that the material costs are approximately $1.25 per square foot (in 1995 prices). Bituminous concrete has an index of 2 (or approximately $2.50 per square foot), poured-in-place concrete has an index of 3, and so forth, up to granite, which has an index of 20. Assuming normal inflation over the years, the differences in cost among the various materials should remain the same. Production, installation, and transportation are the main reasons for this price spread.

Index	Material
1	Crushed stone
2	Bituminous concrete
3	Poured-in-place concrete
4	Exposed-aggregate concrete
5	Precast concrete pavers
6	Unit pavers—asphalt block
6	Unit pavers—precast concrete
6	Brick pavers on stone dust
6	Tile on concrete base
7	Precast pavers on asphalt
7	Brick pavers on asphalt
12	Flagstone on sand
15	Cut stone on sand
18	Slate on concrete base
18	Marble on concrete base
20	Granite on concrete base

other ingredients to give it strength as a paving and structural material.

Aggregate makes up 60 to 80 percent of the volume of concrete. The characteristics of the aggregate thus have a considerable influence on the mix proportions and on the economy of the concrete. Fine aggregates, such as sand, give little structural strength but weigh less. Coarse, angular aggregates, such as crushed stone, give a denser, more solid concrete. There are many choices in between. A ¾-inch stone aggregate is sufficient for most home landscape projects. Aggregate must be free of dirt, silt, clay, mica, salts, and humus—all will affect the bond of the cement paste.

The purpose of water in the concrete mix is to hydrate the cement, coat the aggregate, and permit the mix to be worked. Too much water leads to soupy concrete that will not be strong. Too little water yields a mixture that is too stiff to be workable. Any water that is fit to drink is suitable for mixing with cement. It must not contain sulfates, which contribute to the deterioration or failure of concrete.

Concrete is measured in cubic yards. One cubic yard of concrete will cover 80 square feet (with a 4-inch-thick slab). Concrete is available premixed in bags. Although these bags are expensive, the mix is properly proportioned, and for very small projects it is simpler than mixing your own. It takes about 10 minutes to mix a cubic foot of concrete by hand. Premixed, bagged concrete is not practical for projects that require much more than half a cubic yard. Rent a mixer for small- to medium-sized projects and mix what you need, as you need it. Larger projects will require transit-mix concrete from a truck. These trucks hold 9 cubic yards of concrete. A project requiring the entire contents of a fully loaded transit-mix concrete truck is, in fact, the origin of the phrase "the whole nine yards." Check the Yellow Pages for concrete companies in your area. Some suppliers will deliver only a cubic yard or two, usually with a surcharge for a small quantity.

The mix you choose will depend on the type of construction project. Stiff or heavy aggregate mixes are for foundations and footings; lighter aggregates are for slabs. Check the type on ready-mixed bags; transit-mix suppliers should help you in your selection.

Air-entraining agents and calcium chloride are added to concrete used in cold-weather climates to prevent cracking and to facilitate pouring in cold temperatures. In very hot weather, a retarding agent is used to keep the concrete from setting too fast. When it is critical that the installation be watertight, plasticizing agents are used to minimize shrinkage and cracking due to excessive water. This is especially important next to a house or garage entrance to keep windswept rain and water from leaking into the foundation.

Your building project may necessitate steel reinforcement; concrete has compressive strength (it can handle heavy loads), but it does not have tensile strength. Steel reinforcement in the form of steel rods or mesh provide tensile strength in concrete. Reinforcement is required for many constructed landscape features, such as steps, driveways, and other areas where safety is paramount. Steel bars or rods (often called rebars) will prevent concrete slabs from lifting differentially at cracks or expansion joints. Mesh will not always work as well for this purpose. Concrete shrinks as it cures, and expands and contracts when the temperature changes; this always causes cracking, especially if individual units are large. Place expansion joints at regular intervals.

There are many ways to disguise concrete. It can be divided into sections by using treated wood crosspieces to break up a broad expanse of a patio, for example. Concrete can be colored, stamped with specialized tools to resemble brick or cobblestones, imprinted with designs, or "seeded" on top with bright stones.

Concrete Pavers Although they are somewhat more expensive than poured-in-place concrete, precast pavers, interlocking pavers, and unit pavers can provide a quick and simple installation. They are constructed in a factory under controlled conditions and have a very high tensile strength. They can easily withstand more than 20,000 psi, which is much stronger than concrete poured on-site. Available in a variety of shapes and sizes, concrete pavers can create a multitude of patterns in a landscape. Pavers are widely available in many finishes, textures, and colors. Check local suppliers to see what patterns are available before creating your design.

Building With Concrete Block

Concrete masonry units (CMUs) are commonly called concrete blocks. They are designed for use in all types of masonry construction. Some of the uses include load-bearing and non-load-bearing walls, partition and curtain walls, piers and columns, retaining walls, and pavers. The most common types of units include hollow and solid load-bearing concrete block, hollow non-load-bearing concrete block, concrete building tile, concrete brick, and decorative blocks.

Building With Stone

Although expensive, stone has a permanence that few other materials can rival. There are two types of stone: dimensioned (or quarried) stone and fieldstone. Dimensioned stone has usually been quarried as a block or large piece and then cut into a panel, slab, or other shape according to a specified measurement. The types of quarried stone commonly used in home landscaping are granite, limestone, sandstone, marble, and slate.

Fieldstone is uncut natural stone that is found in fields or along streams and rivers. It has no specific dimensions. When choosing fieldstone, select flat stones—they are much easier to work with than rounded ones. Fieldstone makes wonderful dry-stacked stone walls and can be used for random paving accents, stepping-stones, or edgings. Roughly squared stone is fieldstone that has been "dressed," or chiseled, to remove irregular or rounded sides. Dressed stone is more expensive but easier to work with than stone left in its natural state.

Building With Metal

Unless you take up welding, blacksmithing, or metallurgy, most of the metal materials you will use will be purchased from and perhaps even installed by a metal fabricator. Metal can be used in a number of ways, although it is most commonly seen in fencing.

Wire mesh, including chain link, is commonly used as fencing. Because of the need to keep the mesh taut, these fences should be installed by a professional fence supplier. You can both strengthen and soften the look of chain link fences by purchasing the metal coated in vinyl or threaded with wood lath.

Cast iron is no longer used as much as in the past, but it does have a definite place in the home environment, especially when it complements the landscape style. It makes stylish stair railings and fancy iron work.

Structural steel and aluminum tubing are available in both square and round shapes. These metals can be used for railings, fences, and supports for structures. They must be treated and painted to withstand corrosion. Self-weathering steel is a self-oxidizing metal that does not need treatment;

however, it does stain surrounding surfaces as it begins to weather.

Copper is used for roofs, drains, and special tubes. Copper is quite expensive compared with other metals. With the addition of zinc it becomes brass, and with the addition of tin it becomes bronze. Both can be cast into plates and other shapes. All three of these metals are permanent and will not corrode, although they do discolor with weathering.

Building With Plastic

Of the various clear plastics, acrylic sheets are the most widely used as wind screens and infill panels for outdoor structures. Acrylic is the best plastic for outdoor use because it does not deteriorate from the ultraviolet rays of the sun. Although strong and durable, it does get pitted and sandblasted by the wind. Acrylic ranges in thickness from $\frac{3}{16}$ inch to $\frac{5}{8}$ inch and is available in panels up to 10 feet by 12 feet. Even a very large expanse of plastic will withstand reasonably strong winds. In windy regions, these clear panels allow you to enjoy the outdoors and see the view while shielding yourself from the wind. Acrylic panels can also be used to roof a shade structure or gazebo.

Landscape accents made of plastic, such as patio furniture, pool accessories, temporary lanterns, and plant containers, can be fun, colorful additions to your design. They will not weather as well as similar accents of metal, stone, or wood, however. You may want to consider establishing a place to store plastic items during severe weather.

New products are being introduced every day. Check local building suppliers for lumber products made with wood fiber and plastic resins, called *parallel strand lumber*, for beams of exceptional strength. Look into recycled plastic lumber—it is much more impact resistant than wood, is ultraviolet-proof, comes in nonfade colors, and is generally as strong as lumber for projects such as benches and planters.

Building With Canvas

Canvas, although it breaks down after prolonged exposure to the sun, is a versatile material for outdoor structures. In the form of awnings and umbrellas, canvas gives instant shade and has the advantage of providing color. Because its use is so flexible, it can be custom-sewn for various applications at a fairly low cost. Canvas should not be continuously exposed to the elements, but if it is used only seasonally and, like plastic items, taken in during the winter, it can last a long time. You can purchase ready-made canvas umbrellas from garden centers and catalog outlets. Sailcloth comes in many colors and patterns and can also be used for custom designs. There are many specialty shops that will fabricate them for you.

CONSTRUCTING LANDSCAPE ELEMENTS

Before undertaking any outdoor construction, you must evaluate—realistically—your level of construction expertise. Most outdoor construction projects require a working knowledge of building materials, hardware, and tools; the ability to read architectural plans; and basic carpentry and masonry skills.

Without a doubt, the key to any successful building project is planning. Take the time to make detailed working drawings on complicated projects; you will save time and money in the long run, and your finished product will be of higher quality.

One of the most fundamental skills on projects of this nature is basic carpentry. Wood projects for your landscape are some of the most visible elements in your home. Carpentry is a skill that must be practiced. Using the proper tools and modern building materials, and having an eye for good woodworking, should help you develop your carpentry skills.

Concrete and masonry work requires a great deal of heavy lifting, shoveling, concrete mixing, pattern design, and finishing work—all the rough stuff—as well as a sense of craft and aesthetics. All types of concrete projects require plenty of helpers. The installation of a typical patio slab, for instance, requires a minimum of three people—one of whom must be experienced—working together as the concrete is poured.

Take your time when measuring for the layout of posts and beams, for the placement of hardware, and, especially, for cuts. Double-check all measurements. When building projects that involve tricky cuts, especially with expensive or highly visible wood, you may want to build a scale model, make a

Although canvas may not be the most durable material available for outdoor ceilings, its crisp, traditional feel cannot be matched. Canvas can also be used for side panels that act as windbreaks. Building principles for installing attached shade structures are discussed on page 179.

Throughout this yard various applications of brick— a herringbone-patterned brick-on-sand path, the mortared retaining wall, and the lawn edging—create a unified appearance, although the brick was installed in stages, as time and budget allowed.

template from scrap wood or cardboard, or make the cuts a little long and scribe the materials to fit for perfect joints. You can avoid having to repurchase materials if you practice. When making a layout for concrete construction, be sure to double-check all locations and dimensions, because once concrete or masonry units are installed, it is impossible to move them even a few inches.

Many landscape materials are rough and coarse in nature, and, by virtue of design, precise installation may not be expected or even noticeable. Major structural projects, such as patios, attached shade covers, and decks, require more refined construction skills than simpler accent projects such as reflecting pools and raised planting beds. You must use your best judgment concerning your construction skills. If you plan to install the landscape yourself and are not experienced, consider hiring a contractor or experienced builder on a consulting basis to check your plans and materials list. If you have never completed any construction projects before, you might want to start with small projects, such as the rear corner of the garden, to develop a feel for the tools and materials. Make a few (small enough to move) concrete stepping-stones before pouring a concrete patio.

The following pages discuss the basic construction principles for many popular landscape elements. There is not room here for a full discussion of construction techniques for every type of landscape structure you could build. Many publications go into greater depth on specific elements. Some of these publications are included on the Reading List (see page 320). This section should give you a feel for the proper procedures and

the amount of effort required to install the basic structures, whether you plan to do the work yourself or hire help.

BUILDING FORMS

Concrete is extremely heavy and must be contained by well-braced forms. For patios and paths, you can make excellent forms out of 2×4s. If they are to remain in the concrete, use redwood or cedar. Before starting to pour, cover the top edges of the wood with masking tape to prevent staining.

Hold the forms in place with 1×4 stakes driven every 2 feet. If you will be leaving the forms in the concrete, use redwood or cedar stakes and drive them about 1 inch below the finish elevation. Check the forms with a level to be sure that the proper grade is maintained.

Nail the stakes into the forms with double-headed nails. Steady the stake by placing a crowbar or a length of 2×4 behind it while you hammer.

To make curved forms, cut saw kerfs halfway through the 2×4s every inch or so, then bend the boards so the kerfs close. For gentle curves, you can also use 1×4s; stake them every 2 feet to hold them firmly in place.

For tight curves, use ⅛-inch plywood or redwood benderboards. Put two or three benderboards together against the stakes and nail them in place.

Remember that concrete expands and contracts with changes in temperature. Unless there is room for this movement, the concrete will crack. In paths, place control joints (or crack lines) every 4 to 5 feet; in patios, have one every 8 to 10 feet. Use lengths of either redwood or cedar that you leave in place, or cut expansion joints with a grooving trowel after the concrete has begun to set.

Building Activity Areas

Constructed landscape activity areas fall into two major categories: patios and decks. If you are adding on to an existing patio or deck, there are several things you should check before completing your landscape design. Be sure the old structure will last long enough to warrant remodeling. In some cases decks may not show signs of rot on the surface, but an examination of the footings, posts, and joists reveals signs of advanced rot. Be careful that you do not plan your entire design around building on to an existing structure that will need to be replaced in a year or two.

Another problem with adding to existing features is the need to match materials. Consider providing a contrast with an old patio surface, or re-covering both an older concrete slab and a new slab with decorative brick or other paving units. You can stain an old deck and the addition to match, although you may need to sand the old deck first.

Most important, do not limit your design in order to save an existing deck or patio that may best be removed. Although constructing new patios and decks may be the most challenging aspect of your landscape installation, they are also often the most enjoyed element in the outdoor environment.

Patios To build a patio, you must know how to select materials; cut, saw, nail, and install forms; pour and finish concrete; and possibly cut and install bricks or decorative paving units. Whatever the size, shape, and style of a patio, the basic construction techniques are the same. Style choices include a concrete slab, brick or concrete pavers on a sand base, or a concrete slab with a decorative covering of brick, stone, or pavers. If you are building a patio of brick or some other paver, you need to determine the pattern before beginning the project. Experiment in a small area with dry paving units until you are happy with the pattern.

If you are building a new patio, you must start with an accurately scaled plan. The site should be cleared, the area roughly graded, and the drainage established. If the patio is to be adjacent to the house, the elevation of the patio must be below the finish floor elevation to prevent water damage. (Check local codes for exact dimensions.) If the home is built on a subfloor, you must build stairs or a ramp for access between the house and patio. If the home is built on a slab, the patio elevation should be below the threshold of any doors that open onto the patio, but not more than 6 inches below them, or you will have to provide a step or ramp for access. Determine the exact layout (see page 168) before ordering concrete and beginning construction.

Brick-on-Sand Patios To build a brick- or paver-on-sand patio, put in a sturdy, long-lasting edging (see page 173). With the edging in place, set the finish grade. Add roughly 2 inches of clean sand (or stone dust, if available), dampen thoroughly, and tamp. Level or screed the sand between the edgings. Set bricks or pavers in the desired pattern to the string line within the edging. Sweep additional sand into the joints between bricks or pavers. Walk on the patio to settle the bricks or pavers. Then sweep additional sand into the joints over a period of several days or until the sand works its way fully into the joints.

Concrete-Slab Patios If you have never poured concrete, begin with a small project and seek the help of someone with experience. To build a concrete-slab patio (which can

LAYING OUT A SITE

Before pouring a concrete slab for a patio, building foundation, or other constructed element, you must precisely determine the outside edge of the structure. This process is known as laying out. Laying out the site for constructed elements is more specific than the loose layout of general activity areas you did to determine if you liked your design (see page 149).

To lay out a squared rectangle, first mark the rough position of the area by driving a stake at each corner. Stretch a string from stake to stake. Use a framing square to roughly determine each right angle. Then see how close to square it is by measuring the diagonals. A layout has four square corners when the diagonal measurements are equal. Move the stakes until the measurements fall within a couple of inches of being square. The actual squaring occurs with the batter boards.

Constructing Batter Boards

Batter boards are located at all four corners and consist of 2×4 stakes connected by 1×4 boards. Use a framing square to construct the batter boards at 90-degree angles, but don't waste hours being exact. Make sure that the stakes are driven firmly into the ground, however, so the boards are stable. You will be pulling twine on the batter boards, and if they wobble or shift, your work will be inaccurate.

Two things are important about batter boards: where you position them and how you level them. On a small job where you will be excavating by hand, place the batter boards 4 feet out from the rough perimeter strings. If you are going to dig with a backhoe, set them either 2 feet back so that the backhoe operator can reach over them, or 10 feet back so that the operator can maneuver inside.

Leveling Batter Boards

For an accurate layout, the tops of the crosspieces on the batter boards should all be the same height. Level the tops with a carpenter's level or a line level or rent a builder's transit. Build one batter board, then stretch twine to the other stakes and make a pencil mark on them where level. Nail the crosspieces to the stakes.

Stringing the Perimeter

Once the batter boards are in place, stretch twine between them to mark the outside edges. Stretch the first string above the rough string layout you have on the ground for the baseline side of the structure. Everything else must be square with this line. Drive small nails in the tops of the crosspieces, and attach the string to the nails.

The twine must be pulled taut to eliminate any sags. Tie twine around nail; do not cut it. Cross over to the other crosspiece, tie the twine around the nail, and string the next leg.

Pull the next leg at a right angle to the first by using the 3-4-5 method (see page 170). Do the same on the succeeding legs. Now, to check your work, first measure the edge dimensions, then measure the diagonals. Adjust the strings until the diagonal measurements are equal.

Once you have squared the area, use a saw to cut a shallow notch underneath each string where it crosses the top of the batter board. This is more accurate than relying on nails, which may bend or come loose. If the strings have to be removed for digging the footing ditch, they can be quickly restrung over the notches. Excavate and grade before building any forms.

USING BATTERBOARDS TO PLACE FOOTINGS

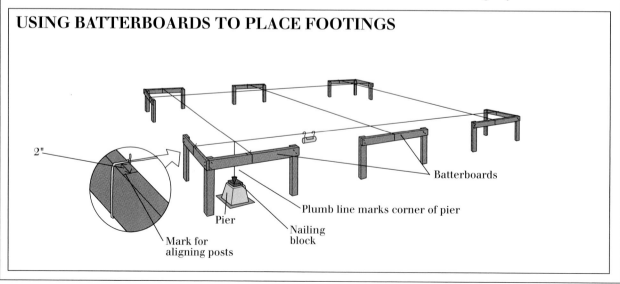

2"

Batterboards

Plumb line marks corner of pier

Pier

Nailing block

Mark for aligning posts

also be used as a foundation for a shade structure or shed), prepare the site and determine the layout. You must decide whether the forms will be permanent or whether they will be removed once the patio is completed. Build forms as described on page 166. To avoid frost heave in areas that freeze in winter, the patio must be placed in a bed of gravel, and the perimeter should be reinforced to prevent cracking.

If your design includes a structure or wall that will be built on top of the slab, you must place posts, hold-downs, footings, or hardware connections before pouring the concrete. You may also want or need to reinforce concrete slabs, especially those that must hold considerable weight (such as driveways or foundations), with rebar or wire mesh.

Decide on the final finish surface of the patio. Your choices include a steel trowel finish; a broomed, salted, exposed-aggregate, or other textured finish; or a finish that is stamped, colored, or both. Very smooth surfaces may be slippery when wet, and salted finishes are not recommended for regions with severe winters, as water in the indentations can freeze and cause cracking. Steel trowel finishes are the most difficult to do correctly. Stamped concrete requires specialized tools. Otherwise, your choice of finish depends only on your landscape style.

You need to order and schedule the delivery of concrete; and you will need help to pour the slab—probably three or four people. For best results, do not pour concrete in the rain or in very hot weather. Place a barricade—strings with brightly colored tags attached—around any concrete project to protect it from unwanted footprints until it is completely cured.

POURING CONCRETE PATIOS

If you are having the concrete delivered, it is essential that you have helpers; at least one of you should be experienced.

As the concrete is poured, shovel and rake it evenly throughout the formed area. Use only a little agitation; too much will cause the gravel to sink. Pour the concrete to about ¼ inch above the forms to allow for settling.

Smooth and level the concrete by pulling a strike-off board across the top in a sawing motion. Immediately after striking off, use a bull float (or darby for small areas) to further level the concrete and fill in any depressions. Push the bull float away with the front edge slightly raised, then draw it back in a sawing motion. Run the tip of a trowel around the edges between the form and concrete to cut the spillover. Make the cut about 1 inch deep, and scrape the form tops clean.

Wait to start the finish work until the water sheen on top of the concrete has evaporated. That may take from a few minutes to several hours. Once the water sheen is gone and the mix has stiffened, work your way around the forms with an edger. Be careful not to push concrete ahead of you. A final edging can be done after texturing.

Cut control joints with a grooving trowel every 4 to 5 feet in paths and every 8 to 10 feet in patios, or as designed. Place a 1×10 board on the concrete to serve as a guide and to distribute your weight so you won't mar the concrete.

Floating adds to the finish. A wood float gives it a rough finish. Moving the float in sweeping curves will give a distinct pattern. For air-entrained concrete, use an aluminum or magnesium float. For a smooth, almost polished finish, use a steel float. Keep the leading edge up, and move in long sweeping strokes. Trowel immediately after floating.

To cure properly, concrete must be kept warm and damp. In warm weather, allow five days for curing; in cold weather, allow seven days.

The key to a proper cure is constant dampness. Cover the top and edges of the concrete with plastic sheeting. This traps the moisture inside and permits a slow, steady curing rate. Weight down the plastic so air does not get in.

Finishing a Concrete Patio With Decorative Pavers Brick, concrete pavers, tiles, dimensioned stone, and other decorative accents can easily be added to an existing or new concrete slab. In either case the slab must be clean, level, and free of debris. If you are resurfacing an existing patio, before applying decorative pavers make sure that the patio is level and all cracks are repaired. The exact method of attaching paving units to concrete depends on the materials. Before

BUILDING FOOTINGS FOR DECKS

Check local codes for footing depths and dimensions. In some regions pressure-treated posts can be buried directly in the ground. To locate the footings, lay out string lines between the ledger and the batter boards, which should represent the outside corners of the posts.

Use a 3-4-5 triangle method to square a corner. To do this, measure 3 feet along one leg and 4 feet along the other. If the diagonal distance between the points is 5 feet, the corner is square. Then excavate the holes and build concrete footings.

Piers

You can either make your own piers or buy precast ones. The cost will be about the same, so it is generally easier to buy piers unless you are pouring a lot of concrete, in which case you can make up some forms and pour your own.

A precast pier has a redwood or pressure-treated woodblock already set into the top, which allows you to either toenail the post to it, as is commonly done, or bolt a metal post connector to the top, which is preferable because it is stronger.

Piers can also be made of hollow-core concrete building blocks. They can be set in place while the footing is still pliable, filled with concrete, and topped with a metal post or connector. For strength, be sure to use standard aggregate blocks and not cinder blocks.

Pouring your own piers allows you to use a drift pin, which provides a secure fitting for the post. The drift pin—either a foundation bolt or length of rebar—extends about 6 inches above the top of the pier. The post is drilled in the center of its base and then set in place over the pin.

Erecting Posts

Cut each post longer than needed, and attach it to its pier. Use the layout strings to align the posts accurately. Plumb each post with a level, then temporarily brace it in both directions with stakes and pieces of scrap lumber.

If the posts are not going to extend to the deck railing, mark them for cutting by measuring down from the level string line a distance equal to the depth of both the joist and the beam. Scribe cutting lines, and saw off the tops of the posts.

order. Apply a bed of thin-set mortar (or the compound recommended for your paving material) to the concrete where you removed the pavers, using the appropriate notched or standard trowel. Use spacers between units for even joints. Where necessary, use string lines to maintain level. String lines are generally needed only for thick units. Fill the joints as applicable for the paving material. Be careful not to let mortar dry on bricks or pavers because it is difficult to remove. For lasting results, seal porous materials with the product recommended by the supplier.

Decks To build a deck, you will have to know how to select, measure, cut, and nail wood. Ground-level decks are fairly simple to design and construct. Raised decks must be properly designed, engineered, and constructed. You must be able to understand and interpret architectural drawings. If you have only rudimentary carpentry skills and equipment, seek professional guidance before attempting to build a raised deck. Most raised decks require permits; check local codes.

Framing materials must be of pressure-treated lumber. For longest life, framing wood should never be directly placed in concrete or buried in soil. For best results, use only exterior-quality framing hardware and hot-dipped galvanized (HDG) nails. Your choice of decking boards will be influenced by your budget and the availability of wood. Construction principles are basically the same for all wood types.

A certain amount of site preparation is necessary before installing a deck. Except for rooftop decks, the area must be roughly graded, and the activity area must be accurately laid out for excavation and proper drainage.

installing bricks and other porous pavers, soak in water until completely saturated.

Always do a test layout on the slab in the desired pattern to ensure proper placement; try out several different patterns. You can cut units as necessary for fit, although this adds to the task, so try to plan a pattern with as few cuts as possible. When you are satisfied with the pattern, remove a small section of pavers, keeping the pattern in

Ground-Level Decks In order to install a deck that will be accessed without steps, you must excavate to a depth of approximately 3 inches and apply a chemical growth retardant or lay down plastic sheeting. Be sure to puncture the sheeting every few feet to provide drainage. Fill the area with gravel, and level it. Portable ground-level decks utilize preassembled modules, which can be placed on the prepared site and fastened together. Portable module decks are also ideal for rooftop and balcony installations. A standard module consists of two 2×4s, called cleats, covered by 2×4 or 2×6 decking. Permanent ground-level decks can be built by laying 4×4s, called sleepers, spaced 2 feet apart on the prepared site. When the sleepers have been installed and leveled, nail decking boards to them in the desired pattern. Unlike portable module decks, permanent ground-level decks are less likely to shift or settle, and they utilize full-length decking boards.

Raised Decks The basic structure of a raised deck consists of a framework of beams and joists that in turn supports the decking boards. The joists are horizontal framing members made from 2×6 or 2×8 pressure-treated lumber. A ledger, normally of the same material as

FRAMING PLAN FOR DECK

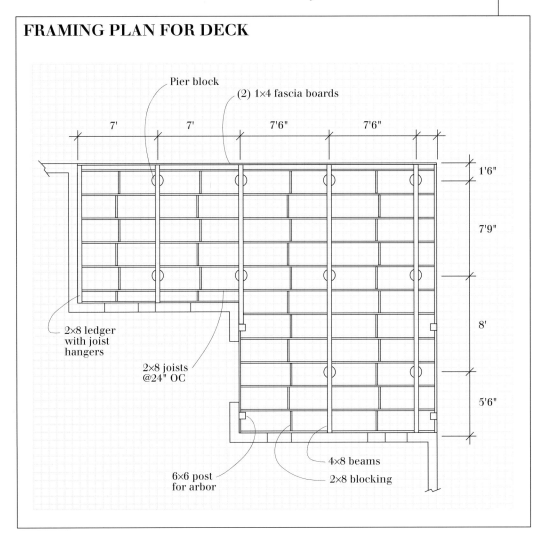

ORTHO'S GUIDE TO CREATIVE HOME LANDSCAPING

the joist, is bolted to the house. (Engineer the connections carefully; decks have been known to tear loose during parties.) The joists are then placed on joist hangers, which are fastened to the ledger. The joists are also supported by beams that rest on posts. The beams should be 4×4s or larger. The posts, which are vertical framing members made of 4×4 boards, are spaced according to the size and spacing of the beams. Joists with spans longer than 10 feet must have blocking to keep the joist system rigid. Blocking should consist of solid pieces of joist material, installed at the midpoint of the joist and over beams. Decking boards are attached to the top of the joist. The most common size of decking board is 2×6, which can span from 2 to 4 feet, depending on species and grade. Narrow boards cup and warp less than wide ones; 2×4s are best. Consider 2×4s on edge for spans up to 6 feet, but install rigid spacers or HDG washers every 3 feet to prevent warping.

Decking boards can be glued, nailed, or screwed in place. Adhesives give a clean appearance; nails work better if some of the boards are crooked. Use corrosion-resistant HDG nails and screws.

Railings Design railings, or have them designed, in conjunction with raised decks. Some areas require railings for decks of a certain height; check local codes. Railings are always a good safety feature. Deck railings are attached either to posts that extend through the deck from the substructure or to posts fastened to the deck. The first method is stronger but somewhat more complicated to construct. Handrails, benches, or planting boxes use these supports. The horizontal boards above the decking boards are the rails. The vertical boards between posts are called balusters.

Although the designs for railings are numerous, some general rules apply. Allow enough space between the decking boards and the bottom rail for cleanup, but not more than 8 inches. The top rail should be no less than 42 inches above the surface of the decking boards. The spaces between baluster and posts should be less than 8 inches. These minimums were designed to prevent children from falling over or through railings. A small child can squeeze through a 4-inch opening, and all railings should be designed to deter climbing. Refer to local building codes again; some jurisdictions are very specific about this. All railings must be strong enough for people to lean against or sit on. Railings are one of the most visible aspects of a deck, so take the time to install them correctly.

Benches built into decks can have backs that form the railing or, if the deck is close to the ground, they can be low, wide platforms that serve as both railings and seats. Construct benches around railing posts. Simply bolt horizontal framing that will support the seat base to posts so that the finished seat height is about 16 inches from the decking boards. Install additional vertical supports at the ends of the seat base to form outer legs. Install decking boards on the seat base to form the seat.

Building Landscape Floors

Constructed garden floors are surfaces for activity areas and connectors between various areas in the landscape. Most garden floors can be built by anyone. All you need is time, a hammer, a shovel, and a pair of gloves. Loose-material areas can be any dimension suitable for your design. Depending on the site, paths, ramps, and steps can be straight or curved. The width and shape of all garden floors should be outlined on your master plan. Paths can be built of concrete, loose material, or brick or paver units on sand, depending on the landscape style. Select an edging material appropriate to the landscape style as well.

Roughly grade all floors for drainage. Be careful not to use a path or ramp as the sole drainage channel, or you may have problems with erosion. Lay out the site according to the specifications of your master plan.

Apply base materials as needed. Base materials are crucial to the permanence of landscape floors. They provide a necessary cushion under the structure that allows water to pass beneath the surface. Almost any open, free-draining material can be used as a base, so long as it is inert and porous enough to allow water to pass through and to counteract frost in cold climates. Sand and gravel are the most common base materials.

Loose-Material Floors Natural materials, such as bark, gravel, crushed stone or seashells, or even pine-needle mulch can be used for attractive garden areas. These paths, play areas, surrounds for planting, or driveways are the simplest and most economical to build, but they require more maintenance than paved surfaces. Keep the grade below 6 percent to avoid washouts. Prepare the subsurface by excavating about 2 inches below the top of the edging. Lay out, excavate, and install the edging of your choice. Apply a chemical growth retardant, or lay down plastic sheeting. Be sure to puncture the sheeting every few feet to provide drainage. Fill with the material of your choice. You may need to rake and refill occasionally.

BUILDING EDGINGS

Edgings are essential for defining ground-level patios and loose-material activity areas. They can range from functional concrete to bold brick and wood beams.

To build any edging, you first need to lay out the site accurately with stakes and string. To install simple plastic or metal edgings or heavy-timber edgings, no reinforcement is necessary. Use a straight-edged shovel to cut a narrow trench under the string line to the width and depth necessary to hold the edging. Place the edging in the trench, and tamp soil around the edging for support.

To build form-reinforced edgings, use a straight-edged shovel to cut a trench about the width of the shovel and the depth of a form board. Place the form in the trench, check that it is level, and support it with 1×4 stakes every 2 feet along the outside. Use two stakes on each side of connecting boards for added support. Nail the stakes into the form with double-headed nails. Steady the stake by placing a crowbar or a length of 2×4 behind it while you hammer.

Drive stakes well below the top of the forms so they will not interfere with surface material. Fill in the backside of the trench flush with the top of the form. Stand the edging against this form. Tamp soil around the edging. The 2×4 form is essential for keeping edgings, such as bricks on end, from working loose and falling over. Forms to be left in place should be redwood, western red cedar (*Thuja plicata*), or pressure-treated lumber.

To build concrete-reinforced edgings, dig a trench to the desired width; make sure it is straight and true. Install forms on each side of the trench as described above. Pour concrete to the top of the forms, strike off and float the concrete, and let it cure for a week.

If an unadorned concrete edging is not attractive to you, finish it with decorative pavers using the method for resurfacing an existing path described on page 174.

Paths Connectors can be built of concrete, wood, decorative pavers on concrete, or bricks or pavers on sand. Sand-based paths are the easiest of these to construct, although they require a certain amount of upkeep. Concrete paths are more difficult and expensive, and require more initial labor to build, but they last virtually forever. If you install a new path of decorative pavers on concrete, you increase the amount of labor because you are actually building the same path twice. However, such paths combine the durability of concrete with a wide variety of design opportunities. Resurfacing an existing concrete

Resurfacing this concrete path with brick greatly enhanced the appeal of the house. Use a carpenter's level, which is also suitable for small masonry jobs, to keep the paving units aligned and even. Kneeling on scraps of carpet will help protect your knees.

path by covering it with decorative pavers is an excellent remodeling project.

Test the paving pattern before you lay out any brick- or paver-covered path, and keep patterns simple to avoid having to cut units. You may want to adjust the width of the path or the paving pattern to accommodate your materials. In most cases paths should be edged. The construction principles for laying out, installing, and finishing paths are basically the same as those for patios made of like materials (see page 169). Wood paths are built in the same manner as permanent ground-level decks (see page 170).

Resurfacing an Existing Concrete Path Perform a visual inspection of the concrete path to determine the quality of the surface. Open and repair any cracks or defects with a suitable patching compound. Simple resurfacing materials are available. Outdoor deck paints can be applied in a variety of colors. Concrete topping mixes, either natural or color matched, are fairly easily to apply. Several epoxy-based resurfacing compounds are available in a wide assortment of

colors and textures. The most popular ones look like wet beach pebbles. These compounds repair and resurface broken, cracked, or soiled concrete and provide a durable, long-lasting, easy-to-clean surface. They should be installed by a professional.

By far the most popular resurfacing materials are brick pavers. They are about half the thickness of standard bricks. You can resurface an existing concrete path with brick pavers if you can measure, cut brick, and work with mortar and hand tools—and if you don't mind working on your hands and knees for a day or two. Once the path is cleaned and repaired, test your paving pattern and determine what brick cuts are necessary. Wet the existing path and soak the brick pavers. Mix the mortar, and lay a thin bed on a small section of path. Lay wet bricks, leaving about ⅜ inch of space between units. Complete the run of the path and allow it to dry thoroughly. Place some dry mortar into a small can; do not mix it with water. Pour dry mortar into the spaces between bricks, filling them completely and being careful not to get any onto the bricks. Brush any spilled mortar off the top surfaces. Wet the mortar with a fine water spray, wait five minutes, then spray again to make sure the water has soaked through to the bottom. Some settling of the mortar is likely after wetting. Carefully add more dry mortar, and wet it again. When the mortar begins to set, use a joint-striking tool to compress the joints; tool the short joints first and then the long joints. To fill small holes and gaps between joints, mix a small amount of mortar with water, and use the jointing tool to smooth it into place. Brush excess mortar off the bricks. If you have trouble cleaning the bricks later

with water, clean them with a mixture of trisodium phosphate (TSP) and water.

Ramps Constructed ramps are built of wood or poured concrete. To build a ramp, you need to know how to interpret building plans, lay out a site, determine the rise and run of a ramp (it should not exceed an 8-percent grade for wheelchair use), select appropriate building materials, and measure, cut, and nail wood. In general, wood or earthen ramps are fairly simple to design and build. Framing members and general construction methods are similar to those used for raised decks (see page 171), although the specifics will vary depending on the site and design.

Poured-concrete ramps require detailed working drawings or experience in form setting and carpentry. This is an advanced building project that requires extensive planning, skills, and specialized tools. The process is to build a series of stepped side walls, backfill the center space with soil, grade the soil to the appropriate slope, and cover the soil with concrete. This type of ramp requires steel rebars to reinforce the footings, perimeter walls, and ramp floor.

Steps Constructing outdoor steps is one of the less difficult landscape projects. To build the simplest outdoor steps, cut a horizontal notch into the hillside as needed and place a paver unit in the cut. This method is not recommended for steep slopes. Notched outdoor steps require constant maintenance to make sure the paver units have not slipped out of place.

A step style that is only slightly more complicated utilizes treated landscape timbers, such as railroad ties, telephone poles, and peeler logs. Drill holes through the tim-

bers approximately 3 inches from each end. Cut rebar stakes to about 16-inch lengths. Set the timbers at appropriate intervals along the hillside. Cut notches in the soil to the desired width. Set the timbers in the cuts, and drive stakes through the holes to attach them to the subsurface. If the hillside is unstable, you may want to pour concrete into each notch, set the rebar stakes in the concrete while it is still wet, allow the concrete to dry, and then set the timbers on top, threading the rebar through the holes.

Stairs Building outdoor stairs is a complex project that requires a knowledge of carpentry, concrete work, layout, equivalent rise and run ratios, and, in the case of concrete stairs, form building and concrete-finishing techniques.

Wood stairs can be built in a variety of styles, depending on the steepness of the slope, the landscape style, and your budget. Very steep slopes and passageways from raised decks to ground level will require stairs. For long runs, wood is usually less expensive than concrete. Wood stairs are built in

Landscape timbers serve many needs. Install them as decorative edgings for steps, or use them to build retaining walls for planting areas filled with loose material.

a manner similar to raised decks (see page 171), using concrete foundations and appropriate framing techniques, hardware, and architectural design.

Concrete stairs require careful and exact design techniques. Basically, these stairs are built by pouring concrete into a form specially designed and built to achieve the desired rise in a given run.

The construction cost of ramps, stairs, and steps is calculated in lineal feet. Height is a big factor in the cost of these features because higher structures may require more support. The lower the structure, the fewer lineal feet of both support and finishing materials are required.

BUILDING FOOTINGS FOR GARDEN WALLS

Except for those made of loose-laid stone or wood, all garden walls should be supported by a continuous concrete footing. The width, depth, and thickness of the footing depend on the height and thickness of the wall, and the depth depends on local soil conditions and climate.

Most footings are twice as wide as the wall, but the width of a footing for a retaining wall is usually two thirds the height of the wall. The footing for a low wall should be at least 8 inches thick; use at least 12-inch-thick footings for walls more than 5 feet high.

The footing should have a 6-inch layer of gravel beneath it. This controls the heaving that occurs in locations with unstable soil or deep frost. Be sure to dig the trench deep enough; in areas that get very cold, the bottom of the footing should be below the frost line. Also be sure that the footing does not encroach on a neighbor's property.

A footing should contain at least one horizontal rebar—two or three would be better. Also place vertical rebar every 24 inches in the footing to protrude up into a brick, concrete, or concrete-block wall. Stone is usually too irregular to accommodate rebar, although you may be able to lay stones around a few bars.

It is necessary to provide drainage behind a retaining wall. If the soil behind the wall becomes saturated, it could force the wall to crack or lean. Weep holes at the bottom of a wall can provide drainage. If the diameter of the holes is 1 inch or larger, space the holes 2 feet apart. Smaller holes require closer spacing. Weep holes tend to clog with debris unless you place fiberglass mesh behind them. In some cases the water that seeps through will be a nuisance. If so, instead of weep holes, bury drainage pipe behind the wall to divert water around it. Cover the back of the wall with a geotextile fabric to lead accumulated water to the drain tile.

Building Landscape Walls

Walls both define your property and divide activity areas within the landscape. Constructed walls are fences, garden walls, or portable screens. Your choice of style and material will depend on your construction skills, budget, and the overall landscape style. Height is a critical factor in landscape walls. Local codes often set limits for fence heights. You will probably need a building permit and expert advice for a garden wall above a certain height, typically 3 feet. If you intend to sit on the wall, keep the height to between 18 and 24 inches.

Garden Walls Most types of masonry and stonework for retaining and freestanding walls require the builder to assemble many fairly heavy units, using mortar, experience, and muscle to build beautiful, functional walls. If you can mix mortar, shovel, measure, and lift, and you have a sense of aesthetics and a strong back, with some education these projects should be attainable.

Garden walls are either retaining walls or freestanding walls. A retaining wall holds back soil from a lower level, taking the place of a bank or slope. Although a retaining wall is more expensive to construct than a common slope, it has the advantage of saving space. A wall takes about 18 inches of width for every 3 feet of height, whereas a sloping bank takes 6 to 9 feet of width for the same height.

Freestanding walls can be used for decoration, privacy, or as windbreaks. It is usually desirable to have some type of planting on or near garden walls to prevent a feeling of coldness and bareness. If vines are to be used for this purpose, it may prove helpful to provide for them during construction.

Inserting wood or plastic plugs at various points throughout the wall will give the vines something to cling to.

Building retaining walls and free-standing walls utilizes many of the same materials and techniques. The materials most commonly used include stone, brick, wood planks, landscape timbers, slump block, reinforced concrete, and concrete block. Popular veneers for concrete and concrete-block walls include brick, stucco, and real or imitation stone.

Wood Walls Retaining walls of landscape timber and pressure-treated plank lumber are popular and are fairly inexpensive to build. The results can be outstanding, even with minimal construction experience. Wood walls are not as durable nor will they bear the same weight load as masonry walls, but they are acceptable for low retaining walls and for raised planting beds. The simplest construction method utilizes 2×10 treated planks set horizontally on 2×4 stakes driven a minimum of 24 inches into undisturbed soil.

A slightly more complicated method uses landscape timbers placed vertically against a hillside. To build this wall, excavate a trench deep enough to bury each timber one half to two thirds of its length. Set the posts so they lean slightly into the hillside, and back-fill the trench with concrete or firmly packed soil. Nail a 2×6 along the back of the wall near the top. Install drainage pipe as needed. Any number of wood landscape walls are possible; you are limited only by your ingenuity and construction expertise.

Masonry Walls To install masonry garden walls, first lay out the wall according to your master plan.

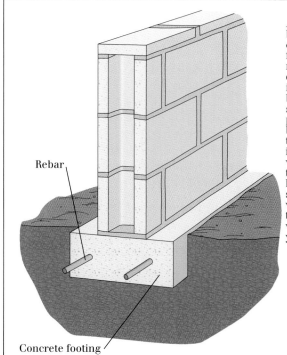

Rebar

Concrete footing

A basic concrete block wall consists of a reinforced footing, blocks, and mortar. It can be disguised by arranging some of the blocks with the cells sideways and making planters out of them; by inserting decorative blocks at regular intervals along the wall; or by covering them with two layers of stucco—the second coat mixed with powdered color to match or contrast with the color of your house.

Mark the location and excavate soil to the proper depth to provide a footing, which should be large enough to bear the weight of the materials and withstand the forces that nature will apply. Retaining walls are actually small dams. They require more resistance to lateral loads than freestanding walls and must be designed to accommodate such stress. Provide drainage or weep holes in walls that will retain soil.

Two popular types of masonry wall are poured reinforced concrete and reinforced concrete block; their construction is similar. Although these walls must be carefully engineered, the stress calculations and design statistics are readily available from professional sources such as landscape architects. They are both less labor intensive than a true stone wall. Once the wall is in place, the addition of a drainage system and stone or brick veneer is all that is needed to complete the project. If budget is a consideration, the veneer can be added at a later date.

True stone walls require a rather large volume of suitable stone. You must be able to develop the skill and craft to build the wall, whether it is to be dry-stacked or mortared.

Brick walls are extremely time-consuming to build and require skill and a lot of practice for a professional-looking installation.

Fences The styles and patterns of fences vary as much as their owners; a fence can be as simple or ornate as you desire. Your choice will depend on your landscape style. Chain link and metal fences should be installed by professionals. To build a basic wood post fence, you need to know how to select, cut, and nail boards and how to install posts.

The basic structure of a fence consists of posts, rails, and infill. Fence posts are commonly made of pressure-treated lumber. Fence rails, also usually of pressure-treated boards, connect the posts and support the infill. Fence styles differ mostly in the infill used; it can be pickets, plywood, lattice, plastic, redwood, or just about anything else you can think of.

Once your layout is complete and the posts are installed (see left), you need to attach the top rail. How this is done depends on your design. The rails can be nailed flush with the posts, on top of the posts, or a few inches below the tops of the posts. You then cut the bottom rails to fit between the posts and attach them with metal fence clips, by toenailing the ends of the rails into the posts, or with dado or mortise-and-tenon joints. Next install the infill to the frame. If your design calls for consistent spaces between boards, be sure to have spacers ready. The top of the fence can be dressed up with a cap board, lattice, roof, or arbor, depending on your design. The more complicated the top, the more difficult the construction.

Gates If you can build a fence, you can build a gate. Gates vary considerably in design; your choice will depend on your landscape style. Whatever type of gate you choose, the basic design and construction considerations are the same. You must consider placement of the gate, direction of swing, and land forms on either side of the opening. Gate construction normally consists of framing, bracing, infill, and hardware. Gate posts should be

INSTALLING FENCE POSTS

The first step in building any kind of fence is to measure the entire area and calculate how many posts you will need. You will have to adjust the bays (openings between posts) near the end so they all appear to be the same width, or you can split the width of the two end bays in half to provide a better visual line. Decide on the placement of any gates, and allow for correct finish opening.

If the fence will turn a corner, mark the corners with stakes and stretch twine between them. Using a framing square, adjust the corners so they are as close to 90 degrees as possible. Use the 3-4-5 method described on page 170 to square the corner.

Set all corner posts. Using a posthole digger (and steel bar for hard ground) dig the posthole at least 18 inches deep, preferably 24 inches deep. Then stretch twine between the posts, if possible. If not, set intermediate posts to support the twine over uneven ground. Make sure that the intermediate posts are in line with the end posts. Keep the twine about 2 feet above the ground.

Mark the proper post spacing along the line of the fence, and dig postholes. The base of the post must be in line with the twine, and the post must be plumb. Carefully check this with a level while the post is being set. Watch that a breeze does not blow the twine out of line.

Shovel a thin layer of rock or gravel into the postholes to keep the posts out of standing water. Place the posts into the holes. Shovel about 6 inches of soil, a little at a time, into the hole around the base of each post. While a helper uses a level to keep the post plumb and in line with the string, tamp in the soil.

Soil must be dry to tamp properly. A post will not set in wet soil, because it won't pack. In heavy clay soil, add some pea gravel. It is best, of course, to set all posts in concrete.

Later, if the posts become slightly wobbly as the soil around them dries and shrinks, pour dry sand in the gap between the post and the surrounding soil to retighten the post.

stronger than line posts; you will want to consider setting them in concrete or planting them deeper in the ground. They must be perfectly vertical and stay that way. The gate itself must be built to minimize sagging. The standard method is to run a diagonal brace inside the gate frame from the bottom of the hinge side to the top of the latch side. This acts like a 45-degree-angle support brace. Carefully measure the distance between the gate posts, and construct the frame slightly smaller than those specifications to allow for swing. Set the gate frame in the post opening, attach the hinges to the frame and gate post, and check for proper swing before installing the infill and latch hardware.

Portable Screens Garden screens are freestanding, portable walls that can be moved around a site as needed. They can block unsightly views or divide a large space when a more intimate area is all you need. You may want to consider constructing a screen to match the fence, or you can make it of other materials to accent the landscape. Build individual frames about 2 feet wide and to the desired height. Attach the infill to the frame. Hinge three frames to form one 6-foot-long freestanding screen.

Building Landscape Ceilings

Constructed landscape ceilings are either attached to the home or mounted on freestanding posts. Although ceilings may be some of the last elements installed in a landscape, it is important to plan for them in conjunction with other construction.

Attached Shade Structures An attached shade structure can be planned as part of a new deck or patio design. It can also be fit to an existing patio through the use of specialized hardware, posts, or both. The most common attached shade structure is built with a post, beam, ledger, and ceiling-joist framing system. This structure can be left open or covered with virtually any type of wood, fiberglass, or other solid, waterproof material. To build an attached shade structure, you must be able to understand working drawings; be able to select, measure, cut, and nail wood; have a working understanding of fastening hardware; know how to install a ledger, framing hardware, and posts; and possibly be able to pour concrete.

Lay out the post-and-beam arrangement on the site according to plan. Attach the ledger to the house at the desired location (usually at the height of the indoor ceiling joists). In most cases you will next install the posts in a straight line parallel to the house wall at the outside edge of the patio. Then fasten the beams to the posts using the appropriate hardware. Install the ceiling-joist system between the ledger and beams. Apply a roof covering, if desired.

Metal framing structures, which you attach to a ledger, are available from home centers and catalog outlets. In general, they can be installed with less construction expertise than their wood equivalents.

Freestanding Shade Structures The construction abilities necessary to build a freestanding shade structure are generally the same as those for an attached one. A freestanding structure requires a minimum of four posts, and shear bracing in two directions is necessary to prevent the structure from swaying.

Gazebos To build a gazebo, you need to know how to read working drawings; be able to measure, cut, and nail wood; have a working knowledge of fastening hardware; and possibly be able to pour concrete. Construction principles for any type of gazebo are basically the same. The more complex the design, the more difficult the project. The type of gazebo you choose will depend on your construction expertise and the style of the landscape. Many prefabricated gazebo kits are available.

Set the gazebo on an existing patio, a new concrete slab, a ground-level deck, or bare ground. Build the roof and supporting structure using standard framing techniques. Most small structures require only four posts for the main frame, which can be of 4×4s or 6×6s. Anchor them onto concrete footings or piers. Cross-beams should be secured with metal connecting devices. Cover the beams or rafters with roofing or shading material. The easiest way to build a gazebo with complex angles is to

assemble it with simple connectors. These are sold in kits that include project books or sets of plans. You have to add roofing, railings, and trim to the basic frame. If the gazebo is to house lights, a hot tub, or an outdoor kitchen, other utility needs will have to be considered.

Building Landscape Accents

Your choice of landscape accents is limited only by your imagination. All landscape accents should be made of quality material to withstand life in an outdoor environment, and they should always fit in with the landscape style. As with landscape ceiling installation, you should plan for accents long before their actual construction, especially those that need utility hookups.

Garden Pools Anyone who can build a simple form and mix and pour concrete can construct a small, cast-concrete molded-saucer reflecting pool. Construct a circular staked form of the desired diameter. Mound soil inside the form with the high point in the center. This is the negative mold of the cast saucer. Pour a 1-inch layer of concrete over the soil inside the form. Add chicken-wire reinforcement to size. Pour a second layer of concrete to the desired thickness. Allow to dry thoroughly. Remove the form, invert the saucer, waterproof it, place it in the desired location, and fill with water.

Another easy way to make a garden pool is with PVC fabric. This durable, flexible plastic sheeting is sold in nurseries and garden centers for making pools. Dig a hole the size and shape you want the pool to be, with a shelf about 2 inches deep and 4 inches wide around the edges. Use a carpenter's level on a board to level the shelf all around. Line the hole with 2 inches of damp sand to cushion the

POND CONSTRUCTION

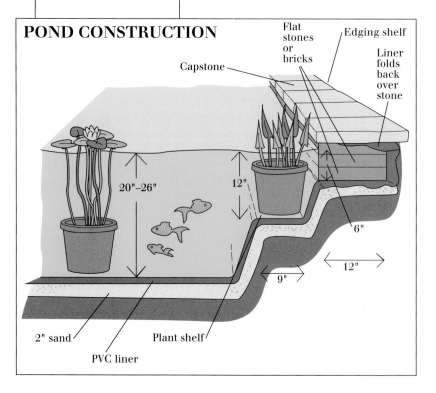

Flat stones or bricks

Edging shelf

Capstone

Liner folds back over stone

20"–26"

12"

6"

12"

9"

2" sand

Plant shelf

PVC liner

fabric. Purchase a piece of fabric the width and length of the hole, plus twice the depth, plus a foot in each dimension. Drape the fabric in the hole, laying the overlap across the shelf. Fill the hole with water to the edge of the shelf. The water will press the fabric against the pool sides, conforming it to the shape of the hole. If the shelf is not completely level, adjust its level now. Line the edge with bricks, laying them on the shelf on top of the overlap. Fold the excess fabric back over the top of the bricks and trim it to the center of the bricks. Add a little more water to the pool, almost to the top of the bricks. Cover the fabric and bricks with flat stones to hide them and make a decorative edge for the pool. This method can be used to make pools of almost any size, shape, and depth.

Waterfalls and Fountains Water accents are easily added to a landscape with the use of a submersible pump that recirculates water. Many styles of fountains are commercially available. Submersible pumps are connected to grounded electrical receptacles, which should be installed by a skilled electrician. To build a waterfall, you must install a basin that holds the pump and water. The water is pumped through a ½-inch plastic hose to the top of a stone or masonry "mountain" from which the water can drop.

Raised Planting Beds Basic carpentry skills are all that is needed to build planting beds. Raised beds are commonly made of rough, decay-resistant 2×12 lumber. Handsome raised beds can also be made from stacked railroad ties, 4×4s, or concrete blocks. Turn raised beds into comfortable garden seats by screwing 2×6s to the tops of 2×12 borders.

PLANTING

PLANTS IN THE LANDSCAPE

Plants perform a variety of practical functions in the landscape. They provide shade, screen objectionable views, shelter areas from harsh winds, prevent soil erosion, create physical barriers, and help to control noise. You must consider more than function in your design, however. Use the design principles beginning on page 53 in combination with this discussion to produce a planting plan that both solves site problems and creates an aesthetically pleasing garden.

Wind reduction is one of the most common functions performed by plants. Trees and shrubs have been used as windbreaks for many years. Plantings that allow a small amount of wind to pass through them are generally more effective than extremely dense plantings or solid barriers such as fences and walls. The ideal windbreak consists of a double row of trees with shrubs beneath them. In general, a windbreak will reduce wind in an area equal to five times its height. For example, a windbreak of 40-foot-high plants will slow the wind down in an area 200 feet beyond it.

Plants are also commonly used to control sun and shade. Shade trees planted in combination with shrubs and turf can reduce the temperature of the area beneath them by as much as 10° F. Trees can also have an impact on the heating and cooling of the house. Deciduous trees planted near windows will allow warming winter sun to enter the house but will shield it from hot summer rays.

A thick planting of ground cover can drastically reduce or even eliminate soil erosion on a steep hillside. The ideal spacing between ground-cover plants varies with the type of plant. In general, the closer the spacing, the better the erosion control.

Plants can be used for noise abatement to some degree. A buffer planting of trees and shrubs between the source of the noise and your garden can significantly decrease the perceptible sound level. If the noise is exceptionally loud, the buffer may have to be as much as 25 feet wide. The creation of mounds of soil with plantings on them will further reduce the noise.

Plants can also enhance attractive views and screen objectionable ones. A dense planting or a planting combined with a fence or wall can provide privacy for the garden.

Finally, plants can act as implied or actual barriers. A low hedge or even a flower bed will create enough of a barrier to control movement. Closely spaced plants with thorns will create a physical barrier to help discourage prowlers and animals from entering your yard.

Drawing Planting Plans

A planting plan is a drawing that indicates the location, type, spacing, and quantity of plants in your design. When you created the master plan, you thought of plants as sculptural masses. Now imagine combinations of individual specimens. Specific plant types are listed in the Landscape Plant Guide beginning on page 211.

To draw a planting plan, make a copy of your master plan. Determine the mature size and location of each plant. Using a circle template and scale, draw a circle to indicate the spread, with a dot in the center to show the exact planting location. Remember to space plants according to their mature size.

Decide on symbols and patterns to indicate different types of plants. It does not matter what markings you use so long as you are consistent and you keep track of what each of them means. Draw a line from each plant or group to the outside of the plan and write the name there. Tally up the plants. This will serve as your shopping list.

TOOLS FOR PLANTING

Having the right tool for the job, one that is neither too small nor too large; keeping tools well sharpened, lubricated, and rust-free; and keeping abreast of innovations in the design of standard tools will reduce the amount of time and energy you spend installing and maintaining your landscape. A judicious selection of tools allows for more efficient use of the time you spend working outdoors, leaving you more time to fully enjoy and appreciate the rewards of having created a beautiful garden.

Power Tools Versus Hand Tools

For those truly interested in minimizing work in the garden, power tools will always be the first choice. However, hand tools have some pluses as well. Even the highest-quality hand tools are less expensive than comparable power tools. Hand tools require less maintenance than power tools, and the maintenance they do require is less complicated. In addition, to many gardeners hand tools are more fitting companions in the garden than their relatively noisy and obtrusive power counterparts. For some landscape jobs, hand tools are all that is available. Other chores can be done with either type of tool. Generally speaking, if you have a large area to cover, or if the job in question is very arduous, consider buying or renting appropriate power equipment.

Choosing Hand Tools

The tools you choose for cultivating or planting will depend on the soil, plant types, and size of your property. If you have a small yard, you may be able to get by with only a shovel, a trowel, and a hose. Larger yards, formal landscapes, and large expanses of lawn may require all of the tools listed below.

Shovel For most gardeners, an all-purpose round-nosed garden shovel is the first tool to buy. The angle between the wood handle and the blade is important. The more pronounced the angle, the greater the leverage when scooping heavy soil. A straighter angle makes it easier to dig deeply into the soil. Handles may either be straight or D-shaped. Long, straight handles allow you to stand more erect, which lessens back strain. D-shaped handles are useful when you are working in close quarters. Look for a sturdy connection between the handle and blade and forged steel.

Spade This tool can be useful for deeply turning heavy soil, for double-digging (see page 192) beds, and when straight soil edging is desired for appearance. Some spades are equipped with a tread, which is a thin metal plate welded to the top of the blade. Treads relieve stress on the bottom of the foot when you step on the spade to force it into the ground. Spades, like shovels, come with straight and D-shaped handles.

Garden Fork A garden fork, or pitchfork, is helpful for digging up plants, cultivating loose soil, and turning compost piles. The tines and base of the sturdier forks are

made as one cast-iron unit. Square-tined English spading forks are heavier and sturdier than flat-tined forks, which sometimes bend out of shape under the stress of working in heavy soil.

Hoe A hoe is useful for breaking up clods after you have turned the soil over with a spade or fork. For heavy cultivating use a stronger hoe with the handle fitted into a heavy socket in the base.

Rake There are two basic styles of rake. Garden rakes have rigid tines and are used for leveling and spreading soil and for preparing seed beds. They may be either bow backed or square backed. Bow-backed garden rakes are sturdier than square-backed ones. Turn either type over to use the back for finishing off a seedbed. Lawn, or leaf, rakes have long, flexible tines of wood or steel and are used for garden cleanup, for raking leaves and lawn clippings, and for lightly loosening lawn soil. Look for

Proper tools make gardening easier, and the time and energy they can save make them well worth the cost. When shopping for garden equipment, always buy the best you can afford, and don't buy tools you don't need. This clamshell posthole digger helps in preparing the ground to receive the container plants nearby.

a strong connection between the head and the handle.

Cultivator A cultivator is useful for light cultivation in well-tilled soil. It also helps break up clods after you have turned the soil over with a spade or fork.

Trowel A trowel is a general-purpose garden tool. It cultivates, plants, digs, weeds, and performs a multitude of other gardening chores. Select one with a strong handle and a sturdy head of forged steel that will not bend during planting.

Crowbar For digging holes, grubbing out stumps, or moving heavy rocks, nothing beats a crowbar. Buy one that is about 5 feet long, with a chisel on one end for prying out impacted material and a point on the other for breaking up compacted soil.

Hand Pruner These are small tools for cutting branches up to ¾ inch thick. Two main types are available. Scissor-style pruners have sharpened blades that overlap in making the cut. This type is liable to twist if forced, making a jagged cut that could injure the plant. If kept sharp and used properly, however, scissor-style pruners give a close, clean cut. Anvil-style pruners have a sharpened top blade that snaps onto a flat plate of softer metal. The disadvantage of anvil-type pruners is that they crush the bark on the anvil side and cannot cut as close as the scissor type. Choose pruners that are light, comfortable in the hand, and have easily replaceable blades and parts.

Lopper This long-handled pruner allows you to cut branches up to 2 inches in diameter. Ratchet loppers add leverage, cutting 2-inch limbs with ease. Look for loppers with

high-alloy steel blades and sturdy wood or steel handles.

Pruning Saw Pruning saws are used to cut branches more than 2 inches in diameter. The teeth of the saw will be either fine or coarse. Choose a saw that is comfortable in your hand, with a curved blade made of high-quality steel.

Hedge Shears (Hedge Trimmers, Hedge Clippers) Hedge shears have long, scissorlike blades used to trim and shape shrubs. To prevent the foliage from slipping away, buy shears on which one blade is notched. Extralong handles are available on most models for tall hedges or short people.

Choosing Power Tools

Power tools are useful when there is a large area to cover or the job is particularly arduous or tedious. Power tools can run on either electricity or gasoline. Electric tools are generally quieter and less expensive than their gasoline counterparts. Their main limitation is that they must be plugged into a power source or recharged from time to time.

Many power tools can be rented. Renting may be especially appropriate for items that are used infrequently, such as a rotary tiller. Check the local garden center or Yellow Pages for businesses that rent equipment.

Rotary Tiller This tool is invaluable for a large, open garden, making it relatively easy to cultivate areas that would take many tedious hours to spade. Tillers are especially good at mixing soil amendments and fertilizer evenly into the top 6 inches of soil, where most root growth occurs. Some rotary tillers have tines in the front, others have tines in the back. Front-end models tend to be best for light jobs, such as loosening soil in a previously used planting bed; rear-end tillers usually work better for heavy-duty tasks, such as creating a new planting bed.

Lawn Mower There are two basic types of lawn mower: reel and rotary. Reel mowers are either operated manually or powered by engines. All rotary mowers are power mowers, with gas or electric engines.

Reel mowers shear the grass with a scissorlike action that produces a very clean cut. They can cut very low and are preferred for grasses which need to be mown to a height of less than 1 inch.

Rotary mowers cut with a high-speed rotating blade. The rotary mower is generally more versatile and easier to handle and maintain than the reel type, but rotary mowers cannot make as sharp or clean a cut. Rotary mowers should not be used to mow lawns lower than 1 inch, or they will scalp the grass.

Both types of mower can be adjusted for the mowing height your grass requires. Place the mower on a level surface. On reel mowers, measure the distance from the surface to the bed knife. Set it to the desired height with a screw adjustment near the roller. On rotary mowers, measure from the edge of the skirt to the surface. Adjust the height by moving the wheels up or down, or measure the height of the grass after mowing and adjust the mower up or down one setting.

Clean the mower with a light spray of water after use. Dry it and spray it lightly with a penetrating oil. Use a knife or screwdriver to remove caked grass from the bottom of a rotary mower. Make sure that the motor oil in power mowers is at the proper level. Never fill the gas tank or oil the mechanism while the mower is on the lawn; spilled gas or oil can kill the grass.

Sharpen mower blades regularly. Dull blades leave crushed and uncut grass, giving the lawn a ragged appearance. To sharpen rotary blades, first disconnect the spark-plug wire, then remove the blade. Use a file or grindstone to sharpen the edge of the blade that comes in contact with the grass; sharpen at a 45-degree angle. Have reel mower blades sharpened professionally.

Hedge Shears (Hedge Trimmers, Hedge Clippers) If your garden contains a long expanse of hedge, power hedge shears may be a good investment; they can be electric or powered by gasoline. Look for shears that are easy to handle, comfortable to hold, and not too heavy.

Choosing a Hose

The decision to install a watering system will cut down but not completely eliminate the need for a garden hose. If you have ever wrestled with a hose full of kinks, you know the importance of a high-quality, pliable hose. The more reinforcement in the hose, the better it will

This open box offers unrestricted use of the hose. When the box is closed, the hose is stored neatly out of sight and protected from the sun.

stand up under pressure. Look for reinforced rubber hoses that will withstand up to 500 pounds of pressure per square inch. Some extra-heavy-duty hoses are doubly reinforced with tire cord. Couplings should be durable octagonal brass that will not crush easily.

When choosing a hose, pay attention to the diameter that best fits your needs. Five basic diameters are sold; the hoses with ⅜-inch and ½-inch diameters are used for watering container plants, the ⅝-inch size is most popular for lawns and gardens, and the ¾-inch and 1-inch hoses are mostly used in commercial applications. The smaller the diameter, the less water the hose will deliver in a given period. Clearly, when you need a large amount of water, a larger hose will save you time.

You can customize your hand-watering system by using a variety of heads, each designed to fill particular garden needs. They are relatively inexpensive, and many will allow you to adjust the flow of water from a fine spray to a hard stream. Sweeper, or cleaning, nozzles are not adjustable, but they are wonderfully effective for jobs that require large volumes of water in powerful streams, such as cleaning driveways, patios, and walls. Fan-spray heads, bubblers or soaker heads, and misting heads all increase your flexibility when it is time to water.

MANAGING YOUR SOIL

Plants and soil are so interrelated that one would not exist without the other. Soil provides plants with water and nutrients. It is also a medium into which plants anchor their roots, giving them the stability to defy gravity and grow upward. And when plants decompose, they turn into humus, the organic component of soil. Understanding and properly managing this precious substance is one of the most important aspects of growing plants.

Because few people are blessed with the "rich, well-drained garden loam" referred to so often on the back of seed packets, most people must improve their soil in one way or another. Do not try to live with problem soil—nothing can dampen enthusiasm more quickly than a soil that does not allow healthy plant growth. You can modify almost any kind of soil to grow any plant that is right for the climate. For all but the worst soils, this is not a particularly extensive or complicated process.

What Is Soil?

Every soil consists of mineral and organic matter, water, air, and living organisms. The proportions may vary, but the major components remain the same. A typical garden soil contains 50 percent solids, 25 percent liquid, and 25 percent air. Minerals account for most soil solids, usually constituting about 45 percent of the soil. Organic solids make up a much smaller portion—5 percent or less. The remaining constituents—water and air—are held on the surfaces of the soil solids or in the spaces between them.

Depth, fertility, texture, and *structure* are terms used to describe important soil characteristics. A good soil for planting landscape plants has a topsoil that is several inches deep, is reasonably fertile, has a good balance of sand, silt, and clay particles (these give it its texture), and has just the right amount of air space between those particles to promote both good drainage and water retention (this is its structure). In addition, good soil has an acceptable pH (acid/alkaline balance) for healthy plant growth.

A Typical Soil Profile

If you dig deeply into your soil, making a vertical section, you will see that there are several distinct layers. The types and sequence of soil layers form what is known as the soil profile. The profile can tell you much about the soil's potential for gardening success. The top few inches, or topsoil, might be a dark, loose soil of fine texture, high in organic material. This layer supports most plant growth and can be manipulated through cultivation and soil amendments. An ideal topsoil is deep, with good texture and structure and an acceptable pH.

Below the topsoil lies the subsoil. Its layers may be more or less impervious. If the subsoil is compacted clay, drainage will be poor. There may be several layers within the subsoil, with varying amounts of sand, silt, and clay. Below the subsoil lies bedrock. This is a layer of solid rock that is relatively impervious to water. The depth of the bedrock may vary from area to area. Bedrock that is close to the surface of the soil will reduce the amount of topsoil and subsoil available for plant growth.

Laboratory Tests

The most accurate way to find out what kind of soil you have is to take samples from the areas in which you intend to plant and have them tested in a soil laboratory. State agricultural colleges usually do soil tests for free or for a nominal charge. Contact the local cooperative extension office for information. In 1995, commercial labs charged about $25 for tests of soil salts and pH and from $25 to $100 for tests to determine levels of soil nutrients. Any labs in your area should be listed in the Yellow Pages.

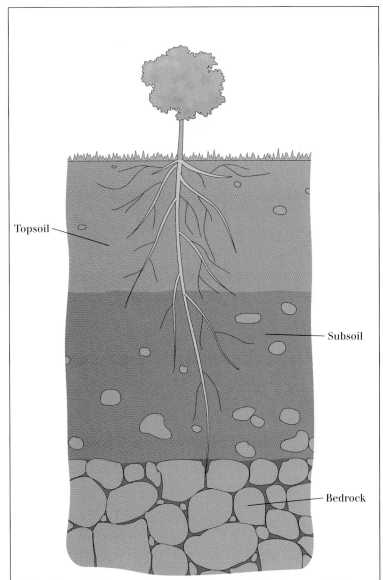

Topsoil

Subsoil

Bedrock

This soil profile shows universal, nonspecific soil horizons—with topsoil, subsoil, and bedrock. The horizons can differ wildly, even in small yards. Horizons can be abrupt or gradual, depending on the location.

Take a soil sample by digging a hole with a shovel and then scraping the side of the hole with a spoon. Take samples from several areas of your yard since soil varies significantly even in a small yard.

SOIL AMENDMENTS

This chart will help you gauge the amount of soil amendment you will need to add before planting landscape plants. A cubic foot of amendment will cover an area of 12 square feet to a depth of 1 inch. A cubic yard is $3 \times 3 \times 3$ cubic feet.

Amendment Needed

Depth of amendment	Volume required to cover 100 sq ft
¼"	2 cu ft
½"	4 cu ft
1"	8 cu ft
2"	17 cu ft
3"	1 cu yd
4"	1¼ cu yd

Soil Amendments

If the results of a soil test indicate that your soil is high in clay or has little topsoil, adding soil amendments should be your next step. Soil amendments are bulk materials that are incorporated into soil to improve drainage, structure, microbial activity, aeration, and other soil properties. They are usually relatively fine-textured decomposed organic materials, such as manure, ground bark, or sawdust. A mulch, by contrast, is a material that is placed on top of the soil for such purposes as reducing erosion, preventing soil crusting, and minimizing weeding. Many of the same materials used for amending soil are also used for mulching.

Mulches are often incorporated into the soil at the end of the gardening season to become amendments. Soil amendments, although usually beneficial, can have some negative side effects, such as introducing weed seeds into the soil, adding salts in amounts harmful to plant growth, or reducing the amount of nitrogen available to the plants. These negative side effects are easily corrected, and the drawbacks of soil amendments are far outweighed by their positive effects on the soil. The most common soil amendments are described below.

Agricultural By-products Agricultural by-products include a wide variety of materials, some of which may be available in your area. Peanut hulls are an excellent amendment. Tobacco stems work well but should be kept away from plants in the same family (tomatoes, potatoes, peppers, and nicotiana) because of diseases. Cottonseed meal has fairly high levels of plant nutrients. Cocoa bean hulls hold water well, have a pleasing appearance and aroma as an amendment or mulch, and are acidic. Rice hulls are sometimes available in the West. Bagasse is a sugarcane by-product that is used as an amendment and mulch in the South. Apple and grape pomace—skins, seeds, and stems left after processing—have been used with good results. Ground corncobs are available in the Midwest. Straw, a traditional soil amendment and mulch, must be supplemented with nitrogen when worked directly into the soil, and it often has weed or grain seeds.

Compost Decomposed organic matter, or compost, is an excellent soil amendment. You can make it yourself by gathering garden refuse, dried leaves, lawn clippings, and organic kitchen refuse and storing these materials in a screened bin or covered container. It can also be purchased. When properly managed, the high heat of decomposition (160° F) will kill most weed seeds, insects, and disease organisms. As a general rule, recycle and reuse—do not remove organic material from the site. All of it is extremely valuable.

Imported Topsoil Imported topsoil is brought in from another location and added to your garden soil. If the layer of topsoil existing in your garden is shallow, you may wish to purchase topsoil to add to it. Bags of topsoil are available at many nurseries and garden centers. You can purchase larger amounts by the truckload. Purchased topsoil may contain weed seeds and may require additional fertilization. If possible, test your soil again, after adding new topsoil. You may wish to add additional soil amendments to it.

Lawn Clippings Lawn clippings are both plentiful and free, if you have a lawn. Moderate amounts of lawn clippings can be worked directly into the soil without composting. If the grass has gone to seed or if it is a variety that grows from its stems, such as bermudagrass (*Cynodon dactylon*), do not use it as a soil amendment without composting it first or you will end up weeding lawn grass out of your planting beds. It is best to cut often and leave the clippings on the lawn itself. Clippings mulch the roots, conserve moisture, and, when decomposed, are organic fertilizer.

Leaf Mold Leaf mold, or decomposed leaf material, is often sold commercially. This material may be acidic, depending on the leaves used, making it a favored amendment for acid-loving plants such as azaleas and blueberries. Make sure that no poison oak or poison ivy has been included in the mix.

Manure Animal manures of all types have long been used as soil conditioners. The commonly used manures all have modest amounts of the major nutrients (nitrogen, phosphorus, and potassium). Chicken manure is the most potent,

so use smaller amounts of it. All manures work better if they are composted first. Manure often carries weed seeds, depending on where the animals were grazing. The amount of salt the animal has eaten will affect the level of salt in the manure. Commercial steer manure usually comes from feedlot steers, which are often fed diets high in salt. A soil amendment will be more successful if you leach water through the manure to dissolve the salt and carry it into the subsoil before planting landscape plants. Check with a local zoo, dairy, or farm for manure that may be available for purchase. Pet rabbits are also a good source of manure for garden soil amendment.

Peat Moss Commonly available at nurseries and garden centers, peat moss is derived from moss from ancient swamps and is an excellent soil amendment. Sphagnum moss is sometimes confused with peat moss; this is moss that is dried but not decomposed. Sphagnum moss is fine when used as a packing material, for making hanging baskets, and to cover the surfaces of pots, but it should not be used as a soil amendment.

Peat moss is relatively expensive, but it retains moisture well, drains

If true gardening—growing food or flowers—is important to you, you know how valuable good compost can be. Consider building a compost storage unit, such as this three-unit bin. It was designed to provide air circulation, which is important for proper decomposition.

superbly, and is lightweight. It has an acidic effect (a pH of 3.5 to 4.5) that may be desirable for certain plants, or you can neutralize this acidity by adding 5 pounds of lime per 100 square feet of 4-inch-deep peat moss. Peat moss is the longest lasting of the organic mulches, minimizing the shrinkage of soil volume that occurs when an organic amendment decomposes. In some areas other types of peat are available, such as sedge peat, but these are inferior to peat moss as a garden soil amendment.

Sand You can add sand to heavy clay soil to improve drainage, but it may have the opposite effect. Unless the resulting blend is more than 80-percent sand, the mix will have worse drainage than clay alone. The clay fills in the spaces between the sand particles, acting like cement. Sand, especially coarse sand, will improve drainage in a container mix that does not include any heavy soil.

Wood By-products Ground bark and sawdust are widely sold as soil amendments. Wood by-products to be used as an amendment should be fortified with nitrogen; if organic materials are not already decomposed, the bacteria that decomposes them will use nitrogen from the soil.

If you use raw sawdust as a soil conditioner, add a nitrogen supplement as well. For every 100 pounds of sawdust, add 1 pound of actual nitrogen. If you are putting 2 inches of sawdust onto a 100-square-foot area, add ½ pound of nitrogen. The amount of nitrogen needed will vary according to the type of sawdust, however. In general, sawdust from coniferous trees will require more added nitrogen than that from hardwood or deciduous trees. Sawdust is often treated with

nitrogen fertilizer and iron sulfate (to make it dark colored) and sold as "soil conditioner." This material needs no extra nitrogen.

Ground redwood or fir bark make excellent soil amendments; they are long lasting, provide good soil aeration, and are easy to use. Ground bark is available at most nurseries and garden centers in bags of varying sizes at a relatively low cost. These products are usually partly decomposed and so require less added nitrogen than sawdust products.

Vermiculite and Perlite These are tiny mineral particles whose sizes have been expanded by a heating process. Vermiculite has a porous structure. It retains water and nutrients very well but is fragile and keeps its structure for only a few months in the soil. Perlite particles are impervious to water and do not retain water or nutrients. Perlite lasts much longer in the soil than vermiculite.

Both perlite and vermiculite provide good soil aeration and are lightweight, making them especially ideal for use in containers and when a sterile soil rather than ordinary garden soil is desired. Use of a sterile soil will reduce plant pathogen problems when seeds are germinating.

Fertilizers as Soil Amendments

Soil amendments function mainly to improve the soil texture, but some of them, such as compost, will release an appreciable amount of nitrogen into the soil as they break down. If your soil tests indicate that additional nutrients are desired or necessary, you can add a fertilizer as a soil amendment during planting.

Most commercial fertilizers contain, among other substances, three primary nutrients: nitrogen, phosphorus, and potassium. Fertilizer labels indicate the percentages of these three nutrients. The percentages may vary, but the listings are always in the same order: nitrogen first, phosphorus second, and potassium third. A 5-10-10 or 10-10-10 fertilizer worked into the soil before planting will get the plants off to a strong start. Spread dry fertilizer evenly over the soil (this can be done when you add the amendments) at the rate called for on the package; then work it in with a spade or rotary tiller.

Many fertilizers supply additional elements, such as iron and zinc, that may be lacking in the soil, some in very minute amounts. If you have tested the soil, the analysis will help you determine the type of fertilizer to use and how much. If you haven't tested the soil, a complete, all-purpose fertilizer will satisfy the requirements of most plants. Phosphorus has been shown to stimulate the early formation and strong growth of roots. For this reason, a superphosphate incorporated into the soil at planting time could prove beneficial. Seedlings almost always benefit from extra phosphorus.

Be careful when planting; fertilizers should not come in direct contact with the roots of the plants. Mix dry fertilizers into the backfill soil or planting beds according to the manufacturer's recommended dosages.

Cultivating Your Soil

Loosening the soil in preparation for planting, or loosening the soil around growing plants, is known as cultivating the soil. Soil cultivation allows you to increase aeration, mix in amendments, and control weeds.

Do not attempt to cultivate soil that is either too wet or too dry. Moisture content is an important

consideration in all but the sandiest soils, but it is especially important in clay soils. When clay soils are too wet, cultivating can compact the particles and destroy the structure of the soil. The hard clods that form as the clay dries will not break down easily. To test the soil, turn over a shovelful and try to break the clod. If it breaks easily, it is ready to work. If it is too sticky to break, wait a few more days.

Cultivating soil that is too dry can also be a problem. If the soil is dry and hard, before cultivating soak it thoroughly and let it drain for a day or two, until a clod breaks easily.

Good soil is essential to growing top-quality plants. Most soils can be greatly improved by the addition of the proper soil amendments before planting. Avoid making the soil more than 50 percent amendments. About 20 to 40 percent is usually appropriate.

Preparing a Bed for Planting

Prepare any area in which you are installing multiple plants, such as a shrub border, in the same manner as for a planting bed. First, clean off any debris from the planting area. Spread soil amendments and fertilizer, and mix them into the soil. Till with a shovel, spade, or fork; if the planting area is large, use a rotary tiller. Smooth the bed with a rake or cultivator.

Tilling With a Shovel, Spade, or Fork Dig one row at a time. Turn each shovelful of soil on its side, so any weeds are buried but do not make a layer in the soil. Forks are effective in light soil and soil with good tilth. Spades work best in clay soil and soil that has not been cultivated before. Shovels can be used in any situation. Shovels and forks turn over about 6 inches of soil; spades, about 8 inches.

Using a Rotary Tiller If the soil is hard or dry, it may be necessary to make several passes across the garden with a rotary tiller, with each pass tilling a couple of inches deeper than the one before. Make these successive passes at right angles to one another. Tillers do not get into corners well, so plan to do the corners by hand. Unless the tiller is extralarge, it will till about 6 inches deep.

Smoothing the Bed After tilling, use a cultivator to smooth the surface. For a seedbed with more finely textured soil, use a garden rake. Bury hard clods and rocks that you rake up below tilling depth at the end of the planting bed.

GETTING LANDSCAPE PLANTS

Timing is all-important in planting. The time to plant varies across the country. Ask your neighbors, the local garden center staff, or your farm adviser when to plant or transplant. Generally, early spring and early fall are recommended as ideal—the planting times of least environmental stress.

In cold-winter areas, small plants, such as ground covers, are usually more successful when planted in the spring. Fall plantings are more likely to suffer from the heaving of the soil caused by freeze/thaw cycles. Young plants may literally be pushed out of the ground; with their roots exposed, they quickly die. If you must plant in the fall, do it as early as possible.

In areas where the soil does not freeze, a fall planting can be very successful; winter rains and cool temperatures help plants adjust to their new home; and when spring comes, they are already established and begin to grow more quickly. Avoid planting in midsummer in dry regions, unless you are prepared to spend a lot of time watering.

Bare-root stock must be planted while it is quiescent and not growing—in the winter or early spring. This allows the root system to become established before top growth occurs. Container-grown and

Tilling with a rotary tiller loosens the soil, mixes in amendments, and is a good initial weed-eradication measure for large areas of your yard. After your landscape is installed, however, you must use other methods of weed control.

balled-and-burlapped plants can be planted almost any time of year, except when the ground is frozen.

During hot weather, plant during the cooler hours of the morning or evening. This will lessen the stress on the plants and reduce wilting. Do not plant if a severe heat spell, morning frost, or stormy weather is predicted. A heavy rainstorm can also damage young seedlings.

Frost Dates and Climate Zones

The U.S. Department of Agriculture has devised a system of plant-hardiness zones (we have amended this system to include southern Canada). A complete discussion of this system, along with a guide to landscape plants that are adaptable to various areas, begins on page 211. Remember, however, that guides for hardiness zones can give only a rough approximation. If your home is on a south-facing hillside or near a large body of water, your location may be 10 degrees warmer than the average temperature in your region. A garden on a north-facing hill can be 10 to 20 degrees cooler than the rest of the region.

Cold, sun, heat, wind, and rain define the limits of outdoor planting activity. Too much of any of these elements can cause stress and leave a plant in a weakened condition, unable to rally effectively against insect or disease attack. To some extent, you can modify outdoor conditions by using protective devices, including shade barriers against the sun or coverings against frost. However, such measures must be heroic to ensure the safety of plants inappropriate for the region. Plants that are too tender for the climate will need to be dug up and brought indoors or carefully protected with mulch if winter temperatures drop too low.

PLANNING FOR THE FUTURE

Landscape design, unlike almost any other creative process, is made of living elements that grow and change in form over time. Before you install your design, it is important to visualize not only how it will look immediately after planting, but also how it will look in 5, 10, or 20 years. The plant that fits so perfectly when young may look radically out of place when it reaches maturity. Before you select plants for your landscape, determine whether their mature form and size are an appropriate fit.

In addition to changing over the years, plants change with the seasons. You can use the seasonal characteristics of plants to your advantage when you are designing the landscape. A deciduous tree may provide the patio with shade from the hot summer sun when it has its leaves and allow the warming winter sun to reach your windows after the leaves fall.

When buying the plants for your new landscape, you may be tempted to get the largest plants available for instant results. This can prove to be expensive and unnecessary, however, as larger plants are more susceptible to transplant shock and may grow slowly and require additional care. One alternative is to plant fast-growing plants to fill in temporarily while the slower-growing, more desirable plants are becoming established. These interim plants are frequently shorter-lived than other garden plants and should be removed once the other plants reach a serviceable size. Interim plantings can also be useful in parts of the garden that are slated for future change, such as an area where you plan to build an addition to the house. Hedges of fast-growing plants, such as Lombardy poplar (*Populus nigra* 'Italica'), or wood fences and screens can help provide temporary barriers if you need privacy while the landscape is maturing.

Consider the maintenance that each plant will require as it matures. Over the years you may decide to change certain plants that prove to be overly aggressive, growing beyond their expected size, or that require excessive work to look attractive. When selecting replacement plants, reconsider the original design intention and choose new plants that complement the existing landscape.

After you have selected plants suitable to your locale, you must find sites in the garden that meet their particular needs for sun and shade. Do not expect a shade plant to thrive in a location where it receives afternoon sun in the summer, especially if the heat reflects off a wall or if searing winds prevail.

Scheduling Your Planting

You will want to have all your plans finished in time to install your plants during their ideal planting time. The dates of the last frost in spring and the first frost in autumn are crucial when planting a garden. Some plants, notably fruit trees, require a winter chill at a specified low temperature for a certain period of time. The temperature and duration should be indicated by the orchardist.

When buying trees or shrubs locally, you can usually assume that the plants are known to flourish in your climate and that the item is ready to plant upon purchase. When buying mail-order trees or shrubs, be especially careful that the plant is adaptable to your region, and check the best planting time for each species.

If the ideal planting time in your area for most plants is early spring, take advantage of the long winter months to develop your design ideas. Planting is among the last of the construction tasks. As soon as weather permits in the spring, you can begin your construction tasks. When the soil starts warming up later in the season, most of your preliminary work will have been done, and you will be ready to install the landscape plants. Begin the installation with trees. Proceed from there to shrubs and vines, and finish up with ground covers and lawns. Installing plants in this order will help you avoid trampling the more fragile ground-cover and lawn plantings during other landscaping and construction tasks.

Plant Costs

In estimating the cost of plants, you need to consider the size and type of plants you need for your design. Smaller plants are, in general, less expensive than larger ones. If you are attempting to fit new plants into an existing landscape, however, you may wish to buy fairly mature plants so the landscape is balanced between new and old.

To save money, install as many of the plants yourself as you can. Buy soil mix in bulk, and rent tree augers or power equipment for digging in difficult soil. Large trees can weigh as much as 3,000 pounds, however, which can pose a problem. Obtain the services of a professional for these special plants. Licensed landscape contractors usually guarantee their work.

In most cases the more exotic the plant, the more expensive it will be, in both initial purchase price and maintenance costs. Buy plants that will grow well in your area. See the Landscape Plant Guide beginning on page 211 for information on the vines, trees, shrubs, ground covers, lawn grasses, and tropical plants that are best suited to your region. As you develop your planting plan, visit local garden centers and take note of the costs and availability of plants you want to use in your landscape; make adjustments in your design if these plants are out of your price range.

Perhaps the best way to save on plant costs is to be somewhat flexible in the type of plants you purchase. Once your landscape planting plan has been determined, watch for sale items that are appropriate for your needs. Check with friends and neighbors for plants that may not fit in their landscapes but would be suitable for your design. Ask the local public park administration and plant societies for cuttings or even whole plants that they may make available at nominal cost.

Buying Plants for Your Landscape

Nurseries and garden centers are delightful places to shop. There is something about being surrounded by living, growing plants that makes a trip to the nursery different from visits to other types of stores. Spend some extra time just looking around.

While you are strolling, keep your eyes open for clues that will tell you something about the nursery and the plants there. Are the growing beds well ordered and easy to walk through? Do the plants look as though they have been well tended? Are the signs and plant labels informative and legible, giving both common and botanical names? More important, is the sales staff helpful and knowledgeable? A short talk with an experienced nursery professional can give you information that would be difficult to find otherwise. If a clerk does not know the answer to a specific question, he or she should be able to find someone who does, or find the information in a reference book. Aside from carrying healthy plants, a highly trained staff is what makes one nursery or garden center better than another. They can be a continuing source of trustworthy information. Use the list from your planting plan and spend time picking out the best specimens, variety by variety, before purchasing plants.

Mail-order Nurseries

For those who don't have the convenience of a local nursery or garden center, mail-order nurseries are a viable alternative. Their colorful catalogs, sent during the cold days of winter, offer an enticement to garden-hungry readers. Mail-order houses often have a limited shipping season and supply of certain plants. On the other hand, they are often good sources of rare or unusual plants that are unavailable at local garden centers.

Many mail-order nurseries have been in business for generations and offer the highest quality of plant material. The fact that it may be sent from some distance away

should not be considered a detriment; many local nurseries also receive their plants from outside the area. Nonetheless, plants that have been shipped through the mail will have undergone a certain amount of stress and should be "babied" as soon as you receive them. Take them out of the shipping containers and get them planted as soon as you can.

If you are ordering plants from a particular mail-order firm for the first time, it might be a good idea to make your initial order a small one. Find out how you like their plants, whether they arrive in good condition, and whether they perform well in your yard before ordering more. Most reputable mail-order companies will stand behind their stock with a reasonable guarantee.

Special Orders

If you are looking for a specific plant that is not in stock at your local nursery, request that the nursery order it for you. Most good nurseries will be able to find what

The roots of this mail-ordered Pseudotsuga menziesii *are protected with a gel that conserves moisture during shipment and immediately after the trees have been transplanted.*

TRANSPLANTING

Transplanting involves moving an established plant from one spot in the garden to another. Transplanting any plant, whether large or small, represents some danger to the plant, though with proper care almost any plant can be moved. Root loss or root damage may seriously affect the plant's ability to reestablish itself.

Try to transplant during cool, moist weather to lessen the stress on the plant. Move plants when they are dormant or as inactive as possible. Dig as large a rootball as you can handle to minimize root loss, and be careful not to break it. Compensate for root loss by pruning the top of the plant proportionally.

Use a compass as part of your tool kit. Tie a red flag (or some other marker) on the north face of the plant and try to orient it similarly in its new location. This reduces shock and lowers the danger of sunburning. This additional precaution is more important for larger, older trees.

If you have lots of time, prune the roots with a sharp shovel two or three times in the year before the transplanting is to occur. Cut the roots where you will finally dig to form a rootball. This early cutting will force the plant to build new fibrous roots in a more confined area. It the plant has a taproot, attempt to dig under it and cut the taproot well in advance of the actual transplanting procedure.

To transplant, first dig a hole in the new location. Then, with a sharp spade, cut around the entire plant you want to move. If the plant is large, dig a ditch around it. Undercut the rootball from one side until the plant can be lifted from the soil. Gently lift the plant onto a piece of burlap and carry it to the new location. Backfill the hole, build a basin, and water the plant as described in Planting Container Plants (see page 204), steps 6 through 10.

you need within a few weeks. Certain types of plants are available only during certain seasons (bare-root trees, for example), so you may have to delay planting. Place special orders early to ensure getting the plants when you need them.

Types of Plants

Plants are sold in many forms, and the type you choose will depend on your situation. Seeds are commonly used to start annual flowering and vegetable plants. Some ground covers and vines are also available in seed form. Flats and cell packs contain seedlings that are usually big enough to plant. Container-grown plants come in plastic or metal pots in a variety of sizes. Most medium-sized shrubs and trees and some

herbaceous perennials are available as container plants. Larger trees and evergreen shrubs are sold with soil wrapped in burlap around their roots. These are called balled-and-burlapped plants. During the winter dormant season, roses, fruit trees, berry plants, and deciduous ornamental trees are sold bare root, meaning the plant is sold while it is dormant with no soil around its roots.

Seeds

Seeds are an economical way of starting certain ground covers and vines. When buying seeds, you must consider the time and care required to germinate and grow them to planting size. Specific growing conditions are frequently necessary for proper seedling growth. These conditions may not be easily achieved. Young seedlings are especially vulnerable to insects and require frequent watering to keep them from drying out. Native grasses and wildflowers are easy to obtain as seeds and can be sown directly on the site. Lawns are commonly started from seed. Selecting a lawn seed requires careful study of the growing conditions and desired use.

Flats and Cell Packs

Ground covers and bedding plants are usually sold in flats or small cell packs. Cell packs may contain 4, 6, or 12 plants. Plants in cell packs are separated into individual plastic cells, making them easy to remove without damaging the roots. Flats generally hold four to five dozen plants that can be separated at planting time.

When selecting flats, look for healthy plants with a good leaf color. Avoid plants that are overgrown, as these may be root bound or may have grown into the soil at the nursery and will have difficulty adjusting. If the plants seem very young, you may wish to leave them in the flat for a week after you take them home. Set them where they will be protected from direct sunlight until you are ready to plant them. Flats dry out very quickly, so be sure to water them frequently, perhaps as often as twice daily during hot weather.

Bare-Root Plants

In the dormant season, you will find a wide variety of bare-root plants at garden centers. Plants that drop their leaves in the winter, such as fruit trees and roses, are completely dormant when out of leaf and can be dug up and transported without any soil around their roots.

A bare-root plant is less expensive than the same kind of plant sold in a container because it is easier to handle, lighter to ship, and requires less attention in the nursery. Bare-root plants are also available in a wider selection.

In the nursery, bare-root plants may be kept in temporary storage in moist sawdust or sand, or the roots may be covered with plastic bags. Even if the plant is prepackaged, try to examine the roots to be sure they are moist and plump, not dry and shriveled. The branches should be evenly spaced so the plant will develop symmetrically.

When you arrive home with your plants, check the roots carefully. With sharp, clean pruning shears, remove any that are broken or damaged. Soak the roots for a couple of hours in a pail of water, and then plant without delay, if possible. If you cannot plant at once because the soil is too wet, plant as soon as the soil can be worked. Meanwhile, store the bare-root plant in a shady location with its roots and some of the stem in a moist medium, such as sawdust,

This healthy bare-root rose displays a well-branched root system.

bark, or in a trench of loose soil. Keep the plant cool until you can install it.

Container Plants

Shrubs and trees are commonly sold in containers. The containers may be metal, plastic, fiber, or wood and are available in many sizes. The most common sizes for shrubs are 1- and 5-gallon containers. Specimen shrubs are often sold in 15-gallon containers. Trees are typically sold in 5-, 10-, or 15-gallon containers. Specimen trees are frequently sold in large wood boxes.

Deciding what size plant to buy can be difficult. The key here is patience. It may be hard to buy a smaller size, knowing that you will have to wait longer for the plant to grow, even though the cost is

Ask garden-center personnel to use a can cutter to slit the sides of container plants for you. Be careful of the sharp edges where the can has been cut when transporting and installing plants in cut containers.

considerably lower. After about three years, however, most plants starting out in both 1-gallon and 5-gallon containers will be about the same size.

Plastic containers allow plants to be slipped out easily, without damage to the root system; an added bonus is that the container can be reused. Metal containers, except those with crimped sides, will have to be cut in order to get the plant out. You can cut them yourself or have it done at the nursery. Wood containers, used for large specimen plants, must be dismantled in order to remove the plants.

Make sure that the container, regardless of the type, is in good shape when you purchase the plant. Rusted metal cans, split plastic, or disintegrated wood usually mean

that the roots of the plant have grown into the ground soil at the nursery. When you take the plant away from its accustomed site, it is likely to suffer severe shock.

The plant should be well anchored in the container, but not to the point of being root bound. Try gently lifting the plant by the trunk. If the soil moves at all, the plant has not had time to develop roots throughout the rootball. If the plant has been in the container too long, growth will have stopped and will be difficult to get started again. Check for thick masses of roots on the soil surface or around the sides of the soil ball. Root-bound plants have more difficulty establishing a normal root system when planted, and their growth may be stunted. Roots that are tightly wrapped around the stem are called girdling roots and will restrict growth as they slowly choke the plant. Avoid plants with this problem, or cut the girdling root when you plant.

Balled-and-Burlapped Plants

So-called B and B plants are trees and shrubs that have been raised in a field. When they are ready for sale, they are extracted from the soil, and the rootball is wrapped in burlap and tied with twine. In mild climates, plants sold balled and burlapped are usually evergreens (such as rhododendrons, azaleas, and conifers) and large deciduous trees that do not tolerate bare-root transplanting. In climates with severe winters, many different types of plants are sold B and B. Because plants raised in fields are much less susceptible to winter freezing than those grown in containers, many plants must be sold balled and burlapped.

The dormant season—autumn and early winter—is the usual time for planting B and B plants because there is less risk of transplant shock. However, because of the protection provided by the soil around the rootball, balled-and-burlapped plants can also be transplanted during the growing season.

Propagation

Plant propagation is the art and science of reproducing plants from seeds, cuttings, division, or grafts. Although some ground covers and vines may be started from seed, other forms of propagation can be difficult, and they are not practical for large-scale landscaping. If you are interested in propagating plants for your garden, many books on propagating and general gardening techniques explain the principles in detail.

Choosing Healthy Nursery Stock

The first question to ask when you are buying the larger types of plants is whether to use seedlings and yearling stock or pay the extra price for larger container-grown or balled-and-burlapped plants. Yearling stock and container-grown or B and B plants are readily available from local sources. Seedlings are generally supplied by mail-order specialists. Buying young plants makes sense when you intend to create a large mass planting and wish to economize.

Plants sold at garden centers are almost always big enough to plant. When selecting plants, check them carefully. The foliage should be healthy; avoid plants with yellowing or spotted leaves. Inspect the stems and the upper and lower surfaces of the leaves for diseases and insects. Plants sold at garden centers are usually either in containers or balled and burlapped. If you will not be able to install the plants right away, do not leave

Evergreen shrubs and trees are often sold balled and burlapped.

them exposed to full sun. Give them shade, and water them regularly until you can place them in their permanent locations.

Selecting Vines Vines are usually sold in flat or cell-pack containers. A well-grown vine will have three or more branches that appear healthy and will have good leaf color. Branches that are twisted together will be more difficult to separate and train after planting and should be avoided. As with other plant types, roots growing from the bottom of the container may mean that the plant is root bound and will have trouble becoming established.

Selecting Trees Trees are commonly available container grown or balled and burlapped. When selecting a tree, look for a straight trunk, a well-balanced branching pattern, and good leaf color. The roots should not encircle the trunk. Likewise, the plant should not be root bound. Avoid trees that have any nicks or cuts in the bark where disease organisms may enter.

ATTRACTING WILDLIFE

If you enjoy observing wildlife and are willing to put up with the damage they may cause, certain plants will enhance the attractiveness of your garden to local birds and animals. In areas where snow covers the ground for much of the winter, leave fruit that has fallen from trees on the ground to provide winter forage for deer and other wildlife. Remember, however, that your prized rhododendrons are also a target for these hungry animals.

Trees

Abies species	Fir
Alnus species	Alder
Amelanchier canadensis	Serviceberry, shadblow
Arbutus menziesii	Madrone, madrona
Arbutus unedo	Strawberry tree
Betula species	Birch
Celtis occidentalis	Common hackberry
Cornus species	Dogwood
Crataegus species	Hawthorn
Ilex species	Holly
Larix kaempferi	Japanese larch
Laurus nobilis	Sweet bay, bay laurel, Grecian laurel
Malus species	Apple
Morus alba (varieties)	Mulberry
Prunus species	

Shrubs

Berberis darwinii	Darwin barberry
Callistemon citrinus	Lemon bottlebrush
Ceanothus species	
Cornus species	Dogwood
Cotoneaster species	
Euonymus species	
Ilex species	Holly species
Lonicera species	Honeysuckle
Mahonia species	Oregon grape
Photinia species	
Pyracantha species	Firethorn
Salix species	Willow species
Vaccinium species	
Weigela florida	Old-fashioned weigela

Vines

Ampelopsis brevipedunculata	Blueberry climber
Lonicera species	Honeysuckle species
Parthenocissus	

Ground Covers

Ceanothus species	
Cotoneaster species	
Euonymus species	
Fragaria chiloensis	Wild strawberry
Heuchera sanguinea	Coralbells
Lonicera japonica	Hall's honeysuckle

Selecting Shrubs

Shrubs may be sold bare root, balled and burlapped, or in containers. When selecting a shrub, look for a healthy plant with few yellow or spotted leaves. The plant should have a well-balanced shape, good leaf color, and should not be too large for its container.

Selecting Ground Covers

Ground covers are usually sold as started seedlings or cuttings in flats or cell packs. When selecting a ground cover that has been grown in a flat or cell pack, look for lush, healthy growth. Individual plants should have good leaf color and should not appear to have outgrown their container.

Selecting Sod

Sod is lawn grass that has been cut into strips and rolled up for easy installation. When purchasing sod, unroll a section to examine the turf. Sod should be a consistent green color, with few yellowed or blackened areas. The soil should be rich and slightly moist and should contain many roots. Sod that has dried out may be yellow-green and more difficult to establish. Blackened, mushy spots in sod may mean that it has been overwatered or that disease organisms are present.

INSTALLING LANDSCAPE PLANTS

The majority of landscape trees and shrubs are sold bare root or balled and burlapped. You will plant ground covers and vines from flats and cell packs or from seed. Lawn grasses are planted from seed, sod, or sprigs. You may also need to transplant some existing plants. See the basic steps described on page 204 for planting container plants, and then apply specific variations for the different types of plants.

Planting Bare-Root Trees and Shrubs

Most garden centers prune a bare-root plant for you after it has been pulled from the holding bed. Sometimes one third or more of the root growth will be cut back, but it will result in a stronger, better-looking plant. Before planting, cut back any additional injured, diseased, twisted, or dead roots to healthy tissue. Store plants in a cool spot with their roots in moist soil, sawdust, or bark to prevent them from drying out until you can put them in the ground.

To install a bare-root plant, dig a hole large enough to accommodate the full span of the roots without

STAKING A TREE

Less than 2" of stake remains above tie

Wind direction

STAKING A SMALL TREE

STAKING A TALL TREE

A larger tree, when transplanted, may need a stronger anchor until the roots secure it in surrounding soil. Attach guy lines to a soft collar around the trunk or to screw eyes. Use a compression spring on each wire for flexibility. Tie rags to the lines to make them easily visible. Guy lines with pins that insert into buried pipes can be removed for lawn-mowing.

bending them. If the roots are radiating in a circle, make a cone-shaped mound in the bottom of the hole, and spread out the roots on this mound. The plant should be at the same depth at which it had been grown. Adjust the mound to raise or lower the plant, if necessary. If you can't find the original soil line, put the top root 1 inch below the surface of the soil. Plant slightly high to allow for some settling.

Do not fertilize bare-root plants when you install them. Dormant plants do not use much fertilizer, and a lot of it will leach away and be wasted before the plant needs it. Instead, fertilize when the first leaves appear on the plant in the spring.

If the plant is grafted, the bud union (which should be clearly visible) must be at least 2 inches above the soil line. The union must remain dry and must not send roots down into the soil.

Prune off any broken or very long roots, and place the plant in the hole, orienting it as desired. When the plant is in place, fill the hole with the amended backfill soil, working soil between the roots with your hands to fill any air pockets.

Build an irrigation basin, as described in step 7 of Planting Container Plants. Fill the basin with water. While the soil is still soupy, wiggle the plant to help eliminate air pockets. Bare-root plants usually do not need staking, and probably will not need to be watered again until leaves appear. Water in the basin.

Planting Balled-and-Burlapped Trees and Shrubs

To plant a B and B tree or shrub, dig a hole and amend the backfill soil in the manner described in

Planting Container Plants, steps 1 through 3. Handling the ball carefully, set it in the hole with the burlap still on. (If the burlap has been treated to retard rotting, you will have to remove it or cut large holes in it. Ask when you buy the plant whether this is necessary. If the plant is wrapped in synthetic material instead of burlap, remove it.) Adjust the height of the rootball and the orientation of the plant, if necessary. Make sure that no part of the trunk is buried.

With the plant in the hole, untie the burlap from the trunk and pull it away from the top of the rootball. If the strings pull away easily, discard them; if not, leave them to decompose in the soil (remove synthetic twine because it does not rot). Cut or fold the burlap back so it will be below the surface of the soil.

Fill the space around the plant with the backfill soil. Because any exposed burlap acts like a wick, drawing water out of the soil, be sure all edges are buried.

Build an irrigation basin as described in Planting Container Plants, step 7, and continue with steps 8 through 10.

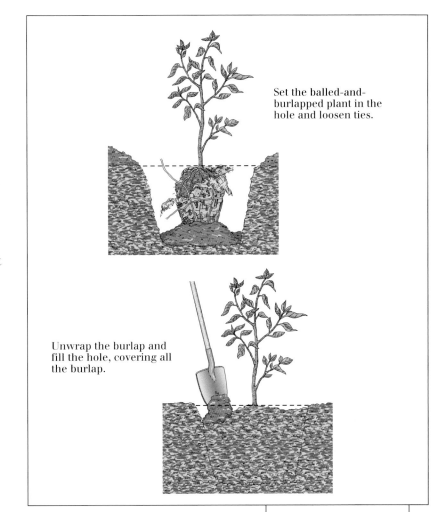

Set the balled-and-burlapped plant in the hole and loosen ties.

Unwrap the burlap and fill the hole, covering all the burlap.

Planting Ground Covers From Flats and Cell Packs

Dig holes that are slightly larger than the rootball, and water them an hour before planting. Do not plant dry plants. Water the flats and allow them to drain for 5 or 10 minutes before you try to take them apart. A damp rootball is less likely to fall apart or stick to the container. If you are planting from flats, gently pull the plants apart with your hands. Plants in six-packs should be turned over and pushed out from the bottom with your thumb. Hold the soil in place with your other hand—never pull the plants out. Place them in the ground, one by one, as you remove them from their containers. This keeps the rootball from drying out and the plants from wilting excessively.

Install the plants slightly deeper than they were growing in the flat, especially if they have long stems. Carefully fill in the hole around the roots, gently firming the soil with your fingers. Water immediately after planting. Some wilting is natural immediately after planting, but you can minimize it by planting during the cooler parts of the day (morning or evening) or by planting on an overcast day. Do not wait for the plants to show signs of wilting before you water them again. Plants may need frequent watering for the first few days after planting.

PLANTING CONTAINER PLANTS

The steps below outline the procedures for planting plants sold in containers. If you follow these 10 steps carefully, your success is practically guaranteed. The procedures for planting bare-root and balled-and-burlapped plants are essentially the same; a few additional instructions for planting them are given in those specific sections.

1. Prepare Beds for Planting

If you are establishing a planting bed, first clear away any debris that you do not want to incorporate into the soil. Then spread the area with fertilizer or soil amendments, and mix them into the soil. Break up clods with a hoe or cultivator, and rake the surface smooth. For all plants, including those not in beds, dig the planting hole approximately twice as wide and either to the same depth as the rootball or 1 inch shallower. Plants have a tendency to sink after they have been planted, and if any of the trunk or stem is below grade, the plant may suffer in time from crown and root rot. The rootball should be resting on firm, undisturbed soil. Roughen the sides of the hole to encourage root penetration into the native soil.

2. Add Soil Amendments

If you are going to prepare a transition soil, this is the time to do it. The soil that you dug from the hole is called backfill soil. Keep the backfill in one pile and make a rough estimate of its volume. Then add an organic soil amendment to the pile, one that decomposes slowly. The proportion of soil conditioner to backfill soil is flexible, but conditioner should make up approximately 25 percent of the final mix.

3. Add Fertilizer

If you are planting in early spring or when you expect leaf growth to begin, now is a good time to add a complete fertilizer. A 5-10-10 or 10-10-10 will meet the requirements for most plants. If you are using a dry fertilizer, add a small amount, according to the manufacturer's recommended ratios. As a rule of thumb, 1 to 2 tablespoons is adequate if the plant you are installing is in a 1-gallon container; ¼ cup is all you need for plants in 5-gallon containers. Stir the fertilizer into the soil so the rootball will not come into direct contact with straight fertilizer.

4. Remove the Plant From the Container

If the plant has been grown in a plastic container, it will slip out easily, especially if the rootball is damp. It is important not to break the rootball trying to get it out—you may permanently damage the root system. If the container is a straight-sided metal can and you are going to install the plant the same day you buy it, have the can cut at the nursery. If you are going to wait, even for only a day or two, leave the can intact, and cut it at home with a large pair of tin snips or a can cutter like the one used at the nursery. Do this cautiously and wear heavy gloves.

5. Place the Plant in the Hole

First, check the rootball. Cut or pull away any circled, matted, or tangled roots so they radiate out from the rootball. Shorten the roots to the width of the planting hole so they will not be bent when planting. Matted roots often stay that way, not venturing into the surrounding soil. If the plant is root bound, prune away the outer ½ inch of rootball, unless the plant is a very sensitive variety. Check the rootball depth in relation to the depth of the planting hole, making sure that the crown of the plant will be above the existing soil level. It is better to plant too high than too low. Determine how the plant will be oriented. For instance, if it is not perfectly symmetrical but has a dominant side branch, orient the plant so the branch will grow in the direction you wish. Place the plant in the hole.

6. Fill the Hole and Tamp the Soil

Fill the hole with the backfill soil to the level of the surrounding soil. Gently press down the backfill soil as you fill the hole, making certain that the roots and soil are in contact with each other.

7. Build a Basin

Build up a ridge of soil to form a shallow basin around the plant so irrigation water will be concentrated in the area where it is needed most. Make sure that water will drain away from the stem of the plant. Use the basin for primary watering until some roots have had a chance to expand into the surrounding soil—this usually takes about 6 weeks—at which time you can break down the basin. If dry weather conditions require continued irrigation, enlarge the basin at that time and continue to use it for watering until regular rainfall resumes.

8. Stake, If Necessary

Recent tests have shown that some back-and-forth movement of the tops of plants actually results in faster and better growth. The only reasons to stake a new plant are if the plant is extremely top-heavy, if it is planted in an area of high winds, or if it is in a high-traffic area where it might get knocked about. If a stake is necessary, place it on the side of prevailing winds, or use two stakes on either side of the plant and tie them loosely to the plant using something that will not damage the surface of the stem, such as an old bicycle inner tube or other suitable material.

Use guy lines to support large trees, if necessary. Three lines, spaced equidistant from one another and staked 5 to 10 feet from the trunk of the tree are typically used. Nylon webbing or rope makes excellent guy lines. Attach the lines to a collar made of soft material, such as nylon webbing, around the tree's trunk. At ground level,

fasten the lines to pins inserted in pipes embedded in the ground, or to pins or 2Χ2 stakes driven into the ground.

Check the ties frequently to make sure that they are not cutting into the growing plant. Remove all stakes after the plant is securely rooted in its new location, usually after the first year.

9. Prune, If Necessary
To compensate for damaged or pruned roots, lightly trim the top of the plant. Even if no roots are lost during planting, top pruning may be necessary to help prevent wilting. Branches that

are close together, that cross one another, or that are broken can be removed without affecting the overall size of the plant. Some pruning may have been done at the nursery. If so, little more need be done. Check for pruning scars, or ask the nursery whether this was done.

10. Water
The last step in planting is to thoroughly water the soil around the root zone. Apply water until the soil is loose and muddy. Gently jiggle the plant until it is positioned exactly how you want it. This action will eliminate any remaining air pockets.

Keep an eye on the plant to see how much water it requires. If a newly planted shrub wilts during the hottest part of the day, the rootball is not getting enough water, even though the surrounding soil may appear wet. Even if it rains or if the plant is in the path of a sprinkler, you may need to water it by hand two or three times a week for the first few weeks, if the soil seems dry. Too much water is as bad as too little, however. If the soil regularly appears soggy, the plant may be receiving too much water. Adjust your watering schedule accordingly.

DISTRACTING WILDLIFE

Young or recently installed plants are more susceptible to damage from animals and birds than are those that have been established for some time. The thin bark of young trees and the tender new shoots of young shrubs and ground covers are delicacies to some animals. In addition, new plantings have fragile root systems that are unlikely to tolerate an animal burrowing near them. These potentially harmful animals may include your family pet as well as wild animals, such as raccoons and deer. Birds are another source of plant damage. New ground-cover plantings and plants with berries may attract birds that will eat most of the aboveground parts of the plant.

The first step toward protection is to provide a physical barrier to prevent animals from reaching the plant. A wire screen around tree trunks, wire mesh covering the ground around shrubs and trees, or even a nylon net on stakes over new plantings will stop most animals. Nylon netting for this purpose is sold in most garden centers. This netting is lighter and more easily managed than wire.

If birds are the major source of damage to your plants, a temporary scarecrow may be all you need to discourage them. A few metal pie tins or cans on strings attached to a post will scare many of them away. Shiny metallic strips of plastic, designed to blow easily in the wind to frighten birds away, are widely sold.

For burrowing animals, such as gophers and moles, traps are sometimes necessary. Spring traps work like mousetraps, injuring or killing the animal when it reaches the bait. Poisoned baits are not recommended if you have young children or pets (including those that may be just visiting). For difficult problems, hire a professional pest eradicator.

Fences can be used to prevent deer and smaller animals, such as rabbits, from entering the garden. The fence should extend about 6 inches into the earth to prevent small animals from burrowing underneath, and should be at least 6 feet high to keep deer from jumping over it. Certain plants are reputed to be deer resistant, but this is not always a reliable method of control. Hungry deer will eat almost any plant.

Planting Seeds

Some ground covers and perennials can be started from seed. You can sow seeds either indoors in a protected environment or outdoors directly in the soil. Starting seeds indoors allows you to get a jump on spring, but this is obviously not practical when sowing seeds on a large scale. Almost any type of container can be used to start seeds, provided it has drainage holes and holds at least 3 tablespoons of soil. The containers should be sterile

and filled with horticultural vermiculite or potting soil. Water the soil and allow it to drain before sowing the seeds. Germinate the seeds in a warm, moist environment. You may wish to cover the containers with plastic, glass, or moist paper towels to prevent them from drying out. Remove the coverings after the seeds germinate. Grow the seedlings in a cool, bright place until they are approximately 2 to 4 inches high. Then harden them off by placing them outside for gradually lengthening intervals until they are ready to plant.

When planting seeds outside, carefully study the instructions on the seed packet. Make sure the season is right for the varieties you are planting. Soil temperature is an important factor in seed germination. Seeds may be planted in rows or blocks, or broadcast onto a loose soil surface. After seeding, be careful not to wash out the seeds or developing seedlings. When the seeds germinate, thin excess seedlings by pulling them out, being careful not to disturb the roots of the remaining plants. Protect the remaining seedlings from insects and animals.

Planting and Supporting Vines

Vines must have some support or structure on which to climb. They can cling to their support by twining or by using tendrils or holdfasts. Twining vines twist around a support—ideally thin, vertical poles or strings. Vines with tendrils need small supports, such as wire or lath, to which they can cling to as they grow. Holdfasts are small roots or tendrils with discs that attach themselves to the support. These vines will climb almost anything, including smooth walls. Some vines have no natural means of clinging to a structure; these must be tied or otherwise attached to the support. Tie lightweight vines to their support with twine, rubber bands, polyethylene tape, or plastic-coated wire ties. For heavier vines use insulated wire, rubber tree ties, or old inner tubes.

When planting a vine, consider the type of support it will need. Have all lath structures or poles in place before planting. After you plant the vine, you will need to train it to direct its growth.

Planting a Lawn

When planting a lawn, adequate soil preparation is critical. In addition to the steps necessary to prepare any activity area, and those necessary to prepare a bed for planting, you must also finely grade the lawn areas.

Lawns can be planted from seed, sod, or sprigs. Once a lawn is established, you cannot tell the difference between the three types of planting.

Because it is relatively economical and allows the widest choice of grasses, seeding is the method most frequently used to install a lawn. Buy the best seed available; it will give you fewer maintenance problems in the future and generally will provide a healthier lawn. Germination can take from 4 to 30 days; after that the lawn will need a 6- to 10-week establishment period before it can be used. Until the lawn has been established, water by hand with a fine spray to minimize soil movement or washing away of seeds. Avoid standing water.

Sod is a lawn grass that has been seeded and grown on a sod farm, then cut loose from the soil and rolled up or stacked. The sod has about ¼ inch of soil attached. Not only does sod produce an instant lawn, it prevents erosion, especially on slopes, and it can be laid at any time of the year that the grass will

grow. The drawbacks of a sod lawn are the initial cost and labor involved; these are substantial compared with a seed lawn.

In areas of the United States where warm-season grasses pre-

This broadcast spreader distributes seed more evenly than casting it by hand.

Top: Sod should be moist, green, and fresh when it is delivered. Before accepting the delivery, check for any problems. Bottom: Roots will emerge from sprigs, forming new plants. Place the sprigs in furrows, positioning them at a slant.

dominate, sprigging and plugging are common methods of starting a lawn. Plugs are small circles or squares of sod. Sprigs are pieces of grass stem that root and spread. Both methods are more economical than sod. Unlike seeds, sprigs and plugs begin to grow immediately, filling in to create an even lawn. The spacing between each plug determines the time it takes to achieve complete coverage. In general, sprigged lawns will fill in within three to four months, and plugged lawns should fill in within a year. In cold-winter areas this may take longer. This planting method is not practiced with most cool-season grasses.

Protect new lawn areas by stringing the entire area and attaching brightly colored flags to warn people away.

Finishing the Planting Job

A few simple steps following planting will increase the chances of healthy and rapid plant growth. These include mulching, protecting plants from the weather, and a final cleanup. Then you can enjoy your beautiful new landscape.

Mulching

A mulch is a material applied to the surface of the soil, and if weed-free is a valuable addition to a new planting. A couple of inches of mulch will keep weeds down and make them easier to pull out if they do appear.

Mulches can be either organic or inorganic. Some of the better-known organic mulches are sawdust, fir bark, ground bark, and tree leaves. Gravel and rocks are common inorganic mulches.

In newly planted beds of ground cover, flowering annuals planted in bare spots will provide a living mulch while the ground cover is filling in.

Protecting Plants From Weather

New plantings are especially vulnerable to climate extremes. The first step in protecting them is to be sure to plant at the right time. Do not install plants that could be damaged by frost until after the last frost in spring. Do not plant during intense heat spells or stormy weather, and avoid planting young plants during the high heat of the afternoon. The cooler temperatures of morning and evening give plants more time to adjust.

If there is a chance of frost, cover sensitive plants with burlap, cardboard, or plastic. A heavy mulch applied to the soil will help prevent soil heaving and will moderate soil temperatures. Small plants can be covered with jars or plastic during the night. Antitranspirant sprays are available to help leaves retain their moisture when the soil is frozen. These are usually valuable only under extreme conditions.

During periods of unusual heat, the most important protection you can give your plants is to keep them well watered. Do not let the soil around the plants dry out. Mulch to keep the soil cool and moist. For plants with particularly tender foliage, erect a simple, temporary structure of four stakes to support a burlap shade.

If high winds are a problem, it is especially important to stake plants properly when you install them. Tender new roots can be seriously damaged if the plants topple over before becoming established.

Final Cleanup
Good sanitation practices are essential in preventing the spread of plant diseases and pests. Many insect eggs and larvae, as well as disease organisms, are deposited on flowers and fruit and mature as the plant materials lie on the ground. After planting, rake all loose soil back into the planting bed. Pick up any debris or plant clippings, and either compost it or remove it with other refuse. Remove dead plant materials frequently, and keep the area clean. Many pests find nesting and hiding places in refuse piles

and then travel out at night in search of live plants to eat. To discourage them, regularly clear leaves, pruning clippings, and other trash from your yard.

CHECKLIST: INSTALLING YOUR LANDSCAPE
(Some of the following happen simultaneously, some overlap . . . so plan your work carefully.)
- ❏ Figure costs against budget.
- ❏ Confirm all local ordinances.
- ❏ Obtain necessary permits.
- ❏ Determine schedule.
- ❏ Clear the site.
- ❏ Lay out the design.
- ❏ Rough-grade.
- ❏ Install first parts of underground drainage system.
- ❏ Install first parts of underground sprinkler pipes, wiring, boxes, and valves.
- ❏ Install first parts of underground lighting conduit and wiring.
- ❏ Build foundations for major structures and walls.
- ❏ Install pool, piping, and electrical systems to serve it.
- ❏ Build paved surfaces.
- ❏ Build fences, gates, and garden walls.
- ❏ Build decks and constructed features.
- ❏ Test and amend soil.
- ❏ Finish-grade.
- ❏ Plant trees and shrubs.
- ❏ Complete drainage system. Test.
- ❏ Complete sprinkler system. Test.
- ❏ Complete other wiring and utilities. Test.
- ❏ Prepare ground-cover and lawn areas.
- ❏ Plant ground covers.
- ❏ Plant lawn.
- ❏ Plant bedding areas.
- ❏ Arrange freestanding features.
- ❏ Adjust lighting.
- ❏ Clean up.
- ❏ Relax and enjoy.

LANDSCAPE PLANT GUIDE

Contrasting textures and forms and a subtle use of color give this secluded patio area the appeal of a wild landscape.

You will find this guide useful throughout the creation of your landscape design. At first you will want to refer to it to get an impression of the forms, textures, and colors that plants bring to the landscape or to identify plants you've seen in other landscapes that you wish to have in your own yard. As you finalize your planting plan, use this guide to make a shopping list. You may make some substitutions once you are at the garden center, but the process will be much easier if you have already compiled a preliminary list.

This guide, describing an assortment of the backbone plants used in landscape design, is divided into six sections: Vines, Trees, Shrubs, Ground Covers, Lawn Grasses, and Tropical Plants. The plants in each section are alphabetized by their scientific names—the names used in plant nurseries throughout the world. One or two common names are also listed for each plant, but these are not reliable—a given plant may have a number of common names, or several plants may all have the same common name. If you want to look up a plant and you know only its common name, refer to the index.

Although scientific plant naming has many fine points, the basics are simple. Plants generally have two-part scientific names. The first name, the *genus*, is the most general. Plants in a genus share a number of characteristics, but sometimes these characteristics are difficult to see unless the plant is blooming. The second name, the *species*, is—as you would expect from the word—more specific. Plants in the same species are related so closely that they are capable of interbreeding. For most plants in the wild, the genus and species names are sufficient for accurate identification, but in some cases a *variety* name is added, indicating a subcategory of the species. All of these names are printed in italic, and variety names are preceded by the abbreviation *var.*

Because landscape plants are commonly bred and selected for characteristics that set them apart from other members of the species, the plants in a garden center almost always have a *cultivar* name in addition to their genus and species names. Like variety names, cultivar names indicate that the plant is a subcategory of the species. However, a cultivar is a plant clone maintained in cultivation; the word *cultivar* is a shortened combination of the words *culti*vated and *var*iety. Cultivar names are enclosed in single quotes.

It is necessary to distinguish cultivars from varieties because, although varieties can usually be grown from seed, many cultivars must be propagated by grafting or cutting. This distinction is not always made, however; the word *variety* is often used to refer to both cultivars and varieties.

Cultivars of a given species can differ in size, form, leaf color, and flower color or size. Some cultivars may be more tolerant of environmental extremes than others, and are thus easier to grow in some areas. The garden center staff can help you determine which cultivars of the plants in this book are best for your area and landscape design.

HOW TO USE THE PLANT GUIDE

Following the plant names in each entry are a few lines of quick-reference information. For the vines, trees, shrubs, ground covers, and tropical plants, this part of the entry tells whether the plant is deciduous or evergreen, how fast it grows, and how large it gets. The growth rate of a plant may change dramatically over its lifetime; the rates in this book refer to the average rate of growth for the first 15 years. Similarly, the size estimates pertain to the size of the plant after about 15 years.

The rest of the entry describes the plant, highlighting its landscape features and pointing out possible problems. The USDA plant-hardiness zones to which the plant is adapted are included at the end of the entry. These zone numbers refer to the northern and southern limit of growth of this plant. See the map on the opposite page to find the zone you live in. These zones are for general reference only. If you live near a large body of water or on a south-facing hillside, you may be able to grow plants that are normally not hardy in your zone. On the other hand, if you live at a high elevation, your zone may be colder than shown on the map. For more specific information about your area, ask your nursery or call the local cooperative extension office.

The lawn grass entries are a little different from the other plant listings. In these entries the quick-reference information tells the type of climate the grass prefers (warm-season or cool-season) and the recommended mowing height. Many cultivars of each grass are available, and new ones are introduced every year.

PLANT CLIMATE ZONES

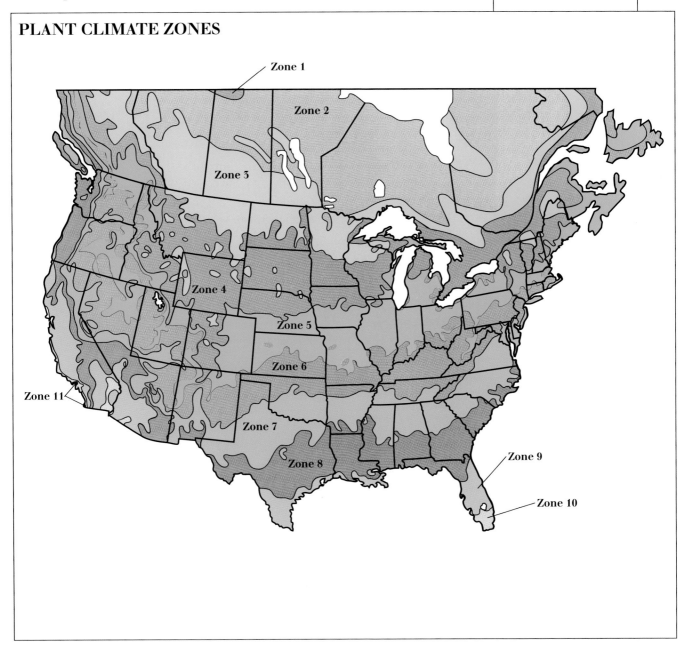

Actinidia arguta

Actinidia chinensis

VINES

Actinidia arguta
Bower actinidia

Deciduous

▮ Rapid growth to 25 to 35 feet.

One of the most cold-hardy deciduous vines. Foliage is dark green and pest-free. Fragrant, white, ¼-inch-diameter flowers bloom in late spring to summer. The lime green fruit offers the combined taste of strawberries, gooseberries, and melons. Will grow under any soil conditions except permanent moisture; tolerates sun or partial shade. A great plant for fences, arbors, pergolas, and general screening. Should be a first choice for difficult sites and cold climates. 'Ananasnaya' is a female cultivar with very sweet fruit.
▮ Zones 4 to 8.

Actinidia chinensis
Kiwifruit, Chinese gooseberry

Deciduous

▮ Rapid growth to 20 to 30 feet.

Famous for its hairy, brownish green, 2-inch-long fruit; best used in the landscape as a quick cover for fences and arbors. The emerging leaves are a rich purplish red and densely hairy, providing interesting color and texture not available from most vines. Male and female plants are required for fruit set. 'Chico-Hayward' and 'Vincent' are popular female cultivars. Native to China.
▮ Zones 8 to 10.

Akebia quinata
Five-leaf akebia

Deciduous

▮ Rapid growth to 15 to 20 feet.

Twines effectively on picket fences and arbors; may also be used as a ground cover. Rich, bluish green foliage emerges early in spring and does not drop until November or December. Evergreen in mild climates. Tolerates extremes of heat and cold as well as moist and dry soil. An excellent choice for shade or sun. Not widely available, but worth looking for. Native to Central China, Japan, and Korea.
▮ Zones 4 to 8.

Ampelopsis brevipedunculata
Blueberry climber

Deciduous

▮ Rapid growth to 10 to 25 feet.

If porcelain blue is your color, the fruit of this vine is sure to please. The ripening fruit progresses through shades of yellow to pale lilac and finally to porcelain blue, and all colors are often present in a single cluster. An ideal candidate for downspouts, railings, trellises, and chain link fences. Clings to structures with tendrils; does not become unruly. Withstands adverse soil conditions; takes full sun to partial shade. Japanese beetles can be troublesome. 'Elegans' (also known as 'Variegata') is a dainty, less vigorous form with white and pink foliage.
▮ Zones 4 to 8.

Akebia quinata

Ampelopsis brevipedunculata

Annona cherimola

Aristolochia macrophylla

Annona cherimola
Cherimoya

Broadleaf deciduous

▌ Moderate growth to 20 feet.

A small, fruiting tree for the warm-climate garden. This is a well-behaved tree maintaining a trim, round head without pruning. Leaves are velvety to 8 inches across. Fruit from 3 to 5 inches is sweet and custardlike. Fragrant, inconspicuous flowers. Prefers rich, loamy soil and moderate watering in a dry, warm climate. Native to the Peruvian Andes.
▌ Zone 10 only.

Aristolochia macrophylla (A. durior)
Dutchman's pipe

Deciduous

▌ Very rapid growth to 20 to 30 feet.

Plant it and stand back; will grow 10 to 20 feet in a single season. A great plant for hiding unsightly features. Often grown in the South on trellises in front of porches to cast shade in the summer months. The 4- to 10-inch, dark green leaves provide a coarse textural effect. Yellowish green, pipe-shaped flowers with brownish purple centers appear in May to June but are hidden beneath the foliage. Excellent in sun or partial shade. Very adaptable; responds vigorously to adequate fertility and moisture.
▌ Zones 4 to 8 (to zone 9 in the West).

Bignonia capreolata
Crossvine

Semievergreen

▌ Moderate growth to 30 to 50 feet.

A stunning vine for both foliage and flowers. Leaves turn reddish purple in winter, are evergreen in mild climates. Orange-red, 2-inch-long, trumpet-shaped flowers appear from April to June. Climbs with tendrils and rootlike holdfasts. Can also be used as a ground cover or allowed to scramble over fences, rocks, and waste areas. Grows well in heavy shade, but foliage and flowers are much more dense in full sun. Requires moist, organic soil for best growth. 'Atrosanguinea' has dark red flowers. Popular in the South, where it is native.
▌ Zones 5 to 8 (to zone 9 in the West).

Bougainvillea glabra
Paper flower

Broadleaf evergreen

▌ Rapid growth to 15 to 30 feet.

Perhaps the most spectacular of all flowering vines. Flower colors range from purple to magenta; cultivars with white, yellow, orange-red, and purple bracts are also available. 'Variegata' offers pretty, white-variegated leaves and brick red flowers. The branches are well armed with sharp spines and need to be tied to a support. Requires warm temperatures and full sun for maximum flowering. Not fussy about soil so long as it is well drained. Transplant carefully—roots are easily damaged. Dies back in zone 9 but can be grown against a protected south wall.
▌ Zone 10.

Bignonia capreolata

Bougainvillea glabra

Campsis radicans

Campsis × tagliabuana

Campsis radicans

Common trumpet vine

Deciduous

▮ Very rapid growth to 20 to 40 feet.

Twines and clings to pergolas, gazebos, lattice, and natural wood structures to provide summer shade. Used effectively on the white picket fences in Colonial Williamsburg. Also an excellent choice for rough areas that simply require a green mantle. Lustrous, dark green leaves appear in late spring. By July brilliant orange-red, 3-inch-long, trumpet-shaped flowers play their soft summer music. 'Crimson Trumpet' has flowers that are a pure, glowing red without a trace of orange. 'Flava' is an orangish yellow form of great beauty.
▮ Zones 4 to 9.

Campsis × tagliabuana

Hybrid trumpet vine

Deciduous

▮ Rapid growth to 10 to 15 feet.

Not as wild and vigorous as *C. radicans;* a better choice for the small garden. Orange flowers are larger than those of *C. radicans.* A hybrid between *C. radicans* and *C. grandiflora* (Chinese trumpet vine); first put into commerce in 1889.
▮ Zones 5 to 8 (to zone 9 in the West).

Celastrus orbiculatus

Oriental bittersweet

Deciduous

▮ Rapid growth to 10 to 20 feet.

Usually grows as a wild, loose shrub or vine. Needs to be restrained in contemporary landscapes but is an excellent choice if trained on handrails, balustrades, or similar structures. The abundant red, yellow, and orange fruit is outstanding in the fall after the leaves drop. Can choke trees and shrubs if allowed to twine around them. Tolerates extremes of soil and climate. Native to Japan and China.
▮ Zones 4 to 8.

Clematis armandii

Evergreen clematis

Broadleaf evergreen

▮ Rapid growth to 10 to 20 feet.

The bold, pleasing foliage is perfect for breaking the monotony of a large expanse of fence or wall. Lustrous, dark green leaves are prominently three-veined, 3 to 6 inches long. Fragrant, white flowers, 2 to 2½ inches in diameter, bloom in March and April. 'Apple Blossom' has broad, white sepals tinged with pink. Roots prefer cool, moist soil—mulch well. Top needs full sun. Dies back in coldest zones. Native to central and western China.
▮ Zones 7 to 9 (to zone 10 in the West).

Celastrus orbiculatus

Clematis armandii

Clematis 'Hagley Hybrid'

Clematis × *jackmanii*

Clematis 'Hagley Hybrid'

Hagley hybrid clematis

Deciduous

▌ Rapid growth to 10 to 15 feet.

One of a large group of single-flowered, deciduous hybrids, it has satin pink flowers with purple anthers; blooms July to October. Roots need cool, moist soil; top needs full sun. As with other summer-flowering clematis, it should be pruned in late fall (after it finishes flowering) or in early spring when the buds begin to swell. Young plants should be cut back drastically—to two or three buds. Established plants (3 or more years old) should be cut to about 2 feet above the ground.
▌ Zones 4 to 9.

Clematis × jackmanii

Jackman's clematis

Deciduous

▌ Rapid growth; often grows 5 to 10 feet in a season.

The grandfather of the large-flowered hybrid clematis. The 4- to 7-inch violet purple flowers appear on new growth from June to July and sporadically until frost. Although usually placed on a trellis, this and other clematis forms are much lovelier—and less gaudy—when allowed to twine between and over the branches of deciduous shrubs and broadleaf evergreens. The shade produced by the clematis foliage does no harm if the shoots are pruned after flowering. 'Alba' has white flowers, and 'Rubra', deep red.
▌ Zones 3 to 9.

Clematis macropetala

Downy clematis

Deciduous

▌ Moderate growth to 6 to 9 feet; can reach 20 feet.

Dainty, charming, and restrained; never overbearing like many of its kin. A beautiful species for a low fence or wall, or cascading from a large urn or planter. Violet blue, 2½- to 3-inch flowers appear in May or June and bloom throughout the summer. Flowers appear double—the stamens are shaped like petals. Even the seeds are attractive; when ripe they become silky, fluffy, and gray. Native to northern China and Siberia.
▌ Zones 4 to 8.

Clematis tangutica

Golden clematis

Deciduous

▌ Rapid growth to 10 to 15 feet.

An extremely accommodating species that is incredibly easy to cultivate. Bears nodding, 1½- to 2-inch-long, rich yellow flowers on a background of sea green foliage in June and July. Later, silky seed heads develop and decorate the vine into fall. A superb vine for banks, large boulders, trellises, fences, walls, and other suitable structures. Native to Mongolia and northwestern China.
▌ Zones 4 to 8 (to zone 9 in the West).

Clematis macropetala

Clematis tangutica

Distictis buccinatoria

× *Fatshedera lizei*

Distictis buccinatoria
Blood trumpet vine

Broadleaf evergreen

▮ Very rapid growth to 20 to 30 feet.

A rampant climber; clings with tendrils to walls, arbors, trellises, and lattice. Climbs up to 20 feet in a season; prune annually to keep it under control. Funnel-shaped, 4-inch-long flowers are a rich purplish red with a yellow base; they bloom off and on throughout the summer. Grows only in the warmest parts of the United States. Prefers ample moisture, fertile soil, and full sun or partial shade. 'Rivers' bears mauve to purple flowers with a golden throat in late summer into fall. Native to Mexico.

▮ Zone 10 (to zone 9 in the West).

× Fatshedera lizei
Fatshedera

Broadleaf evergreen

▮ Moderate growth to 10 to 15 feet.

Provides the perfect textural touch for deeply shaded areas of the landscape. Used abundantly in southern gardens to soften large expanses of brick. The 4- to 10-inch, lustrous, five-lobed leaves develop a bronzy purple tinge in cold weather. Requires moist, organic, well-drained soil; partial to heavy shade. Temperatures below 10° F often kill the plant to the ground. Raised in France in 1910; the result of a cross between *Fatsia japonica* 'Moseri' and *Hedera helix* 'Hibernica' (English ivy). 'Variegata' has leaves with an irregular white border.

▮ Zones 8 to 10.

Ficus pumila
Creeping fig, climbing fig

Broadleaf evergreen

▮ Moderate growth to 20 to 30 feet or more.

Has been likened to a green carpet on a vertical floor. It affixes itself to almost any material by rootlike holdfasts and never lets go. Juvenile shoots form delicate tracery on walls; they bear small, oval, dark green leaves. When mature, the vine grows more vigorously, producing larger, light green leaves on a woody framework. Should be cut to the ground every few years to maintain juvenile growth; otherwise, the vine will bury the structure. Takes partial to heavy shade. Native to China, Taiwan, and Japan.

▮ Zones 7 to 10.

Gelsemium sempervirens
Carolina jessamine

Broadleaf evergreen

▮ Rapid growth to 10 to 20 feet.

Impressive in late winter (March), when its bright yellow, fragrant, trumpet-shaped flowers are often the sole beacon in the landscape. Very durable, but unruly twining growth must be restrained by frequent pruning. Used in southern states on mailboxes, light poles, and trellises. Often trained over entryways and garages. Tolerates diverse soils and full sun or partial shade. In nature, often scrambles up trees and is rather pretty when combined with redbuds, because their flowering sequences overlap. All parts are poisonous.

▮ Zones 6 to 9 (to zone 10 in the West).

Ficus pumila

Gelsemium sempervirens

Hardenbergia violacea

Hedera helix

Hardenbergia violacea

Coral pea

Broadleaf evergreen

▋ Moderate growth to 10 feet.

An unusual shrub-vine with pendulous clusters of pealike flowers in late winter to early spring. Flower colors range from white to rose and violet with a yellow basal blotch. Blooms at an early age. Requires a peaty, well-drained soil in full sun, partial shade in hot areas. Both nematodes and mites can be troublesome. Native to eastern Australia and Tasmania.

▋ Zones 9 and 10.

Hedera helix

English ivy

Broadleaf evergreen

▋ Rapid growth; height limited by structure.

Commonly used as a ground cover, but will climb any porous structure with rootlike holdfasts. An excellent vine for the north side of a building where light is minimal. Has grown as high as 90 feet in trees. Leaves are lustrous, dark green, often with white or light green veins. Well-drained, organic, moist soil is preferable. 'Baltica', 'Bulgaria', 'Hebron', 'Rochester', 'Thorndale', and 'Wilson' are the hardiest cultivars.

▋ Zones 5 to 10.

Hydrangea anomala ssp. petiolaris

Climbing hydrangea

Deciduous

▋ Slow growth at first, rapid thereafter; height limited by structure.

One of the most elegant clinging vines; never appears unkempt or disheveled. Used extensively in the eastern United States on walls, stone fences, buildings, and trees. Affixes itself by rootlike holdfasts. The trunk becomes quite woody and thick; it is covered with flaking, cinnamon brown bark. Lustrous, dark green leaves are 6 to 10 inches in diameter. Flat, pinwheel-shaped clusters of white flowers bloom in June and July. Needs rich, moist soil; grows well in sun or shade. Slow to establish, but worth the wait. Native to Japan and China.

▋ Zones 4 to 8 (to zone 9 in the West).

Jasminum polyanthum

Pink jasmine

Broadleaf evergreen

▋ Rapid growth to 15 to 20 feet.

Pinkish white, ¾-inch-long flowers fill the air with delicious fragrance throughout the spring and summer months. Ideal near a patio, porch, or other area where its fragrance can be enjoyed. The compound, blue-green leaves are fine textured and handsome. Blooms best in moist soil, with full sun. Flowers appear on new growth; prune annually in early spring to prevent an unkempt, tangled mess from developing. Native to China.

▋ Zones 9 and 10.

Jasminum polyanthum

Hydrangea anomala ssp. *petiolaris*

Lapageria rosea

Lonicera × brownii

Lapageria rosea
Chilean bellflower

Broadleaf evergreen

▮ Rapid growth to 10 to 20 feet.

One of the most beautiful flowering vines for warm climates. The leaves are especially attractive—pointed, leathery, and glossy, dark green. The flowers are bell-shaped, rose to rose crimson, and waxy. Bloom lasts from late spring to fall. Flowers are good for arrangements, lasting for as long as two weeks after cutting. Needs partial shade. The variety *albiflora* is white flowered. Native to southern Chile.

▮ Zone 10.

Lonicera × brownii
Brown's honeysuckle

Deciduous

▮ Moderate growth to 8 to 10 feet.

A hybrid between *L. sempervirens* (trumpet honeysuckle) and *L. hirsuta* (hairy honeysuckle); resembles the first in most characteristics. The orange-red flowers are borne in whorls at the ends of the stems from June or July into late summer. Generally not as desirable as *L. sempervirens*, but the cultivar 'Dropmore Scarlet' is the hardiest vine honeysuckle and thus is preferable in areas where temperatures drop below –20° F. The red flowers of 'Dropmore Scarlet' appear in May or June and continue blooming into October.

▮ Zones 3 to 8.

Lonicera japonica
Japanese honeysuckle

Deciduous to evergreen

▮ Very rapid growth to 20 to 30 feet.

Exceedingly aggressive and adaptable; a good choice for difficult areas of the landscape if restrained. Wonderfully fragrant flowers open white and mature to yellow; they bloom from June until frost. Tolerates full sun or shade, dry or moist soil, high or low pH. Unless controlled by frequent pruning, it will overgrow shrubs and eventually smother them. 'Halliana' is a particularly vigorous cultivar. 'Purpurea' has purple-tinged foliage and purplish red flowers.

▮ Zones 4 to 9.

Lonicera sempervirens
Trumpet honeysuckle

Deciduous

▮ Moderate growth to 10 to 20 feet.

Spectacular in bloom, when brilliant red flowers cover the bluish green foliage. Weaves tapestries on white picket fences throughout the South. Must be trained on a trellis, fence, wall, or other suitable structure; otherwise, it grows in a heap. Almost as tolerant of poor soil as *L. japonica*, but needs full sun for best flowering. Flowers are not fragrant. 'Superba', with bright red flowers, and 'Sulphurea', with rich yellow flowers, are fine alternatives to the species. All bear bright red fruit that persists into late fall.

▮ Zones 4 to 9.

Lonicera japonica

Lonicera sempervirens

Polygonum aubertii

*Parthenocissus
quinquefolia*

Parthenocissus quinquefolia
Virginia creeper

Deciduous

▊ Very rapid growth; height limited by structure.

New growth emerges bronze red, matures to a lustrous deep green in summer, and turns red in the fall. Flowers and fruit are insignificant. Will cover any structure in a short time; often grows 6 to 10 feet in a single season. Also serves as a functional ground cover. Japanese beetles are serious pests; they can defoliate large plantings in a matter of weeks. The variety *engelmannii* has smaller leaves and clings more tenaciously than the species. Native from New England to Florida and Mexico and west to Ohio, Illinois, and Missouri.

▊ Zones 3 to 9.

Parthenocissus tricuspidata
Boston ivy

Deciduous

▊ Very rapid growth; height limited by structure.

Boston ivy thrives in the same situations as *P. quinquefolia*, but may not be quite as rampant—although some homeowners will challenge this contention. The foliage is perhaps a degree more lustrous; fall color can be equally outstanding. 'Beverley Brook' has large leaves that turn brilliant shades of red and scarlet in the fall. 'Veitchii' has red new growth, smaller leaves, and good red fall color. 'Lowii' has small, 3- to 7-lobed leaves.

▊ Zones 4 to 8.

Passiflora caerulea
Blue passion flower

Broadleaf evergreen

▊ Rapid growth to 10 to 20 feet or more.

A choice vine for chain link fences and other architectural misfits. Its large, 5- to 9-lobed, bluish green leaves hide unsightly structures well. The bluish white flowers are 2 to 4 inches in diameter and bloom throughout the summer and into the fall. The oval, 2½-inch-long fruit ripens yellow to orange. Climbs with tendrils. Generally requires average soil and full sun. No special care is required. Will die back to the roots in the coldest areas, but regrows rapidly. Native to Brazil and Argentina.

▊ Zones 7 to 10.

Polygonum aubertii
Silver lace vine

Deciduous

▊ Rapid growth; grows 10 to 15 feet in a season.

Has a rampant, twining growth habit; should be limited to fringe areas or areas where soil conditions do not permit planting of more aesthetically pleasing species. When used on fences, walls, and vertical structures, some pruning is required. Glossy, green, wavy-margined foliage is attractive, and from July or August into fall the greenish white to white flowers turn the plant into a low-slung cloud. Can be cut to the ground in late winter; will be flowering again by August. Japanese beetles can present a problem. Native to western China.

▊ Zones 4 to 8.

Passiflora caerulea

*Parthenocissus
tricuspidata*

Rosa banksiae

Rosa hybrida

Rosa banksiae
Banks rose

Evergreen (semievergreen in colder areas)

▌ Rapid growth to 18 feet or more.

A popular climbing species rose in mild climates. The stems are nearly thornless. The flowers are borne in unbelievable profusion. Requires full sun. Practically pest- and disease-free. The 'Albo-Plena' variety has fragrant, double, white flowers. 'Lutea' has scentless, double, yellow flowers. Native to China.
▌ Zones 8 to 10.

Rosa hybrida
Rose climbing hybrids

Deciduous

▌ Rapid growth to 8 to 20 feet.

Spectacular in flower when trained on fences, trellises, arbors, and pergolas. Must be tied into place, for they neither twine nor cling. Like their hybrid tea and floribunda counterparts, these plants require considerable disease control and careful pruning. All need full sun and moist, organic, moderately fertile, well-drained soil. Spring-flowering types produce one magnificent burst of color in May or June; prune these immediately after flowering. Other types flower most heavily in May or June, taper off in summer, and bloom again in fall; prune these in late winter.
▌ Zones 4 to 9.

Solandra maxima
Cup-of-gold

Broadleaf evergreen

▌ Sprawling growth to 25 feet.

Stiff branches need tying—provide sturdy trellis or strong anchors. Large, dark green leaves to 8 inches in length. Big, yellow, trumpet-shaped flowers to 10 inches long and 6 inches across. Winter flowering. This is a spectacular plant for California or Florida gardens. Native of Mexico and Central America.
▌ Zone 10.

Thunbergia alata
Black-eyed-susan

Perennial (often grown as annual)

▌ Rapid growth; often grows 10 to 20 feet in a season.

A handsome vine; throughout the summer bears white to orange-yellow, trumpet-shaped flowers with purple throats. A great choice for covering trellises, lattice, porches, and chain link fences. Growth is extremely vigorous in moist, fertile, well-drained soil. 'Alba' has white flowers with dark centers; 'Bakeri' has pure white flowers; 'Aurantiaca' produces orange-yellow flowers with dark centers. Native to tropical Africa.
▌ Zone 10.

Solandra maxima

Thunbergia alata

Wisteria floribunda

Trachelospermum jasminoides

Trachelospermum jasminoides
Starjasmine

Broadleaf evergreen

▌ Moderate growth to 10 to 15 feet.

Usually grown as a ground cover, but can also be trained on a trellis. The leathery, dark green leaves have a light green vein pattern. Five-petaled, fragrant, white flowers appear in May or June and sporadically thereafter throughout the summer. Their scent is delightful; plant where you can enjoy their fragrance, such as in an area near a patio or window. Leaves brown at temperatures below 10° F. Requires partial shade in summer and winter. The leaves of 'Variegatum' have gray-white margins and blotches. Native to Japan and China.
▌ Zones 8 to 10.

Wisteria floribunda
Japanese wisteria

Deciduous

▌ Rapid growth; height limited by structure.

Long (8- to 20-inch) clusters of violet blue flowers emerge with or before leaves, perfume entire garden. Bright green foliage may develop a yellowish tinge in fall. Purchase named cultivars that have been grafted or rooted from cuttings; seedling-grown plants often disappoint. Blooms best in full sun. 'Alba' and 'Longissima Alba' are fine, white-flowered cultivars; 'Macrobotrys' bears violet flower clusters; 'Rosea' offers pale rose flowers. 'Royal Purple' and 'Texas Purple' have violet purple flowers. Native to Japan.
▌ Zones 4 to 9.

Wisteria sinensis
Chinese wisteria

Deciduous

▌ Rapid growth; height limited by structure.

Flower clusters are shorter than those of *W. floribunda*, but open all at once along the length of the stem. Also has fewer leaflets (7 to 13, compared with 13 to 19) and grows less vigorously. Adapts to a variety of soils; needs good drainage. Grows and blooms well in full sun or partial shade. The violet blue flowers of the species are only weakly fragrant. 'Alba' has white flowers; 'Jako' is a selected form of 'Alba' with extremely fragrant, white flowers; 'Black Dragon' has double, dark purple flowers. Native to China.
▌ Zones 5 to 9.

Wisteria venusta
Silky wisteria

Deciduous

▌ Rapid growth; height limited by structure.

Leaflets are larger than those of *W. floribunda* or *W. sinensis* and are covered with silky hairs. Large, white, fragrant flowers are borne in clusters 4 to 6 inches long that open all at once. Like other wisterias, can be trained as a vine, shrub, or small tree. Adapts to a variety of soils; needs good drainage. Plants bloom best in full sun. The variety *violacea* is a wild form with fragrant, purple-blue flowers. Native to Japan.
▌ Zones 5 to 8.

Wisteria sinensis

Wisteria venusta

Abies concolor

Abies procera

TREES

Abies concolor
White fir

Needle evergreen

▮ Moderate growth to 80 to 100 feet high; can reach 200 feet.

Tolerates heat, drought, and city conditions better than most other native firs. Horizontal branches are covered with 2-inch-long, blue-green or gray-green needles. Upright, cylindrical cones are borne in clusters on the upper branches. Young trees have smooth, gray bark and make fragrant container Christmas trees. 'Conica' is a dwarf form. Native to the western United States.
▮ Zones 4 to 8.

Abies procera
Noble fir

Needle evergreen

▮ Rapid growth to 100 to 150 feet high.

One of the most handsome of all the firs. A narrow tree with stiff branches that are thickly covered with blue-green foliage. Needs a cool climate in order to thrive. Native to the mountains of the northwestern United States.
▮ Zones 5 to 7.

Acacia baileyana
Bailey acacia, cootamundra wattle

Broadleaf evergreen

▮ Rapid growth to 20 feet high, equally wide.

Blooms at an early age with daffodil yellow flowers that completely eclipse the fine, blue-gray foliage. Virtually foolproof but grows best in dry, well-drained soil. May also be trained as a multi-stemmed shrub. 'Purpurea' is named for its purple spring growth. Native to Australia.
▮ Zones 9 and 10.

Acacia melanoxylon
Blackwood acacia

Broadleaf evergreen

▮ Rapid growth to 40 feet high or higher.

This tough, upright tree will stand all types of abuse. Use as a fast-growing wind-break or screen, or for erosion control. The dark green leaves are 2 to 4 inches long. Flowers are inconspicuous. Roots can break up pavement and compete vigorously with other plants in shallow soil. Native to Australia.
▮ Zones 9 and 10.

Acacia baileyana

Acacia melanoxylon

Acacia pendula

Acer buergerianum

Acacia pendula
Weeping myall

Broadleaf evergreen

▌Moderate growth to 20 to 25 feet high, 10 to 12 feet wide.

A choice, silvery gray accent tree. Yellow flowers bloom sporadically in the spring. Usually has a strong weeping form, but may be dense and spreading. May be espaliered. Native to eastern Australia.
▌Zones 9 and 10.

Acer buergerianum
Trident maple

Deciduous

▌Moderate growth to 35 feet high.

Named for its three-pointed, glossy leaves, which turn yellow to red before falling from the tree in autumn. Usually grows with multiple trunks and low branches, but can easily be trained as a shade tree with a single trunk. Excellent drought tolerance. Native to Japan and China.
▌Zones 6 to 9.

Acer campestre
Hedge maple

Deciduous

▌Slow to moderate growth to 25 to 40 feet high, 20 to 25 feet wide.

Often trained as a hedge but also useful as a small street tree. Grows best in well-drained soil; will tolerate dry, poor, or sandy soil. Small, 2- to 4-inch, dull green leaves turn yellow in the fall. Native to Europe and Turkey.
▌Zones 5 to 8.

Acer palmatum
Japanese maple

Deciduous

▌Slow growth to 20 feet high, equally wide.

Offers a variety of leaf shapes and colors. The leaves may have lobes that are indistinct or deeply incised, and they vary in length from 2 to 4 inches. Leaf colors range from yellow-green to dark maroon in solid colors; variegated leaves may be highlighted with white and pink. Leaves develop best colors in full sun, but will burn in hot, dry, or windy areas unless given partial shade. Native to China and Japan. 'Atropurpureum' is one of the hardiest purple-leaved forms. 'Dissectum' has finely divided green or red leaves. 'Senaki' has green leaves and contrasting coral bark.
▌Zones 6 to 9 (to zone 10 in the West).

Acer campestre

Acer palmatum

Acer platanoides

Acer rubrum

Acer platanoides
Norway maple

Deciduous

▌ Growth rate and size depend on cultivar.

Many have been selected; some for their growth form, others for their foliage color. Dense foliage combined with a vigorous root system make it difficult to grow grass or other plants under this tree. 'Crimson King' grows slowly to between 35 and 40 feet high and 50 feet wide; leaves are maroon throughout the growing season. 'Emerald Queen' grows rapidly to 50 feet high and wide; has excellent yellow fall color. 'Summer Shade' grows rapidly to 45 to 50 feet high and 60 to 70 feet wide; its heavy-textured leaves are more heat tolerant than most other selections.
▌ Zones 3 to 9.

Acer rubrum
Red maple, swamp maple

Deciduous

▌ Rapid growth to 50 to 60 feet high, 40 to 60 feet wide.

Its common names describe two of its best landscape features: attractive, small red flowers in early spring, and adaptability to poorly drained soil. Many varieties have been selected for form and fall color. 'Autumn Flame' is round headed; the leaves turn orange-red 1 to 2 weeks before most other maples—they also fall 1 to 2 weeks earlier. 'Bowhall' has a narrow, pyramidal form appropriate for areas near buildings and streets. 'Red Sunset' and 'October Glory' offer brilliant red fall colors. Native to the eastern United States from Maine to Florida.
▌ Zones 3 to 9.

Acer saccharinum
Silver maple, soft maple

Deciduous

▌ Rapid growth to 100 feet high, 70 feet wide.

More tolerant of heat and dry winds than other maples; used for quick shade where other trees fail. As with many other fast-growing tree species, limb breakage in wind or storms is a serious problem. Some cities have prohibited planting *A. saccharinum* as a street tree; check local ordinances before planting. Native to the flood plains of the midwestern, northeastern, and southern United States.
▌ Zones 3 to 9.

Acer saccharum
Sugar maple, rock maple

Deciduous

▌ Grows slowly to 50 to 60 feet high, equally wide.

Lights up New England with its yellow, orange, and red fall colors. Also the source of maple syrup and the lumber for maple furniture. Sensitive to soil compaction and hot, dry conditions; does not grow well in the city. The dark green leaves of 'Green Mountain' are more tolerant of hot, dry conditions than most other varieties. Native to the midwestern, northeastern, and southern United States.
▌ Zones 3 to 8.

Acer saccharinum

Acer saccharum

Aesculus × *carnea*

Acer tataricum ssp.
ginnala

Acer tataricum ssp. *ginnala*
Amur maple

Deciduous

▌ Moderate growth to 20 feet high, equally wide.

The fragrant, creamy white flowers of this multi-stemmed tree are unusual among maples. Summer color is provided by the bright red fruit; later, the foliage also turns yellow to bright red. Shape is a broad oval or globe. Tolerant of wind and cold; a useful substitute for Japanese maple in cold regions. Native to Siberia.
▌ Zones 3 to 8.

Aesculus × *carnea*
Red horsechestnut

Deciduous

▌ Slow to moderate growth to 30 to 50 feet high, 30 to 50 feet wide.

A spectacular flowering tree, at its best in midspring when it bears upright, 8- to 10-inch-long, pink to red flower spikes. Five-fingered leaves cast dense shade in summer, and fall from the tree in autumn. A very manageable garden, street, or park tree. Pyramidal when young, erect with a round crown when mature. Best adapted to cool areas with moist summers and protected locations; the leaves are easily scorched by hot, dry winds. Hybrid of *A. hippocastanum* (common horsechestnut—native to southern Europe) and *A. pavia* (red buckeye—native to the southeastern United States).
▌ Zones 4 to 8.

Albizia julibrissin
Silk tree, mimosa

Deciduous

▌ Rapid growth to 25 to 40 feet high, occasionally twice as wide.

Horizontal layers of branches form an umbrellalike canopy of feathery, light green leaves. In summer the branches are covered with showy pink flowers that resemble powder puffs. Adapts well to lawn areas. Achieves its best form when allowed to grow naturally with multiple trunks. Problems include weak wood, messy flowers, and susceptibility to wilt and twig girdlers. Native to Asia from Iran through Japan. 'Rosea' is the hardiest cultivar.
▌ Zones 6 to 10.

Alnus cordata
Italian alder

Deciduous

▌ Rapid to moderate growth to 40 to 70 feet high.

The best-behaved alder, although like other alders, its roots are invasive. Tasslelike catkins decorate the branches after the leaves fall. Has a pyramidal habit. Native to Corsica and southern Italy.
▌ Zones 5 to 8 (to zone 10 in the West).

Albizia julibrissin

Alnus cordata

Alnus rhombifolia

Amelanchier canadensis

Alnus rhombifolia
White alder

Deciduous

▌Rapid growth to 60 to 70 feet high, about two thirds as wide.

Valuable for quick screening in poorly drained soil. Has an irregular, upright form and gracefully pendulous branch tips. The leaves are dark green above, paler beneath. Catkins add a purple tinge in winter. Native to the northwestern United States and Canada.
▌Zones 4 to 7.

Amelanchier canadensis
Serviceberry, shadblow

Deciduous

▌Moderate growth to 20 to 40 feet high.

One of the earliest trees to flower in the East. Snow white blossoms appear just after the flowers of dogwood, but before those of eastern redbud. A durable, all-season performer; displays beautiful autumn color. Twiggy, upright, often multi-stemmed. Native to Canada and the northern and mid-western United States.
▌Zones 4 to 8.

Araucaria araucana
Monkeypuzzle tree

Needle evergreen

▌Slow growth to 60 to 70 feet high, 30 to 35 feet wide (grows to about 20 feet in 15 years).

Stiff, sharp needles give the branches of this tree a tubular look that is often considered exotic. Has a pyramidal habit, but lower whorls of branches tend to die as the tree grows, particularly if crowded. The common name is derived from a saying that once a monkey climbs up this tree, it can't climb down again. Needs well-drained soil and plenty of water. Native to Chile.
▌Zones 7 to 10.

Araucaria heterophylla
Norfolk Island pine

Needle evergreen

▌Moderate growth to 60 to 70 feet high, half as wide (grows to about 25 feet in 15 years).

Popular in Victorian times for its soft, formal, horizontal tiers of symmetrical branches, this tree has regained popularity as an indoor plant. Grows well in containers. Tolerates coastal conditions. Native to Norfolk Island (1,000 miles east of Australia).
▌Zone 10.

Araucaria araucana

Araucaria heterophylla

Arbutus menziesii

Arbutus unedo

Arbutus menziesii

Madrone, madrona

Broadleaf evergreen

▌ Slow to moderate growth to 20 to 40 feet high, equally wide (grows to about 25 feet in 15 years).

Colorful throughout the year. Soft, light green to copper new leaves become leathery and dark green with gray undersides when mature. The smooth, reddish brown bark peels off in thin flakes. The irregular round head is usually as wide as the tree is high. Difficult to establish; does not tolerate garden watering. Native to the Pacific Northwest and southern California.
▌ Zones 7 to 9.

Arbutus unedo

Strawberry tree

Broadleaf evergreen

▌ Slow to moderate growth to 10 to 25 feet high, equally wide.

Has a shrubby habit; suckers easily, but may be pruned into a well-formed tree. Once trained, the twisting, bonsai-like form becomes more attractive with age. Bark is smooth, deep red to brownish red. Leaves are dark green with red stems. Small, white, urn-shaped flowers are followed by edible fruit that looks like strawberries but tastes like cotton. Best placed where it can be looked up into, such as in a patio or lawn. Adapts to a variety of soils and climates. Native to the Mediterranean region and Ireland.
▌ Zones 7 to 9.

Bauhinia variegata

Purple orchid tree

Deciduous

▌ Moderate growth to 20 to 30 feet high.

The *Bauhinia* most common to southern California. Flowers appear in January to April; colors range from white to lavender or purple. Double-lobed leaves drop for a brief period in midwinter. Fruit is foot-long pods. Needs staking and training to form a single-stemmed tree; otherwise, forms a multistemmed shrub. Requires full sun, moderate watering. A mild, dry winter produces the most spectacular bloom. Makes an excellent street tree. Select grafted cultivars for consistent flower color. 'Candida' has white flowers.
▌ Zone 10.

Betula papyrifera

Paper birch, canoe birch

Deciduous

▌ Moderate growth to 40 to 60 feet high.

Called "the lady of the forest" in the far north. White bark brings a lively grace to a group of needle evergreens, and in winter the white bark and blue-gray branches contrast with the typically dark brown bark of other leafless trees. Has an open, erect habit. Usually planted in clumps of several trees, as found in nature. Borers can cause severe injury in southeastern, mild-winter areas. Native to North America from eastern Canada to Alaska.
▌ Zones 3 to 8.

Bauhinia variegata

Betula papyrifera

Betula pendula

Brachychiton acerifolius

Betula pendula

European white birch

Deciduous

▌ Moderate growth to 60 feet high (grows to about 35 feet in 15 years).

Rough, warty twigs and white bark with vertical black markings distinguish this birch. Mature trees have pendulous branches. Unfortunately, this species is often plagued by pests; bronze birch borers infest mature trees; aphids and leaf miners may also cause problems. The larvae of another pest, the black sawfly, produce blotches or blisters on young leaves. 'Fastigiata' is columnar when young, pyramidal when mature. 'Pyramidalis' is also pyramidal and is resistant to the bronze birch borer. 'Gracilis' has finely dissected leaves. 'Tristis' is a tall, graceful cultivar with slender, pendulous branches. Native to Europe and Asia Minor.

▌ Zones 2 to 7 (to zone 8 in the West).

Brachychiton acerifolius

Flame tree

Deciduous

▌ Moderate growth to 55 to 60 feet high (grows to about 25 feet in 15 years).

Produces an incredible number of small, almost tubular, scarlet to orange flowers in late spring or early summer. Ten-inch-long, shiny, green leaves have five to seven lobes and drop just before the tree flowers. Seedpods resemble boats. The thick, green trunk supports an upright, pyramidal form. Withhold water in spring for best flowering. Native to Australia.

▌ Zones 9 and 10.

Brachychiton populneus

Bottle tree, kurrajong

Broadleaf evergreen

▌ Slow to moderate growth to 25 to 50 feet high.

Named for its heavy, tapering trunk. The crown is dense and conical; the leaves are variously lobed and resemble those of a poplar. Small, white, bell-shaped flowers are followed by canoe-shaped seedpods. Pods are attractive in dried arrangements but litter the area under the tree. Drought resistant; extremely useful in hot, dry climates. Native to Australia.

▌ Zones 9 and 10.

Callistemon citrinus

Lemon bottlebrush

Broadleaf evergreen

▌ Rapid growth to 10 to 15 feet high.

Common in the gardens of southern California and Florida. Displays bright red, brushlike flowers throughout most of the year. Flowers attract hummingbirds. Fragrant leaves are lemon scented, coppery when young. Has a round-headed, open form; needs training to form a small tree. Prefers good drainage and full sun. Tolerates drought and a wide range of soils, including those that are alkaline or saline. Excellent for desert landscapes. Cultivars vary in their compactness, flower color, and size. Native to Australia.

▌ Zones 8 to 10.

Brachychiton populneus

Callistemon citrinus

Calocedrus decurrens

Carya illinoinensis

Calocedrus decurrens

Incense cedar

Needle evergreen

▮ Slow to establish, later grows rapidly to 70 to 90 feet high (grows to 10 feet in 15 years).

Fans of foliage are richly aromatic—particularly in hot weather—and grow so densely that they usually conceal the attractive reddish brown bark. Has a handsome pyramidal form when standing on its own, but several can be planted together to form a tall hedge or windbreak. Native to the mountains of southern Oregon, California, western Nevada, and Baja California.
▮ Zones 5 to 8 (to zone 9 in the West).

Carya illinoinensis (C. illinoensis)

Pecan

Deciduous

▮ Moderate growth to 80 feet high (grows to about 25 feet in 15 years).

Has held its place in the affection of home gardeners in spite of its susceptibility to diseases—most notably scab. Quite cold tolerant, but the nuts need a long growing season to mature properly. Has a wide, rounded crown. In alkaline soil of arid Arizona and New Mexico, pecans should be fertilized or sprayed to prevent zinc deficiency.
▮ Zones 5 to 9.

Casuarina cunninghamiana

River she-oak, beefwood

Narrowleaf evergreen

▮ Rapid growth to 70 feet high.

A rugged tree, valuable in arid or saline areas where little else will grow. Its long, drooping branches have slender, dark green branchlets similar to pine needles. The fruit is woody, grayish, and conelike. It is the tallest and most graceful *Casuarina*. Native to Queensland and New South Wales.
▮ Zones 9 and 10.

Cedrus deodara

Deodar cedar

Needle evergreen

▮ Grows rapidly 40 to 70 feet high, 20 to 45 feet wide.

A refined, graceful, soft-textured cedar. The lower branches sweep to the ground; upper branches are evenly spaced and well defined. Needles are light blue-green. The nodding tip makes it very recognizable on the skyline. Has the fastest growth rate of any of the cedars. It will quickly fill a small yard with spreading limbs. Can be slowed down, however, by pinching one half of the new growth before the needles unfurl in spring. Drought resistant if established by deep, infrequent waterings. Native to the Himalayas.
▮ Zones 7 to 10.

Cedrus deodara

Casuarina cunninghamiana

Cedrus libani

Cedrus libani ssp.
atlantica

Cedrus libani

Cedar-of-Lebanon

Needle evergreen

▌ Slow growth to 40 to 70 feet high; branches spread widely.

A striking skyline tree, but less commonly planted than other cedars due to its slow growth. Young trees have bright green foliage and a pyramidal form similar to those of *C. libani* ssp. *atlantica*. Dwarf cultivars—where available—are popular rock-garden plants. Native to Asia Minor.
▌ Zones 5 to 7.

Cedrus libani ssp. *atlantica*

Atlas cedar

Needle evergreen

▌ Slow to moderate growth to 40 to 60 feet high, 30 to 40 feet wide (grows to about 25 feet in 15 years).

An open, pyramidal tree when young, it fills in with age to form a picturesque skyline tree. Wide-spreading branches make it unsuitable for small city lots, but it is excellent for parks, large gardens, or along boulevards. The most popular of the blue conifers, its fine-textured, bluish green needles are borne in stiff clusters. Moderately drought resistant. 'Glauca' has the richest blue tinge. Native to the Middle East and North Africa.
▌ Zones 7 to 9.

Celtis occidentalis

Common hackberry

Deciduous

▌ Moderate growth to 40 to 60 feet high, equally wide.

Hackberries are known for their persistence in tough situations, withstanding drought, wind, and city conditions. Leaves are bright green with finely toothed edges. Branches are spreading, sometimes pendulous. The dark purple berries attract birds. Although relatively pest-free, its one drawback is "witches' broom," a foliage and branch deformation to which the cultivar 'Prairie Pride' is resistant. Native to the central and southeastern United States.
▌ Zones 5 to 9.

Ceratonia siliqua

Carob, St. John's bread

Broadleaf evergreen

▌ Slow growth to 25 to 40 feet high, equally wide (grows to about 15 feet in 15 years).

Naturally shrubby but easily trained into a dense, round-headed tree. Leaves are divided into 4 to 10 leaflets. Inconspicuous flowers are foul-smelling on male trees. On females, flowers are followed by long, twisting, dark brown seedpods, which can be a nuisance when they drop in the garden or on the street. Effective as a shrubby hedge or screen, it takes well to shearing and casts deep shade. Widely adapted; grows wherever olive will, withstanding heat, drought, and city conditions. Pods are ground into powder and used as a chocolate substitute. Native to the eastern Mediterranean region.
▌ Zones 9 and 10.

Celtis occidentalis

Ceratonia siliqua

Cercis canadensis

Chamaecyparis lawsoniana

Cercis canadensis

Eastern redbud

Deciduous

▮ Moderate growth to 25 to 35 feet high, equally wide.

An all-seasons performer. Best known for its rosy pink flowers that bloom on bare branches—even on the trunk—in spring, a few weeks before dogwood. Has attractive dark green, heart-shaped leaves, yellow fall color, and interesting seedpods. In winter, the lovely reddish brown bark highlights the horizontal zigzag structure of the branches. Will grow under almost any conditions: sun, shade, acid soil, alkaline soil, and moist soil. Native from southeastern Canada to northern Florida.
▮ Zones 5 to 9.

Chamaecyparis lawsoniana

Lawson's cypress

Needle evergreen

▮ Rapid growth to 60 to 70 feet high, one third as wide (grows to about 30 feet in 15 years).

A graceful, pyramidal tree with wide-spreading, pendulous branches. Lacy sprays of bright green to blue-green, scalelike leaves, a nodding tip, and soft brown to reddish brown fibrous bark contribute to its softness and elegance. Many cultivars are available, varying in form and foliage color. Subject to cypress root rot in the Northwest; ask for resistant cultivars in that area. Susceptible to root rot in the southeastern United States. Native to southwestern Oregon and northwestern California.
▮ Zones 6 to 9.

Chamaecyparis obtusa

Hinoki false-cypress

Needle evergreen

▮ Slow growth to 40 to 50 feet high, 15 to 25 feet wide.

Many cultivars, including dwarf forms, are usually more readily available than the species. Most have flattened sprays of shiny, deep green foliage. Branch tips are slightly pendulous, but not so distinctly as *C. lawsoniana.* Has a pyramidal habit. 'Gracilis' has very dark green foliage and grows to 20 feet high, 4 to 5 feet wide. 'Nana Gracilis' is a very slow-growing dwarf. A specimen at the Secrest Arboretum in Wooster, Ohio, took 66 years to grow 9 feet. 'Crippsii' has golden new growth and reaches 30 feet high. Native to Japan.
▮ Zones 5 to 8 (to zone 9 in the West).

Chamaecyparis pisifera

Sawara false-cypress

Needle evergreen

▮ Moderate growth to 20 to 30 feet high, half as wide.

Less dense than *C. obtusa.* Loosely arranged branchlets have glossy, bright green foliage. Lower branches are lost early in life, revealing reddish brown bark that peels in long strips. Inner branches often die out; encourage new growth with heavy annual pruning. Native to Japan.
▮ Zones 4 to 8.

Chamaecyparis obtusa

Chamaecyparis pisifera

Cinnamomum camphora

Citrus limon

Cinnamomum camphora

Camphor tree

Broadleaf evergreen

▮ Slow growth to 50 feet high or higher, wider spread (grows to about 25 feet in 15 years).

A deservedly popular residential and street tree. Has a round-headed form; the upward-spreading limbs provide dense shade. Attractive, aromatic, dark yellow-green foliage contrasts with bronzy new leaves. Yellow flower clusters are fragrant, although not showy. Grows poorly in heavy alkaline or sandy soil. Native to China and Japan.
▮ Zones 9 and 10.

Citrus limon

Lemon

Broadleaf evergreen

▮ Growth rate and size depend on cultivar.

Of the many cultivars available, two are especially popular for home landscapes. 'Improved Meyer' is the most widely adapted cultivar, growing to 12 feet high with equal or wider spread. A dwarf form reaches half that size. Good for hedges and containers. Nearly everblooming. The fruit is very juicy, sweeter than commercial lemons, and holds well on the tree. 'Ponderosa' grows 7 to 10 feet high; dwarf forms grow half that size. The grapefruit-sized fruit is juicy and acidic, but has a milder flavor than commercial lemons; it holds well on the tree.
▮ Zones 9 and 10.

Cladrastis lutea

American yellowwood

Deciduous

▮ Slow to moderate growth to 30 to 50 feet high, 40 to 55 feet wide.

This eastern native has smooth, beechlike gray bark and bright green foliage that turns clear yellow in the fall. In June white, intensely fragrant, pea-shaped flowers are borne in pendant clusters. Usually flowers most heavily every third year. The brown pods and zigzagging branches are interesting in winter. A good lawn, patio, or park tree; best used as a specimen. When mature it withstands drought, heat, and extreme cold, and tolerates alkaline and wet soil.
▮ Zones 4 to 8.

Cornus florida

Flowering dogwood

Deciduous

▮ Moderate growth; rarely exceeds 30 feet high.

The dogwood varies from pyramidal to umbrella shaped to wide spreading and flat, depending on the cultivar. May be susceptible to fungal wilt diseases and borer problems. Dogwood anthracnose is a serious problem. Of the pink forms, *C. florida* var. *rubra* is probably the most common. The flowers of 'Cherokee Chief' are deeper pink than those of *rubra*, but the tree is not quite as hardy. 'Cloud Nine' bears white flowers and grows more slowly than most other cultivars. 'White Wonder' has the largest flowers and is hardier than most. 'New Hampshire', can be grown in zone 4. Native to the eastern United States.
▮ Zones 5 to 9.

Cladrastis lutea

Cornus florida

Crataegus laevigata

Crataegus × lavallei

Crataegus laevigata
English hawthorn

Deciduous

■ Moderate growth to 15 to 25 feet high, equally wide.

Abundant in Europe, a common country hedge throughout England. The most variable hawthorn; white, pink, or red flowers may be single or double. Its habit is shrublike and round headed. Performs poorly in summer heat and humidity, where foliar fungus diseases may leave the twigs bare during most of the summer months. 'Plena' bears myriad double, pure white flowers in late May, followed by a few red fruit. 'Autumn Glory' bears single, white flowers but is noted for its very large and long-lasting red fruit. 'Paul's Scarlet' has double, rosy red flowers but no fruit; its habit is full and rounded.
■ Zones 5 to 8 (to zone 9 in the West).

Crataegus × lavallei
Lavalle hawthorn

Deciduous

■ Moderate growth to 20 feet high.

Has large, abundant white flowers. Dense, oval head; more erect than other hawthorns. Glossy, green foliage turns bronze red in the fall. Large, orange to red fruit lasts well into the winter. A cross between *C. crus-galli* (cockspur hawthorn) and *C. pubescens*.
■ Zones 5 to 8 (to zone 9 in the West).

Crataegus phaenopyrum
Washington thorn

Deciduous

■ Moderate growth to 20 to 30 feet high, 20 to 25 feet wide.

The best hawthorn for fall color—glossy, orange-red leaves complement the scarlet fruit. Abundant, pure white flowers. Dense with thorns. Narrow and upright when young, broadens with age. Resistant to fire blight. Grows exceptionally well in the city—specimens many decades old are still thriving in downtown New York City. Native to the south central United States.
■ Zones 5 to 8 (to zone 9 in the West).

Cryptomeria japonica
Japanese cedar

Needle evergreen

■ Moderate growth to 50 to 60 feet high, half as wide.

Small, lustrous, light green to bluish green needles and drooping branches combine to give this tree a soft, graceful look. The needles are tinged with purple in winter. Reddish brown bark peels in strips. Needs ample water and well-drained soil; does not like arid climates. Relatively pest-free. Native to Japan and China. 'Elegans' is a small, slow-growing cultivar; it eventually forms a 20- to 25-foot pyramid. Soft, feathery foliage turns bronze in winter. Other cultivars, including dwarf forms, are available.
■ Zones 6 to 9.

Crataegus phaenopyrum

Cryptomeria japonica

Cupressus macrocarpa

× Cupressocyparis leylandii

× *Cupressocyparis leylandii*
Leyland cypress

Needle evergreen

▌ Rapid growth to 40 to 50 feet high (grows 3 to 5 feet per year).

One of the best fast-growing columnar plants for tall hedges and screens. Its branching pattern is graceful, spreading in horizontal fans of gray-green to pale green foliage. Has a dense, pyramidal habit. Tolerates a wide range of soils and climates. A cross of *Chamaecyparis nootkatensis* (yellow cypress) and *Cupressus macrocarpa*.
▌ Zones 6 to 10.

Cupressus macrocarpa
Monterey cypress

Needle evergreen

▌ Slow to moderate growth to 40 to 70 feet high.

The postcard tree of the California coastline. Young trees are symmetrical and narrowly pyramidal. Windswept habit develops only in high winds near the coast, and then only with age. Valuable as a windbreak, but subject to a fatal canker disease if grown away from cool ocean breezes. Native to the Monterey Peninsula of California.
▌ Zones 8 to 10 in the West only.

Cupressus sempervirens
Italian cypress

Needle evergreen

▌ Rapid growth to 30 to 40 feet high, 3 to 6 feet wide.

A dominant vertical element in any landscape, too stiff and formal for anything but a large garden or formal driveway approach. Often planted inappropriately along short walkways and under eaves. Tolerates drought and a wide range of soils, but not poor drainage. Several cultivars are commonly available; most have tighter habits than the species and vary in foliage color from bright green to blue. Native to southern Europe and western Asia.
▌ Zones 8 to 10.

Diospyros kaki
Japanese persimmon

Deciduous

▌ Moderate growth to 20 to 30 feet high, equally wide.

A fine small-garden tree. The new leaves are light green, gradually turning darker in summer, then to shades of yellow, red, and orange before dropping in the fall. In winter, bright orange fruit decorates the bare branches like Christmas tree ornaments. The shapely branches and handsome bark are also attractive in winter. Fruit is very sweet—excellent fresh or dried. Choice fruiting varieties include 'Chocolate', 'Fuyu', and 'Hachiya', which is also the most valuable as an ornamental tree. Constant moisture and early spring fertilization help reduce fruit drop. Native to China and Korea.
▌ Zones 7 to 9.

Cupressus sempervirens

Diospyros kaki

Diospyros virginiana

Elaeagnus angustifolia

Diospyros virginiana
American persimmon, common persimmon

Deciduous

▮ Moderate growth to 30 to 50 feet high, half as wide.

Not as showy in fruit as *D. kaki*, but hardier and more adaptable to various soils and climates. Easily identified by the blocky patterns in the bark. Fruit is astringent until very soft and ripe. Male and female trees are required for fruit production. Native to the eastern United States.
▮ Zones 5 to 9.

Elaeagnus angustifolia
Russian olive

Deciduous

▮ Rapid growth to 20 to 25 feet high, equally wide.

Widely adapted to cold regions or hot, dry areas, and to all but poorly drained soils. Excellent hedge or screen; takes well to clipping even when espaliered. Also good for erosion control or slope cover. Leaves are willowlike, olive green above and silvery beneath. The twisted trunk has attractive, shedding, dark brown bark. Branches are thorny. Greenish yellow flowers appear in early summer. Produces yellowish red berries that furnish winter food for birds. Verticillium wilt can be a serious problem. Native to Europe and western Asia.
▮ Zones 2 to 8.

Eriobotrya japonica
Loquat

Broadleaf evergreen

▮ Moderate growth to 20 to 30 feet high, equally wide.

An ornamental tree with edible fruit. Very large leaves, prominently veined and serrated, are dark green above with downy, rust-colored undersides. Small, fragrant, white flowers are borne in fall to winter. Abundant, orange to yellow fruit ripens in late winter or early spring. The fruit has a large seed and is astringent if picked green, but delicious when ripe. Amenable to pruning; can be trained as a landscape or container specimen, or espalier. Tolerates alkaline soil but needs good drainage. Sometimes subject to fire blight. Seedlings are unpredictable; 'Gold Nugget' and 'Champagne' produce good fruit. Native to China and Japan.
▮ Zones 8 to 10.

Erythrina caffra
Kafferboom coral tree

Deciduous

▮ Rapid growth to as high as 40 feet, but usually smaller; wider spread.

The best *Erythrina* for the coast. Produces spectacular scarlet blossoms. Its bold, twisted habit is as unique and identifiable as that of olive. Dark green leaves drop from thorny branches prior to flowering in January and reappear in March. Demands full sun and moist, well-drained, rich soil. Native to South Africa.
▮ Zone 10.

Eriobotrya japonica

Erythrina caffra

Eucalyptus cinerea

Eucalyptus ficifolia

Eucalyptus cinerea
Silver-dollar tree

Broadleaf evergreen

▌ Moderate to rapid growth to 30 to 40 feet high.

One of the best of the blue-gray group. Perfoliate (impaled on stems, like a shish kebab), juvenile leaves are used for interior decorating. Many of these leaves are retained on the tree as the long, narrow, mature leaves develop. The rough, brown bark has a distinctive ashen tone—hence, the name *cinerea* ("ashen" in Latin). Tends to have multiple trunks but can be pruned to one. Remains garden sized for at least the first 10 years; juvenile leaves make it a striking specimen for at least the first 5.
▌ Zones 9 and 10.

Eucalyptus ficifolia
Flaming gum, red-flowering gum

Broadleaf evergreen

▌ Rapid growth to 25 feet high.

The small, chunky form of this tree is less graceful than that of other eucalyptus, but is sensational when in fiery full bloom. The flowers are white, pink, or red. Large, heavy, dark green leaves are similar to the leaves of *Ficus*. Branches are thick. Sensitive to frost; coastal zones are best.
▌ Zones 9 and 10.

Eucalyptus gunnii
Cider gum

Broadleaf evergreen

▌ Rapid growth to 50 feet high.

One of the hardiest of the eucalyptus; has been known to withstand temperatures as low as 0° F when established. Upright, sturdy, and strong; makes a good windbreak. Leaves are typical for the genus—long, narrow, medium green. Best used in areas that are too cold for other species.
▌ Zones 8 and 9.

Eucalyptus polyanthemos
Round-leaved eucalyptus

Broadleaf evergreen

▌ Rapid growth to 40 to 50 feet high.

The silvery gray, rounded juvenile leaves of this tree rustle in the lightest breeze. A tough tree; at home on the sea coast or in the desert, where it grows quite rapidly. Gray-green foliage is most attractive when the tree is young; it loses some of its charm with age.
▌ Zones 8 to 10.

Eucalyptus gunnii

Eucalyptus polyanthemos

Eucalyptus sideroxylon

Fagus sylvatica

Eucalyptus sideroxylon
Red ironbark

Broadleaf evergreen

▮ Moderate growth to 40 to 50 feet high.

Normally grows very large, but individuals vary widely in size as well as in foliage and flower color. Has a narrowly upright form. Foliage is usually gray-green and pendulous; attractive flowers are usually rose red. Commonly planted along old city streets, in parks, and on golf courses. Particularly tough, but does not grow as rapidly as other large species.
▮ Zones 9 and 10.

Fagus sylvatica
European beech

Deciduous

▮ Slow growth to 70 to 80 feet high, 60 feet wide.

The bark of a venerable old beech looks like the hide of an elephant—some parts are silvery gray and smooth, others look like wrinkled skin. Also like the elephant, beeches need a great deal of room when mature. Glossy leaves turn rich, golden brown in fall. Nuts attract birds. Native to central and southern Europe. 'Asplenifolia', the fernleaf beech, has narrow leaves with delicate lobes. 'Atropunicea' has purple foliage, does well in containers, resists drought, and tolerates moist soil conditions.
▮ Zones 5 to 7.

Ficus elastica
Rubber plant

Broadleaf evergreen

▮ Moderate growth to 45 feet high or more.

Popular as a potted plant, this tree grows large in warm climates. It is a vigorous ground feeder, and it's difficult to grow other plants in its heavy shade and strong root system. Leaves are large and glossy, to 12 inches long and 5 inches wide. It is a handsome specimen tree, pest-free and salt tolerant though not as much as *F. microcarpa.* An excellent patio tree, it will lift paving when it is older. Native to India and Malaya.
▮ Zones 9 and 10.

Ficus microcarpa (F. retusa)
Indian laurel

Broadleaf evergreen

▮ Moderate growth to 35 feet high.

A member of the fig or rubber tree family, this one is an excellent tree for the patio or the street in warm climates. It is pest-free and clean with glossy pointed leaves to 2½ inches, about ¾ inch wide. Very salt tolerant, this tree can be grown close to the beach line, where most trees cannot survive. Provide ample amounts of water but do not overfertilize. *F. benjamina* (weeping fig) is similar but not as hardy. Native to India and Malaya.
▮ Zones 9 and 10.

Ficus elastica

Ficus microcarpa

Franklinia alatamaha

Fraxinus pennsylvanica

Franklinia alatamaha
Franklinia

Deciduous

▌ Slow to moderate growth to 20 to 25 feet high.

Considered extinct until discovered in Georgia in the nineteenth century. Beautiful white flowers are similar to camellias and are often borne at the same time as the brilliant orange-red fall foliage. Has an upright, open, pyramidal habit. Makes an unusual lawn or patio tree. Somewhat of a challenge to grow—has been known to die suddenly—but worth the effort. Prefers rich, acid, moist, well-drained soil, partial shade, and protection from wind.
▌ Zones 6 to 8.

Fraxinus pennsylvanica
Green ash

Deciduous

▌ Moderate growth to 30 to 50 feet high.

Very popular and easy to grow—withstands wet soil and severe cold. Narrowly upright when young; has a compact, oval to rounded habit when mature. Check its cultivars—there are many excellent varieties. Native to the eastern United States.
▌ Zones 3 to 9.

Fraxinus velutina var. glabra 'Modesto'
Modesto ash

Deciduous

▌ Rapid growth to 50 feet high.

Popular in mild climates because of its bright yellow fall color, even though it has weak wood and is susceptible to anthracnose and mistletoe. When pruning young trees, select branches with wide angles of attachment to the trunk to minimize limb breakage. Resistant to oak root fungus. A selection of (*F. velutina* var. *glabra*) Arizona ash, originally grown in Modesto, California. Native to Arizona and New Mexico.
▌ Zones 7 to 10 in the West only.

Ginkgo biloba
Maidenhair tree

Deciduous

▌ Slow growth to 60 to 100 feet high (grows to 20 feet in 15 years).

One of the oldest living trees; fossils date back 200 million years. Conical and sparsely branched in youth, spreading and dense with age. Bright green, fan-shaped leaves turn brilliant yellow in the fall and may drop all at once, making for easy autumn cleanup. A remarkably tough tree, it withstands smoke and air pollution and is pest-free. Widely adaptable; demands only well-drained soil. Slow to establish after transplanting; needs careful watering. Be sure to get a male cultivar, such as 'Fairmont' or 'Autumn Gold'; berries of female trees have a rancid odor when crushed. Native to China.
▌ Zones 4 to 9.

Ginkgo biloba

Fraxinus velutina var. *glabra* 'Modesto'

Grevillea robusta

Gleditsia triacanthos var. *inermis*

Gleditsia triacanthos var. *inermis*

Thornless honeylocust

Deciduous

▌ Moderate to rapid growth to 30 to 60 feet high, equally wide.

An excellent lawn tree. Delicate, compound leaves open late in spring after turf has started growing, and cast light shade in summer. Leaves drop early in the fall and are easy to rake. In midsummer, thin out about half of the new growth to keep the tree from becoming overgrown. Tolerant of environmental stresses. Mimosa webworm, pod gall midge, and plant bugs can be troublesome; wilt has become a serious problem along the East Coast. Native to the eastern and central United States.
▌ Zones 4 to 9.

Grevillea robusta

Silk oak

Broadleaf evergreen

▌ Rapid growth to 50 to 60 feet high, 20 to 35 feet wide.

Fast growth makes this an excellent temporary tree for use while permanent trees develop. Makes a fine background plant, hedge, or screen. Fernlike leaves and golden orange flowers are used by florists. Habit is pyramidal in youth, eventually becoming round headed. Not a true oak, but the silky-smooth wood has the grain and color of oak. Tolerates compacted soil and drought, but not the constant watering of a lawn. Flowers best with summer heat. The brittle wood is easily damaged by wind. Judicious pruning helps, but also induces heavy suckering. Native to Australia.
▌ Zone 10.

Halesia tetraptera (H. carolina)

Snowdrop tree, wild olive

Deciduous

▌ Moderate growth to 25 to 30 feet high, 20 to 25 feet wide.

One of the most attractive American native trees. In mid-May each twig bears a string of 1-inch-long white flowers that resemble little wedding bells hanging from slender stems. Habit is pyramidal when young, becoming round headed with age. Grows naturally as a clump of several trunks; makes a fine shelter for a planting of azaleas or rhododendrons. Native to southeastern United States, but popular in England and on the European continent.
▌ Zones 5 to 10.

Ilex aquifolium

English holly

Broadleaf evergreen

▌ Moderate growth to 30 to 60 feet high, 15 to 20 feet wide.

The species most often used for Christmas decorations. Normally has spiny, undulating, glossy, dark green leaves, but many spineless and variegated forms are available. Berry colors vary from red to cream. 'Angustifolia' has a narrow, conical form with narrow, spiny leaves. 'Boulder Creek' has very large, dark green, glossy leaves and brilliant red berries. 'Little Bull' is a good pollenizer with a compact, upright habit that fits nicely into landscape plantings. Native to southern Europe and northern Africa.
▌ Zones 7 to 9.

Halesia tetraptera

Ilex aquifolium

Ilex 'Nellie R. Stevens'

Ilex opaca

Ilex 'Nellie R. Stevens'

'Nellie Stevens' holly

Broadleaf evergreen

▍ Rapid growth to 25 feet high.

One of the nicest heat-tolerant hollies. This hybrid of *I. cornuta* (Chinese holly) and *I. aquifolium* may be trained as a small tree; otherwise, it forms a large, pyramidal shrub. Bears colorful red berries.
▍ Zones 6 to 8.

Ilex opaca

American holly

Broadleaf evergreen

▍ Slow growth to 45 to 50 feet high.

Through the selection of hardy cultivars, this holly has been successfully grown north of its original habitat. Has a pyramidal habit. Leaves are usually spiny. Berries vary from red through orange to yellow, but are usually red. Often found in low, moist areas, but grows best in moist, well-drained, acid soil. More than a thousand selections have been named. Consult a nursery for the cultivars best adapted to your area. Native to the eastern United States.
▍ Zones 6 to 9.

Ilex pedunculosa

Long-stalk holly

Broadleaf evergreen

▍ Slow growth to 20 to 30 feet high.

This hardy holly has spineless leaves, 1½ to 3 inches long, and bright red berries on 1- to 2-inch stems. Usually a shrub, but may be trained as a small tree. Habit is usually narrow and upright. Most often used as a specimen. Native to China and Japan.
▍ Zones 6 and 7.

Jacaranda mimosifolia (J. acutifolia)

Jacaranda

Briefly deciduous

▍ Moderate to rapid growth to 25 to 50 feet high, two thirds as wide.

A popular tree in warm climates. Flowers over a long period, generally from May to July. Flowers are usually lavender blue; pink and white forms are also available. Interesting seedpods are attractive in dried arrangements. Tolerates a variety of conditions, but is choosy about watering: becomes floppy with too much water, dwarfed with too little; needs good drainage. Not recommended for very windy areas. A good choice for the garden or along the street. Has an open, irregular head; often has multiple trunks. Train for best form. Native to Brazil.
▍ Zone 10.

Ilex pedunculosa

Jacaranda mimosifolia

Juglans nigra

Juniperus scopulorum

Juglans varieties
Walnut

Deciduous

▌ Moderate growth to more than 100 feet high.

The Juglandaceae family is a large one, and *J. nigra* (black walnut) and *J. regia* (English walnut) should be mentioned here. Both are stately trees. Black walnut leaves are compound, dark green, and shiny. The nuts have thick, hard shells and are difficult to break. English walnut has large, dull, light green leaves and thin-shelled nuts. Both are stately and effective shade trees for larger gardens. The nut-covering sheaths of both stain anything they touch; plant far away from patios or sidewalks.
▌ English walnut zones 6 to 10; black walnut zones 4 to 10.

Juniperus scopulorum
Rocky Mountain juniper

Needle evergreen

▌ Slow growth to 35 to 45 feet high.

A good juniper for heat and drought. The broad, pyramidal form becomes round headed with age. An excellent choice for a tall hedge, screen, or windbreak. Has blue-gray foliage with brownish red bark, but many selections are available, varying in foliage color and plant habit. Susceptible to root rot and other diseases in areas of high summer rainfall or humidity. Native to the Rocky Mountains.
▌ Zones 4 to 7 (to zone 10 in the West).

Juniperus virginiana
Eastern red cedar

Needle evergreen

▌ Slow growth to 35 to 45 feet high.

Adaptable to a remarkable range of soils and climates. Unlike *J. scopulorum*, this tree grows in areas with summer rain. Normally has bright green foliage, but several selected varieties vary in both foliage color and form. Foliage turns yellow to brown in cold weather. Attractive blue cones are a favorite food for birds in winter. Excellent as a tall, long-living hedge, screen, or windbreak. Native to the eastern United States.
▌ Zones 3 to 9.

Koelreuteria paniculata
Goldenrain tree

Deciduous

▌ Moderate growth to 25 to 35 feet high.

A good lawn tree; its deep root system and open branching habit permit healthy lawn growth. Rounded outline and wide-spreading branches eventually give the tree a flat top. Tolerates alkaline soil, drought, and winter cold, but branches tend to be brittle. Named for the delicate drizzle of golden flower petals following late-spring bloom. Papery, copper fruit, resembling Japanese lanterns, hangs in clusters late into fall. Native to China, Japan, and Korea.
▌ Zones 5 to 9.

Juniperus virginiana

Koelreuteria paniculata

Laburnum × watereri

Lagerstroemia indica

Laburnum × watereri
Goldenchain tree

Deciduous

▌Moderate growth to 20 to 30 feet high.

Its blooms are this tree's main attraction. In May, graceful 18-inch chains of rich yellow, pea-shaped flowers make a spectacular show. Habit is dense and upright with a vase-shaped crown. Good subject for espalier. A hybrid of *L. alpinum* (Scotch laburnum) and *L. anagyroides* (common laburnum). The leaves, fruit, and flowers are poisonous. Does not do well in hot climates. The most popular cultivar, 'Vossii', has chains of flowers up to 2 feet long.
▌Zones 5 to 7 (to zone 9 in the West).

Lagerstroemia indica
Crape myrtle

Deciduous

▌Slow growth to 10 to 30 feet high.

Best known for its late-summer profusion of showy flowers in electric shades of pink, red, lavender, or white. Flowers are crinkled and ruffled like crepe paper and are held high above the foliage. The mottled, red and brown bark is attractive year around, but is especially striking in winter. Vase shaped if grown with multiple trunks; round headed when trained to a single stem. Fall color is good but inconsistent. Mildews in humid climates. The "Indian tribe" group of crape myrtle cultivars, introduced by the National Arboretum, have improved hardiness and mildew resistance. Native to China.
▌Zones 8 to 10.

Larix kaempferi
Japanese larch

Deciduous

▌Rapid growth to 50 to 60 feet high, 25 to 40 feet wide.

Unique deciduous conifer. Its habit is pyramidal and spreading. Has feathery, blue-green foliage with excellent ocher to yellow fall color. Cones hang on tree in winter. Needs ample moisture; adapts well to lawn watering. Grows in a variety of soils. Attracts birds. Native to Japan.
▌Zones 4 to 7.

Laurus nobilis
Sweet bay, bay laurel, Grecian laurel

Broadleaf evergreen

▌Slow growth to 12 to 30 feet high.

A well-behaved, indoor/outdoor tree. Its compact, conical form takes well to shearing into hedges, screens, or other formal shapes. Dark green leaves are aromatic, used in cooking. Flowers are insignificant. Small, dark berries attract birds. Withstands city conditions but requires well-drained soil.
▌Zones 9 and 10.

Larix kaempferi

Laurus nobilis

Liquidambar styraciflua

Leptospermum laevigatum

Leptospermum laevigatum
Australian tea tree

Broadleaf evergreen

▌ Moderate growth to 30 feet high.

This sculptural tree has a twisted trunk and a dense, rounded canopy. The leaves are stiff and gray-green. A good specimen tree, especially in the spring when covered with tiny white, red, or pink flowers. Keep on the dry side when mature. Best in well-drained, acid soil. Native to Australia.
▌ Zones 9 and 10.

Liquidambar styraciflua
American sweet gum

Deciduous

▌ Moderate to rapid growth to 60 to 75 feet high.

Popular in mild climates for its bright fall color. Star-shaped leaves turn rich shades of yellow, crimson, and purple, and decorate tree for up to 6 weeks. A symmetrical pyramid when young, becoming irregular with maturity. The fruit is like prickly golf balls, a nuisance when it drops in the fall. Will grow in many soils, but does best in rich clay or loam. Often planted as a street tree, but roots damage sidewalks and driveways. 'Burgundy', 'Festival', and 'Palo Alto' are popular in the West; 'Moraine' is hardier, commonly planted in the East. Native to the United States and Mexico.
▌ Zones 6 to 9.

Liriodendron tulipifera
Tulip tree, yellow poplar, tulip poplar

Deciduous

▌ Rapid growth; some have grown 60 to 70 feet high in 70 years.

Tallest of the eastern hardwoods; needs plenty of room to develop properly. Uniquely shaped, bright green leaves form a light, beautiful canopy. Fall color is bright yellow. Large, tulip-shaped, greenish yellow flowers with an orange blotch at the base are borne in late spring. The branches are somewhat brittle. Roots are invasive. Does poorly in dry and alkaline soil. Aphids may cause problems; honeydew prohibits its being planted over patios and parking areas. 'Fastigiatum' reaches 50 feet, has a narrow, columnar form. Native to the eastern United States.
▌ Zones 5 to 9.

Magnolia acuminata
Cucumber tree

Deciduous

▌ Rapid growth to 50 to 80 feet high, half as wide.

The stateliest of the hardy magnolias. A vigorous tree—needs room to develop properly. Pyramidal when young, becomes rounded with maturity. Its common name is derived from the shape and color of the fruitclusters. Inconspicuous greenish yellow flowers appear after the foliage unfurls in the spring. Native to the eastern United States.
▌ Zones 4 to 8.

Liriodendron tulipifera

Magnolia acuminata

Magnolia grandiflora

Magnolia kobus var.
stellata

Magnolia grandiflora
Southern magnolia

Broadleaf evergreen

▌Moderate growth to
60 to 75 feet high,
35 to 55 feet wide.

Popular in the West as well
as in the southern United
States. Many varieties are
available. Flowers are generally large (8 inches or
more), fragrant, and creamy
white. Leaves are lustrous,
leathery, and large (5 to 8
inches); they tatter in windy
areas. 'Victoria' and 'Edith
Bogue' are cold-hardy forms.
'St. Mary' is a small variety
(to 20 feet), grown for its
abundant blooms and pre-
dictable shape. Normally a
large shrub, usually trained
as a small tree. Native to the
southern United States.
▌Zones 7 to 9.

Magnolia kobus var. stellata
Star magnolia

Deciduous

▌Moderate growth to
15 to 20 feet high.

Another early bloomer; fragrant, white flowers with
12 to 15 strap-shaped petals
appear before the leaves in
late winter or early spring.
Like *M. × soulangiana*,
flowers can be damaged by
frost. Avoid southern exposures that encourage buds
to develop early and flowers
to open too fast. A hardy,
small tree with a rounded
habit. Good specimen plant.
Native to Japan.
▌Zones 5 to 9.

Magnolia × soulangiana
Saucer magnolia

Deciduous

▌Moderate growth to
20 to 30 feet high, often
equally wide.

Probably the most widely
planted and best known of
the magnolias. Flower colors of the different varieties
range from white to dark
reddish purple. Most bloom
well when very young. Plant
in an open area where it
will have room to spread.
Avoid planting in protected
locations; heat hastens
spring bloom, which may
easily be damaged by frost.
The foliage of this tree is
not the most attractive of
the magnolia, but the flowers and winter branch
form are stunning.
▌Zones 5 to 9.

Magnolia virginiana
Sweet bay magnolia

Broadleaf, deciduous, or
evergreen

▌Moderate growth to 10 to
20 feet high in the North,
40 to 60 feet in the South.

Evergreen in zone 9, but
also a popular magnolia in
the colder areas, where it
is deciduous. Fragrant,
creamy white flowers are
similar to but smaller than
those of *M. grandiflora*.
Leaves are also similar but
are smaller and glossy
above, blue-white beneath.
Prefers rich, moist, acid
soil. Native to the lowlands
of the southern and eastern
United States.
▌Zones 5 to 9.

Magnolia × soulangiana

Magnolia virginiana

Malus × atrosanguinea

Malus floribunda

Malus × atrosanguinea
Carmine flowering crab apple

Deciduous

▌ Slow growth to 15 to 20 feet high.

One of the better disease-resistant, pink-flowered crabs. The rose pink flowers average 1¼ inches in diameter. The small, dark red fruit is seldom abundant. Habit is usually rounded with wide-spreading, architectural branches. ▌ Zones 4 to 8.

Malus floribunda
Japanese flowering crab apple

Deciduous

▌ Slow growth to 15 to 25 feet high.

This is the crab apple against which all others are measured. Rich red buds open pinkish white to white. Each flower averages 1 to 1½ inches in diameter. The ⅜-inch fruit vary from yellow to red. Its habit is broad, rounded, and densely branched. Native to Japan. ▌ Zones 4 and 5.

Malus hupehensis
Tea flowering crab apple

Deciduous

▌ Slow growth to 20 to 25 feet high.

When fully grown, it offers a vase-shaped, decidedly picturesque habit that makes it unique among crab apples. The long branches are smothered with deep pink buds that open to fragrant, white flowers, 1½ inches in diameter. The greenish yellow to red-tinged fruit is seldom abundant. Fire blight can be a problem. Native to China. ▌ Zones 4 to 8.

Malus sargentii
Sargent flowering crab apple

Deciduous

▌ Slow growth rate; seldom grows more than 8 feet high.

This is a dense, wide-spreading, shrubby species. Bears elegant ¾- to 1-inch, fragrant, white flowers and bright red, ¼- to ⅜-inch-diameter fruit. It is a choice plant for small residential landscapes. Often grown in containers. Native to Japan. ▌ Zones 4 to 8.

Malus hupehensis

Malus sargentii

Maytenus boaria

Malus zumi var. *calocarpa*

Malus zumi var. *calocarpa*
Redbud flowering crab apple

Deciduous

▎ Slow growth to 25 feet high.

Deep red buds give way to 1½-inch, white flowers, providing a great spring spectacle. The ⅜- to ½-inch, bright red fruit persists into winter, tends to be borne heavily in alternate years.
▎ Zones 5 to 9.

Maytenus boaria
Mayten tree

Broadleaf evergreen

▎ Slow growth to 30 to 40 feet high.

A great tree for mild climates. Takes heat and tolerates salinity and seaside conditions. Interesting bark and weeping form—reminiscent of weeping willow without all the problems. A good patio or driveway tree. Native to Chile.
▎ Zones 9 and 10.

Melaleuca linariifolia
Snow-in-summer, flaxleaf paperbark

Broadleaf evergreen

▎ Slow to moderate growth to 70 feet high.

Distinguished in all seasons by its texture and subtle coloring. Thin, pale beige branchlets and clusters of delicately pointed, blue-green leaves contrast with the honey brown, papery bark that peels from the trunk and old limbs. Becomes truly spectacular in early summer, when its full bloom of white flowers looks like a blanket of snow. Habit is narrow, upright, and open when young; becomes dense and round headed with age. Native to Australia.
▎ Zones 9 and 10.

Metasequoia glyptostroboides
Dawn redwood

Deciduous

▎ Very rapid growth to 80 to 100 feet high.

Resembles the deciduous bald cypress in foliage character, although its flat, needlelike leaves are more the size of hemlock needles. The trunk shape differs considerably from that of bald cypress. Has a buttress-shaped trunk, deeply fluted and very wide at the base. Its overall shape is pyramidal. The horizontal branches have pendulous tips. Bark is deep reddish brown on trunk, lighter on twigs. Foliage is light green in summer, bronze in the fall. Native to China.
▎ Zones 6 to 8.

Melaleuca linariifolia

Metasequoia glyptostroboides

Nyssa sylvatica

Morus alba, weeping form

Morus alba varieties
Mulberry

Deciduous

▮ Moderate growth from 20 to 80 feet, depending on variety.

This species comes in a wide spectrum of varieties, from large upright trees to relatively small weeping types. Their leaves are usually about 4 inches long and sometimes deeply toothed. The purple fruit are up to 2 inches long and some varieties are very sweet, much like boysenberries. Be careful where you plant mulberries—the fruit stains everything nearby and attracts a large variety of birds. Native over a wide area of America, Europe, and Asia.
▮ Depending on varieties, hardy in zones 5 to 10.

Nyssa sylvatica
Black tupelo, black gum, sour gum, pepperidge

Deciduous

▮ Moderate growth to 30 to 50 feet high, about half as wide.

Has a dense, pendulous canopy of glossy, green foliage. Scarlet autumn leaves look marvelous against the foliage of evergreens; the leaves turn bright colors even in mild climates. Has a pyramidal habit. The naked winter branches make a lovely silhouette against the sky and bear attractive red buds in spring. Very adaptable. Native to the eastern United States.
▮ Zones 5 to 9.

Olea europaea
Olive

Broadleaf evergreen

▮ Fairly rapid growth in youth, slowing down with age, to 20 to 30 feet high.

The gnarled, gray trunk and gray-green leaves are familiar throughout the Southwest and California. Has a rounded head. Adaptable to a variety of soils, but needs full sun. Easily transplanted when mature. Fruit stains pavement, will harm lawns if not raked up. Select fruitless varieties for these areas. 'Swan Hill' is a full-sized, fruitless tree. 'Skylark Dwarf' is also fruitless, but is grown as a shrub. 'Ascolano' is an attractive fruiting variety. Native to the Mediterranean region and western Asia.
▮ Zones 9 and 10.

Oxydendrum arboreum
Sourwood

Deciduous

▮ Slow growth to 30 to 40 feet high.

One of the most beautiful American flowering trees. Leaves are translucent amber red as they unfold in the spring, scarlet in autumn. Pendulous sprays of white flowers are borne for a long period in July. Has a light, feathery habit; looks more like an oriental specimen than a shade tree. Its delicate and enduring beauty is best enjoyed at close hand on a terrace or patio. The common name is derived from the very sour-tasting foliage. Requires acid soil; resents competition from lawns or other plants. Native to the eastern United States.
▮ Zones 6 to 9.

Olea europaea

Oxydendrum arboreum

Phoenix canariensis

Picea abies

Phoenix canariensis
Canary Island date palm

Broadleaf evergreen

▮ Slow growth to 60 feet high (grows to about 20 feet in 15 years).

A stately palm with feathery, arching leaves. Bears pendulous clusters of orange-yellow fruit. Has a wide-spreading head; best suited to large areas, but may be grown for years in a pot. Native to the Canary Islands.
▮ Zone 10.

Picea abies
Norway spruce

Needle evergreen

▮ Rapid growth to 40 to 60 feet high.

A very good landscape specimen where space permits. Makes an excellent windbreak or tall screen. Retains lower branches and needles well. Has a pyramidal form; becomes more pleasing as it ages and the branches become more pendulous. In addition to its fine foliar features, bears attractive cones 4 to 7 inches long. Prefers cool, moist conditions; avoid planting in hot areas and dry, infertile soil. Varieties range from dwarf to weeping, from compact to spreading. Many, especially the weeping forms, require staking to bring them up to the desired height. Native to Europe.
▮ Zones 3 to 8.

Picea glauca
White spruce

Needle evergreen

▮ Slow to moderate growth to 40 to 60 feet high, 10 to 20 feet wide.

Extremely hardy, withstanding both very cold and very hot, dry conditions. Habit is formal, conical. Needles are short and soft. Grows well in containers—can be used as a miniature Christmas tree for several years. Mites can be a problem. 'Densata', the Black Hills spruce, is a popular compact form that grows slowly to about 20 feet high. 'Conica', a shrub-sized cultivar, is described on page 280. Native to Alaska, Canada, and the northern United States.
▮ Zones 3 to 6.

Picea pungens
Colorado spruce

Needle evergreen

▮ Slow growth to 30 to 60 feet high, 10 to 20 feet wide.

When young, Colorado spruce is a beautiful, narrow to broad, pyramidal tree with stiff branches, but after about 15 to 20 years it begins to lose its lower branches and becomes less attractive. The blue-needled varieties are the most widely available, but they should be placed very carefully in the landscape—the rich blue pyramids often look out of place. 'Glauca' has excellent soil and climatic tolerances. Native to Wyoming, Utah, Colorado, and New Mexico.
▮ Zones 3 to 8.

Picea glauca

Picea pungens

Pinus bungeana

Pinus densiflora

Pinus bungeana
Lacebark pine

Needle evergreen

▌ Slow growth to 30 to 50 feet high.

Often overlooked, but very desirable as a landscape tree. Pyramidal to rounded in youth, often with many trunks; becomes more open and irregular with age. Bark peels off in patches, exposing areas of gray, grayish green, and brown. Tolerates acid, limestone, and relatively dry soil. An excellent specimen plant—its use is limited only by the imagination of the gardener. Native to northwest China.
▌ Zones 5 to 8.

Pinus densiflora
Japanese red pine

Needle evergreen

▌ Rapid growth to 50 to 60 feet high, equally wide.

A splendid pine with rich foliage, attractive bark, and a unique growth habit. The needles appear to be tufted and seem perched like butterflies on the branches. Usually forms two or more crooked, leaning trunks. The branches spread horizontally, giving the tree an open, loose habit and a flat top. Orangish to reddish bark brightens the winter landscape. Dwarf varieties include 'Globosa' and 'Umbraculifera'. 'Oculis-Draconis' is an oddity with yellow-banded needles that make the branch tips look like dragon's eyes. Native to Japan.
▌ Zones 5 to 8.

Pinus nigra
Austrian pine

Needle evergreen

▌ Slow to moderate growth to 35 to 50 feet high, 15 to 25 feet wide.

An important pine in the East and Midwest; tolerant of drought, salt, sand, clay, and city conditions. Becomes flat topped at maturity, but is densely pyramidal and wide spreading in youth. Bark is mottled with gray, white, and brown. The sharp, stiff needles are 4 to 8 inches long. Oval cones grow to about 3 inches long. A choice evergreen for screens, windbreaks, and specimen use, but its susceptibility to diplodia tip blight and nematodes limits its use in the East. Native to central and southern Europe and Asia Minor.
▌ Zones 4 to 8.

Pinus radiata
Monterey pine

Needle evergreen

▌ Rapid growth to 60 to 80 feet high.

This tree is normally pyramidal when young, but develops a rounded, flattened crown with age, often contorted by the wind. Used for windbreaks, screens, and large hedges. Deep green needles may be 3 to 7 inches long. Clusters of 3- to 5-inch cones stay on the tree for many years. Native to California.
▌ Zones 8 to 10.

Pinus nigra

Pinus radiata

Pinus strobus

Pinus sylvestris

Pinus strobus
Eastern white pine

Needle evergreen

▌ Moderate to rapid growth to 50 to 80 feet high, 20 to 40 feet wide.

Has a graceful, dignified appearance. Forms a pyramid of soft, almost furry foliage in youth. With age the crown becomes open, the branches grow almost horizontally, and the needles are borne in graceful plumes. A superior specimen tree; can also be used for screens, hedges, and groupings. Tolerates many kinds of soil, but may become chlorotic in alkaline soil. Performs well in the East, Midwest, and upper South. 'Fastigiata' is columnar, 'Glauca' has bluish green needles, and 'Pendula' has long branches that sweep the ground.
▌ Zones 3 to 8.

Pinus sylvestris
Scotch pine, Scots pine

Needle evergreen

▌ Slow to moderate growth to 30 to 60 feet high.

Often grown as Christmas trees, Scotch pine also make excellent landscape plants. Rich, blue needles contrast with the sea of green produced by most pines. Irregularly pyramidal in youth; the crown eventually becomes open and wide spreading, flat, or rounded. The peeling bark is reddish orange at first, maturing to a grayish red-brown. Species is variable; many strains and cultivars have been selected. 'Fastigiata' is columnar, 'Argentea' has silver needles, 'Nana' and 'Watereri' are dwarfs. Native to Europe and Asia.
▌ Zones 3 to 8.

Pinus thunbergii
Japanese black pine

Needle evergreen

▌ Moderate growth to 20 to 40 feet high.

An elegant, artistic addition to any garden. Its habit is broadly pyramidal, but the branches may dip, dive, spread, and turn. Frequently ungainly in youth. The crown becomes irregular and spreading as it approaches maturity. Salt tolerant, ideal for sandy soil in coastal areas. Not particularly cold tolerant; needles may brown severely when temperatures drop below –10° F. Native to Japan.
▌ Zones 5 to 8.

Pinus wallichiana
Himalayan pine

Needle evergreen

▌ Slow to moderate growth to 30 to 40 feet high, 10 to 30 feet wide.

The graceful, broadly pyramidal habit provides a framework for slender, arching needles. Should be grown as a specimen; allow considerable space for spreading growth. Needles are bluish green, 6 to 8 inches long. Tan cones are long and slender. Grows best on moist, acid, well-drained loam. Native to the Himalayas.
▌ Zones 5 to 7.

Pinus thunbergii

Pinus wallichiana

Pistacia chinensis

Pittosporum undulatum

Pistacia chinensis
Chinese pistache

Deciduous

∎ Moderate growth to 30 to 40 feet high, equally wide.

A fine lawn or street tree; one of the best trees for providing filtered shade. The bright green, compound leaves grow up to 12 inches long; they have a pink tinge in the spring, turn brilliant shades of yellow, orange, and red in the fall—even in mild climates. Zigzag branching pattern adds winter character to the landscape. Widely adapted; grows best with summer heat. Has no serious disease problems. Because of its uneven growth habit, needs shaping when young to develop good form. Native to China.
∎ Zones 6 to 10.

Pittosporum undulatum
Victorian box

Broadleaf evergreen

∎ Moderate growth to 40 feet high.

A most useful tree for tall screen and background plantings. The canopy is rounded. May be grown with one or multiple trunks. The glossy, 5-inch, deep green leaves have wavy edges. The sticky, orange seeds create a mess on walkways. Native to Australia.
∎ Zones 9 and 10.

Platanus × acerifolia
London plane tree

Deciduous

∎ Rapid growth to 60 to 100 feet high.

Versatile and widely adapted; takes harsh city conditions, drought, and poor soil. Widely used as a street tree and in malls. Has a naturally rounded, open crown. Often pollarded to produce a dense ball of green, but the resulting club-shaped branches are unattractive in winter. The green and creamy white bark looks like dappled sunlight. Large leaves have lobes similar to those of maples. Brown, ball-shaped clusters of fruit hang on the branches through winter. Susceptible to anthracnose, which causes leaves to fall in spring. A hybrid of *P. occidentalis* (American sycamore) and *P. orientalis* (oriental plane tree).
∎ Zones 5 to 9.

Podocarpus elongatus
African yellowwood

Broadleaf evergreen

∎ Moderate growth to 40 feet high.

A well-behaved, round-headed tree with narrow, 3-inch, dark green leaves growing in a whorled pattern. Pest-free and hardier than its cousin *P. macrophyllus.* Grows well in containers for patio specimens when young. Not fussy about soil, but needs adequate drainage. Native to South Africa.
∎ Zones 9 and 10; an adventurous spirit might try it in protected parts of zone 8.

Platanus × acerifolia

Podocarpus elongatus

Populus alba

Podocarpus macrophyllus

Podocarpus macrophyllus
Yew-pine

Broadleaf evergreen

▌ Slow growth to 50 feet high.

A columnar to oval evergreen used for screening, hedging, and espaliers. May be pruned to create interesting patterns against walls or fences. Also well suited to containers—indoors and out—and for use in entryways. Airy foliage grows on slightly drooping branches. Waxy fruit has a bluish tinge. Pest-free and widely adapted, but may show chlorosis in alkaline or heavy soil. Plant in a protected location to extend hardiness. Native to Japan.
▌ Zones 9 and 10.

Populus alba
White poplar

Deciduous

▌ Rapid growth to 50 to 90 feet high.

The foliage of this tree is the prettiest of all the poplars. The slightest breeze makes the leaves flash and flicker. Grows exceptionally well in the desert or near the seashore. Its greatest fault is the persistent sprouting of shoots from the widespreading root system. Rapid growth makes it a useful windbreak in areas where few trees will grow at all. 'Pyramidalis', the bolleana poplar, is distinctly upright, has the fine foliage of white poplar, and does not sucker as badly. Native to Europe and Asia.
▌ Zones 4 to 10.

Populus nigra 'Italica'
Lombardy poplar

Deciduous

▌ Rapid growth to 70 feet high.

Valuable for poor soil in the Midwest and Southeast. Its narrow, columnar form and fast growth make it unbeatable as a tall screen. However, it is very susceptible to stem canker disease in southern areas. But even where disease is a problem, a row can provide an ideal temporary windbreak or screen when planted adjacent to a row of arborvitae, spruce, or columnar junipers. By the time the poplars begin to decline (usually in 15 to 20 years), the evergreens will be tall enough to take over the job. *P. nigra* var. *thevestina* has white bark, a broader habit, and some canker resistance.
▌ Zones 3 to 9.

Prunus caroliniana
Carolina cherry laurel

Broadleaf evergreen

▌ Rapid growth to 20 to 30 feet high, 15 to 20 feet wide.

Typically a small tree with a dense, pyramidal to oval outline. Has much to offer as a single specimen, in informal groupings, or as a screen. Fragrant, white flowers are followed by lustrous, black fruit that attracts birds. Adapts to wide range of soil types. 'Bright 'n Tight' is a compact form with smaller leaves than the original species and is probably a better choice for contemporary landscapes.
▌ Zones 7 to 10.

Prunus caroliniana

Populus nigra 'Italica'

Prunus ilicifolia

Prunus serrulata

Prunus ilicifolia
Hollyleaf cherry

Broadleaf evergreen

▮ Moderate growth to 12 to 35 feet high.

Hollyleaf cherry has dark green, hollylike leaves. The new growth is lighter green, giving a soft look to the tree. Small clusters of attractive, white flowers are followed by edible red cherries that gradually turn a deep reddish purple. Native to the California coast and Baja California.
▮ Zones 9 and 10.

Prunus serrulata
Japanese flowering cherry

Deciduous

▮ Moderate to fast growth to 20 to 25 feet high.

The species is rarely grown, but more than 120 cultivars have been selected; many are widely available. Tree habits range from stiffly upright to open and spreading. Spreading forms make good shade trees. Flowers are usually pink, fading to white, and may be single or double. Requires well-drained soil. 'Amanogawa' grows to 20 feet and is the narrowest and most upright of the cultivars. Flowers are pale pink. 'Kwanzan', the most popular and hardy of the double-flowered cultivars, grows to 12 to 18 feet high and has deep pink flowers. Native to eastern Asia.
▮ Zones 6 to 9.

Prunus × yedoensis
Yoshino cherry

Deciduous

▮ Rapid growth to 40 feet high.

One of the fastest-growing cherries. Usually wide spreading, flat topped when mature. Single, white flowers are borne in abundance early in the season. Makes up the main part of the cherry display in Washington, D.C. Native to Japan.
▮ Zones 6 to 8.

Pseudotsuga menziesii
Douglas fir

Needle evergreen

▮ Moderate growth to 40 to 80 feet high, 12 to 20 feet wide.

Not many evergreens can compete effectively for landscape attention with Douglas fir. Gracefully pyramidal in youth, it will maintain this outline if grown in moist, acid, deep, well-drained soil. Most effectively used as a specimen, in an informal screen, or as a Christmas tree. Species is best adapted to the West, but the cultivar 'Glauca', which has bluish green needles, is considered the hardiest and the best adapted to the Midwest and East. Native to Alaska through the western United States into Mexico.
▮ Zones 4 to 8.

Prunus × yedoensis

Pseudotsuga menziesii

Pyrus calleryana

Pyrus kawakamii

Pyrus calleryana
Callery pear

Deciduous

▌ Moderate growth to 25 to 50 feet high, 15 to 20 feet wide.

Has outstanding landscape qualities: abundant white flowers in early spring; shiny, dark green leaves with scalloped edges; brilliant crimson-red fall color; and impressive adaptability. Stands up to pollution and other city stresses; can take wind. Adapts to most soils. Requires little maintenance; relatively pest-free. 'Bradford' grows to 50 feet high and 30 feet wide and has an oval shape and spectacular fall color. 'Chanticleer' is narrower and more pyramidal. 'Aristocrat' is pyramidal and has very glossy leaves with wavy edges. 'Fauriei' flowers profusely and grows to 30 to 40 feet high.
▌ Zones 5 to 9.

Pyrus kawakamii
Evergreen pear

Broadleaf evergreen

▌ Moderate growth to 30 feet high.

One of the most widely used trees in California. Has an open, irregular habit. Commonly pruned into a single or multitrunked tree; forms a spreading shrub if untrained. A showy mass of white blossoms covers the tree from late winter through spring. Leaves are shiny, light green, with wavy edges. Adaptable to many soil types; needs minimum care. Easy to espalier, and good in containers. Susceptible to aphids and fire blight. Native to Taiwan.
▌ Zones 9 and 10.

Quercus agrifolia
California live oak

Broadleaf evergreen

▌ Slow growth to 20 to 75 feet high, equal or wider spread.

A massive, dense, wide-spreading tree. The heavy, twisted branches are covered with dark gray bark. Has a picturesque outline. The shiny, hollylike leaves are 1 to 2½ inches long. Needs a great deal of room to mature. Requires a mild Mediterranean climate and well-drained soil; will not tolerate moisture at base of trunk. Native to California.
▌ Zones 9 and 10.

Quercus alba
White oak

Deciduous

▌ Slow growth to 60 to 80 feet high, equally wide.

White oak has a pyramidal shape when young but matures slowly to form a dense, broadly rounded tree. Autumn color is purplish red. Has little trouble with pests or diseases but must have well-drained, nonalkaline soil and plenty of moisture. Native to the eastern and midwestern United States.
▌ Zones 4 to 9.

Quercus agrifolia

Quercus alba

Quercus coccinea

Quercus palustris

Quercus coccinea

Scarlet oak

Deciduous

▌ Rapid growth to 50 to 80 feet high.

Named for its outstanding fall color. Has an open habit. Fast growing and relatively pest-free, but difficult to transplant. Requires neutral or acid soil. Native to the eastern and southern United States.
▌ Zones 4 to 9.

Quercus palustris

Pin oak

Deciduous

▌ Fairly rapid growth to 60 to 80 feet high.

The most popular native oak. Has a dense, pyramidal habit; the drooping branches will sweep to the ground. Glossy, deeply lobed foliage turns brilliant red in the fall in cold climates, but may turn brown and hang on the tree through the winter in mild areas. The easiest oak to transplant. Tolerates a variety of sites, but subject to iron chlorosis in alkaline soil. The drooping habit of the lower branches makes this tree a poor choice where automobile or foot traffic must pass close by or underneath. Native to the eastern United States.
▌ Zones 5 to 9.

Quercus robur

English oak

Deciduous

▌ Moderate growth to 80 feet high.

A stately tree with a wide, open head and a short, thick trunk. Little or no fall color; does not drop leaves until very late in the season. Very susceptible to powdery mildew, which is unsightly but not fatal. 'Fastigiata' is an upright, columnar cultivar. Native to Africa, Europe, and Asia.
▌ Zones 5 to 9.

Quercus rubra

Northern red oak

Deciduous

▌ Rapid growth to 60 to 80 feet high.

Adaptable, fast-growing, and easy to transplant. Pyramidal in youth, rounded in maturity. Second only to *Q. coccinea* in intensity of fall color. Native to eastern North America.
▌ Zones 3 to 9.

Quercus robur

Quercus rubra

Rhamnus alaternus

Robinia pseudoacacia

Rhamnus alaternus
Italian buckthorn

Broadleaf evergreen

▌ Rapid growth to 12 to 20 feet high, equally wide.

Most often used as a high screen or hedge; responds well to shearing to almost any shape. Can be trained as single- or multitrunked tree. Has small, shiny, green leaves. Bears inconspicuous spring flowers and tiny, black fruit. Susceptible to verticillium wilt. Native to southern Europe.
▌ Zones 7 to 9.

Robinia pseudoacacia
Black locust

Deciduous

▌ Rapid growth to 40 to 75 feet high, 30 to 60 feet wide.

A good choice for difficult situations. Takes heat, drought, and almost all types of soil. Often has multiple trunks; its habit is sparse and open. Bears pendulous, fragrant clusters of white or pink flowers that attract bees. Young leaflets are silvery gray-green, turning dark green with age and yellow in the fall. Use as a last resort for difficult sites; its weak wood, invasive root system, and susceptibility to borers limit its landscape usefulness to areas where other trees would not survive. Native to the east central United States.
▌ Zones 4 to 9.

Salix babylonica
Weeping willow

Deciduous

▌ Rapid growth to 30 to 50 feet high, wider spread.

Named for its pendulous branchlets that droop to the ground. Long leaves are medium olive green, turning yellow in the fall. Branchlets are green to brown. Needs room to grow; may need training to develop a single trunk. Drooping habit makes an interesting winter silhouette. Widely adapted to a variety of soils and climates; needs abundant moisture. Wood is brittle, roots invasive. Tree is short lived; most specimens last 15 to 20 years. Native to China.
▌ Zones 5 to 9.

Sapium sebiferum
Chinese tallow tree

Deciduous

▌ Rapid growth to 35 feet high, equally wide.

A good lawn or street tree; can also be used as a shade tree on a patio or terrace, or as a screen. Its habit is round headed to conical. Fast growth and freedom from pests and diseases make it a good substitute for poplars. Foliage provides light shade, turns bronze to bright red after a sharp frost. Prune and stake in early stages for a single trunk. Tolerates moist soil, prefers acid conditions. Ample water will encourage fast growth. Native to China.
▌ Zones 8 and 9.

Salix babylonica

Sapium sebiferum

Manilkara zapota (Sapota achras)
Sapodilla

Broadleaf evergreen

▌Robust and fast growth up to 75 feet high.

Grown in tropical regions for its delicious fruit, whose texture is like firm custard; great for fruit salads. Trees are often heavily laden with 3- to 4-inch fruit in midsummer and fall. Light green leaves to 5 inches. Tolerant of most soils and requires only moderate watering. Appreciates ample fertilizing for best fruiting. Pest-free. Its sap is a milk latex that produces gum chicle, the base product in chewing gum.
▌Zones 9 and 10.

Schinus molle
Pepper tree

Broadleaf evergreen

▌Rapid growth to 20 to 50 feet high.

Has a well-deserved reputation for growing rapidly with very little encouragement, accepting poor soil, scant rainfall, strong winds, and occasional frost. Its habit is rounded; branches spread wide, branchlets weep. Despite invasive roots, messy fruit, and susceptibility to scale and aphids, this tree has a place in desert landscapes where it will have room to grow. Native to Peru, Bolivia, and Chile.
▌Zones 9 and 10.

Schinus terebinthifolius
Brazil pepper tree

Broadleaf evergreen

▌Fast growing to 25 feet high.

A more compact tree than its cousin *S. molle.* Larger compound leaves. An excellent tree for the small garden, tidy and well behaved. Small, bright red, decorative berries. It accepts poor soil and little water but is brittle in high winds. Native to Brazil.
▌Zone 9 and 10.

Sequoia sempervirens
Coast redwood

Needle evergreen

▌Rapid growth, usually to 75 to 100 feet high.

Best adapted to the fog belt of northern California and Oregon, where it can receive year-round moisture. Its fast growth; fibrous, red bark; and attractive, narrow, pyramidal form have prompted plantings throughout California. Seedlings are variable; choose a named cultivar. 'Aptos Blue' has heavy, blue-green foliage. 'Santa Cruz' is a full, dense tree with soft, light green foliage. 'Los Altos' has glossy foliage with a rich green color that persists even in winter. Its cousin *Sequoiadendron gigantea* (Sierra redwood) is slower growing, broader, and more compact.
▌Zones 7 to 10.

Manilkara zapota

Schinus molle

Schinus terebinthifolius

Sequoia sempervirens

Sophora japonica

Sorbus aucuparia

Sophora japonica
Japanese pagoda tree

Deciduous

▮ Moderate growth to 20 to 30 feet high, then slow growth to 50 to 70 feet high, equally wide.

Does not begin blooming until it is 8 to 10 years old, but when it does, the large, loose clusters of creamy white blossoms can last for more than 6 weeks. Blooms in late spring or early summer. Dense and upright when young, becoming rounded and spreading with age. Pods look like strings of green beads. Leaves cast filtered shade; good for lawn or patio. Withstands city conditions, subject to no serious pest or disease problems. Native to Japan and Korea.
▮ Zones 5 to 8 (to zone 10 in the West).

Sorbus aucuparia
European mountain ash

Deciduous

▮ Moderate growth to 25 to 30 feet high.

The most popular mountain ash. Symmetrical and fast growing; has an upright habit that becomes round headed with age. Bears clusters of white flowers in late spring, maturing to bright orange or red berries in late summer and early fall. Its great enemies are borer insects, which invade the tree when it is stressed. Fire blight is also a problem, particularly in hot, humid areas. 'Xanthocarpa' has yellow fruit. 'Asplenifolia' has lacy, doubly-serrate leaflets. 'Fastigiata' has a narrow habit. Native to Europe and Asia.
▮ Zones 2 to 7.

Styrax japonicum
Japanese snowbell, Japanese snowdrop tree

Deciduous

▮ Slow to moderate growth to 15 to 20 feet tall, 20 to 25 feet wide.

One of the choicest small-garden trees. Excellent patio tree; its pendant flowers are especially attractive when viewed from below. Also grows well in lawns. Flowers are borne in great abundance in early June; the whole tree looks white when in bloom. Branches have a zigzag habit, giving the tree a broad, flat-topped crown. Tolerates shade and grows best in rich, well-drained soil. Needs training to control its natural tendency toward shrubbiness.
▮ Zones 5 to 9.

Taxodium distichum
Bald cypress

Deciduous

▮ Moderate to rapid growth to 50 to 70 feet high.

Few trees can survive in standing water, but this one thrives in soggy sites as well as in drier areas. Its slender, pyramidal shape allows it to fit into the landscape where space is limited. Makes a good lawn tree, but knees (woody growths from the root system) cause mowing problems in wet lawns. Needles turn bronze in autumn. Native to the eastern United States from Delaware to Florida.
▮ Zones 5 to 10.

Styrax japonicum

Taxodium distichum

Thuja occidentalis

Thuja plicata

Thuja occidentalis

American arborvitae, eastern arborvitae

Needle evergreen

▌Slow to moderate growth to 40 to 50 feet high.

May appear as a column or broad pyramid in the landscape. Usually dense and full to the ground—excellent for screens and hedges. The habit opens as the tree matures, showing attractive grayish to reddish brown bark. Tolerates most soil conditions, but deep, moist, well-drained soil is ideal. Needles burn in cold winds. 'Nigra' and 'Techny' are dense, pyramidal, grow to 20 feet high, and hold dark green color throughout winter. Many other cultivars are available, varying in foliage color and habit.
▌Zones 3 to 8.

Thuja plicata

Western red cedar, giant arborvitae, canoe cedar

Needle evergreen

▌Slow growth to 50 to 70 feet high, 15 to 25 feet wide.

One of the most beautiful arborvitaes. Distinctly pyramidal in youth and old age. Retains lower branches, remains dense and full throughout crown. A good choice as a specimen, screen, or grouping. More sensitive to heat than *T. occidentalis*. Tolerates wet soil, but may blow over if grown in wet soil in a windy area. 'Fastigiata' has an upright, columnar form and is especially effective for tall screens. Native from Alaska through northern California.
▌Zones 5 to 8.

Tilia cordata

Littleleaf linden

Deciduous

▌Moderate to rapid growth to 60 to 70 feet high.

Its fine texture and symmetrical habit make this a popular street, lawn, or shade tree. Dark green, heart-shaped leaves are 1¼ to 2½ inches long—about half the size of most linden leaves. Like other lindens, it can stand adverse city conditions, heat and drought, and a wide variety of soils, but grows best in moist, fertile soil. Bears clusters of very fragrant, yellow flowers in late spring or early summer; flowers attract bees. Small, papery bracts are similar to maple samaras. Native to Europe.
▌Zones 4 to 8.

Trachycarpus fortunei

Windmill palm

Broadleaf evergreen

▌Moderate to rapid growth to 15 to 30 feet high.

One of the hardiest palms; its broad, fan-shaped leaves survive temperatures as low as 10° F. The trunk is thinner at its base than at the top and is covered with thick, dark brown fiber. Native to China.
▌Zones 8 to 10.

Tilia cordata

Trachycarpus fortunei

Tsuga canadensis

Tsuga caroliniana

Tsuga canadensis
Eastern hemlock,
Canadian hemlock

Needle evergreen

▮ Moderate growth to
40 to 70 feet high, 25 to
35 feet wide.

The aristocrat of conifers.
Softly and gracefully pyramidal in youth; becomes
more pendulous with age.
New spring growth is light
green, changes to lustrous
dark green. Has no rival for
screens and hedges; also
makes a fine specimen, accent, or foundation plant. A
moist, acid, well-drained
soil is essential for landscape success. Sensitive to
dry winds, salt, and pollution. Hemlock scale is a
problem in New York, New
Jersey, Connecticut, and
Pennsylvania. 'Sargentii' has
a magnificent, broadly
weeping form. Native to
northeastern North America.
▮ Zones 3 to 8.

Tsuga caroliniana
Carolina hemlock

Needle evergreen

▮ Slow growth to 45 to 60
feet high, 20 to 25 feet wide.

Seldom a landscape match
for *T. canadensis*. Airy,
open, and pyramidal, with
short, stout, often semipen-
dulous branches. Deserves
consideration for specimen
use, but may be difficult to
locate commercially. Soil
and climate requirements
are similar to those of *T.
canadensis*, but *T. caroliniana* is more tolerant of
urban environments. Native
to the mountains of Virginia
through Georgia.
▮ Zones 4 to 7.

Ulmus parvifolia
Chinese elm

Deciduous (nearly
evergreen in the
warmest zones)

▮ Rapid growth to 40 to
60 feet high.

A medium-sized, oval to
rounded tree with many desirable landscape features.
Small leaves form an open
canopy, turn pale yellow to
purple in the fall. Brown
outer bark peels in circular
plates to reveal yellow inner
bark. Very tolerant of alkaline, poor, and compacted
soil, as well as heat and
drought; grows rapidly
under good conditions.
Highly resistant to Dutch
elm disease and the elm
leaf beetle. The elm phobia
caused by Dutch elm dis-
ease should be ignored in
the case of this fine tree.
Native to China and Japan.
▮ Zones 5 to 9.

Vitex agnus-castus
Chaste tree

Deciduous

▮ Slow growth in cold
climates, more rapid in
warm climates, to 6 to
20 feet high.

Often multitrunked; broad
and spreading. Leaflets are
dark blue-green above, and
gray beneath. Flowers best
with summer heat; showy,
lilac blue flowers bloom in
late summer and early fall.
Can be trained high as a
shade tree. Native to southern Europe.
▮ Zones 6 to 10.

Ulmus parvifolia

Vitex agnus-castus

Washingtonia filifera

Washingtonia robusta

Washingtonia filifera
California fan palm

Broadleaf evergreen

▮ Moderate growth to 60 to 80 feet high (grows to about 20 feet in 15 years).

Has a large, open head of fan-shaped leaves. If unpruned, old leaves hang down in layers like a grass skirt. Usually pruned, though, due to fire hazard. Use as a specimen in a large yard; otherwise, best suited to streetside plantings. Drought tolerant, but does best in moist, well-drained soil. Native to the western United States.
▮ Zones 9 and 10.

Washingtonia robusta
Mexican fan palm

Broadleaf evergreen

▮ Moderate growth to 100 feet high (grows to about 25 feet in 15 years).

Similar to *W. filifera*, but grows taller and has a more slender trunk and a smaller crown. Widely planted in southern California—the tall, curved trunks are a Hollywood hallmark. Like *W. filifera*, the old leaves form a skirt, which should be pruned up at least 10 feet high to reduce fire hazard. Not for the small garden—has the character of a telephone pole when viewed from a close distance. Native to Mexico.
▮ Zones 9 and 10.

Zelkova serrata
Sawleaf zelkova, Japanese zelkova

Deciduous

▮ Moderate to rapid growth to 50 to 60 feet high, equally wide.

Heavily planted as a substitute for its close relative, American elm. Its habit is round headed, eventually becoming vase shaped. The foliage is similar to that of elms; it turns shades of yellow or red in the fall, most commonly russet. With age, the gray bark takes on an attractive mottling. Although not totally immune to Dutch elm disease, has a far better chance of surviving than American elm. Susceptible to wilt disease in some areas. Native to Japan and Korea.
▮ Zones 5 to 9.

Ziziphus jujuba
Chinese jujube

Deciduous

▮ Grows to 15 to 25 feet high.

A widely adapted, dual-purpose tree. Has a vase-shaped form. Especially valuable in the high and low desert; able to withstand alkaline or saline soil and drought. The small, glossy, green leaves are markedly veined. Small, yellow flowers are followed by a fall crop of fruit with the fresh taste of a meaty apple. When dried and candied, they taste like dates. The rough, gnarled trunk and drooping branches are picturesque in winter. Native to southeastern Europe and China.
▮ Zones 6 to 9.

Zelkova serrata

Ziziphus jujuba

Abelia × grandiflora

Acca sellowiana

SHRUBS

Abelia × *grandiflora*
Glossy abelia

Broadleaf evergreen (deciduous in the North)

▌ Moderate to rapid growth to 4 to 8 feet high, equally wide.

Hardiest and most free flowering of the Abelias. Makes an effective specimen, informal hedge, or mass; combines particularly well with other broadleaf evergreens. Showy, pinkish white flowers cover the plant from July until frost. Finely textured, glossy, deep green summer foliage turns an attractive bronze in the fall. Habit is graceful, rounded, and arching. Easy to grow; needs well-drained soil, full sun to partial shade, and average watering. Takes formal shearing, but at the expense of flowering. Best if allowed to achieve its natural, graceful shape.
▌ Zones 6 to 10.

Acca sellowiana (*Feijoa sellowiana*)
Pineapple guava

Broadleaf evergreen

▌ Moderate growth to 10 feet high, equally wide.

Dark green leaves to 3 inches long, nearly silver or white below. Long-stamened, red flowers followed by fruit up to 3½ inches long and 1½ inches in diameter. Fruit is excellent, sweet flavored, and only faintly tasting of pineapple. Plant in sandy loam rich in organic material. Requires only moderate watering. A tough, warm-climate plant. Good for background and informal hedging. Native to Brazil.
▌ Zones 8 to 10.

Aesculus parviflora
Dwarf horsechestnut

Deciduous

▌ Moderate growth to 8 to 12 feet high, about twice as wide.

Its spectacular July flowers, trouble-free foliage (unusual for *Aesculus* species), and adaptability to heavy shade make this shrub excellent for specimen plantings and for massing in problem shady areas, such as under large shade trees. Its habit is open, wide spreading, and suckering. The flowers are white with red anthers, and are borne in erect clusters 8 to 12 inches long from early to late July. Prefers moist, well-drained soil high in organic matter; tolerates full sun to heavy shade. 'Rogers' has 15-inch flower clusters.
▌ Zones 5 to 9.

Aucuba japonica
Japanese aucuba, spotted laurel

Broadleaf evergreen

▌ Moderate growth to 6 to 10 feet if unpruned.

Valued for its tolerance of heavy shade, large leathery leaves, and adaptability to adverse growing conditions. Use in problem shady areas, such as dim, north-facing entryways or under dense trees—it competes well with tree roots. Leaves burn in full sun. Keep the plant dense by selectively cutting branches back to leaf nodes. Drought tolerant once established. Performs well in any soil. Amend soil with organic matter when planting. Numerous cultivars are available with different leaf shapes, colors, and variegation patterns.
▌ Zones 7 to 9 (to zone 10 in the West).

Aesculus parviflora

Aucuba japonica

Berberis darwinii

Berberis thunbergii

Berberis darwinii

Darwin barberry

Broadleaf evergreen

▮ Rapid growth to 5 to 10 feet high, 4 to 7 feet wide.

This is the showiest barberry in flower; it is covered with bright yellow-orange flowers in early March. Forms an arching, loose shrub. Dark blue berries are an asset; they are beautiful and they attract birds. Tends to spread by underground stolons, becoming loose and open in old age unless pruned regularly. Like all barberries, it is not particular about its soil and withstands drought well. Does not grow well on the East Coast. 'Corallina Compacta' is favored for its dense, compact, rounded shape.
▮ Zones 8 to 10 in the West only.

Berberis thunbergii

Japanese barberry

Deciduous

▮ Moderate growth to 3 to 6 feet high, 4 to 7 feet wide.

Extremely easy to grow. Impenetrable thorns and dense, shearable foliage make this one of the most popular hedge and barrier plants around. Has outstanding, reddish purple fall color and red winter fruit. The thorny branches tend to collect trash; cleanup can be painful. Adapts to nearly any soil, withstands drought well, and performs admirably in either full sun or partial shade. Red-, yellow-, and variegated-leafed cultivars are available; these need full sun.
▮ Zones 5 to 9.

Buddleia davidii

Butterfly bush

Deciduous

▮ Rapid growth to 6 to 10 feet high.

An old-time favorite. Pretty, fragrant flowers attract multitudes of butterflies. Coarse texture; wild, unruly growth habit. Flowers bloom from July or August into fall on current season's growth. Best treated as an herbaceous perennial in the rear of a perennial border. Prune to within 6 to 12 inches of the ground in late winter. Numerous cultivars are available; flower colors range from white through pink and lavender to deep reddish purple. Native to China.
▮ Zones 5 to 10.

Buxus microphylla var. koreana

Korean littleleaf boxwood

Broadleaf evergreen

▮ Slow growth to 3 to 4 feet high, equally wide.

Similar to *B. sempervirens,* (common boxwood), but hardier and more finely textured. The foliage usually turns yellow-brown in cold weather. Cultural instructions and landscape uses are the same as for *B. sempervirens.* 'Tide Hill' and 'Wintergreen' are hardy to zone 5 and do not brown in winter. Native to Korea and Japan.
▮ Zones 6 to 8 (to zone 10 in the West).

Buddleia davidii

Buxus microphylla var. *koreana*

Buxus sempervirens

Calluna vulgaris

Buxus sempervirens
Common boxwood

Broadleaf evergreen

▌ Slow growth to 10 to 20 feet high.

Most often grown as a dainty, compact shrub, sheared into formal shapes such as globes, cubes, and teddy bears. If allowed to grow naturally, becomes a beautifully gnarled, spreading, open shrub. Limited to mild, moist climates; susceptible to a variety of insect pests and diseases. Plant in well-drained soil amended with organic matter; mulch heavily to keep roots cool and moist. Prune out dead twigs to prevent twig canker disease, a common problem in the East. Takes full sun to partial shade. 'Northern Find' and 'Vardar Valley' are hardy to zone 5. Native to Europe, Africa, and western Asia.
▌ Zones 6 to 10.

Calluna vulgaris
Scotch heather

Narrowleaf evergreen

▌ Slow growth to 4 to 20 inches high.

Treasured for its finely textured foliage, dainty, rose pink flowers, and low, restrained habit, but can be finicky and difficult to grow. *Must* have acid, perfectly drained soil with high moisture retention. Best in full sun; flowers less in partial shade. Prune or shear each fall after flowering to maintain compactness and encourage heavier blooming. Cultivars vary in size, flower color, blooming season, and foliage color. Native to Europe and Asia Minor.
▌ Zones 5 to 9.

Camellia japonica
Common camellia

Broadleaf evergreen

▌ Moderate growth to 6 to 12 feet high.

Especially effective when massed in shady woodland gardens; blends nicely with other broadleaf evergreens. Bears large, symmetrical flowers and dense, polished, dark foliage. Flowers are extremely variable: more than 3,000 cultivars offer single and double forms with varying degrees of flutes and frills. Flower colors range from white to red; sizes range from 2½ to 5 inches in diameter. Culture is similar to that of *Rhododendron* species. Native to China and Japan.
▌ Zones 9 and 10.

Camellia sasanqua
Sasanqua camellia

Broadleaf evergreen

▌ Moderate growth rate; size depends on cultivar.

Similar to *C. japonica*, but foliage texture is more refined. This plant also blooms earlier, from autumn to early winter. Like the *C. japonica*, cultivars vary widely in flower and form. Some are low-growing, sprawling shrubs that are useful for ground covers and espaliers; others make good hedges or screens. All make good specimens. Native to China and Japan.
▌ Zones 9 and 10.

Camellia japonica

Camellia sasanqua

Carissa macrocarpa

Ceanothus species

Carissa macrocarpa (*C. grandiflora*)
Natal plum

Broadleaf evergreen

▮ Moderate growth rate to 3 to 5 feet high, equally wide.

Dark green, glossy-leaved shrub, well behaved but spiny. White flowers, 1 inch across and plentiful. Bright red fruit ripens over a long period and provides good color. The fruit when cooked is almost identical to cranberry sauce. Excellent in California and Florida gardens. Native to South Africa.
▮ Zone 10.

Ceanothus species
Wild lilac

Broadleaf evergreen

▮ Growth rate and size vary among species.

Very useful in West Coast gardens, where more than 40 species can be grown. Its hallmarks are fragrant, blue or white flowers and glossy, dark green leaves. Cultivars range in size from 8-inch ground covers to 30-foot trees. Most effective in large masses; occasionally used as specimens. Plant in full sun in well-drained soil, away from sprinklers. Do not overwater. Prune only during the dry summer months to avoid transmitting a deadly canker disease. 'Julia Phelps' grows 4 to 6 feet high, 6 to 8 feet wide; blooms dependably.
▮ Zones 8 to 10 in the West only.

Choisya ternata
Mexican orange

Broadleaf evergreen

▮ Slow to moderate growth to 5 to 7 feet high, equally wide.

The deliciously scented, white flowers are a delight near entryways, outdoor living areas, windows, walkways, and paths—wherever their fragrance can be enjoyed. Effective as an informal hedge or screen; fan-shaped, trifoliate leaves create an interesting layered texture. Touchy about soil conditions: needs well-drained, acid soil that is rich in organic matter; intolerant of alkaline or saline soil. Tolerates full sun on the coast, needs partial shade in hot-summer climates. Water infrequently but deeply. Native to Mexico.
▮ Zones 8 to 10 in the West only.

Cistus purpureus
Rock rose

Broadleaf evergreen

▮ Rapid growth to 3 to 4 feet high, 4 to 5 feet wide.

Dense, rounded shrub; excellent when massed. Low in maintenance and big in spring color. Billowy foliage is dark green or gray-green, and fragrant—especially on hot days. Drought resistant and adaptable to salt spray, ocean winds, and desert heat. Needs fast-draining soil. Pinch the tips of young plants to encourage dense growth. Native to the Mediterranean region.
▮ Zones 8 to 10 in the West only.

Choisya ternata

Cistus purpureus

Coprosma repens

Cornus stolonifera

Coprosma repens
Mirror plant

Broadleaf evergreen

■ Rapid growth to 10 feet high, 6 feet wide.

When restrained by pruning, *C. repens* makes an excellent hedge, screen, foundation plant, or espalier. Leaves are very shiny. Flowers and fruit are inconspicuous. The habit is rangy and open if neglected. Adapts particularly well to seashore conditions and is drought tolerant once established. Needs full sun on the coast, partial shade in hot inland areas. Performs well in nearly any soil. Susceptible to powdery mildew. Cultivars with yellow or white variegated leaves are widely available. Native to New Zealand.
■ Zones 9 and 10.

Cornus stolonifera
Redosier dogwood

Deciduous

■ Rapid growth to 15 feet high, at least twice as wide.

Grows into a large, multi-stemmed shrub. Has exceptional fall color, and its red stems are vivid against snow. Spreads by underground stems and rooting branches. Prefers water-logged soil. 'Isanti' is a dwarf form. 'Flavirmea' has unusual, bright yellow stem color in winter, but must be heavily pruned in spring to prevent twig blights. Native to North America.
■ Zones 2 to 7.

Corylus avellana 'Contorta'
Harry Lauder's walking stick; corkscrew hazel

Deciduous

■ Rapid growth to 8 to 10 feet high, equally wide.

Thoroughly distinctive. The twisted stems and leaves of this plant make it an excellent accent or focal point in an entryway or courtyard. Its winter silhouette is especially effective against a light-colored wall. Flowers are pendulous, yellowish brown catkins, appearing in March before leaves. Easy to grow; adapts to a wide range of soil types and light intensities. Remove suckers that arise from below the graft union of grafted specimens—the more vigorous understock has a tendency to overtake the contorted top growth.
■ Zones 5 to 8 (to zone 9 in the West).

Cotinus coggygria
Smoke tree

Deciduous

■ Moderate growth to 10 to 15 feet high.

A long-time favorite for the low-maintenance garden. Puffs of purple flower stalks smolder through the summer; the foliage catches fire in the fall in shades of red, purple, or yellow. Usually a loose, open shrub with many upright stems. Most useful for a shrub border as a textural and color accent. Not a good single specimen. Takes full sun; adapts to a variety of soil types. Needs deep, frequent watering when young; drought tolerant once established. 'Velvet Cloak' is one of the best purple-leafed varieties.
■ Zones 5 to 8 (to zone 9 in the West).

Cotinus coggygria

Corylus avellana 'Contorta'

Cotoneaster horizontalis

Cytisus × praecox

Cotoneaster horizontalis
Rock cotoneaster

Deciduous

▌ Moderate growth to 2 to 3 feet high, 5 to 8 feet wide.

The angular, layered form of this shrub adds an unusual texture to the garden. Pink flowers attract bees from late May to early June. Red berries dot the plant from late August through November. Glossy foliage turns orange and red in the fall in northern areas. May be semievergreen in mild climates. Also excellent as a large-scale bank or ground cover. Needs full sun and good drainage. The many cultivars offer a variety of forms and foliage colors. Native to China.
▌ Zones 5 to 7 (to zone 9 in the West).

Cytisus × praecox
Warminster broom

Deciduous
(stems are evergreen)

▌ Moderate growth to 4 to 6 feet high, equal or wider spread.

A rounded thicket of green stems provides an interesting accent in winter and bears pale yellow flowers in the spring. Foliage is sparse. Works well in a shrub border, or in a large rock garden. Needs full sun and well-drained soil. Does well in infertile soil. The tips of young plants can be pinched to encourage compactness, but older plants do not respond well to pruning of any kind; allow them to develop their natural form. Native to the Mediterranean region.
▌ Zones 6 to 8 (to zone 10 in the West).

Daphne cneorum
Garland flower

Broadleaf evergreen

▌ Slow growth to 6 to 12 inches high, 2 or more feet wide.

Rosy pink clusters of flowers fill the garden with delicious fragrance in April and May. Forms a low, loose, trailing mass that is perfect for rock gardens, for covering small areas, or in groupings with other shrubs. Grow in the shade and keep protected from hot sun and drying winds. Mulch to keep roots cool and moist. Plant fairly high to reduce the chances of crown rot. Native to central and southern Europe.
▌ Zones 5 to 7.

Daphne odora
Winter daphne

Broadleaf evergreen

▌ Slow growth to about 3 feet, wider spread.

The most popular daphne in mild areas despite its reputation for being unpredictable and frustrating. The fragrance of the rose pink flowers permeates the garden in February and March. Lustrous leaves are attractive the year around. Must have perfect drainage; plant high to keep water away from crown. Water infrequently during summer months to increase flowering and prevent root rot. 'Aureomarginata' has yellow-edged leaves and is reputedly hardier and easier to grow. Native to Japan and China.
▌ Zones 8 and 9 (to zone 10 in the West).

Daphne cneorum

Daphne odora

Elaeagnus pungens

Escallonia rubra

Elaeagnus pungens
Silverberry

Broadleaf evergreen

▌Rapid growth to 6 to 15 feet, wider spread.

This tough shrub has white, powerfully fragrant flowers, olive-colored foliage, thorny branches, and red fruit. Without pruning, it becomes a rigid, sprawling mass. Responds well to shearing; a good hedge plant. Thorny branches form an impenetrable barrier. Adapts to problem areas of heat, wind, and drought; does well in poor, infertile soil. The leaves of 'Maculata' have gold centers; those of 'Aurea' are bordered with yellow. 'Variegata' has leaves with yellow and white edges. Native to Japan.

▌Zones 7 to 10.

Escallonia rubra
Red escallonia

Broadleaf evergreen

▌Rapid growth to 6 to 15 feet high if unpruned.

Produces fragrant, attractive red flowers in the summer and fall (year-round in mild climates). Excellent for screens or windbreaks; useful for massing and for integrating into a shrub border. Dark, evergreen foliage responds well to pruning, although with a corresponding reduction in blooming. Prune lightly once a year to maintain compact form. Tolerates wind and salt spray of coastal gardens, but won't tolerate highly alkaline soil. Needs partial shade in hot inland gardens. 'C. F. Boll' and 'Terri' are dwarf varieties that grow to about 3 feet high. Native to South America.

▌Zones 8 to 10 in the West only.

Euonymus alatus
Burning bush, winged euonymus

Deciduous

▌Moderate growth to 15 to 20 feet high, equally wide.

Popular for its brilliant fall color, its open, vase-shaped habit, and its clean, pest-free foliage. Its branches are corky, broadly winged, and provide an unusual winter character. Use as an unclipped hedge or screen, in a shrub border, or as a specimen. Adaptable to many growing conditions and soil types, except very wet ones. Grows well in full sun or heavy shade, but develops brightest autumn hues in full sun. Pruning causes uneven growth. 'Compactus' is often sold as a dwarf, but actually grows to 10 feet high and wide. Native to China.

▌Zones 4 to 8.

Euonymus fortunei
Wintercreeper

Broadleaf evergreen

▌Moderate growth rate, low and spreading.

One of the hardiest broadleaf evergreens. Cultivars range in habit from mounding shrubs to vines and ground covers, and are quite variable in their habit and size. Some cultivars do not fruit; others bear heavy crops of bright orange fruit in the fall and winter. Tolerant of all but the wettest soil; withstands full sun to heavy shade. Susceptible to mildew, anthracnose, crown gall, scale, and other pests. *E. fortunei* 'Vegetus' has an irregular, mounding habit and bright orange fruit. Native to China.

▌Zones 5 to 9 (to zone 10 in the West).

Euonymus alatus

Euonymus fortunei

Euonymus japonicus

Forsythia × intermedia

Euonymus japonicus
Evergreen euonymus

Broadleaf evergreen

■ Moderate growth to 8 feet high, 15 feet wide.

A tough, low-maintenance plant for harsh situations and poor soil. Notoriously susceptible to mildew and many sucking insects—especially scale, aphids, mites, and thrips. Plant where air circulation is good and where water does not stand. Many cultivars are available. The strongly variegated forms, such as 'Aureomarginatus' (golden) and 'Albomarginatus' (white) are among the most popular.
■ Zones 7 to 9 (to zone 10 in the West).

Forsythia × intermedia
Border forsythia

Deciduous

■ Rapid growth to 8 to 10 feet high, 10 to 12 feet wide.

Forsythia's bright yellow burst is a harbinger of spring. Its habit is upright, arching, and vigorous. Grows in nearly any soil; give it plenty of water and fertilizer. Plant in full sun for maximum flowering. Prune annually, right after flowering, by removing one third of the oldest canes. Give plenty of room and allow to grow naturally; do not shear. Cultivars vary in hardiness, growth habit, and bloom characteristics. In northern zones, select hardy varieties such as 'Karl Sax' and 'Beatrix Farrand'.
■ Zones 5 to 9.

Fothergilla major
Large fothergilla

Deciduous

■ Moderate growth to 6 to 10 feet high, slightly narrower spread.

One of the most attractive of the southeastern native shrubs. White, honey-scented blooms resembling small, round bottlebrushes appear in late April to early May. Clean, pest-free, dark green foliage consistently provides a showy fall display of electric yellow, orange, and scarlet. The neat, rounded habit makes it suitable for groups, masses, and foundation plantings. Especially attractive as a specimen or when integrated into a shrub border. Acid, well-drained soil is a must. Grows well in partial shade and dry, rocky soil, but full sun and rich soil improve flowers and fall color.
■ Zones 5 to 8 (to zone 9 in the West).

Fuchsia hybrida
Common fuchsia hybrids

Deciduous to evergreen

■ Rapid growth from 3 to 12 feet high.

A widely variable group of plants with bright, multicolored flowers and trailing to upright habits. Blooms from early summer until frost. Flowers vary in color, size, and shape; all attract hummingbirds. Shrub forms can be used as upright specimens or integrated into a shrub border. They are also often espaliered. Performs best in areas with cool summers and high humidity. Needs filtered shade and moist, rich soil. More than 500 cultivars are available.
■ Zones 9 and 10 in the West only.

Fothergilla major

Fuchsia hybrida

Gardenia augusta

Genista hispanica

Gardenia augusta (G. jasminoides)

Gardenia

Broadleaf evergreen

▌ Rapid growth to 3 to 6 feet high, equally wide.

Gardenias have waxy, white flowers with a heady, sweet fragrance and superb, glossy leaves. Use as a specimen in a container or raised bed, for a hedge or low screen, or espalier. Quite finicky—requires highly organic, acid soil. Sensitive to saline water, poor drainage, and drought. Prefers a protected location with partial shade. Susceptible to sucking insects—may need to be sprayed regularly. Will not bloom well in cool-summer areas. Native to China.

▌ Zones 9 and 10.

Genista hispanica

Spanish broom, Spanish gorse

Narrowleaf evergreen

▌ Moderate growth to 1 to 2 feet high, wider spread.

Features spectacular yellow flowers in June on strongly vertical, nearly leafless, evergreen stems. Requires full sun and sharp drainage, but is adaptable and easy to grow, actually preferring poor, dry, infertile soil. Tolerates drought and coastal conditions well. Leave alone after it becomes established—*Genistas* do not move easily. Native to the Mediterranean region.

▌ Zones 6 to 9.

Hamamelis × intermedia

Hybrid witch hazel

Deciduous

▌ Moderate growth to 15 to 20 feet high, equally wide.

The showiest witch hazel available in the United States. As early as February, its leafless branches are covered with deep yellow, spicily fragrant blossoms that last about a month. Vivid yellow to orange-red fall color. Use as a screen, background, or large focal point. Excellent choice for a naturalized woodland understory. Consider planting near a window where it can be seen from indoors on cold, wintry days. Plant in deep, rich soil with abundant moisture. Virtually pest-free. 'Jelena' has coppery orange flowers. 'Diane' has red flowers.

▌ Zones 6 to 8 (to zone 9 in the West).

Hamamelis vernalis

Vernal witch hazel

Deciduous

▌ Moderate growth to 6 to 10 feet high, wider spread.

The habit of this shrub is rounder and denser than that of other *Hamamelis* species. It bears small, powerfully fragrant, yellow to orange-red flowers in January and February. The leaves turn a clear yellow in the fall. Native to gravely, often-flooded stream banks in the Ozark Mountains.

▌ Zones 4 to 9.

Hamamelis × intermedia

Hamamelis vernalis

Hamamelis virginiana

Hibiscus rosa-sinensis

Hamamelis virginiana

Virginia witch hazel

Deciduous

▌ Moderate growth to 20 to 30 feet high, equally wide.

The hardiest but also the largest and rangiest of the *Hamamelis* species. Yellow flowers are often borne along with yellow fall foliage in October through December, and are quite fragrant. Native to forest understories from Canada to Georgia and west to Nebraska.
▌ Zones 3 to 9.

Hibiscus rosa-sinensis

Chinese hibiscus

Broadleaf evergreen

▌ Rapid growth to 15 to 30 feet high.

Popular shrub in Florida, California, Texas, and Hawaii. The thousands of available cultivars have large, platelike flowers in whites, pinks, reds, and yellows. All cultivars need good drainage, abundant moisture, sun, heat, and protection from wind and frost. Seldom blooms in cool-summer areas. Native to China.
▌ Zones 9 and 10.

Hibiscus syriacus

Shrub althea, rose-of-Sharon

Deciduous

▌ Moderate growth to 8 to 12 feet high, 6 to 10 feet wide.

Traditionally used as a focal specimen, but much more effective when grouped or massed in a shrub border. Flowers appear in late summer; they are white, red, purple, violet, or a combination of these (depending on the cultivar). Habit is very erect and round headed. Extremely tolerant of the salt and wind of coastal gardens. Prefers a hot summer. Best in full sun, but tolerates partial shade. Leaves drop early in the fall, appear late in spring. Needs regular spraying for pests and diseases in most climates. Native to China and India.
▌ Zones 6 to 9.

Hydrangea macrophylla

Bigleaf hydrangea

Deciduous

▌ Moderate growth to 4 to 6 feet high, equally wide.

Excellent late-summer floral display (June to August) and lustrous, neat foliage. Has a rounded habit with many erect, infrequently branched stems. Suckers vigorously. 'Hortensia' ('mophead') cultivars have large, globular flower heads; 'lacecap' cultivars have a delicate ring of large flowers surrounding a cluster of tiny ones. Flowers can be single or double; are pink in alkaline soil, blue in acid soil. Native to Japan.
▌ Zones 7 to 10.

Hibiscus syriacus

Hydrangea macrophylla

Ilex cornuta

Hydrangea paniculata 'Grandiflora'

Hydrangea paniculata 'Grandiflora'
Peegee hydrangea

Deciduous

■ Large shrub or small tree to 20 feet.

Elliptic leaves to 4 inches long are pubescent beneath. Bold panicles of flowers up to 12 or more inches long and 8 inches across. Flowers are white to pinkish and long lasting in August and September. Prefers rich, moist soil and some shade. Prune hard in spring for heavy blooming. Native to China and Japan.
■ Zones 4 to 8.

Hypericum × moserianum
Goldflower

Broadleaf evergreen

■ Moderate growth to 3 feet high, wider spread.

This shrub requires very little maintenance. The gold flowers bloom almost continuously throughout the summer months. Arching stems are red when young. Dies back in colder zones. One of the few plants that will do well under eucalyptus trees.
■ Zones 8 to 10.

Ilex cornuta
Chinese holly

Broadleaf evergreen

■ Moderate growth to 10 to 15 feet high (cultivars are smaller).

Leaves are a handsome, dark, polished green in all seasons; they are larger and coarser than those of *I. crenata*. Profuse berries are normally brilliant red. Much more tolerant of heat and drought than *I. crenata*. 'Dwarf Burford' (10 feet high), and 'Dazzler' (6 feet high) are slow-growing dwarf forms. 'Rotunda', an especially dense dwarf, grows to 3 to 5 feet high. 'Carissa' grows to 3 feet high. 'Burfordii' (20 feet high) is reputedly hardier—it performs well in zone 6. Native to eastern China and Korea.
■ Zones 7 to 10.

Ilex crenata
Japanese holly

Broadleaf evergreen

■ Slow growth to 5 to 10 feet high, wider spread.

Commonly mistaken for boxwood due to its neat, rounded shape and dense, lustrous, finely textured foliage. Use for hedges, foundation plantings, massing, and for texture in a shrub border. Responds well to pruning. Often sheared into formal shapes. Transplants easily into moist, well-drained, slightly acid soil. Does well in sun or shade; appears to be tolerant of pollution. Fruit is black and inconspicuous. 'Black Beauty', 'Hetzii', and 'Helleri' are three of the hardiest compact types. 'Microphylla' and 'Convexa' are hardy large forms. Native to Japan.
■ Zones 6 to 8 (to zone 10 in the West).

Ilex crenata

Hypericum × moserianum

Ilex vomitoria

Juniperus chinensis

Ilex vomitoria
Yaupon

Broadleaf evergreen

▮ Slow growth to 15 to 20 feet high.

The species is a small evergreen tree, but several cultivars, such as 'Nana' and 'Stoke's', are dwarf (to 3 feet or shorter) and compact. More tolerant of alkaline soil, salt, and drought than other holly species; also resists nematodes. Finely textured foliage can easily be sheared into formal shapes. Species fruits heavily, but dwarf forms are generally sterile. Native to the southeastern United States.
▮ Zones 7 to 10.

Juniperus chinensis
Chinese juniper

Needle evergreen

▮ Moderate growth rate; size depends on cultivar.

An extremely diverse species that includes many of the most popular shrub forms. Grows in well-drained acid or alkaline soil. Prone to root rot if planted near a lawn. Needs full sun in cool-summer areas, partial shade in desert and other hot areas. 'Pfitzeriana' grows 5 to 6 feet high, spreads about 15 feet, and has arching branches. Many other forms of the 'Pfitzer' juniper are available; most are compact; some, such as 'Pfitzeriana Aurea', have golden new growth. 'Hetzii' has bluish foliage and grows to 15 feet high. 'Torulosa' has an irregular, twisted branching habit and grows to 15 feet high. Native to China, Mongolia, and Japan.
▮ Zones 4 to 9 (to zone 10 in the West).

Juniperus communis
Common juniper

Needle evergreen

▮ Moderate growth rate; size varies, generally 5 to 10 feet high, 8 to 12 feet wide.

Extremely hardy and adaptable to the poorest soil. Has a spreading habit. Spiny leaves are gray- or blue-green in the summer and turn yellowish or brownish green in winter. All cultivars are very susceptible to phomopsis blight. 'Compressa' has silvery green leaves and grows to 2 to 3 feet high. Subspecies *depressa* rarely grows over 4 feet high, but spreads up to 15 feet wide; 'Depressa Aurea' is similar but has yellow foliage. Native to the United States, Europe, and Asia.
▮ Zones 2 to 7 (to zone 10 in the West).

Juniperus sabina
Savin juniper

Needle evergreen

▮ Moderate growth to 4 to 6 feet high, 10 to 15 feet wide.

Tolerant of urban pollution. Stiff, spreading branches form a low-growing vase shape. Foliage is dark green in summer, often turning brownish green in cold weather. The following varieties are resistant to phomopsis blight: 'Von Ehron' grows 5 feet high and equally wide. 'Broadmoor' grows 18 inches high (center of plant mounds higher with age) and spreads 10 to 15 feet. 'Arcadia', an excellent dwarf form, grows 1 foot high and 4 feet wide; 'Skandia' is similar but has bluish foliage. Native to Europe.
▮ Zones 5 to 10.

Juniperus communis

Juniperus sabina

Kalmia latifolia

Leptospermum scoparium

Kalmia latifolia

Mountain laurel

Broadleaf evergreen

▮ Slow growth to 7 to 15 feet high.

An undisputed treasure. Spectacular white to deep pink flowers are framed by excellent evergreen foliage. Use as a specimen or as a companion for rhododendrons and azaleas. Dense, rounded, and neat in youth, it becomes gnarled, picturesque, and open in old age. Plant in cool, moist, acid, well-drained soil that is high in organic matter; give it full sun for optimum flowering in most areas, partial shade in hot areas. Cultivars have flower colors ranging from white to deep, bright pink. Native to the eastern United States.
▮ Zones 5 to 9.

Leptospermum scoparium

New Zealand tea tree

Narrowleaf evergreen

▮ Moderate growth rate, usually to 6 to 10 feet high, equally wide.

Displays outstanding flowers from late winter to spring; finely textured, fragrant foliage is effective the rest of the year. Use as a specimen, an accent, or a focal point in a shrub border. Must have excellent drainage; prefers full sun. Drought tolerant once established. Pest-free. Flower colors of cultivars are commonly red, pink, or white; habits range from upright shrubs to prostrate ground covers. Native to New Zealand.
▮ Zones 9 and 10.

Ligustrum japonicum

Japanese privet

Broadleaf evergreen

▮ Rapid growth to 6 to 12 feet high.

This shrub makes an excellent hedge or screen in southern or western gardens because of its lustrous leaves, dense, compact habit, and responsiveness to pruning. Also commonly trained as topiary. Grows well in containers. Looks best when given plenty of water and protected from hot sun. Many cultivars are available. 'Silver Star' is a variegated form. Native to Japan and Korea.
▮ Zones 8 to 10.

Ligustrum lucidum

Glossy privet, Chinese privet

Broadleaf evergreen

▮ Rapid growth to 20 to 25 feet high.

Similar to *L. japonicum* but grows much taller. Often grown as a small tree, but makes a good large shrub. To differentiate this plant from *L. japonicum* among young nursery plants, feel the undersides of the leaves. If the veins are raised, it is *L. japonicum;* if they are sunken, it is *L. lucidum.* Native to China and Korea.
▮ Zones 8 to 10.

Ligustrum japonicum

Ligustrum lucidum

Ligustrum obtusifolium

Lonicera nitida

Ligustrum obtusifolium

Border privet

Deciduous

▌Rapid growth to 10 to 12 feet high, 12 to 15 feet wide.

One of the hardiest and most attractive of the privets. Has a broad, horizontal growth habit and dark green foliage. Size is easily managed. *L. obtusifolium* var. *regelianum* is a low, 4- to 5-foot-high shrub with unusual, horizontally spreading branches that are most attractive if allowed to grow naturally. Native to Japan.
▌Zones 4 to 10.

Lonicera nitida

Box honeysuckle

Broadleaf evergreen

▌Rapid growth to 6 feet high.

Unlike other honeysuckles, *L. nitida* presents a neat, refined appearance. Its foliage is finely textured. The creamy white flowers bloom in June. Tolerant of coastal conditions. Responds well to pruning and makes an excellent hedge. Native to China.
▌Zones 8 to 10.

Lonicera tatarica

Tatarian honeysuckle

Deciduous

▌Rapid growth to 10 to 12 feet.

The chief attributes of this species are early May flowers in white, pink, or red, and showy red berries in June and July. Dense, bluish green foliage has a medium texture. Its habit is upright and arching. Becomes quite leggy and, like most honeysuckle species, has an impossible winter appearance. Best used in a shrub border where these faults can be hidden. Adaptable to many soils; prefers full sun. Susceptible to honeysuckle aphid, a major problem in the Midwest. 'Arnold's Red' has the darkest red flowers of any honeysuckle. 'Nana' has pink flowers and grows only 3 feet high. Native to central Asia.
▌Zones 3 to 9.

Magnolia stellata

Star magnolia

Deciduous

▌Slow growth to 15 to 20 feet high, 10 to 15 feet wide.

Large, fragrant, white flowers are set off well by a background of evergreens or a dark wall. Use as a specimen, as a focal point in a shrub border, or in foundation plantings. Needs deep, rich, moist soil; takes full sun to partial shade. 'Rosea' has pink buds that fade to white as the flower opens. 'Ann' is 8 to 12 feet high, has a superior uniform, upright habit, and bears pink (almost magenta) flowers. Native to Japan.
▌Zones 5 to 9 (to zone 10 in the West).

Lonicera tatarica

Magnolia stellata

Mahonia aquifolium

Mahonia bealei

Mahonia aquifolium

Oregon grape

Broadleaf evergreen

▮ Moderate growth to 3 to 6 feet high.

Popularly used as a ground cover in shady areas, but its irregular, spreading habit and relatively high growth make it quite suitable for shrub borders and foundation plantings. Open, upright branches bear bright yellow flowers in late April. Spiny, hollylike leaves often turn purplish bronze at the onset of cold weather. Dark blue fruit makes good jelly. Plant in shade in moist, acid soil; leaves scorch in hot sun and wind. Native to damp forests from British Columbia to Oregon.
▮ Zones 5 to 9.

Mahonia bealei

Leatherleaf mahonia

Broadleaf evergreen

▮ Moderate growth to 10 to 12 feet high.

A striking structure is this plant's chief attribute. Large, compound leaves are held horizontally on vertical stems, producing an exotic tropical effect, especially when displayed against a wall or dramatically lit at night. Produces showy clusters of yellow flowers and powdery blue, grapelike fruit. Will not tolerate drought, hot sun, or winter sun. Should be planted in rich, moist soil and given plenty of water. Difficult to prune correctly; consider ultimate size before planting. Native to China.
▮ Zones 7 to 10.

Myrica pensylvanica

Northern bayberry

Deciduous

▮ Moderate growth to 5 to 12 feet high.

Its billowy masses of clean, lustrous green foliage make this plant excellent for large-scale plantings. Tends to sucker and form large colonies, but still works in a shrub border or as an informal hedge. Adapted to poor soil; grows well in coastal areas, difficult urban sites. Takes full sun or partial shade. Fruit is waxy, grayish white berries that persist through the winter. The berries are used to make fragrant candles, but all parts of the plant are aromatic. Does not tolerate alkaline soil. Native to the eastern United States.
▮ Zones 2 to 7.

Myrtus communis

Myrtle

Broadleaf evergreen

▮ Moderate growth to 5 to 10 feet high, 4 to 5 feet wide or wider.

Glossy, bright green foliage is delightfully fragrant when bruised. Commonly grown in hot, dry areas and coastal gardens in Arizona and California as formal or informal hedges, screens, masses, or backgrounds. Accepts shearing extremely well; is easily trained into a formal hedge. Sweetly scented, mildly attractive flowers are produced in the summer. Smooth, rusty tan bark is showy on older specimens. Other than requiring fast drainage, it is not particular about soil. Native to the Mediterranean region.
▮ Zones 9 and 10.

Myrica pensylvanica

Myrtus communis

Nandina domestica

Nerium oleander

Nandina domestica
Nandina, heavenly-bamboo

Broadleaf evergreen (deciduous in the North)

❚ Moderate growth to 8 feet high, 2½ to 3 feet wide.

Popular in southern gardens for its variety of ornamental assets and easy care. Its strongly vertical form contrasts nicely with the delicate, wispy foliage. Bears creamy white flower spikes and bright red berries. Fall colors are brilliant crimson to purple. Effective as a hedge or screen, in a grouping, or as a solitary specimen. Performs well in nearly any soil and in sun or shade, but shade is best in hot climates. Established plants tolerate drought well. Native to central China and Japan.
❚ Zones 7 to 10.

Nerium oleander
Oleander

Broadleaf evergreen

❚ Very rapid growth to 8 to 12 feet high, 6 to 10 feet wide.

Commonly used shrub in the Deep South and west of the Rockies. Easy to care for, particularly in hot, dry climates. Has deep green foliage; bears attractive red, pink, white, or yellow flowers throughout the summer. Broad, rounded, bulky habit. Plant in full sun, in any soil from dry sand to wet clay. Plagued by many insects and diseases, particularly in shady or humid environments. All parts are poisonous. Contact with leaves can cause dermatitis. Ingestion may be fatal. 'Petite Pink' and 'Mrs. Roeding' are compact cultivars; 'Mrs. Roeding' has pink, double flowers. Native to the Mediterranean region.
❚ Zones 9 and 10.

Osmanthus fragrans
Sweet olive

Broadleaf evergreen

❚ Moderate growth to 20 to 30 feet high, equally wide.

Powerfully fragrant flowers, borne in spring and early summer, are the main attraction of this shrub. Has a compact habit and glossy foliage; makes an outstanding hedge, screen, background, espalier, or container plant. Easy to care for and adaptable to any soil from sand to clay. Needs partial shade. Size is easily controlled; responds well to shearing. 'Aurantiacus' has orange blossoms with an astonishing fragrance. Native to eastern Asia.
❚ Zones 9 and 10.

Paeonia suffruticosa
Tree peony

Deciduous

❚ Moderate growth to 4 feet high, equally wide.

Although its curiously textured foliage is a decided asset, it is grown chiefly for its huge (6- to 10-inch) flowers with their exquisitely intergraded coloring and delicate crepe paper texture. Its habit is usually open and leggy. An astounding array of cultivars are available, from white, yellow, pink, and red to maroon, violet, and purple. Single or semidouble forms are preferable; fully double blossoms are so heavy they require individual staking. Plant in moist, rich, well-drained soil that is amply amended with organic matter. Native from Bhutan to Tibet and China.
❚ Zones 5 to 8 (to zone 9 in the West).

Osmanthus fragrans

Paeonia suffruticosa

Photinia × fraseri

Photinia serratifolia

Photinia × fraseri
Fraser photinia

Broadleaf evergreen

▌ Moderate growth to 10 feet high, 12 feet wide.

In spring, the new, bronzy red foliage of this plant is showier than many flowers. Also produces attractive, ivory-colored flowers in many 4-inch clusters in late March and April. Use as a screen, a formal or informal hedge, or an espalier. Lustrous, dark green foliage makes an excellent background. Size is easily restrained. Needs well-drained soil amended with organic matter. Tolerates heat, but only if watered generously. Susceptible to fire blight, aphids, scale, and leaf spot—a severe problem in the Southeast.
▌ Zones 7 to 10.

Photinia serratifolia (P. serrulata)
Chinese photinia

Broadleaf evergreen

▌ Moderate growth to 20 to 25 feet high.

An extremely large shrub or small tree. Makes a good screen. Large (8-inch), lustrous, coarsely textured leaves are bronzy when new. White, malodorous flowers are showy in spring; bright red berries are most effective in fall and winter. Needs well-drained soil; in summer needs ample (but not excessive) moisture. Native to China.
▌ Zones 7 to 10.

Picea glauca var. albertiana 'Conica'
Dwarf white spruce

Needle evergreen

▌ Very slow growth to 6 to 8 feet high.

Stiffly conical—looks like an upside-down ice-cream cone. Finely textured, light green needles and unusual form make this an interesting specimen or oddity. Best used as a focal point in a grouping. Susceptible to spider mites, especially in hot, dry areas. Native to the northern United States and southern Canada.
▌ Zones 2 to 6 (to zone 8 on the West Coast).

Pieris japonica
Japanese andromeda; lily-of-the-valley shrub

Broadleaf evergreen

▌ Slow growth to 9 to 12 feet high, 6 to 8 feet wide.

Beautiful broadleaf evergreen related to rhododendrons and mountain laurel (*Kalmia*). Delicate, white or pinkish white, pendulous panicles of flowers bloom in early spring. Deep green foliage is bronzy when new. Has an upright, irregular, rounded outline; useful as a specimen, in shrub borders, or in groups or masses. Combines especially well with other acid-loving, broadleaf evergreens. Prefers moist, acid soil, but not quite as particular as other members of the heath family. Protect from wind and winter sun. Native to Japan.
▌ Zones 6 and 7 (to zone 9 in the West).

Pieris japonica

Picea glauca var. *albertiana* 'Conica'

Rhododendron minus

P.J.M hybrids

Rhododendron minus (R. carolinianum)

Carolina rhododendron

Broadleaf evergreen

▌ Slow to moderate growth to 3 to 6 feet high.

This restrained, rounded shrub bears funnel-shaped, pink or white flowers that are 1½ inches wide. The leaves are dark green and 3 to 4 inches long. Does well on both the East and West Coasts, but cannot tolerate the heat of the extreme Southeast. Native to the Blue Ridge Mountains of Tennessee and the Carolinas.
▌ Zones 4 to 8 (to zone 9 in the West).

Rhododendron, P.J.M hybrids

P.J.M. hybrid rhododendron

Broadleaf evergreen

▌ Moderate growth to 3 to 6 feet high.

The vivid, purple-pink flowers of these popular cold-hardy hybrids are 1½ inches wide. Plant forms a rounded, relatively dense mass. Dark green foliage turns purple in winter. Specimens vary in the intensity of their flower color, so it is best to buy them when in bloom.
▌ Zones 4 to 8 (to zone 9 in the West).

Rhus aromatica

Fragrant sumac

Deciduous

▌ Moderate growth to 3 feet with 5 foot spread.

An excellent rough bank cover. Good for erosion control. Fragrant, small, yellow flowers in the spring; small, red fruit later. The leaves are deep green and in leaflets of three. Brilliant fall colors from orange to reddish purple. Drought resistant. Native to North America.
▌ Zones 4 to 9.

Rhus typhina

Staghorn sumac

Deciduous

▌ Moderate growth to 15 feet.

A sprawling, suckering large shrub for rough places. Compound, bold leaves on velvety stems. Stems resemble hairy antlers during the deciduous period. Striking fall colors are brilliant orange-red. Red fruit. Drought resistant. Native to North America.
▌ Zones 3 to 8.

Rhus aromatica

Rhus typhina

Rosa carolina

Rosa rugosa

Rosa carolina
Carolina rose

Deciduous

▌ Rapid to moderate growth to 3 to 4 feet high.

A wonderful native rose with single, pink, 2- to 2½-inch flowers borne in June to July. A multistemmed shrub, it forms large thickets due to its suckering habit. An excellent plant for banks and slopes. In the wild, grows in low, wet areas and at the borders of swamps and streams. Native from Maine to Texas.
▌ Zones 4 to 8 (to zone 10 in the West).

Rosa rugosa
Japanese rose

Deciduous

▌ Rapid growth to 4 to 6 feet high, equally wide.

Especially well adapted to the sandy soil and saline environment of coastal gardens; probably also the easiest rose to grow. Flowers range from reddish purple to white, and may be single or double, depending on the cultivar. Everblooming. Plant forms a dense bramble; the stout, upright, prickly canes withstand pruning well and make an effective barrier hedge. Leaves are a lustrous green, changing to yellow-orange in the fall. They make an effective backdrop for the brick red hips. An excellent choice for difficult rocky or sandy soil. Native to northern China, Korea, and Japan.
▌ Zones 2 to 10.

Rosa xanthina f. hugonis (R. hugonis)
Father Hugo rose

Deciduous

▌ Rapid growth to 6 to 8 feet high, often wider spread.

One of the best and most popular of the yellow-blooming species roses. Single, canary blossoms appear in May—at the same time as the last tulips. The buds are exquisite. Habit is upright, arching, and twiggy. The finely cut foliage is attractive, but the plant tends toward raggedness when not in bloom. Use as a screen or informal hedge, in a shrub border, or espaliered on a trellis. Native to central China.
▌ Zones 5 to 10.

Rosmarinus officinalis
Rosemary

Narrowleaf evergreen

▌ Growth rate and size depend on cultivar.

A common herb in the kitchen, also very useful in dry landscapes. Leaves are grayish green, have fine texture, and clip and shear well. Large forms may be grown as a hedge or in a dry shrub border; lower types make excellent, erosion-controlling bank or ground covers, spilling over rocks and walls. The showy flowers are light blue and appear in late winter or very early spring; they attract birds and bees. Tolerates heat, sun, infertile soil, and drought. Must have sharp drainage; overwatering and overfertilizing will result in rank, stretchy growth. Native to southern Europe and Asia Minor.
▌ Zones 7 to 10.

Rosa xanthina f. hugonis

Rosmarinus officinalis

Salix discolor

Salix discolor
Pussy willow

Deciduous

▮ Rapid growth to 20 feet high, equally wide.

Grown principally for its winter display of fuzzy gray catkins. Branches may be cut in winter and forced indoors for early spring bouquets. The plant is a wild, unruly mass of upright stems. Constantly drops twigs, leaves, and branches. Grows well in poor, wet soil. This species is often grown in northern areas as a substitute for the more tender *S. caprea* (French pussy willow). Native throughout eastern North America.

▮ Zones 2 to 7 (to zone 9 in the West).

Sarcococca ruscifolia
Sweet box

Broadleaf evergreen

▮ Slow, compact growth to 3 to 5 feet

A dark green, handsome shrub for shady areas. Very refined foliage about 1½ inches long and densely clustered along the stems. Tiny, fragrant, white flowers and shiny, red berrylike fruit in winter. Good for massing. Excellent companion plant with camellias and rhododendrons. Native to China.

▮ Zones 8 and 9.

Spiraea japonica 'Bumalda'
Japanese spirea

Deciduous

▮ Rapid growth to 2 to 3 feet high, 3 to 5 feet wide.

Low, spreading shrub. White to deep pink flowers bloom from June to August on the current season's growth. 'Anthony Waterer' is a popular cultivar with deep rose flowers. Other superior cultivars include 'Crispa', a 2-foot-high shrub with twisted leaves, 'Goldflame', which bears brightly colored red, copper, and orange foliage in early spring and fall, and 'Nyewoods', an especially dense and compact plant with pink flowers. 'Froebelii' is also an excellent cultivar.

▮ Zones 4 to 8 (to zone 10 in the West).

Spiraea × vanhouttei
Vanhoutte spirea

Deciduous

▮ Rapid growth to 8 to 10 feet high, 10 to 12 feet wide.

The most popular spirea; often used in shrub borders and for massing. Has a graceful, arching habit. Dense growth; may also be sheared. Very tough and easy to grow. White flowers are borne on the previous season's growth from early April to May.

▮ Zones 5 to 10.

Spiraea × vanhouttei

Spiraea japonica 'Bumalda'

Syringa vulgaris

Tamarix hispida

Syringa vulgaris

Common lilac

Deciduous

▋ Moderate growth to 8 to 15 feet high, 12 to 15 feet wide.

The main attractions of *S. vulgaris* are its lavender, powerfully fragrant flowers, borne mid- to late May. Not a suitable specimen plant; it has little to offer when not in flower. Best located in the rear of a shrub border. Its habit is upright, often irregular. Leaves may be covered with powdery mildew by midsummer. Plant in full sun in neutral, rich soil. Most lilacs do not perform well in warm climates. Exceptions are 'Lavender Lady', 'Blue Boy', 'Chiffon', 'Mrs. Forrest K. Smith', and 'Sylvan Beauty', a group of hybrids developed in southern California. Native to southern Europe.
▋ Zones 3 to 7.

Tamarix hispida

Kashgar tree

Deciduous

▋ Rapid growth to 4 to 6 feet high.

For a bright pink fall display under the harshest seashore conditions, try this wispy, slender shrub. This is the neatest and most restrained of the tamarixes, but its winter appearance is impossible; it needs to be well hidden in a shrub border. Must have well-drained soil, but is extremely tolerant of salty, sandy soil and harsh, dry wind. Can stand considerable drought. Excellent choice for desert gardens, but needs periodic watering. Native to the region near the Caspian Sea.
▋ Zones 5 to 10.

Taxus cuspidata

Japanese yew

Needle evergreen

▋ Slow growth rate; size depends on cultivar.

Hardier than *T. baccata*. Many excellent cultivars of this species are available, ranging from 'Aurescens'—a low, 1-foot-high, 3-foot-wide form with yellow new growth—to 'Capitata', which grows 10 to 25 feet high and has a pyramidal form. Native to Japan and Korea.
▋ Zones 4 to 7.

Taxus × media

Anglojapanese yew

Needle evergreen

▋ Slow growth rate; size depends on cultivar.

This is a hybrid between *T. baccata* and *T. cuspidata*. An extremely wide variety of cultivars is available, from low, spreading types to tall, narrow ones. 'Hicksii' is columnar. 'Brownii' has a mounded habit. 'Wordin' has a wide-spreading, dense form. 'Hatfieldii' has a broad, compact, columnar form.
▋ Zones 5 to 7.

Taxus cuspidata

Taxus × media

Vaccinium corymbosum

Tsuga canadensis
'Pendula'

Tsuga canadensis 'Pendula'

Sargent's weeping hemlock

Needle evergreen

❚ Very slow growth to 6 to 10 feet high, 8 to 14 feet wide.

One of the most common hemlocks. Displays a graceful, pendulous habit and refined, evergreen foliage. An outstanding focal specimen in a border, by an entryway, in a raised bed, or in a container. Needs well-drained, moist, acid soil. Prefers partial shade, tolerates full shade. Leaves scorch at temperatures over 95° F or in polluted air. Native from Nova Scotia to Minnesota, and south to Alabama and Georgia.
❚ Zones 4 to 8.

Vaccinium corymbosum

Highbush blueberry

Deciduous

❚ Slow growth to 6 to 12 feet high, 8 to 12 feet wide.

Grown primarily for its delicious fruit, also an outstanding ornamental plant when given the right growing conditions. Rounded, compact form is easily restrained. Foliage provides bright red fall color. Small, white flowers are borne in great quantities as leaves emerge in spring. Fruit ripens in late July through August. A single mature bush will usually provide enough berries for a few pies, some jam, and the birds. Easy to grow in full sun to partial shade in moist, acid (pH 4.5 to 5.5), well-drained soil. Native from Maine to Minnesota and south to Florida and Louisiana.
❚ Zones 4 to 9.

Viburnum × burkwoodii

Burkwood viburnum

Deciduous

❚ Moderate growth to 8 to 10 feet high, 5 to 7 feet wide.

Upright, straggly shrub with powerfully fragrant blossoms. Flowers are pink in bud, white when open; they appear in early to late April before the plant leafs out. Fine plant for a shrub border; its fragrance will perfume an entire garden. Semievergreen in the South.
❚ Zones 5 to 8.

Viburnum carlesii

Korean spice viburnum

Deciduous

❚ Moderate growth to 4 to 5 feet high, 4 to 8 feet wide.

Considered the most fragrant of all the viburnums. The pinkish white flowers appear in late April to early May and have a sweet, spicy scent. Dark green leaves may develop reddish purple fall color. Habit is rounded and dense. Native to Korea.
❚ Zones 5 to 8.

Viburnum × burkwoodii

Viburnum carlesii

Viburnum davidii

Viburnum opulus

Viburnum davidii
David viburnum

Broadleaf evergreen

▌ Moderate growth to 2 to 3 feet high, 3 to 4 feet wide.

A handsome foliage plant suitable for western gardens. Its leaves are large, dark green, and leathery; the habit is very dense. Flowers are dull white, but the metallic-blue fruit is very appealing. Plant in partial shade. Native to China.
▌ Zones 8 to 10.

Viburnum opulus
European cranberrybush

Deciduous

▌ Moderate growth to 8 to 12 feet high, 10 to 15 feet wide.

Delicate, pinwheel-shaped clusters of white flowers put on a beautiful show in mid-May. Bright red fruit, borne September to November, is often accompanied by good fall foliage color. Best used in large gardens in a border, as a screen, or for massing. Terribly susceptible to aphids; needs to be sprayed regularly. For this reason, *V. trilobum*, a nearly identical American native, is often planted instead. 'Compactum' is a dense, dwarf cultivar about half the size of the species; 'Nanum' is a dwarf form.
▌ Zones 4 to 8 (to zone 10 in the West).

Viburnum plicatum var. tomentosum
Doublefile viburnum

Deciduous

▌ Moderate growth to 8 to 10 feet high, slightly wider spread.

One of the best deciduous flowering shrubs for the home garden. In May, pure white flowers are borne along tiers of branches. Summer foliage is dark green; fall colors are tints of rust to purplish red. The bright red fruit ripens in July and August, attracts birds. Makes an excellent specimen, also a good horizontal element in an otherwise upright shrub border. Combines well with broadleaf evergreens. In fertile, well-drained, moist soil, this is an easily maintained, trouble-free plant. Native to China and Japan.
▌ Zones 5 to 9.

Viburnum tinus
Laurustinus

Broadleaf evergreen

▌ Moderate growth to 6 to 12 feet high.

An upright shrub grown in southern and western gardens for its dark green foliage, pink to white flowers, and bright metallic-blue fruit. Clean, dense foliage hugs the ground; excellent for screens and hedges. Responds well to formal pruning. Adapts to shade, but flowers best in full sun. Native to the Mediterranean region.
▌ Zones 8 and 9 (to zone 10 in the West).

Viburnum tinus

Viburnum plicatum var. *tomentosum*

Weigela florida

Xylosma congestum

Weigela florida
Old-fashioned weigela

Deciduous

▌ Moderate growth to 6 to 9 feet high, 9 to 12 feet wide.

Out of bloom, this is a coarse, rangy shrub, but it is spectacular in late May to early June when laden with rosy pink flowers. Use in a shrub border, in masses, and in groupings, where its awkward form and coarse texture can be hidden when not in bloom. Prefers well-drained soil and full sun, but will adapt to less favorable conditions. Practically pest-free. Many cultivars and hybrids are available; flower colors range from white to deep red. *W. florida* var. *venusta* is hardy to zone 4. Native to northern China and Korea.
▌ Zones 5 to 8.

Xylosma congestum
Shiny xylosma

Broadleaf evergreen

▌ Slow growth to 8 to 10 feet high, equally wide.

Valued for its shiny, yellow-green foliage in all seasons. Habit is rounded and loose. Use in a shrub border or foundation planting, as a container plant, or as a formal or informal hedge. The spiny forms are useful barriers. Responds well to pruning; easily trained into an espalier. Adapts to almost any soil. Will tolerate heat and drought, but looks best when it has adequate water. Native to southern China.
▌ Zones 8 to 10.

GROUND COVERS

Achillea tomentosa
Woolly yarrow

Broadleaf evergreen

▌ Spreads rapidly, 8 to 12 inches high.

A sturdy, low-maintenance herb with soft, feathery, gray-green leaves 1 to 4 inches long. Commonly used in rock gardens and as a border plant. Tight clumps form a dense mat. Tolerates light traffic; may be used as a lawn substitute. Controls erosion on moderate slopes. From spring through summer, flat clusters of tiny, yellow blossoms are borne at the top of 4- to 10-inch stems. Requires full sun and well-drained soil. Fairly drought tolerant; needs only moderate watering during the summer.
▌ Zones 3 to 9.

Adiantum pedatum
Five-finger maidenhair fern

Deciduous

▌ Spreads slowly, to 2 feet high.

The hardiest *Adiantum.* Adapts well as an understory ground cover; lovely in the shade of trees and shrubs. May be interplanted with flowers or tucked into the pockets of a stone wall. Delicate foliage and thin, black stems give the plant a fine, airy texture. Spreads by creeping rootstocks. Thrives in shade to partial sun; needs soil rich in humus. Keep soil moist and apply a leaf mold mulch to prevent the delicate, fibrous roots from drying out.
▌ Zones 3 to 9 (to zone 10 in the West).

Achillea tomentosa

Adiantum pedatum

Agapanthus praecox ssp. *orientalis*

Ajuga reptans

Agapanthus praecox ssp. orientalis

Lily-of-the-Nile

Broadleaf evergreen

▌ Spreads rapidly, to 2 feet high.

This summer-flowering perennial features tall (4- to 5-foot) flower stalks with large, spherical clusters of tubular flowers in shades of white or blue. Leathery, straplike leaves. Mass plantings provide dramatic displays when plants are in bloom. Needs full sun for best flowers, but adapts to partial shade. Tolerates heavy soil. Needs ample water, especially when in flower. *A. africanus*, a smaller version, grows to about 20 inches high. An even smaller form, *A.* 'Peter Pan', grows to 14 inches high and is widely planted in the West.

▌ Zones 9 and 10.

Ajuga reptans

Carpet bugle

Broadleaf evergreen

▌ Spreads rapidly, 4 to 12 inches high.

Particularly effective when planted in the shade of other plants or buildings. Blue flowers are a short-term bonus; landscape value is based on handsome foliage—tight clusters of oval, wavy leaves 2 to 4 inches long that form a thick, low mat. Best in partial sun to light shade. Needs well-drained soil. Water moderately, more in full sun—plants should not be allowed to dry out. Protect from winter winds in cold areas. Rejuvenate by mowing lightly after blooming. Susceptible to fungus disease in the warm Southeast.

▌ Zones 5 to 8 (to zone 10 in the West).

Arctostaphylos uva-ursi

Bearberry, kinnikinick

Broadleaf evergreen

▌ Spreads slowly, to 10 inches high.

Effective as a large-scale planting in informal or native gardens, particularly on slopes or trailing over walls. Sturdy; drought tolerant. Branches can spread to 15 feet, are covered with oval, leathery, bright green leaves up to 1 inch long that turn bronze red where winters are cold. In spring, bell-shaped, white or light pink flowers appear at branch ends, followed by red fruit. Needs full sun in mild-summer areas, partial shade in hot-summer areas. Requires well-drained soil. Prune to remove deadwood only. Two cultivars for the West are 'Point Reyes' and 'Radiant'.

▌ Zones 3 to 6 (to zone 9 in the West).

Armeria maritima

Thrift

Perennial

▌ Spreads slowly; clumps reach 5 to 10 inches high, 15 inches wide.

Grows in dense, grassy clumps. Blooms in spring, into summer in inland areas; even longer in cool-summer areas. Delicate pink or white flowers are borne on long, thick stems. Thrives in medium shade or full sun. Prefers well-drained soil; requires moderate watering during summer months. Very salt tolerant. Common cultivars are 'Alba' (white flowers), 'Californica' (short stems, large white flowers), and 'Purpurea' (purple flowers).

▌ Zones 2 to 7 (to zone 10 in the West).

Arctostaphylos uva-ursi

Armeria maritima

Asarum caudatum

Asparagus densiflorus
'Sprengeri'

Asarum caudatum
British Columbia
wild ginger

Broadleaf evergreen

▮ Spreads moderately,
to 7 inches high.

A ground cover for heavily
shaded, woodland areas.
Forms a dense mat. Com-
bines well with evergreen
shrubs or wildflowers. Although not related to *Zin-
giber* (culinary ginger), its
creeping rootstocks and
pungent leaves have a gin-
gerlike fragrance. Slow to
establish, but grows rapidly
thereafter. With lots of
water, can grow in heavy
soil low in organic matter,
but thrives in soil that
is either naturally high in
humus or generously
amended. Locations pro-
tected from drying winds
are best. The species *A. eu-
ropaeum, A. shuttleworthii,*
and *A. virginicum* are
grown in the East.
▮ Zones 5 to 8.

*Asparagus densi-
florus* '**Sprengeri**'
Sprenger asparagus fern

Needlelike evergreen

▮ Moderate growth rate;
billows to 18 inches high.

The trailing growth habit
and arching sprays of light
green, slender leaves also
make these plants useful as
small-area ground covers
in mild climates. Effective in
a raised bed; cascade nicely
over a low wall. Best grown
alone—tend to climb other
plants. Clusters of tiny, pinkish white flowers bloom
in spring and early summer,
followed by equally small,
bright red berries that soon
drop off. Grow well in full
sun or light shade in any
good garden soil.
▮ Zones 9 and 10.

Athyrium filix-femina
Lady fern, Japanese
painted fern

Deciduous

▮ Moderate growth to
4 feet high.

Very easy to grow; tolerates
more sun and less moisture
than most ferns and is thick
enough to outcompete most
weeds. Arching, yellow-
green fronds give plant a
vase shape. Makes a fine
ground cover for woodland
gardens or along streams.
As with most ferns, ideal
conditions include partial
sun to shade, good garden
soil, and lots of moisture.
Fronds become ragged
looking unless protected
from wind.
▮ Zones 4 to 8 (to zone 10 in
the West).

*Aurinia saxatilis
(Alyssum saxatile)*
Basket-of-gold, golddust,
madwort

Broadleaf evergreen

▮ Moderate growth to
6 inches high.

Classic rock-garden plant,
best known for its spring
bloom of bright golden yellow flower clusters. Plant
in a prominent spot in the
front of a garden or along
a border to show off its brilliant color. Can also be
grown in containers and
moved to suitable spots in
the landscape. Grayish
green leaves are 2 to 5 inches long. Thrives in full sun
and well-drained soil. Keep
it on the dry side. Self-sows
freely once established in
the garden. Stimulate compact growth by cutting back
stems after flowering.
▮ Zones 4 to 8.

Athyrium filix-femina

Aurinia saxatilis

Baccharis pilularis

Bergenia cordifolia

Baccharis pilularis
Dwarf coyotebrush

Broadleaf evergreen

▌ Rapid growth to 3 to 8 feet wide, 2 feet high.

Reliable, drought-tolerant ground cover. Provides erosion control; widely used as a bank cover. Fire resistant. Dark green leaves are small, lightly toothed, and closely set on woody branches. Inconspicuous flowers appear at the leaf ends in summer. Widely planted in the West, where it is remarkably adaptable, growing equally well in sun or light shade and in almost any type of soil. 'Twin Peaks' has a compact growth habit. 'Pigeon Point' is greener, grows faster, and mounds higher.

▌ Zones 7 to 10 in the West only.

Bergenia cordifolia
Heartleaf bergenia

Broadleaf evergreen

▌ Spreads slowly; reaches 20 inches high.

Commonly used for shady borders, in clumps among smaller-leafed ground covers, around irregular surfaces such as rocks, and by pools and streams. Leaves are large and leathery, have heart-shaped bases. Handsome pink, white, or rose flower spikes appear in the spring. Plant in partial shade, protected from wind. Takes full sun in cool coastal areas. Best in moist, well-drained soil. Water and fertilize regularly, and bait for snails and slugs. Cut plants back when the thick, woody rhizomes become leggy. Divide clumps if they become crowded.

▌ Zones 3 to 8 (to zone 10 in the West).

Bergenia crassifolia
Siberian tea

Broadleaf evergreen

▌ Spreads slowly; clumps reach 18 to 20 inches high.

Quite similar to *B. cordifolia*, but unlike that plant, its finely toothed leaves are shorter by 2 or 3 inches and do not have heart-shaped bases. Flower spikes, borne well above the foliage, emerge in January and February in mild-climate areas. Flowers may be rose, deep pink, lilac, or purple. Most popular *Bergenia* species; hybrids are also available. Needs same culture as *B. cordifolia*.

▌ Zones 3 to 8 (to zone 10 in the West).

Campanula poscharskyana
Serbian bellflower

Perennial

▌ Spreads rapidly, to 1 foot high.

Best for small-scale plantings; needs to be seen up close to be appreciated. Forms a loose mat of heart-shaped, 1½-inch-long leaves. Blooms from spring into early summer. Flowers are star-shaped (one of several exceptions in the genus), and lavender blue. Makes an attractive accent in any shaded garden area. Needs full sun in cool climates and coastal areas, light shade in warmer climates. Drought tolerant; needs good drainage. Can be invasive; plants should be contained by a header or divider.

▌ Zones 3 to 10 in the West only.

Bergenia crassifolia

Campanula poscharskyana

Ceanothus gloriosus

Ceanothus griseus var. *horizontalis*

Ceanothus gloriosus
Point Reyes creeper

Broadleaf evergreen

▮ Spreads slowly, to 5 feet wide, 1 to 1½ feet high.

Forms a dense, evergreen mat. Leathery, dark green leaves are 1½ inches long and mostly round. Blooms in late spring, producing clusters of violet blue flowers. Needs a sunny location and light, well-drained soil. Does not tolerate wet conditions; can develop root rot from too much summer water. Once plants are established, two deep waterings a month in hot-summer areas are plenty. Native to southern California.
▮ Not recommended in the East; zones 8 to 10 in the West only.

Ceanothus griseus var. horizontalis
Carmel creeper

Broadleaf evergreen

Spreads slowly to 5 to 15 feet wide, 1½ to 2½ feet high.

A dense, spreading mat. Oval leaves are 2 inches wide. Violet blue flowers are borne in clusters 2 to 3 inches long. Like *C. gloriosus*, this plant needs a sunny location and light, well-drained soil. Does not tolerate wet conditions; can develop root rot from too much summer water. Browsed by deer. A more compact cultivar, 'Compacta', grows only 1 foot high.
▮ Not recommended in the East; zones 7 to 10 in the West only.

Cerastium tomentosum
Snow-in-summer

Broadleaf evergreen

▮ Spreads about 2 feet per year, 4 to 6 inches high.

A popular ground cover because of its striking, light gray foliage, its toughness, and its adaptability to almost any growing condition. Slender stems turn upward at the ends; upper sections are covered with narrow, woolly, ¾-inch-long leaves. Foliage is covered with white, ½-inch flowers from spring into summer. Grows well on slopes, level ground, or among stepping-stones. Needs full sun and well-drained soil. Set plants 1 to 2 feet apart in the spring.
▮ Zones 3 to 8 (to zone 10 in the West).

Ceratostigma plumbaginoides
Dwarf plumbago, blue leadwort

Perennial

▮ Spreads rapidly, 8 to 12 inches high.

Easy-to-grow, valued for its long-lasting, blue, ½-inch flowers, which appear in late summer and last until fall. Tufting growth; spreads by underground stems. Dark green leaves are about 3 inches long; they develop a reddish purple tint in the fall. Dies to the ground in all but the mildest areas; cut back to the ground after flowering. Takes full sun or light shade. Use to cover large areas, or tuck into corners or under shrubs. Combines well with boxwood, ajuga, and *Sempervivum*.
▮ Zones 6 to 9 (to zone 10 in the West).

Cerastium tomentosum

Ceratostigma plumbaginoides

Chamaemelum nobile
Chamomile

Perennial

▌ Moderate growth to 3 to 12 inches high.

A perennial herb, popular in Europe as a lawn substitute. Also famous for chamomile tea, made from the dried flowers. Lacy, lustrous leaves form a soft mat. Good cover for small areas if left to grow naturally. Suitable for paths and areas between stepping-stones if sheared and rolled. During summer, small green or yellow flower heads with white petals appear at the tops of slender stalks. Best in light, sandy soil and full sun. Tolerates light shade. Drought tolerant; requires only moderate watering in summer. Set plants 6 to 12 inches apart.
▌ Zones 7 to 10.

Convallaria majalis
Lily-of-the-valley

Deciduous

▌ Moderate growth to 8 inches high.

One of the hardiest and most adaptable ground covers. Thrives in partial or full shade; develops a dense mass of soil-holding roots in just about any soil. Fragrant, ¼-inch, bell-shaped flowers, usually white, appear in spring. Typically planted around shrubs, such as the taller rhododendrons and camellias; also effective with ferns. The *Rosea* variety has pale pink flowers. 'Fortin's Giant' has larger flowers. 'Striata' has white-striped leaves.
▌ Zones 3 to 8.

Chamaemelum nobile

Convallaria majalis

Coprosma × kirkii
Kirk's coprosma

Broadleaf evergreen

▌ Moderate growth to 1½ to 2½ feet high.

A small, spreading shrub composed of woody, upright, heavily branched stems lined with yellow-green, oblong leaves that are ¼ inch long. Makes a tough ground or bank cover for small areas; withstands wind and salt spray. Grows in sun or partial shade. Adapts to almost any soil. Drought resistant; needs only light summer watering.
▌ Zones 9 and 10.

Coronilla varia
Crown vetch

Deciduous

▌ Spreads rapidly, to 2 feet high.

Deep, soil-building roots and dense, weed-choking foliage make this one of the most popular ground covers for erosion control, particularly in large, difficult-to-maintain areas. The foliage consists of ½-inch, oval leaflets. Pinkish flowers appear in summer. Dies back in winter; the mass of brown stems can be a fire hazard. Drought resistant. Prefers full sun but tolerates partial shade. Spreads by underground runners; can be invasive and difficult to eradicate.
▌ Zones 3 to 8.

Coprosma × kirkii

Coronilla varia

Cotoneaster dammeri

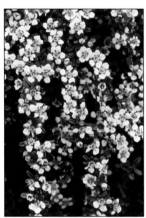

Cotoneaster conspicuus 'Decorus'

Cotoneaster conspicuus 'Decorus'

Necklace cotoneaster

Broadleaf evergreen

▌ Spreads slowly to 6 to 8 feet wide, 1 to 1½ feet high.

An extremely prostrate cultivar of *C. conspicuus.* Very attractive ground cover, but its open branches do not completely shade out weeds. Best in small areas, on slopes, and in rock gardens. Flowers are white. Scarlet, ⅓-inch berries cover branches in fall. Leaves are ¼ inch long, dark green on top and paler underneath. Susceptible to fire blight, especially in zones 8 and 9 in the Southeast.
▌ Zones 7 to 9.

Cotoneaster dammeri

Bearberry cotoneaster

Broadleaf evergreen

▌ Spreads rapidly to 6 feet wide, 1 to 1½ feet high.

One of the best hardy, broadleaf evergreen ground covers. The foliage is dense and glossy, and the plant stays low and fills in rapidly. Use on banks and slopes, in masses, in a shrub border, or as a low facing plant for tall, leggy shrubs. White flowers speckle the plant in late May. Bright red fruit resembling tiny apples develops in late summer. Adaptable to many soils; prefers fast drainage. An excellent choice for dry, rocky soil in an exposed, sunny location. 'Royal Beauty' and 'Skogholm' have superior foliage and grow more rapidly than the species. 'Lowfast' is hardy to zone 5.
▌ Zones 6 to 9.

Cotoneaster horizontalis

Rock cotoneaster

Deciduous (semievergreen in mild climates)

▌ Spreads moderately to 8 to 10 feet wide, 2 to 3 feet high.

Perhaps the most widely grown of all the cotoneasters. Semievergreen in mild climates; where deciduous it's so heavily covered with bright red berries that leaves aren't missed. Flowers and fruit are small; leaves are round, ½ inch across, become reddish before falling. Combines well with fine-textured species such as the low-growing junipers. Stiff growth discourages traffic on banks and low dividers.
▌ Zones 5 to 8 (to zone 9 in the West).

Cotoneaster microphyllus

Littleleaf cotoneaster

Broadleaf evergreen

▌ Spreads moderately to 6 feet wide, 2 to 3 feet high.

The finest-textured *Cotoneaster.* Tangled, intermingling branches are well suited for banks or around rocks. White flowers appear in June; scarlet-red berries mature in the fall. Fine hairs on the undersides of the glossy leaves give them a grayish cast. *C. cashmiriensis* 'Cochleatus' is a dwarf form, often used for bonsai. *C. linearifolius* (*C. microphyllus* f. *thymifolius*) is a very compact form with stiff, upright branches. 'Emerald Spray' is resistant to fire blight. Hardy to −10° F.
▌ Zones 6 to 8 (to zone 9 in the West).

Cotoneaster horizontalis

Cotoneaster microphyllus

Cyrtomium falcatum

Cytisus × kewensis

Cyrtomium falcatum
Japanese holly fern

Broadleaf evergreen

▮ Moderate growth to 2 to 3 feet high.

A common houseplant; makes a handsome ground cover outdoors in mild climates. Effective border for walks and paths. Attractive under camellias. Light yellow-green fronds are about 2½ feet long. Tolerates drier air and more sun than many ferns, but prefers shade and a rich, moist soil. Plant on 1½-foot centers for solid cover. Susceptible to brown scale.
▮ Zones 9 and 10.

Cytisus × kewensis
Kew broom

Deciduous
(stems are evergreen)

▮ Spreads rapidly to 3 feet wide, 6 to 10 inches high.

An excellent plant for hot, dry, sunny locations; also tolerates salt-laden air and sandy soil. Combines well with drought-tolerant southwestern natives. Trailing branches cascade handsomely over low walls. Leaves are tiny. Pale yellow, ½-inch flowers cover the plant in May. Very adaptable; generally does best in dry, poor, slightly acid soil. Tolerates heavy rainfall if the soil drains well.
▮ Zones 6 to 8 (to zone 10 in the West).

Dianthus deltoides
Maiden pink

Perennial

▮ Spreads slowly, to 6 inches high.

Forms a thick carpet of blue-green, grasslike leaves. Growth is persistent and invasive; plant in contained areas. Red or pink ¾-inch flowers are borne on stalks above the foliage in May to June. Needs full sun and light soil. Mow after flowering to maintain even, compact growth; may be kept at 2 to 3 inches by frequent mowing.
▮ Zones 2 to 8 (to zone 10 in the West).

Dicentra eximia
Fringed bleeding-heart; turkey corn

Perennial

▮ Clumps reach 2 feet wide, 1 to 2 feet high.

This easily grown perennial is perfectly suited to beautifying shady corners. Combines well with ferns and wildflowers. Pink flowers, borne on 6- to 8-inch spikes, appear in May and last until first frost. Fernlike leaves are blue or gray-green. Both flowers and foliage are long lasting in flower arrangements. Best in rich humus and partial shade. Many varieties are available; 'Bountiful' has rich pink flowers. For a solid cover, plant clumps about 8 inches apart.
▮ Zones 3 to 8 (to zone 10 in the West).

Dianthus deltoides

Dicentra eximia

Duchesnea indica

*Epimedium
grandiflorum*

Duchesnea indica
Mock strawberry

Perennial

∎ Spreads rapidly, to 2 inches high.

Superficially resembles *Fragaria chiloensis* (wild strawberry), but the fruit is inedible and borne above the foliage. (The delicious fruit of *F. chiloensis* is borne within the foliage.) Leaves are smaller than those of *F. chiloensis;* flowers are yellow. Takes full sun, but in most areas is best in light shade. Attractive when planted in the filtered shade of trees and shrubs.
∎ Zones 5 to 8 (to zone 10 in the West).

Epimedium grandiflorum
Bishop's-cap, barrenwort

Semievergreen perennial

∎ Moderate growth to 1 foot high.

Easy to grow; should be used more. Good cover for areas under rhododendrons and camellias; competes well with the roots of trees. Best in light shade, takes full sun in northern zones if soil is rich and moist. Best in acid soil. Flowers appear in May; they resemble orchids, are shaped like a bishop's miter. 'Rose Queen' has bright, rose-colored flowers with white-tipped spurs. The hybrid *E. × versicolor* 'Sulphureum' has yellow flowers. *E. × youngianum* 'Niveum' has a compact form and white flowers.
∎ Zones 3 to 8.

Erica carnea (E. herbacea)
Spring or Christmas heath, bell heather

Narrowleaf evergreen

∎ Spreads slowly to 2 to 3 feet wide, 6 to 12 inches high.

An excellent low-maintenance ground cover. Tightly woven roots hold soil well on slopes. Foliage is very fine. Flowers may be red, pink, or white. Blooms as early as November in mild-winter areas; pendulous flower clusters are 1 to 2 inches long. Prefers infertile, acid soil, but will tolerate slight alkalinity. Takes full sun, partial shade in hot climates. Tolerates salty air and wind. Plant on 2½-foot centers.
∎ Zones 6 and 7 (to zone 10 in the West.)

Euonymus fortunei
Wintercreeper

Broadleaf evergreen

∎ Spreads rapidly; size depends on cultivar.

Often grown as vine or shrub; some cultivars are useful ground covers. Hardy and sturdy; grows in many parts of the country, in sun or shade, and in good or poor soil. 'Coloratus' grows 6 to 10 inches high and has striking purple foliage in the fall. Good for mass planting, erosion control. 'Gracilis' is smaller and less vigorous, with variegated, whitish leaves that take on a pink tinge in winter. 'Kewensis' and 'Minimus' are dwarf, slow-growing types, reaching little more than 2 inches high. The dwarf varieties are best planted in small areas.
∎ Zones 5 to 9 (to zone 10 in the West).

Erica carnea

Euonymus fortunei

Festuca glauca

Fragaria chiloensis

Festuca glauca (F. ovina var. glauca)

Blue fescue

Narrowleaf evergreen

▌ Slow growth; forms 4- to 10-inch tufts.

An attractive ornamental grass composed of bluish gray tufts of hairlike blades. Although a true grass, it is not a practical lawn substitute because of its mounding habit. Plant in geometric patterns in large areas. Small clumps are effective accents. Successfully grown in ordinary, well-drained soil and full sun. Minimize weeding among tufts by applying a light mulch.
▌ Zones 3 to 8 (to zone 10 in the West).

Fragaria chiloensis

Wild strawberry, sand strawberry

Broadleaf evergreen

▌ Spreads rapidly, to 6 inches high.

The parent of all commercial strawberries. Contributes a delightful, woodsy effect to the landscape. Tolerates occasional traffic. Thick mat of 2-inch, dark green leaves turns reddish in winter. A profusion of white, 1-inch-wide flowers appears in spring, followed by small fruit. Grows in full sun and in most well-drained soils; does particularly well in sand dunes at the beach. Needs regular watering throughout the year. Susceptible to red spider mites. Choose a cultivar for your area for best fruit.
▌ Zones 6 to 10.

Gaultheria procumbens

Wintergreen, teaberry, checkerberry

Broadleaf evergreen

▌ Spreads moderately, to 6 inches high.

Native wintergreen, common in the woods of the Northeast. Excellent companion for rhododendrons and azaleas or as a ground cover in native gardens. Drooping flowers, similar to those of *Convallaria majalis* (lily-of-the-valley), bloom in May; they are followed by edible, scarlet berries in the fall. Leaves are leathery, dark green, about 1½ inches long. Spreads by underground runners. Needs partial shade and moist, acid soil.
▌ Zones 4 to 8 (to zone 10 in the West).

Gelsemium sempervirens

Carolina jessamine

Broadleaf evergreen

▌ Spreads rapidly; mounds 3 to 4 feet high.

The state flower of South Carolina. Usually evergreen, but loses its shiny green, finely textured leaves in winter in cold climates. Most appreciated for its fragrant, yellow, early-spring flowers. Tolerates some shade but flowers more profusely in full sun. Prune selectively and frequently to keep it low (about 3 feet high), and to encourage new growth from the base. Adapts to almost any soil. Generally best used as cover for large areas.
▌ Zones 6 to 9 (to zone 10 in the West).

Gaultheria procumbens

Gelsemium sempervirens

Genista pilosa

Hedera canariensis

Genista pilosa
Silky-leaf woadwaxen

Deciduous
(stems are evergreen)

▌Spreads moderately to 7 feet wide, 1 foot high.

Very similar to *Cytisus* × *kewensis* (kew broom). Blends into the landscape for most of the year, but stands out in spring with a vivid display of yellow blooms. Adapts well to poor and dry soil and to dry-summer, Mediterranean climates. Leaves are about ½ inch long. Needs hot, dry, sunny exposure. Infertile, well-drained soil is best. Very drought tolerant once established.
▌Zones 6 to 8 (to zone 10 in the West).

Hedera canariensis
Algerian ivy

Broadleaf evergreen

▌Spreads rapidly, 6 to 8 inches high.

Tougher, coarser, and more aggressive than *H. helix*—best viewed from a distance. Shiny, green leaves are up to 8 inches across, but most are about half that size. Better adapted to sunny locations than *H. helix*, but requires more water. The most common cultivar, 'Variegata', has leaves edged with yellowish white. Set young plants 18 inches apart.
▌Zones 9 and 10.

Hedera helix
English ivy

Broadleaf evergreen

▌Spreads rapidly, 6 to 8 inches high.

Dark green, lobed leaves are generally 2 to 4 inches long. Succeeds in most climates, in full sun to heavy shade. Requires minimal maintenance. Mow every other year with the mower at the highest setting to prevent growth from becoming too dense. 'Baltica' has smaller leaves (1 to 2 inches long). 'Green Feather' is a compact form with bird's-foot-shaped leaves. Many variegated forms are also available. Set young plants 12 inches apart.
▌Zones 5 to 10.

Helianthemum nummularium
Common sunrose

Broadleaf evergreen

▌Spreads moderately to 3 feet wide, 6 to 8 inches high.

Fine, low-maintenance, fire-retardant ground cover. Bright, 1- to 2-inch flowers are single or double and come in shades of pink, red, and yellow. Delicate blossoms last only a day, but new flowers open so regularly that their short life goes unnoticed. Leaves are glossy or dull green, depending on the variety. Needs neutral to alkaline soil with good drainage and full sun. Can be grown in acid soil in areas of high rainfall if soil has excellent drainage and is amended with lime before planting. Where winters are cold and there is no snow, cover plants with a layer of straw or similar material to protect them.
▌Zones 5 to 10 in the West only.

Hedera helix

Helianthemum nummularium

Heuchera sanguinea

Hosta lancifolia

Heuchera sanguinea
Coralbells

Perennial

▌Spreads slowly, to 12 to 18 inches high.

Distinctive ground cover for small areas. Bell-shaped, coral pink or red flowers are favored by humming-birds, suitable for arrange-ments. Blooms June to September; may bloom all year in mild areas. Remove faded flowers to extend blooming season. Grows best in partial shade—pro-tect from hot afternoon sun. Many cultivars, varying in flower color, are available. Plant on 1-foot centers.
▌Zones 3 to 8 (to zone 10 in the West).

Hosta lancifolia
Narrowleaf plantain lily

Deciduous

▌Spreads slowly; clumps reach 2 feet wide, 1½ to 2 feet high.

Has narrow, pointed leaves, 4 to 6 inches long. Flowers, which appear in summer, are a light shade of blue-purple. Easy to grow in sandy or loamy soil with plenty of organic matter. Medium to dense shade is a necessity. Performs best in cold-winter areas. Snails and slugs love the leaves. *H. sieboldii* (*H. lancifolia* var. *albomarginata*) has leaves edged with white.
▌Zones 3 to 8.

Hosta plantaginea
Fragrant plantain lily

Deciduous

▌Spreads slowly; clumps reach 2 feet wide, 10 inches high.

The only fragrant plantain lily. Has large (4- to 5-inch-wide), white flowers that ap-pear in late summer or early fall. Heart-shaped leaves are up to 10 inches long and 6 inches wide. Easy to grow in sandy or loamy soil with plenty of organic matter. Medium to dense shade is a necessity. Snails and slugs love the leaves.
▌Zones 3 to 8.

Hosta sieboldiana
Siebold plantain lily

Deciduous

▌Spreads slowly; clumps reach 2 feet wide, 18 inches high.

Has the most impressive foliage of its genus. Makes a dramatic accent by a shaded pool. Leaves are blue-green, 10 to 15 inches long, and heavily veined. White flowers are much less significant than those of *H. plantaginea*, and are usually borne down in the foliage. Easy to grow in sandy or loamy soil with plenty of organic matter. Must have medium to dense shade. Leaves attract snails and slugs. The leaves of 'Frances Williams' have creamy yellow borders.
▌Zones 3 to 8.

Hosta plantaginea

Hosta sieboldiana

Hypericum calycinum

Iberis sempervirens

Hypericum calycinum

Aaron's-beard, Saint John's wort

Broadleaf evergreen

❚ Spreads rapidly, 10 to 15 inches high.

A dense ground cover, excellent for mass planting. Very handsome and easy to grow. Oblong, bright green leaves are 2 to 3 inches long. Flowers are about 3½ inches across and have bright yellow petals with delicate tufts of orange-yellow stamens rising from the center. Blooms almost all summer. Needs partial shade in warm areas. Can be invasive; use a header board or other divider to contain the plants. Plant 12 to 18 inches apart.
❚ Zones 6 to 9 (to zone 10 in the West).

Iberis sempervirens

Evergreen candytuft

Broadleaf evergreen

❚ Spreads rapidly to 6 to 12 inches wide, equally high.

Small-scale ground cover blanketed with white, flat flower clusters in early spring. The foliage forms a dense mat as the long stems bend to the ground and root. Spills gracefully over walls. Grows best in full sun. Needs regular watering throughout the year. Compact cultivars include 'Snowflake', which grows to about 9 inches high; 'Little Gem', about 6 inches high; and 'Little Cushion', which also is about 6 inches high and spreads 1 foot or more.
❚ Zones 3 to 9 (to zone 10 in the West).

Iris cristata

Crested iris

Deciduous perennial

❚ Spreads rapidly, 4 to 6 inches high.

Forms a thick mat of slender, greenish rhizomes on the surface of the soil. Rhizomes will creep into cracks and crevices in stones and at the edges of walkways; plants are also attractive in mass plantings. Upright, sword-shaped leaves contrast well with smaller-leaved ground covers. Blooms profusely in May to June. Prefers cool, moist soil; tolerates acid soil. Takes full sun, but does best with some shade. 'Alba' has white flowers. 'Caerulea' has blue flowers. Native to eastern North America.
❚ Zones 3 to 8.

Juniperus communis var. saxatilis

Common juniper

Needle evergreen

❚ Spreads slowly to 6 feet wide, 1 foot high.

This variety is a prostrate form of an extremely variable species. The gray-green foliage is composed of prickly clusters of tiny, needlelike leaves. Branches turn up at the ends. Requires full sun and good drainage. Not widely planted in the East.
❚ Zones 5 to 7 (to zone 10 in the West).

Iris cristata

Juniperus communis var. *saxatilis*

Juniperus conferta

Juniperus horizontalis

Juniperus conferta
Shore juniper

Needle evergreen

■ Spreads moderately to 10 feet wide, 10 inches high.

A handsome, low creeper. Has a compact habit and prickly foliage. An obvious choice for coastal areas and sandy soil; can also be grown successfully inland. Particularly attractive when allowed to cascade over low stone or concrete walls. Drought tolerant. 'Blue Pacific' has blue-green foliage.
■ Zones 6 to 10.

Juniperus horizontalis
Creeping juniper

Needle evergreen

■ Growth rate and size depend on cultivar.

Commonly available in many forms. 'Blue Chip' has bluish green foliage, mounds to 8 inches high, and spreads to about 2 feet. 'Bar Harbour' has a distinctive, flat-branching growth habit and silver blue foliage; reaches 12 inches high. 'Emerson's Creeper' has gray-green foliage, grows 8 inches high, and spreads 6 to 8 feet wide. 'Emerald Spreader' has delicate, emerald green foliage, grows 10 inches high, and spreads 4 to 6 feet wide. 'Wiltonii' (also known as 'Blue Rug') grows to only 4 inches high.
■ Zones 5 to 9 (to zone 10 in the West).

Juniperus procumbens 'Nana'
Japanese garden juniper

Needle evergreen

■ Spreads slowly to 4 to 5 feet wide, 6 to 12 inches high.

Has a flat, creeping habit; a prized juniper for rock gardens. The foliage is bluish green, dense, and somewhat prickly. Needs full sun and well-drained soil. 'Variegata' has a higher, slightly mounding habit and gray-green foliage with patches of light yellow.
■ Zones 5 to 8 (to zone 10 in the West).

Lantana montevidensis
Trailing lantana

Perennial

■ Spreads rapidly to 3 to 4 feet wide, 1½ to 2 feet high.

Tough and ever-blooming; good for large-scale plantings, particularly on steep banks where maintenance is a problem. One-inch clusters of tiny, lavender flowers appear along the ends of vinelike stems lined with oval, dark green, 1-inch leaves. Texture is coarse. Needs sun to thrive. Grows well in poor soil; needs only occasional watering. Old plants become woody; dead patches should be cut out in early spring. Many flower colors are available.
■ Zones 9 and 10.

Lantana montevidensis

Juniperus procumbens 'Nana'

Lavandula angustifolia

Liriope muscari

Lavandula angustifolia

English lavender

Broadleaf evergreen

■ Moderate growth rate; dwarf varieties reach 1 to 2 feet wide, equally high.

Cultivated for centuries as an ornamental herb and for its aromatic oil. Dwarf varieties make good ground covers, grow at a moderate rate. Lance-shaped, gray-green leaves are 1 to 2 inches long and ½ inch wide. Flowers are blue to purple, borne on spikes 8 to 24 inches high. Collect flowers for sachets just as buds open. Needs full sun. 'Carroll Gardens' has pale purple flowers. 'Dutch' has deep blue flowers. 'Fragrance' is heavily scented. 'Hidcote' has deep purple flowers, grows 12 inches high. 'Munstead' bears lilac blue flowers. 'Twickel Purple' has dark purple flowers in fanlike clusters.
■ Zones 5 to 8 (to zone 10 in the West).

Liriope muscari

Big blue lilyturf

Broadleaf evergreen

■ Slow growth; clumps reach 10 to 15 inches wide, 2 feet high.

Use as an informal filler for small areas or along paths. Dark green, grassy leaves grow in tufts. Violet flowers bloom from July into September. Takes full sun to partial shade. Leaves turn yellow in cold winters; clip off before growth resumes in spring. Sometimes sold as *Ophiopogon jaburan.*
■ Zones 6 to 9.

Liriope spicata

Creeping lilyturf

Broadleaf evergreen

■ Spreads moderately, to 8 to 9 inches high.

Smaller and hardier than *L. muscari.* Forms a dense cover and spreads widely by underground stems. Flowers are pale lavender to white. Mow in early spring to stimulate fresh new growth.
■ Zones 4 to 9.

Lobularia maritima

Sweet alyssum

Annual

■ Slow growth to 3 to 10 inches high.

Commonly used as a bedding plant; works well when planted as a temporary cover to discourage weeds between young plants of a slow-growing ground-cover species. Quarter-sized flowers appear in clusters all season long. Colors vary from dark purple to white. Easy to grow in full sun to partial shade. Perennial in mild climates. 'Carpet of Snow' has white flowers, grows 4 inches high. 'Oriental Nights' has dark purple flowers, grows 4 inches high.
■ Zones 2 to 10.

Liriope spicata

Lobularia maritima

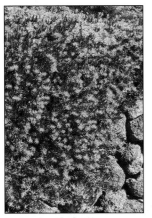

Lotus berthelotii

Lonicera japonica 'Halliana'

Lonicera japonica 'Halliana'

Hall's honeysuckle

Deciduous

▮ Spreads very rapidly; mounds to 6 feet high.

An exceptionally vigorous vine, often used as a ground cover. Twining habit, will climb and strangle trees and shrubs if allowed. Leaves are soft and downy, evergreen in warm climates. Fragrant, trumpet-shaped, white flowers appear in summer, turn yellow with age. Grows in most soil in sun or light shade; resists drought. Becomes woody and scraggly if not cut back occasionally. Because of its invasive habit, it has become a pest in some parts of the country. Choose less vigorous, locally available cultivars.
▮ Zones 4 to 10.

Lotus berthelotii

Parrot's beak

Narrowleaf evergreen

▮ Spreads rapidly to 1 to 2 feet wide, 3 to 4 inches high.

Has a delightful, trailing habit; makes an excellent bank cover. Flat, gray-brown branches are covered with clusters of silvery, needlelike leaves ¾ inch long. Brilliant, deep scarlet flowers with petals shaped somewhat like a parrot's beak bloom from late spring to summer. Grows in full sun; needs moderate to light watering. Cut plants back occasionally to encourage dense growth. *L. corniculatus*, the bird's-foot trefoil, is a related species that is hardy to zone 5.
▮ Zone 10.

Lysimachia nummularia

Creeping-jenny, moneywort

Perennial

▮ Spreads rapidly, to 4 inches high.

One of those rapidly spreading creepers that is a weed where you don't want it (in a lawn) and a ground cover where you do. Its small, bright green leaves and slender stems form a wavy carpet a few inches high. Bright yellow flowers, about ¾ inch in diameter, bloom throughout the summer. Plant in moist, shady places where other plants, such as grass, won't grow. A natural place would be around small pools or rocky areas. Tolerates light traffic. Prefers shade but will grow in full sun if soil is always moist to wet. Propagate by division; start new plants at any time.
▮ Zones 3 to 10.

Mahonia repens

Creeping mahonia

Broadleaf evergreen

▮ Spreads rapidly, 1 to 2 feet high.

A good ground cover for small to medium-sized areas, such as beds bordering patios. Leaves are bluish green and spiny, turn bronzy in winter. Bears 1- to 3-inch clusters of bright yellow flowers in the spring, dark purple berries in the fall. Can be planted in full sun, but grows equally well—and looks better— in filtered shade. Plant 10 inches apart in spring.
▮ Zones 5 to 8 (to zone 10 in the West).

Lysimachia nummularia

Mahonia repens

Mentha requienii

Nandina domestica
'Harbour Dwarf'

Mentha requienii
Corsican mint

Perennial

▮ Spreads rapidly, 1 to 3 inches high.

The lowest growing of the many species and dozens of cultivars of mint. Makes a delightful ground cover for small patches anywhere in the garden, especially among stepping-stones. Tiny, oval leaves are soft, give off a strong minty fragrance when bruised. Bears miniature lavender flowers in midsummer. Grows vigorously in sun or light shade. Needs ample soil moisture. Dies to the ground in freezing temperatures, but returns in the spring.
▮ Zones 6 to 10.

Nandina domestica 'Harbour Dwarf'
Nandina, heavenly-bamboo

Broadleaf evergreen

▮ Spreads moderately, 12 to 18 inches high

An unusual, very low cultivar of the well-known landscape shrub. Dense; spreads by underground rhizomes. Plant near the house or anywhere that its lacy foliage can be appreciated at a close distance. Semievergreen in colder zones; turns orange to bronzy red in fall. Tolerates partial shade, but foliage colors are more dramatic in full sun.
▮ Zones 7 to 10.

Ophiopogon japonicus
Mondograss

Narrowleaf evergreen

▮ Spreads slowly, 8 to 10 inches high.

A popular ground cover for sun or shade. Dense clumps of long, coarse, ⅛-inch-wide leaves arch over to form mounds 8 to 10 inches high. Small, pale purple flowers, mostly hidden among the leaves, appear in July and August, followed by pea-sized blue fruit. Spreads by means of fleshy, subsurface stems. Suitable for sizable plantings in the shade of large trees. In a shaded patio setting, a few dozen plants placed about 8 inches apart with *Soleirolia soleirolii* (baby's tears) in between will produce a lovely, cool effect.
▮ Zones 7 to 10.

Pachysandra terminalis
Japanese spurge

Perennial

▮ Spreads rapidly, 6 to 8 inches high.

Spreads by underground runners to form a dense cover of essentially uniform height. Use for large-scale plantings under trees or, on a small scale, in the shade of evergreen shrubs. Remains evergreen in the most severe winters. Veined, dark green, oval leaves, 1½ to 4 inches long and lightly toothed near the ends, grow in clusters at the top of upright stems 6 to 8 inches high. Needs partial to full shade and good, somewhat moist, acid soil. 'Green Carpet' is darker green and bears more flowers.
▮ Zones 4 to 8 (to zone 10 in the West).

Ophiopogon japonicus

Pachysandra terminalis

Phlox subulata

Phyla nodiflora

Phlox subulata
Moss phlox

Perennial

▌Spreads slowly, 4 to 6 inches high.

A mat-forming perennial, attractive in small- or large-scale plantings, as well as in rock gardens. The flowers, ranging from white to various shades of pink and red, cover the needlelike foliage completely for about a month in late spring or mid-summer. Individual plants grow in clumps, spreading rapidly by means of trailing stems. Needs full sun; adapts to most soils. Different color cultivars are available, including 'White Delight', 'Red Wings', and 'Emerald Blue'.
▌Zones 3 to 9.

Phyla nodiflora
Lippia, matgrass, capeweed

Broadleaf evergreen

▌Spreads moderately, 1 to 2 inches high.

Forms a dense mat; makes a good lawn substitute in warm climates. Tiny, lavender flowers spotted with yellow appear from spring through summer. Flowers attract bees, a liability when using the plant as a lawn substitute unless flowers are removed by regular mowings. Also effective around small garden pools, where it can creep among rocks and up little slopes. Leaves turn brownish in cold weather. Grows well in most soil; takes partial shade, but does better in sun. Withstands extreme heat and is very drought resistant.
▌Zones 9 and 10.

Polygonum capitatum
Knotweed, pink clover blossom

Perennial

▌Spreads rapidly, 5 to 8 inches high.

An informal ground cover. Wiry, trailing, reddish stems are loosely covered by 1-inch-long, elliptical, dark green to pinkish leaves. Small, pink flowers bloom most of the year. The overall effect is of a wine red, mounding tangle. Grows best in full sun, in any soil that has good drainage. Occasional watering in dry-summer areas is the only maintenance requirement.
▌Zones 6 to 10.

Potentilla neumanniana (P. tabernaemontani)
Spring cinquefoil

Perennial

▌Spreads moderately, 3 to 6 inches high.

The lowest-growing cinquefoil; forms a dense, matlike cover. Bright yellow flowers, about ⅛ inch across, bloom in great numbers from spring well into summer. Takes full sun in all but desert areas; also does well in shade. An excellent plant for medium-scale plantings on slopes, under high-branched trees, or among clusters of rocks.
▌Zones 6 to 10.

Polygonum capitatum

Potentilla neumanniana

Rosa wichuraiana

Rosmarinus officinalis
'Prostratus'

Rosa wichuraiana
Memorial rose

Deciduous to evergreen

▮ Spreads about 10 feet
a year, 1 foot high.

Many *Rosa* species can
be used as ground covers,
but this is the only truly
procumbent species. Its fast
growth can cause trouble;
use only in large areas
where the plant has plenty
of room to ramble. Ever-
green in mild climates.
White, 2-inch flowers are
produced in late summer;
this is one of the last roses
to bloom. Best in prepared
soil and full sun, but tolerates poor soil. Plant 4 to
5 feet apart.
▮ Zones 5 to 8 (to zone 10 in
the West).

Rosmarinus officinalis 'Prostratus'
Dwarf rosemary

Broadleaf evergreen

▮ Spreads slowly to
4 to 8 feet wide, 8 to
24 inches high.

A dwarf, low-growing
form of the popular herb.
Bears narrow, aromatic,
deep green leaves and tiny
clusters of light blue, ½-inch
flowers. Blooms most of the
year, most heavily in winter
and spring. Prevents ero-
sion on slopes, cascades
beautifully over walls.
Drought tolerant; must have
good drainage. This cultivar
is similar to the widely
planted 'Lockwood de For-
est', but stays closer to the
ground. Set new plants 2
feet apart.
▮ Zones 8 to 10.

Sagina subulata
Irish moss, Scotch moss,
pearlwort

Narrowleaf evergreen

▮ Spreads rapidly, 3 to
4 inches high.

Ideal for rocky areas—particularly among stepping-
stones. Awl-shaped leaves
grow in dense, rounded
tufts. Produces tiny, white
flowers in summer. Grows
equally well in full sun
or light shade. To thrive,
plants need rich, well-
drained soil and enough
water to keep it moist but
not soggy. The leaves of
'Aurea' have a yellow tinge.
▮ Zones 4 to 10.

Santolina chamaecyparissus
Lavender cotton

Broadleaf evergreen

▮ Spreads rapidly, 1½ to
2 feet high.

Grown chiefly for its distinctive light gray, aromatic
foliage. For a month or so in
summer, the foliage is partially covered by a profusion
of small, round, bright yellow flowers. Grows in any
well-drained soil (including
sandy or gravely soil) in full
sun. Exceptionally drought
resistant; requires only
occasional watering in the
summer. Adapts well to
seashore conditions. Dies to
the ground in very cold
areas, but usually recovers.
Plant on 3-foot centers.
▮ Zones 6 to 9 (to zone 10
in the West).

Sagina subulata

Santolina chamaecyparissus

Sedum acre

Sarcococca hookeriana var. *humilis*

Sarcococca hookeriana var. humilis

Small Himalayan sarcococca

Broadleaf evergreen

▌ Spreads moderately, 1 to 2 feet high.

An attractive choice for heavy shade. Spreads several feet by underground runners. Its most attractive feature is its glossy, dark green foliage. Fragrant, white flowers in spring are followed by black berries. Needs acid soil generously amended with organic matter. Will not withstand direct sunlight. Susceptible to scale.
▌ Zones 5 to 8.

Sedum acre
Mossy stonecrop

Evergreen succulent

▌ Spreads rapidly, to 2 inches high.

An ideal plant for areas among stepping-stones or tucked into rock crevices. Has tiny leaves less than ¼ inch long. Flowers are yellow, bloom in spring. Stays green through the coldest of winters. Not particular about soil or water; as a guide, use the least amount of water that will keep it healthy and colorful.
▌ Zones 3 to 10.

Sempervivum tectorum
Hen-and-chickens

Evergreen succulent

▌ Spreads rapidly; mounds to 1 foot high.

Well known to American gardeners, having arrived with the earliest settlers. Its fleshy leaves grow in rosettes. Binds soil well—served this purpose on the roofs of medieval cottages; *tectorum* is the Latin word for roof. Easy to grow; requires only full sun and good drainage. On dry slopes it can outgrow most weeds. Many cultivars are available, offering a variety of leaf colors and patterns.
▌ Zones 4 to 10.

Soleirolia soleirolii
Baby's tears

Broadleaf evergreen

▌ Spreads slowly, 1 to 3 inches high.

A creeping, mosslike plant. Leaves are tiny, light green; forms a dense, soft, carpet. Provides a cool, delicate effect when planted at the base of trees or shade plants such as ferns, camellias, and azaleas. Easily bruised by footsteps. Requires shade, rich soil, and moisture.
▌ Zone 10.

Sempervivum tectorum

Soleirolia soleirolii

Stachys byzantina

Tanacetum parthenium

Stachys byzantina
Lamb's ears

Perennial

▌ Clumps grow moderately to 3 feet wide, 18 inches high.

Woolly leaves are soft and silvery gray—they contrast well with green plants. Stands out dramatically against the foliage of *Fragaria chiloensis* (wild strawberry). Purple flowers appear in summer on 1-foot spikes. Easy to grow, requiring only good drainage and full sun. Cold winters may damage some leaves; plants are usually cut back in the spring.

▌ Zones 4 to 9 (to zone 10 in the West).

Tanacetum parthenium
Feverfew

Broadleaf evergreen

▌ Rapid growth to 8 to 36 inches high, depending on cultivar.

Used chiefly as filler or for contrast among bedding plants. Aggressive; can grow in a crack in a driveway and reappear even after it presumably has been completely ripped out. Has a compact, upright habit. Bears great numbers of small (¼- to ½-inch), white, daisylike flowers throughout the summer. 'Golden Ball' has yellow flowers. 'Silver Ball' has double, white flowers. 'Golden Feather' has chartreuse foliage, grows 8 to 10 inches high.

▌ Zones 6 to 8 (to zone 10 in the West).

Thymus pseudolanuginosus
Woolly thyme

Broadleaf evergreen

▌ Spreads slowly, 2 to 3 inches high.

Tiny, gray-green leaves form a dense, soft carpet. Strikingly effective among stepping-stones, spilling over a boulder or low bank, or simply alone as a cover for small areas. Tolerates light traffic. Its tiny, pink flowers appear only occasionally. Needs the same culture as *T. serpyllum*.

▌ Zones 4 to 10.

Thymus serpyllum
Creeping thyme, mother-of-thyme, wild thyme

Broadleaf evergreen

▌ Spreads slowly, 3 to 6 inches high.

Forms a flat, green mat; tolerates light traffic. Upright stems bear tiny, pale lavender flowers from late spring through summer. Excellent in the border, in a rock garden, or on a dry slope. Best in full sun, takes light shade. Needs regular watering in hot-summer areas. Set young plants 6 to 12 inches apart. Trim periodically to keep plants neat.

▌ Zones 4 to 10.

Thymus serpyllum

Thymus pseudolanuginosus

Verbena peruviana

Trachelospermum jasminoides

Trachelospermum jasminoides

Starjasmine, Asiatic jasmine

Broadleaf evergreen

▮ Spreads slowly, about 2 feet high.

One of the most widely used plants in mild-winter areas, usually as a ground cover, but sometimes as a vine. Long, woody stems twine and ramble. Leaves are glossy, deep green. Bears small, sweetly fragrant, star-shaped flowers from early spring through summer. Needs shade in desert areas; partial shade elsewhere. Requires regular watering throughout the year. Plants become chlorotic in alkaline soil. Plant on 2-foot centers in spring. Some weeding is necessary until plants fill in.
▮ Zones 8 to 10.

Verbena peruviana

Peruvian verbena

Perennial

▮ Spreads rapidly, 4 to 6 inches high.

Spectacular flower colors, a long blooming season, and a rapid growth rate make this one of the most popular ground covers. Crimson-red flowers rise above the foliage in flat-topped clusters, blooming almost continuously from spring through fall. Grown as an annual in cold-winter areas, or as a short-lived perennial in warmer climates. Thrives in hot sun; drought tolerant once established. Water infrequently during summer to avoid problems with mildew and other fungus diseases. A number of excellent hybrids offer a wide array of flower colors.
▮ Zones 9 and 10.

Veronica prostrata

Hungarian speedwell

Perennial

▮ Spreads rapidly, to 6 inches high.

A good paving plant, particularly in shady areas. Softens the edges of steps or paved areas and can serve as bulb covers. Shiny, green, notched leaves are oval to lance-shaped and form a thick, dark mat. Dotted in spring and early summer with clusters of bright blue flowers. Serves as a lawn substitute, but takes no traffic. Grows in full sun or partial shade. Needs good soil and regular watering throughout the year.
▮ Zones 6 to 10.

Vinca major

Big periwinkle

Broadleaf evergreen

▮ Spreads very rapidly, to 2 feet high.

Invasive, fast-spreading; useful as a large-scale ground cover on slopes, particularly in naturalistic gardens and around country homes. Leaves falling from overhead trees vanish beneath its glossy, dark green foliage. Trailing stems root as they grow. Bears lilac blue flowers in the spring. Grows best in light shade and moist, well-drained soil. Two-color variants having leaves mottled with white or gold are also available.
▮ Zones 7 to 10.

Veronica prostrata

Vinca major

Vinca minor

Viola odorata

Vinca minor
Periwinkle

Broadleaf evergreen

▌Spreads rapidly, to 6 inches high.

Smaller, hardier, and less invasive than *V. major*. Among the best of the evergreen ground covers, not only because of its hardiness, but also because of its quiet, cool beauty. An excellent choice for medium-scale plantings, particularly in the filtered shade of large trees or shrubs. 'Alba' has white flowers. 'Atropurpurea' has purple flowers. The leaves of 'Aureovariegata' are spotted with yellow.
▌Zones 4 to 9 (to zone 10 in the West).

Viola odorata
Sweet violet

Perennial

▌Spreads moderately, 3 to 8 inches high.

The classic fragrant violet used by florists. Makes a good small-scale ground cover for partially shaded areas. Spreads by runners. Cultivars vary in height as well as in flower size, color, and intensity of fragrance. Among them are 'Royal Robe', with large, deep blue flowers; 'Marie Louise', which has fragrant, double, white and lavender flowers; 'Royal Elk', with long-stemmed, single, fragrant, violet flowers; 'Charm', with small, white flowers; and 'Rosina', which has pink flowers.
▌Zones 6 to 10.

Viola sororaria
Confederate violet

Perennial

▌Spreads moderately, 6 to 8 inches high.

A common violet in the Northeast. Stemless plant with large leaves (up to 5 inches wide). Flowers are usually deep blue. Self-sows readily; a good small-scale ground cover for borders, beds, and below large-leafed evergreen shrubs. To look their best, they need partial shade, plenty of water, and rich, moist soil.
▌Zones 4 to 10.

Zoysia tenuifolia
Koreangrass, Mascarene grass

Narrowleaf evergreen

▌Spreads slowly, 3 to 5 inches high.

Although a true grass, it is suitable for use only as a ground cover (not as a mowed lawn grass) due to its mounding growth habit. Most effective in small patio settings, among stepping-stones or railroad ties, or on a slope. Tolerates light traffic. Must have well-drained soil; takes sun or light shade. Remains evergreen as long as temperatures remain above freezing, but browns in frost. Slow to establish; set new plants about 6 inches apart.
▌Zones 9 and 10.

Viola sororaria

Zoysia tenuifolia

Agrostis palustris

Cynodon dactylon

LAWN GRASSES

Agrostis palustris
Creeping bentgrass

Cool-season

▮ Mow ¼ to 1 inch high.

The grass of choice in cool climates for golf course putting greens, lawn bowling, and similar uses. Fair wearability. Quickly builds an extensive thatch layer unless mowed very short. Best in full sun, tolerates some shade. Needs plenty of water, and ½ to 1 pound of actual nitrogen per 1,000 square feet per growing month.

Cynodon dactylon
Common bermudagrass

Warm-season

▮ Mow ¾ to 1½ inches high.

Likes heat, is easy to grow in most soils, takes considerable abuse, and makes a handsome lawn when given extra care. Wearability is outstanding. Poor shade tolerance, and invasive; browns in fall until spring. Tolerates drought. Needs ½ to 1 pound of actual nitrogen per 1,000 square feet per growing month.

Cynodon species
Improved bermudagrass

Warm-season

▮ Mow ½ to 1 inch high.

Has most of the same virtues of *C. dactylon*, but has a softer, finer texture and is dormant for a shorter time. Relatively drought tolerant, but needs more water, fertilizer, and mowing than *C. dactylon*. Also susceptible to more pests and diseases. Extremely intolerant of shade. Many cultivars are available. Needs 1 pound or more of actual nitrogen per 1,000 square feet per growing month.

Dichondra micrantha
Dichondra

Warm-season

▮ 1 to 3 inches high.

A popular lawn substitute in mild areas; rarely needs mowing. Takes light traffic. Dark green, cupped, horseshoe-shaped leaves are ¼ to ¾ inch across; they grow atop delicate stems. Takes full sun or light shade, light or heavy soil. Soil should be prepared as for a lawn and kept evenly moist but not soggy. Grow from seeds, plugs, or sod. Does not resist weed invasion as well as most lawn grasses. Formerly known as *D. repens*.

Cynodon species

Dichondra micrantha

Eremochloa ophiuroides

Festuca elatior

Eremochloa ophiuroides

Centipedegrass

Warm-season

■ Mow 1 to 2 inches high.

A good low-maintenance, general-purpose lawn grass. Adapts to infertile, acid soil. Aggressive enough to crowd out weeds. Needs less mowing than most grasses. Resistant to chinch bugs and rhizoctonia; provides an alternative to *Stenotaphrum secundatum* (St. Augustine grass). Coarse textured; fair to poor wearability. Light green color; tends to yellow from chlorosis. Sensitive to low temperatures. Fair shade tolerance. Needs less than ⅓ pound of actual nitrogen per 1,000 square feet per growing month.

Festuca elatior (F. arundinacea)

Tall fescue, meadow fescue

Cool-season

■ Mow 2 to 3 inches high.

A good, tough play lawn. Stays green all year; has some disease and insect resistance. Good shade tolerance; often used where it is too shady for St. Augustine grass. Wearability is good in spring and fall, fair in summer. Medium to coarse textured; tends to clump. Annual overseeding may be necessary to maintain density. Needs less than ½ pound of actual nitrogen per 1,000 square feet per growing month.

Festuca longifolia

Hard fescue

Cool-season

■ Mow 1 to 2½ inches high.

Performs better than most other finely textured fescues due to its better tolerance of heat and drought and its resistance to leaf spot, anthracnose, red thread, and dollar spot. Excellent shade tolerance if grown in well-drained soil. Good drought tolerance. Fair wearability. Adaptable to many climates; needs moderate night temperatures. Needs less than ⅓ pound of actual nitrogen per 1,000 square feet per growing month.

Festuca rubra var. *commutata*

Chewings fescue

Cool-season

■ Mow 1 to 2½ inches high.

A finely textured fescue. Tolerates close mowing in cool climates. Good shade and drought tolerance. Very susceptible to summer diseases in hot climates, especially in moist, fertile soil. Competitiveness can be a disadvantage in mixtures or blends with Kentucky bluegrass. Poor wearability. Needs less than ½ pound of actual nitrogen per 1,000 square feet per growing month.

Festuca longifolia

Festuca rubra var. *commutata*

Festuca rubra ssp. *rubra*

Lolium perenne

Festuca rubra ssp. *rubra*

Creeping red fescue

Cool-season

▌ Mow 1½ to 2½ inches high.

This fescue is a common component of bluegrass mixtures. Blends well and does what some bluegrass species cannot do—grows well in shade or dry soil. Has a fine texture and deep green color. Tolerates acid soil. Preferable to *F. rubra* in a mix. Very susceptible to summer diseases in hot climates, especially in moist, fertile soil. Poor wearability. Needs less than ½ pound of actual nitrogen per 1,000 square feet per growing month.

Lolium perenne

Turf-type perennial ryegrass

Cool-season

▌ Mow 1 to 2 inches high.

Tough play lawn. Germinates and establishes quickly. Improved heat and cold tolerance. Compatible in mixtures with Kentucky bluegrass and fine fescues. Suffers from winterkill in the coldest climates. Medium shade tolerance; poor drought tolerance. Excellent for overseeding dormant bermudagrass in the South and Southwest. Apply ⅓ to ½ pound of actual nitrogen per 1,000 square feet per growing month.

Paspalum notatum

Bahiagrass

Warm-season

▌ Mow 2 to 3 inches high.

A tough, low-maintenance lawn grass. Extensive root system is valuable for erosion control. Fair to good drought tolerance. Moderately aggressive. Forms a coarse, open lawn. Adapts to infertile, sandy soil. Tall, fast-growing seed stalks need frequent mowing. Susceptible to iron chlorosis, dollar spot, and mole crickets. Needs ½ pound of actual nitrogen per 1,000 square feet per growing month.

Poa pratensis

Kentucky bluegrass

Cool-season

▌ Mow 1½ to 3 inches high.

Improved cultivars of this grass resist drought and wear and have greater resistance to leaf spot, stripe smut, and summer patch. These cultivars also require more frequent fertilizing and dethatching. Shade tolerance depends on the cultivar. Adapted to cool-summer areas. Needs ⅓ to ⅔ pound of actual nitrogen per 1,000 square feet per growing month.

Paspalum notatum

Poa pratensis

Poa trivialis

*Stenotaphrum
secundatum*

Poa trivialis
Rough bluegrass

Cool-season

▮ Mow 1 to 2 inches high.

A common component of shady lawn mixtures due to its excellent shade tolerance. Shallow root system does not tolerate drought. Poor wearability. Contaminates perennial ryegrass in sunny areas. Adapts to wet, shaded sites in the northern states. Needs ⅓ to ½ pound of actual nitrogen per 1,000 square feet per growing month.

Stenotaphrum secundatum
St. Augustine grass

Warm-season

▮ Mow 2 to 3 inches high.

A robust, fast-growing grass with excellent shade tolerance. Tolerates salty soil. Poor wearability. Tends to thatch badly. Susceptible to chinch bugs and virus diseases. Best adapted to southern California, Hawaii, mild areas of the Southwest, and the Gulf Coast states. Best in neutral to alkaline soil. Needs about ⅓ to ⅔ pound of actual nitrogen per 1,000 square feet per growing month.

Zoysia species
Zoysiagrass

Warm-season

▮ Mow 1 to 2 inches high.

Forms a dense, fine-textured, weed-resistant lawn with good wearability. Heat and drought tolerant—needs long, warm summers. Relatively free of diseases and insect pests, although billbugs sometimes cause problems. Very slow to establish. Tends to build thatch. Grows slowly in shade, but better than bermudagrass. Needs ⅓ to ½ pound of actual nitrogen per 1,000 square feet per growing month.

Zoysia species

Alpinea zerumbet

Cyathea australis

TROPICAL PLANTS

This section includes only a small number of plants and could have been absorbed into the shrub list. The difference is that most of these are not technically shrubs. They are grasses, herbs, and long-lived perennials that are treated as shrubs in the subtropical or tropical garden.

Alpinea zerumbet (A. speciosa)

Shellflower, shell-ginger

Herbaceous broadleaf

▮ Rapid growth to 10 or 12 feet.

Multiple stemmed, broadleaf plant for the shade garden or greenhouse. The leaves are continuous on stems from 6 to 12 feet, the individual leaves 24 inches long and 6 inches wide. The flowers are white tinged with purple, edged with yellow, red, and brown, and borne in long racemes. *A. zerumbet* is very fragrant, spicy, and ginger-like. Native to East Asia.
▮ Zone 10.

Cyathea australis (Alsophila australis)

Australian tree fern

Broadleaf fern

▮ This tree fern grows up to 20 feet in height with large fronds to 12 feet in length on a fibrous trunk.

A group of them is spectacular in a shade garden with other tropical plants and flowering shrubs such as camellias and begonias. Tree ferns like their trunks kept moist and do best in partial shade, in moist peaty soil, with nitrogen-rich fertilizers. Native to Australia.
▮ Zones 9 and 10.

Philodendron bipinnatifidum (P. selloum)

Bigleaf evergreen

▮ Dark green specimen plant with deeply lobed leaves to 30 inches long.

Prefers dappled sunlight in a warm location. Excellent in a protected patio in southern climates. Needs rich soil and lots of moisture. Native to Brazil and Paraguay.
▮ Zone 10.

Phormium tenax (varieties)

New Zealand flax

Evergreen large herb

▮ Moderate growth to 6 feet tall (clump).

This member of the flax family has straplike leaves from the base, and attains a width of up to 4 inches. Strikingly bold specimen plants. Varieties have leaves with bronze, purple, and white stripping. Normally grown as specimen plants and treated as shrubs. Prefers soil rich in organic humus and moderate amounts of water. Native to New Zealand.
▮ Zones 9 and 10.

Phormium tenax

Philodendron bipinnatifidum

Phyllostachys aurea

Strelitzia nicolai

Phyllostachys aurea

Golden bamboo,
fishpole bamboo

Tall woody grass

▮ Moderate growth to
15 feet tall (clump).

Leaves to 5 inches long and
¼ inches wide. Light green
with golden segmented
stems up to 1 inch in diameter. A striking accent plant
in a tropical or oriental
garden. Spreads slowly by
underground runners.
Same family as *P. bambusoi-
dies*, which grows to 45 feet
and has 4-inch stems.
Prefers rich, well-drained
soil and moderate moisture.
Native to China and Japan.
▮ Zones 9 and 10.

Strelitzia nicolai

Giant bird-of-paradise

Broadleaf

▮ This member of banana
family grows up to 25 feet
with solid trunks.

Leaves to 4 feet long and 2
feet wide. Strong bold form
for the subtropical garden.
Flowers and bracts are 15 to
18 inches long. Flowers are
white with blue tongue
and purplish bracts. Plant
in well-drained soil rich
in humus, and keep well watered. Native to South Africa.
▮ Zones 9 and 10.

Strelitzia reginae

Bird-of-paradise flower

Broadleaf

▮ Clump-type growth
(with no trunk) to 4 feet.

Strong vertical accent plant
with dark green leaves
12 inches long and 6 inches
wide on 2- to 3-foot stems.
Large flowers rise above
the leaves. Flowers are
deep yellow to orange with
a bright blue tongue. Bracts
are purplish and up to
8 inches long. Prefers rich,
loamy soil. Keep well
watered. Native to South
Africa.
▮ Zones 9 and 10.

Strelitzia regina

READING LIST

There are many fine books available about home landscaping. Many concentrate on more technical aspects of landscape design, outdoor construction, and plants and gardening than provided here. The following list is composed of those found to be most helpful during the writing and editing of this book. Look for these publications at your local bookstore and public library.

Additional Reading on Landscape Design

Gardens Are for People, second edition, by Thomas D. Church, Grace Hall, and Michael Laurie. McGraw-Hill Book Co., 1983.

The History of Gardens by Christopher Thacker. University of California Press, 1979.

Landscape Plans. Ortho Books, 1989.

Landscaping With Wildflowers & Native Plants. Ortho Books, 1984.

All About Landscaping. Ortho Books, 1988.

Outdoor Storage. Ortho Books, 1983.

How to Design & Build Children's Play Equipment. Ortho Books, 1986.

Landscape Architecture: A Manual of Site Planning & Design by John O. Simonds, McGraw-Hill Book Co., 1983.

Residential Landscapes: Graphics, Planning & Design by Greg Pierceall. Reston Publishing Co., 1983.

Additional Reading on Outdoor Construction

Basic Carpentry Techniques. Ortho Books, 1981.

Basic Masonry Techniques. Ortho Books, 1985.

Garden Construction. Ortho Books, 1985.

How to Design & Build Decks. Ortho Books, 1995.

How to Design & Build Decks & Patios. Ortho Books, 1979.

How to Design & Build Fences & Gates. Ortho Books, 1985.

How to Design & Install Outdoor Lighting. Ortho Books, 1984.

Landscape Architecture Construction by Harlow C. Landphair and Fred Klatt, Jr. Elsevier North Holland Publishing Co., 1979.

Lawn & Garden Construction by Robert F. Baudendistel. Reston Publishing Co., 1983.

Ortho's Home Improvement Encyclopedia. Ortho Books, 1994.

Principles of Grading, Drainage and Road Alignment: An Ecological Approach by Richard K. Untermann. Reston Publishing Co., 1978.

Additional Reading on Plants and Gardening

All About Azaleas, Camellias & Rhododendrons. Ortho Books, 1995.

All About Ground Covers. Ortho Books, 1993.

All About Lawns. Ortho Books, 1994.

All About Trees. Ortho Books, 1992.

All About Evergreens. Ortho Books, 1984.

Gardening in Containers. Ortho Books, 1983.

Hortus Third, A Concise Dictionary of Plants Cultivated in the United States and Canada by Liberty Hyde Bailey, Ethel Zoe Bailey, and the Staff of the Liberty Hyde Bailey Hortorium. Macmillan Publishing Co., 1976.

Shrubs & Hedges. Ortho Books, 1990.

The Ortho Book of Gardening Basics. Ortho Books, 1991.

Sunset Western Garden Book, fifth edition. Lane Publishing Co., 1995.

Wyman's Gardening Encyclopedia, by Donald Wyman Macmillan Publishing, 1977.

Fescue (*continued*)
creeping red (*Festuca rubra* ssp. *rubra*), *316*, **316**
hard (*Festuca longifolia*), *315*, **315**
meadow. *See Festuca elatior*
tall; meadow fescue (*Festuca elatior*), *315*, **315**
Festuca
arundinacea. See *Festuca elatior*
elatior (*F. arundinacea*) (meadow fescue; tall fescue), *315*, **315**
glauca (*F. ovina* var. *glauca*) (blue fescue), 46, 129, *300*, **300**
longifolia (hard fescue), *315*, **315**
ovina var. *glauca*. See *F. glauca*
rubra
var. *commutata* (chewings fescue), *315*, **315**, 316
ssp. *rubra* (creeping red fescue), *316*, **316**
Feverfew (*Tanacetum parthenium*), *311*, **311**
Ficus, 238
benjamina (weeping fig), 239
elastica (rubber plant), 23, *239*, **239**
microcarpa (*F. retusa*) (Indian laurel), *239*, **239**
pumila (climbing fig; creeping fig), 23, 43, 73, *218*, **218**
retusa. See *F. microcarpa*
Fieldstone, 163, 164
Fig
climbing. See *Ficus pumila*
creeping; climbing fig (*Ficus pumila*), 23, 43, 73, *218*, **218**
weeping (*Ficus benjamina*), 239
Files, carpenter's, 154
Filter cloth, for drainage, 118
Finish, for concrete patios, 169
Fir, 45, 200
Douglas (*Pseudotsuga menziesii*), 84, 158, *255*, **255**
noble (*Abies procera*), *224*, **224**
white (*Abies concolor*), 84, *224*, **224**
dwarf, 23
Fir lumber, 158

Firethorn, 129, 200
scarlet (*Pyracantha coccinea*), *282*, **282**
Fit, appropriate, in landscaping, 54–55
Fittings, for watering systems, 138
Fixture, light, 121, *125*, *130*
Flagstone, cost of, 162
Flame tree (*Brachychiton acerifolius*), *230*, **230**
Flats, buying, 196–97
Flax, New Zealand (*Phormium tenax* varieties), 129, *318*, **318**
Floats, 155
Floors, landscape, 22, 67–70
building, 172–76
materials for, 69
plants as, 67–68
Flowers
beds of, as accents, 78, *85*
landscaping for, 36–37, *36*
uses of, 85, *85*
Flow rate, watering systems and, 142, 146
Footcandle, 121, 123
Footings
for decks, 170
for garden walls, 176, *177*
to place, *168*
Force mains, 134
Fork, garden (pitchfork), 183
Form
in landscaping design, 56–57
in plants, 57
Forms, building, 166, 169, 173
Forsythia × *intermedia* (border forsythia), *271*, **271**
'Beatrix Farrand', 271
'Karl Sax', 271
Forsythia, 72
border (*Forsythia* × *intermedia*), *271*, **271**
Fothergilla major (large fothergilla), 61, *271*, **271**
Fothergilla, large (*Fothergilla major*), 61, *271*, **271**
Foundation planting, 82–83
Fountains, *30*, *50*, *60*, *79*, 82
to build, 181
Fragaria chiloensis (sand strawberry; wild strawberry), 200, 299, *300*, **300**, 311
Fragrance, plants for (*list*), 84
Framing square, 153
Franklinia alatamaha (franklinia), 61, *240*, **240**
Franklinia (*Franklinia alatamaha*), 61, *240*, **240**

Fraxinus
pennsylvanica (green ash), *240*, **240**
velutina var. *glabra*, 'Modesto' (Modesto ash), *240*, **240**
velutina var. *glabra* (Arizona ash), 240
Frequency, watering systems and, 142
Frost, protecting plants from, 209
Frost line, 113, 133
Fruit trees, landscaping for, 38
Fuchsia hybrida (common fuchsia hybrids), 23, *271*, **271**
Fuchsia, common hybrids (*Fuchsia hybrida*), 23, *271*, **271**

G

Garbage cans, hiding, *132*, 133
Garden, shared, *22*
Garden center, advice from, 13
Garden house, *76*
Gardenia
augusta (*G. jasminoides*) (gardenia), 23, 43, 84, *272*, **272**
jasminoides. See *G. augusta*
Gardenia (*Gardenia augusta* [*G. jasminoides*]), 23, 43, 84, *272*, **272**
Gardening, books on (*list*), 320
Garland flower (*Daphne cneorum*), 47, *269*, **269**
Gas
lines for, *134*, 135
methane, to vent, 112
Gates
to build, 178–79
planning, 74
standard dimensions of, 92
wood, *29*, 74
wrought iron, *47*
Gaultheria procumbens (checkerberry; teaberry; wintergreen), 61, *300*, **300**
Gazebo (belvedere), *76*, 76, 179–80
Gelsemium sempervirens (Carolina jessamine), 84, *218*, **218**, *300*, **300**
Genista
hispanica (Spanish broom; Spanish gorse), 48, *272*, **272**
pilosa (silky-leaf woadwaxen), *301*, **301**

Ginger, British Columbia wild (*Asarum caudatum*), *293*, **293**
Ginkgo biloba (maidenhair tree), 46, 61, *240*, **240**
'Autumn Gold', 240
'Fairmont', 240
Glare, 121
Gleditsia triacanthos (honeylocust)
'Sunburst', 78
var. *inermis* (thornless honeylocust), 129, *241*, **241**
Golddust. *See Aurinia saxatilis*
Goldenchain tree (*Laburnum* × *watereri*), *244*, **244**
Goldenrain tree (*Koelreuteria paniculata*), *243*, **243**
Goldflower (*Hypericum* × *moserianum*), *274*, **274**
Gorse, Spanish. *See Genista hispanica*
Gradient. *See* slope
Grading, 109–20
costs of, 116
finish, 113, 114
mature trees and, 148
planning, 112–18
plan of, 95
procedure for, 114–16
rough, 113, 114
underground utilities and, 133
see also drainage
Grain, of wood, 157–58
Granite, 162, 163
Grass/es
for lawns, 207–208, **314–17**
Mascarene. *See Zoysia tenuifolia*
ornamental, *27*
St. Augustine (*Stenotaphrum secundatum*), *315*, *317*, **317**
for sports lawns, *33*
wild, *63*
Gravel, *65*, 74, 173
Grevillea robusta (silk oak), *241*, **241**
Ground covers, 68
to attract wildlife (*list*), 200
for controlling erosion, 26, 181–82
for fall color (*list*), 61
for formal gardens (*list*), 43
for fragrance (*list*), 84
in a landscape, 83
landscaping styles and, 42, 46, 47

She-oak, river; beefwood
(*Casuarina cunning-
hamiana*), 48, *231*, **231**
Shovels, 155, *155*, 183
Shrub heads, 140–41
Shrubs
to attract wildlife
(*list*), 200
container-grown, 197,
202–203
for containers (*list*), 23
for fall color (*list*), 61
for formal gardens
(*list*), 43
for fragrance (*list*), 84
in a landscape, 82–83
landscaping styles and, 42,
44, 45, 46, 47, 48
for lighting (*list*), 129
low-maintenance, 37
for patios, 35
for play areas, 34
to remove, 149
to select, 201
sprinklers for, 140–41, *141*
as walls, 72–73
Siberian tea (*Bergenia
crassifolia*), *294*, **294**
Side yard, landscaping, 25
Silhouetting, 125–26, *125*
Silk oak (*Grevillea robusta*),
241, **241**
Silk tree; mimosa (*Albizia
julibrissin*), 23, 48,
227, **227**
Silverberry (*Elaeagnus
pungens*), 84, *270*, **270**
Silver-dollar tree (*Eucalyptus cinerea*), *238*, **238**
Silver lace vine (*Polygonum
aubertii*), 129, *221*, **221**
Site
analyzing, 89–90, *89*
to lay out, 168, *168*
to measure, 88–89, *110*,
152–53, 165
preparation of,
147–49, 170
Size, form and, 56
see also scale
Slate, *14*, 162, *163*
Slope
defined, 113
landscaping, 26
to measure, *110*, *115*
watering systems and, 145
Smoke tree (*Cotinus
coggygria*), 61, 129,
268, **268**
Snowbell, Japanese;
Japanese snowdrop tree
(*Styrax japonicum*),
260, **260**
Snowdrop tree
Japanese. *See Styrax
japonicum*
(wild olive) (*Halesia
tetraptera*), *241*, **241**

Snow-in-summer; flaxleaf
paperbark (*Melaleuca
linariifolia*), *248*, **248**
Snow-in-summer (*Cerastium
tomentosum*), *295*, **295**
Sod
planting a lawn from,
207, *208*
to save, 149
to select, 201
Software, CAD (computer-
aided design), 86
Soil, *191*
amendments for, 188–90,
191, 204
quantities needed
(*table*), 188
conditioner, 190
cultivating, 191
described, 186
drainage of, to test, 111
grading and, 110–11
managing, 186–92
profile, 187, *187*
purchasing, 115
testing, 187, *187*
toxicity in, 112
types of, and watering
systems, 145
see also topsoil
Solandra maxima (cup-of-
gold), *222*, **222**
Soleirolia soleirolii (baby's
tears), 307, *310*, **310**
Sophora japonica (Japanese
pagoda tree), *260*, **260**
Sorbus aucuparia (European
mountain ash), *260*, **260**
'Fastigiata', 260
'Xanthocarpa', 260
Sour gum. *See Nyssa
sylvatica*
Sourwood (*Oxydendrum
arboreum*), *249*, **249**
Spa, *54*
lighting, 127
Space
for children's activities, 67
to enlarge, 8, 22–23, *25*
large, to landscape, 24, *25*
small, to landscape,
22–23, *22*
Spade, 155, 183
Speedwell, Hungarian
(*Veronica prostrata*),
312, **312**
Sphagnum moss, 189
*Spiraea
japonica* 'Bumalda'
(Japanese spirea), 61,
287, **287**
'Anthony Waterer', 287
'Crispa', 287
'Froebelii', 287
'Goldflame', 287
'Nyewoods', 287
× *vanhouttei* (Vanhoutte
spirea), *287*, **287**

Spirea
Japanese (*Spiraea
japonica* 'Bumalda'), 61,
287, **287**
Vanhoutte (*Spiraea ×
vanhouttei*), *287*, **287**
Spotlighting, 125
Sprigs, planting a lawn from,
208, *208*
Spring heath; Christmas
heath; bell heather
(*Erica carnea* [*E.
herbacea*]), *299*, **299**
Sprinkler system, *134*,
136, *137*
heads for, *139*, 140–41
Spruce, 43, 77
Black Hills (*Picea glauca
'Densata'*), 250
Colorado (*Picea pungens*),
250, **250**
dwarf white (*Picea glauca
var. albertiana
'Conica'*), *280*, **280**
Norway (*Picea abies*),
250, **250**
white (*Picea glauca*), 23,
35, *250*, **250**
Spurge, Japanese
(*Pachysandra
terminalis*), 36, *307*, **307**
Stachys byzantina (lamb's
ears), 34, *311*, **311**
Stairs
to build, 175–76
concrete, 176
cost of, 176
wood, 175–76
Stakes
for plants, *201*, *202*,
204–205
surveyor's, to use, 116
Starjasmine; Asiatic jasmine
(*Trachelospermum
jasminoides*), 23, 84,
129, *223*, **223**, *312*, **312**
Statues. *See* sculpture
Steel, structural, 164
Stella garden, *51*
Stenotaphrum secundatum
(St. Augustine grass),
315, *317*, **317**
Steps, *36*
brick, *175*
to build, 175, *175*
cost of, 176
planning, 71
and planter boxes, *62*
standard dimensions of,
71, *92*
Stone
bridge, *45*
building with, 163–64
cost of, 162
crushed, 162, 173
cut, cost of, 162
dimensioned
(quarried), 163

Stone (*continued*)
path, *39*, *73*
patio, *52–53*, *83*
quarried. *See* stone,
dimensioned
walls, *64*, 178
see also fieldstone
Stonecrop, mossy (*Sedum
acre*), *310*, **310**
Storm sewer, 135
Straw, as a soil
amendment, 188
Strawberry
mock (*Duchesnea indica*),
299, **299**
sand. *See Fragaria
chiloensis*
wild; sand strawberry
(*Fragaria chiloensis*),
200, 299, *300*, **300**, 311
Strawberry tree (*Arbutus
unedo*), 26, 37, 129,
200, *229*, **229**
Streets, drainage and, 112
*Strelitzia
nicolai* (giant bird-of-
paradise), *319*, **319**
reginae (bird-of-paradise
flower), *319*, **319**
Style, landscaping, 40–50,
54–55
Styrax japonicum (Japanese
snowbell; Japanese
snowdrop tree),
260, **260**
Subgrade, defined, 113
Subsoil, 187
*Suggested Minimum
Standards for
Residential Swimming
Pools* (National Spa and
Pool Institute), 81
Sumac
fragrant (*Rhus aromatica*),
61, 84, *285*, **285**
staghorn (*Rhus typhina*),
61, *285*, **285**
Summer house, 76
Sump (dry well), 113
Sunrose, common (*Helian-
themum nummularium*),
301, **301**
Survey, certified land, 99
Swale, 113, *117*
Sweet bay; bay laurel;
Grecian laurel (*Laurus
nobilis*), 200, *244*, **244**
Sweet gum, American
(*Liquidambar
styraciflua*), 61, 129,
245, **245**
Swimming pool, 6, *16*
cover, 81
landscaping for, 35
lighting, *126*, 127
planning, 81
plants near, 81
size of, 81